THE IMPORTANCE OF ASTROLOGY IN YOUR LIFE

The stars impel; they don't compel. What does compel is the force of your will, and astrology is a tool for helping you get in control of it.

Astrology is important, not because it tells you what is going to happen, but rather because it illuminates what is already there. Planetary forces are like ocean waves. They can bring about movement, tensions and dynamic situations in your life. It is up to you where you let them take you. *Robin MacNaughton's Sun Sign Personality Guide* is not about fate or a predetermined future. It is simply your key to a creative, disciplined, more meaningful life.

ROBIN MacNAUGHTON'S
SUN SIGN
PERSONALITY GUIDE
Robin MacNaughton

BANTAM BOOKS
NEW YORK · TORONTO · LONDON · SYDNEY · AUCKLAND

ROBIN MACNAUGHTON'S SUN SIGN PERSONALITY GUIDE
A Bantam Book / October 1978

Portions of this book appear in Bantam's twelve-book astrological forecast series for
1978, Robin MacNaughton's Guide to The Complete (sun sign) Personality.

ISBN 0-553-27380-9

Published simultaneously in the United States and Canada

Bantam Books are published by Bantam Books, a division of Bantam Doubleday Dell
Publishing Group, Inc. Its trademark, consisting of the words "Bantam Books" and
the portrayal of a rooster, is Registered in U.S. Patent and Trademark Office and in
other countries. Marca Registrada. Bantam Books, 1540 Broadway, New York, New
York 10036.

PRINTED IN THE UNITED STATES OF AMERICA

KR   25   24   23   22   21   20   19

CONTENTS

I

YOU
AND
ASTROLOGY

WHAT IS A HOROSCOPE?

Your personal horoscope, also called your natal chart, is a symbolic, graphic representation of the planets' positions in the sky at the minute you were born. With the latitude of your birthplace, the time and the day you were born, an astrologer, after making mathematical calculations and consulting astronomical tables, is able to create your horoscope. By carefully studying the relationships of the planets to each other at the moment you officially entered the world, the trained astrologer is able to read your character and tell you specific facts about your life.

What most people don't understand is that each of these planets represents a specific energy field. And when all of the ten planets are combined in a chart, this energy field is intensified and becomes very complex. Each individual has a unique pattern of energies represented symbolically by the markings of an astrological chart. And what this symbolic representation stands for is the sum total of potentialities of your life.

There is very little in life that is fated. However, there is much that is planned. What is the difference? Well, almost everyone knows that the energy of the moon rules the ocean tides. The water is not a conscious being, so it churns and rushes from the strength of the lunar vibrations. We, however, are conscious beings, so we have a choice every time a strong influence is forcing us in a certain direction. Most of the time we do not think of resisting the force, so we give in to the vibration that seems to be directing us, but that does not mean that we *have* to give in to it. Just think of the Yogis who can walk on nails and the trained Buddhist monks who can douse their hands in flame and emerge without injury.

When an astrologer reads your future from a horoscope, the predictions are based on the strength of the planetary energies presently operating in the sky rather than on the potential strength of the human will. However, any fine astrologer will attempt to help you creatively control these energies rather than glibly tell you that it will be a bad period. The planets moving about in the sky at the time of birth will make their influence known for an entire human lifetime. After the moment of birth, these planets are referred to as the transits and will serve to intensify or modify the basic birth influences. These energy waves lose their force only at the moment of death. Up until that moment, the horoscope is only a potential for various action patterns. Therefore, what the stars really have to say for you can very well be nothing more than what you will them to say. Your mind is a minute model of the entire universe. Learn to use it well, and astrology can be your guide to greater happiness rather than an awesome harbinger of doom.

THE IMPORTANCE OF
ASTROLOGY IN YOUR LIFE

The stars impel; they don't compel. What does compel is the force of your will, and astrology is a tool for helping you to get in control of it. Palmists will tell you that the lines on your hand can change in a matter of days. Tarot readers will tell you that you can alter the meaning of your cards. And any good astrologer will tell you that there really are no negative transits.

Despite what you may feel, planetary energies are totally impersonal. The way you deal with these energies as they radiate in your life is nothing but a matter of your choice. It is your choice whether you *will* that these energies work for you. Never think that the power of the planets is stronger than the power that already exists within your own mind. Astrology is important, not because it tells what is going to happen, but rather because it illuminates what is already there. Planetary forces are like ocean waves. They can bring about movement, tensions, and dynamic situations in your life. However, it is truly up to you where you let them take you. Remember that to be able to ride on the crest of planetary waves requires diligence and discipline. Critically decide what you want for a more meaningful life. Then, using all of the powers of your mental faculties, will that this be so. Never compromise. And never sit back and wait. Use these planetary insights to help you achieve your goals. Synthesize their energies in your mind so that you come to be in command of your private universe. Remember, before the planets can guide you to a happier and more fulfilled existence, you first must allow it to happen.

THE INFLUENCE OF PLANETARY CYCLES

THE INFLUENCE OF PLANETARY CYCLES

The laws of astrology operating on a daily basis bring into focus all the cycles of becoming that we will experience in a lifetime. At the moment of birth, the cycles begin as we enter the flow of the energies of the universe. The symbol for the cumulative number of cycles that we can experience on earth is the zodiacal circle, known as the horoscope. All cycles through time are framed by its geometry, which functions as a prism for the flow of planetary energies.

The reason why the horoscope is a circle and not a square is that it signifies that man is ever becoming. There are no stopping points, not even in death. There is only change and transmutation. Change is the force of the planetary energies pulling man forward to each new hour, day, decade, lifetime. Transmutation is the new portion of his higher self that unfolds and enlarges with each new change. On a very deep level, man's consciousness is also a circle, mirroring the vast, limitless circle of the zodiac in space. This is what is meant by the ancient Hermetic axiom, "As above, so below"—what is "out there" in space is exactly what is archetypally embedded in man's brain. Therefore, the human mind mirrors the universe on a minute scale. And like the vast, mysterious universe, it is naturally limitless. The only limits it ever comes to know are what man chooses to impose upon it. Sometimes those limits are fear, pain, or obsession. Or they can even be the limitations of pleasure, perverted into pain through excess. The truly liberated man imposes no limitations. He thrives on the freedom issuing from a state of inner balance. His mental energies no longer control him; he has learned through study and discipline how to control them.

In doing so, he has become master of his own universe, and thus, master of change. At this point, his name is no longer man, it is God, living in the flesh of a man's body.

When man completes the 360 degrees of the archetypal circle of his existence, death occurs. And at the moment of death, he experiences the first degree of a new cycle of existence. In doing so, he undergoes physical changes as well as the transmutation of his consciousness. In numerology, 360 reduces to the number 9, and 9 is the universal number of completion. But because the laws of the universe illustrate that matter cannot be destroyed, but only transformed, 9 is really the step before rebirth. All endings lead *only* to new experiences. This is the law of change. And it can be a comforting thought in a moment of emotional crisis.

It is interesting that even the orbit of each of the planets in space follows the path of an ellipse. And as each planet completes its arc in the solar system, it represents a different cycle in the life of the individual. The passage of the moon through the degrees represents our hourly cycles; and the passage of the sun from one degree to the next represents our daily, or diurnal, cycle. As a matter of fact, every hour and every day are under the influence of a planet. The seven days of the week were originally named after the planets that ruled the first hour of each day: Sunday, ruled by the sun; Monday, the moon; Tuesday, Mars; Wednesday, Mercury; Thursday, Jupiter; Friday, Venus; and Saturday, Saturn. It is true that each of these days carries the vibrations of its planetary ruler and can bring us from one brief mood cycle to another. For instance, it is clearly noticeable that people have a tendency to feel blue or moody on Monday, but ready for a social celebration on Friday. This is because of the influence of the energies of the moon and Venus, respectively.

The moon completes its arc every twenty-eight days, and at that time returns to the same sign it occupied twenty-eight days before. This, of course, constitutes the monthly cycle, which greatly influences the sexual physiology of women. The female is symbolized in astrology by the moon. Therefore, there is also a very close archetypal link between the orbit of this planet and the feminine polarity of our personality, regardless of the nature of our sex.

Approximately every 363 days the sun completes its passage around the ecliptic. This constitutes our year.

However, the astrologer measures the yearly and monthly cycles at different points than the average person. In the astrologer's frame of reference, the new year begins at the moment when the transiting sun in the sky returns to the individual's zodiacal sun-sign position to the second. Likewise, the new month begins when the transiting moon returns to its natal position by the minute. Mathematically, the astrologer is able to calculate the moment of both occurrences, and from there can erect a yearly and a monthly horoscope, called the solar and lunar return. These charts detail the influences of both yearly and monthly cycles, and can prove to be indispensable tools for predicting events. You can watch this on a practical level by noticing if you have experienced significant internal change around your birthday. Some years, this change is not as salient as it is in other years. But often it can be manifested as a long-term depression suddenly lifting; emotional chaos starting noticeably to sort itself out; new attitudes about life, career, love emerging; a sudden rise in drives and ambitions. Unfortunately, the new solar influences can also usher in unexpected chaos where there was once stability, repeated deathlike situations, rapid forced change, loneliness, and confusion. In a lifetime, each human being must pass through the experiences of both the pain and the pleasure cycles if there is to be expansion of consciousness manifested by inward growth and wisdom. Each experience in a cycle of time should become a learning one, leading to a greater awareness, which, in turn, should slowly lead to a more dispassionate view of personal experience and a release from self-imposed sorrow.

The cycle of Saturn, which returns to its natal position approximately every twenty-eight years, critically brings to our attention the areas where we need to focus our energies to create greater personal growth. Astrologically speaking, the Saturn return marks our entrance into adulthood. As Saturn is the severe taskmaster of the zodiac, this period can be marked by greater responsibility, hard work, and serious evaluation of future life goals. For those who have been evading their responsibilities up till this point, emotional pain, anxiety, crisis, and depression are often the price to pay for remaining a child too long.

On the other hand, those who have already learned the lesson of discipline, and have channeled the restrictive energies of the natal Saturn for greater perseverance and structure, will not only reap during this transit, but may also find that they are gaining the opportunities and achievements of long-awaited desires.

When a person is between forty-two and forty-five, Uranus, the planet of sudden change, reaches the midpoint of its complete orbit around the zodiac. At this time, it moves into a 180-degreee opposition from its natal position, bringing about a peak point in life marked by abrupt change, crisis, and upheaval. It can also bring a whirlwind of excitement or mark a point of adulthood when excitement is restlessly sought. This cycle, which makes the transition to middle age, is accompanied by internal changes that often have their outlet in altered relationships. Frequently, this is a time of divorce, infidelity, a "fated" love affair, and even the death of the partner. Uranus uproots the illusion of stability that the individual has been drowsing under, forcing a search of the inner self for more meaningful foundations. Uranus is new experience at its most dramatic. For many, it ushers in a totally different life-style in which one seems to begin a new life all over again, creating new relationships and formulating new goals.

At about age fifty-six, Saturn returns to its natal position for the second time, bringing with it the peak material rewards and prestige accrued from an adulthood of hard work. But since Saturn also rules structure, its transit can shatter situations still controlled by youthful folly. This is the beginning of the cycle of old age. To some, it may bring burdens; to others, it can bring a much-needed rest from the onerous tasks and duties of adulthood. With the transformation brought about through retirement, many new hobbies and pastimes can be enjoyably pursued after years of postponement due to the time demands of the material world. During the following years of this transit, Saturn functions on the highest level by slowly unraveling the material from the spiritual being. And if one has learned the lessons of his lifetime, Saturn now lifts the soul away from the burdens that he had earlier imposed. With death, Saturn culminates the severance cycle and allows the spirit to rise and relinquish its material limitations. The four primal energies—fire, air, earth, and water—that once comprised a human experience now disintegrate and transmute. The spirit soars to a different plane of existence, and once again the death cycle culminates in the mysterious cycle of life.

THE ELEMENTS IN THE ZODIAC

There are four elements in the universe: fire, air, earth, and water. These elements in combination make up our total experience. When someone says that he is a fire sign or a water sign, for example, what he is saying is that the position of the sun at his birth fell into one of these categories. Each of the elements has specific properties that identify an individual with a mode of behavior.

FIRE

Fire is aggression, energy, enthusiasm, warlike qualities, fearlessness, courage, strength, selfishness, restlessness, insensitivity, animation, vitality, action, passion, leadership, temperamental behavior, willfulness.

Fire-sign people, born under the sign Aries, Leo, or Sagittarius, tend to display these characteristics, modified by other factors in the horoscope. These people love challenges and are impulsive, self-reliant, and goal-oriented. They are associated with a high degree of success and leadership, and enjoy driving themselves to their limits to attain their desires. They often act before they think, and because they are connected with the fire energy, can have strong tempers that quickly explode and blow off steam. Immediate ego expression is the motivating factor, and often an instantaneous gratification is the expectation.

AIR

Air is intellect, logic, communication, changeability, superficiality, sociability, enthusiasm, tentativeness, capriciousness, emotional detachment, adaptability, articulation, analysis.

Air-sign people, born under the sign Gemini, Libra, or Aquarius, are the most superficially agreeable, but the most uncertain. They operate from the mental rather than the emotional plane, and generally tend to analyze all personal experience. These people are talkative, amusing, and extremely sociable. Because they enjoy brief, surface interactions with others, they are often heavy partygoers. Mentally, they are restless, easily bored, and continually seeking stimulation. In romance, they tend toward fickleness, since their thoughts get confused with their feelings, and they tend to be indecisive and changeable.

EARTH

Earth is practicality, perseverance, building, materialism, structure, realization, conservation, caution, material creation, stability, strength, durability.

Earth-sign people, born under the sign Taurus, Virgo, or Capricorn, are the most practical people in the zodiac. They are purposeful, patient, and well-grounded in realistic perspectives. These people have highly focused goals and will tenaciously work toward them, despite many obstacles. Often they are good at details and will make a slow, yet steady progress in areas that others would tend to forsake. Their limitation is that they can become confined by the petty details of day-to-day experience. However, of all the elements in the zodiac, earth has the greatest staying power.

WATER

Water is emotion, love, intuition, feeling, psychic ability, empathy, moodiness, introversion, mediumship, occultism, warmth, creativity, artistic ability, sensitivity, compassion, self-sacrifice, wisdom, healing ability, jealousy, manipulation.

Water-sign people, who are born under the sign Cancer, Scorpio, or Pisces, are the most emotional inhabitants of the zodiac. These people can use their potent feelings to travel to higher realms of experience, either in the arts or in occult fields. Or they can pervert the flow of their emotions by seeking the false intensification of all experience through drugs, alcohol, sexual promiscuity, and romantic fantasy. Their principal life task is searching for the most satisfactory kind of emotional outlet. Sometimes, in the signs Cancer and Scorpio, the feelings become blocked within the psyche, and direct expression is exceedingly difficult. These people may be accused of being cold and distant, but, in fact, they are the most intensely emotional and the most vulnerable, if stripped of all controls. Water signs are the most enigmatic because of their acute ability to sense, perceive, emote, and manipulate. They have an uncanny understanding of how to control and influence others. Those who use this gift to its highest ends are often the outstanding spiritual leaders of our time.

four areas exert a more dominant influence on the individual. The first house, carries an additional significance,
since it may have a special influence on conduct ... health.

THE HOUSES

While the planets in the signs have specific meanings,
their placement in the horoscope is of prime significance.
The zodiac is symbolically divided into twelve segments,
referred to as "houses." The houses determine the affairs
of life that the plenet will influence when positioned
there at the time of birth. However, this is not as simple
as it may sound. To begin with, each house has many
meanings, and the more time one devotes to the experimental side of astrology, the more meanings come into
focus. Therefore, to ensure correct chart interpretation, it
is necessary that the astrologer determine the most relevant
meaning or meanings for each planet at the time of the
reading. This is especially crucial in predictive work.

THE FIRST HOUSE

The sign and degree of the cusp of this house are also
loosely referred to as the ascendant. This house signifies
the outward personality that the world sees, but not necessarily the expression of the inner being. This is the behavior that we want to show to the world or that we
feel a compulsion to show to the world. The sign on this
house indicates how we tend to express ourselves in our
environment—but this is also modified by any planets
placed in the house, especially near the cusp. Since the
first house has to do with the sense of self and the concept
of I, it also rules the physical body and is an indication of
personal appearance. However, this too is modified by
planetary placement. This area of the horoscope is of
prime importance, since it is considered to be one of the
four angular houses, and any planet placed in one of these

four areas exerts a more dominant influence on the individual. The first house carries an additional importance, since it can have a crucial influence in matters of health.

THE SECOND HOUSE

This house is associated with matters of money, possessions, wealth, values, and self-value. It also has to do with heredity and social advantages, and shows what one has to build on in a lifetime to establish a maximum sense of self-worth.

THE THIRD HOUSE

This is the house of communication, learning, teaching, writing, and logical interaction with the environment. It is one of many factors in the horoscope that indicate the ways in which one tends to use the logical mind—creatively, critically, expressively, etc. The third house expresses the kind of experience involved in the early years of education. At a later point in life, it reveals attitudes built from these experiences, as well as the kind of mental frameworks operating in the day-to-day existence.

THE FOURTH HOUSE

This is the second of the four angular houses, and therefore carries considerable importance in the horoscope. On the most salient level, it refers to the home, the family, and the more passive parent. On a deeper level, it is tied to the deepest unconscious needs, the individual's sense of security, and the preconscious foundations for all motivations. This is the house of the soul, and shows where and how we must recognize and satisfy our deepest needs in order to find satisfaction and pleasure in the fifth house.

THE FIFTH HOUSE

Loosely termed, this is the house of pleasure. It is also the playground for the working out of the fourth-house subconscious drives. The sign on the cusp of the house will indicate the area of life where these efforts will be most fruitful. Fifth-house activities include all kinds of pleasureful pastimes, from sports to gambling, from active creative endeavors to vicarious enjoyment at a film or the theater. This is also the house of love and romance. Often the sign on the cusp will indicate the type of person that one is most attracted to. Planets positioned within, their signs and aspects, will show whether one tends to be romantically fortunate or unfortunate, and how the will can be guided to alter the negative course of events. This is also the house of children, and when the sun, which symbolizes the ego drive, is afflicted in this house, the result is often an individual who behaves like a spoiled child.

THE SIXTH HOUSE

This is the house of routine work, health, service, pets, and hygiene. It is also associated with emotional adjustments necessary for proper health. When one fails to make these necessary mental-emotional adjustments, one gets sick, often psychosomatically. Therefore, the operations of this house are intrinsic to a healthy, functioning mind and body.

THE SEVENTH HOUSE

This is the house of marriage, partnership, committed relationships, and legal matters. In general, this house has to do with all of the others involved, on both a personal and impersonal basis. Since the seventh house is also associated with the public, the moon or sun placed here in favorable aspect can denote potential fame. The sign and element on the cusp often indicate the kind of marriage partner the individual will tend to seek. Afflicted planets located within are most often glaring signs of an individual who brings about perpetual broken relationships. Since this is the third of the four angular houses, planets placed here have a predominant importance in the judgment of the entire horoscope.

THE EIGHTH HOUSE

This is the house of death, sex, regeneration, and un-earned income. It also rules occult forces, activities, and groups. Within the larger framework, the meaning of this house is change through transformation of values. In this respect, it shows our potential for both personal and spiritual rebirth. As it follows the seventh house of partnership, it is also associated with the profound psychological effects of the activities that have gone on in the seventh house. On a more mundane level, it also rules the partner's income—both in business and in the marital situation.

THE NINTH HOUSE

This is the house of travel, religion, ethics, philosophy, higher education, and mental expansion. Its activities are associated with growth and higher awareness. Satisfaction in the ninth house can be experienced only when one has transcended the limitations of the eighth.

THE TENTH HOUSE

This house is also loosely referred to as the midheaven, because when the sun is positioned at its cusp, it is noon and at its highest point in the heavens. This is the place where subjective aspirations seek objective reward. It is the house of the profession, the reputation, the more powerful parent, the significant authority figures; it represents the challenge for the individual to become his own parent and authority figure. This house is the most significant of the four angular houses, and planets contained within can be of great importance.

THE ELEVENTH HOUSE

This is the house of hopes, wishes, dreams, friendships, collective associations, and clubs. Social activities and group functions fall within this domain. In addition, both public contacts and public awareness are associated with this house, which is often the solar domicile in the charts of celebrities.

THE TWELFTH HOUSE

This is the house of self-imposed limitations, sorrow from self-undoing, secrets, imprisonment, confinement, large institutions, and hospitals. On an occult level, twelfth-house experiences can involve mysticism, astral travel, spiritual retreat, karma, experience from past lives, and mediumship. The twelfth house completes a cycle of experience and requires self-evaluation in respect to past relationships. Since the twelfth house opposes the sixth, it also involves a serious readjustment of values and behavior. Its challenge is the transcendence of self-limitation to achieve the goal of growth and greater self-development.

CUSPS

When people chat about astrology in cocktail conversations, the word "cusp" always seems to crop up. This most often occurs when the individual would really like to be another sign. "I'm a Virgo, but on the cusp of Leo" means "I was born on the day that separates the sign Leo from Virgo, and therefore must have a strong Leo influence in my chart, because it's so close, and I hate being a Virgo."

There are two basic meanings of "cusp." The first one concerns the day that either ends or begins a sign. For example, August 22 is the cusp of Leo and Virgo, since it is the last day of the sun's transit through the sign of Leo. And August 23 is the cusp of Virgo and Leo, since it is the first day of the sun's transit into the sign of Virgo. What most people fail to realize is that neither position necessarily implies an influence from the other by the mere fact of the next sign's proximity. A Leo born on the cusp of Virgo may or may not have planets placed in Virgo, and vice versa. The deciding factor is the specific year and date that are in question, and this can be determined only by checking an ephemeris—a book of tables indicating the daily planetary positions, as expressed in degrees of longitude and based on Greenwich time.

The other meaning of "cusp" is more technical and refers to the degree of a sign separating one house from the next in the horoscope. This is a term used by astrologers to indicate the change in polarity from one energy level to the next. Planets positioned on this point are especially significant, as they have a much greater potency in the affairs of the particular house than planets positioned within.

THE PLANETS

Each of the zodiacal signs is ruled by one, sometimes two planets, and the meaning of each sign is influenced by the nature of the planet that rules it. Every horoscope comprises ten planets sitting in one of twelve signs, falling in a degree from zero to twenty-nine. When a planet in the individual horoscope falls in a sign that it naturally rules, it is most powerfully placed and will promise the individual greater benefit.

PLANETARY RULERSHIP

Aries is ruled by Mars.

Taurus is ruled by Venus.

Gemini is ruled by Mercury.

Cancer is ruled by the Moon.

Leo is ruled by the Sun.

Virgo is ruled by Mercury.

Libra is ruled by Venus.

Scorpio is ruled by Mars and Pluto.

Sagittarius is ruled by Jupiter.

Capricorn is ruled by Saturn.

Aquarius is ruled by Uranus and Saturn.

Pisces is ruled by Neptune and Jupiter.

THE SUN

The position of the sun in the horoscope reveals the nature of the individual's will. It is the motivating force behind all action, and in the solar system it represents the single most powerful force. The sun is associated with the life force, vitality, ideals, inner purpose, and drive for significance in the social environment. As a planet of such potency, it signifies leadership, power, and creativity when strongly placed by sign and aspect. On its highest level, it represents the potential of the higher self to control the lower self, and the domination of spirit over matter. Because the sun is also associated with the ego, when afflicted it can denote a bombastic, arrogant individual who is self-conscious and consumed by conceit. The sun is the energy of life, the key to attainment, the spark of authority. When it illuminates the character, love, faith, honor, and the most exalted human principles are evinced by the individual.

THE MOON

The moon lights up our darkness and represents the nocturnal side of awareness, or the unconscious. It rules the emotions, the moods, and the ability to express personal desires. It directs the will of the sun and determines the path of attainment for the sun's needs. Thus, it is associated with instinct, habit, heredity, memory, imagination, feeling, and receptivity. The placement of the moon in the horoscope is the key to behavior, and its aspects illuminate emotional problems, complexes, blockages, and impulses. This planet is the fastest-moving body in the zodiac, changing signs every two days. Thus, its meaning is associated with personal change and the desire for new experience. When it is afflicted in a horoscope, it signifies a moody, enigmatic temperament that can be capricious, restless, and inconstant. When well-aspected, it denotes a fine intelligence, an excellent imagination, a well-integrated personality, emotional stability, sensitivity, and compassion.

The moon also rules the female body and the feminine experience. In a man's horoscope, its sign indicates the ideal qualities he is searching for in a woman. In addition, the moon has to do with the public, and is often seen to be in a prominent position in horoscopes of famous personalities.

MERCURY

Mercury represents the channels of communication, understanding, interpretation, translation, and intelligence. It transmits the energies of the moon into communicative frameworks, and its tools are language, writing, broadcasting, books, newspapers, magazines, and transportation systems. A common misconception concerning this planet is that it rules the individual's intelligence. Actually, Mercury is merely the ruler of the logical processes that function in concrete, day-to-day situations that do not involve abstract thought. The moon rules the philosophical intelligence that considers values and that evaluates purpose. These energies are translated to the world by Mercury, which is concerned only with how the individual expresses himself. Mercury rules quick-wittedness, verbal abilities, adaptability, mechanical learning tasks, skillfulness, coordination, thought patterns, ingenuity, and logic. When afflicted in a chart, it can show the daydreamer, the liar, and the compulsive talker. It indicates how people tend to communicate, whether they favor intense discussions or chatter away about superficials. Teachers, writers, broadcasters, translators, and scholars all come under the domain of this planet. When Mercury is prominent and rising, it shows a nervous mind that will not easily rest. If afflicted in this position, it can indicate someone who has a tendency to live through thought more than emotion.

VENUS

Venus is the traditional goddess of love and romance. Within the horoscope, it shows the individual's capacity for affection, warmth, and love. It also indicates the personal values that one seeks to satisfy in the love experience, and the kind of person one wishes to attract as an emblem of these values. Venus also shows how one demonstrates affection and communicates the deep emotions of the moon.

On another level, it is associated with all artistic expression, aesthetics, beauty, refinement, harmony, fashion, ornaments, parties, social occasions, and luxuries. When afflicted in a chart, it can indicate self-indulgence, perpetual flirtation, laziness, romantic fickleness, sexual aberrations, and an unbalanced passion for pleasure.

A well-aspected Venus promises creative talent, artistic ability, harmonious love experiences, and often a good fortune in monetary undertakings. The world's great artists, musicians, poets, novelists, actors, and actresses usually have a prominent Venus in the chart. However, interestingly enough, in many cases Venus is afflicted, and the energy devoted to the arts is a sublimation resulting from a sorrowful love life. At its highest, Venus is the principle of universal love, expressed in the sign of Pisces, where it is exalted. However, few can rise to the self-sacrifice required as a higher expression of this position. And thus, the sign Pisces assumes the mundane connotation of sorrow, self-delusion, and vicarious expression of the love urge—seen on a higher level in the artistic endeavor, and on the lower level in excessive fantasy and romantic idealism.

MARS

Mars stands for the principle of assertive energy as expressed in both aggression and sex. In the horoscope, Mars's sign and aspects indicate the specific channels through which both anger and sexuality are most likely expressed. As Mars was the god of war, this planet is best placed when its sign and aspects allow it to easily release the energies of aggression, courage, passion, ambition, assertiveness, and sexuality. When the energies are blocked, because of an affliction, by sign or aspect, anger is reduced to either silence or sarcasm, sexual passion is reduced to frigidity and impotence, courage is reduced to passivity, and driving ambition is dissipated by half-hearted and spurious attempts at accomplishment. On a more aggressive level, when this energy is misdirected, the personality is argumentative, temperamental, rash, and pushy. Personal activities are undertaken in convulsive fits and starts, only to be ultimately abandoned.

Mars rules athletes, dancers, policemen, firearms, fire, and fever. However, aside from its connotation of heat, energy, and aggression, Mars has a decidedly cutting aspect, and also is associated with sarcasm, sharp instruments, surgeons, butchers, brutality, and accidents. This planet is considered malefic by nature, and when negatively aspecting a personal point in the natal chart by transit, it has the force to be severely disruptive.

JUPITER

Jupiter is the great benefic in the solar system, and even in bad aspect does not bode a sorrowful situation. It is the planet of expansion, which applies to all levels of experience, from gaining weight to gaining cosmic bliss, through transcending personal awareness. It rules travel, religion, philosophy, higher education, wealth, wisdom, knowledge, and all activities through which the individual ventures beyond the static limitations of his private universe. This is the planet of luck, good fortune, and unearned opportunity. It is associated with happiness, optimism, laughter, faith, joviality, generosity, and success. Jupiter predominates in the chart of the multimillionaire, and is noticeably influential in the horoscopes of philosophers, professors, comedians, occultists, and those who are consumed by the desire to travel.

At its highest, it denotes enthusiasm, a strong spirituality, love of knowledge, the highest wisdom and human understanding, and the kind of joy that issues from within an elevated state of mind. On its lowest level, Jupiter is extravagance, laziness, exaggeration, overindulgence, waste, frivolity, behavioral excess. Its danger is that it can sometimes make things look too easy, which obviates the inclination toward asserted effort. It can also make unearned opportunities and rewards manifest, setting up a situation that stifles personal growth and leads to indolence.

SATURN

Saturn is the teacher and taskmaster of the zodiac. Because of its restrictive nature, the ancients considered it to be a malefic. However, once the energies of Saturn are properly channeled and the individual seeks to move with Saturn's vibrations rather than against them, this planet can bring the most lasting rewards of a lifetime.

When prominently placed in the horoscope, Saturn can bring either constant trials or creative challenges. The difference depends on the development of the individual. Since its energies are limiting in nature, Saturn can instill points of constriction or concentration.

It can slow things down, bring about disappointments, delays, obstacles, anxiety, depression. Used positively, it can provide the discipline, tenacity, and inner strength that can bring about great accomplishments. Extremely Saturnian people appear cold, rigid, serious, and self-effacing. Often they have problems in allowing their emotions to show. They are responsible and often critical, having high standards for the people with whom they interact closely.

Saturn strongly placed in the chart is an indication of stability, endurance, and determination. If it is in bad aspect with the sun or moon, ego problems and pessimism are qualities often evidenced.

Saturn is the planet of time. It teaches the positive aspects of patience and perseverance. Its principle is crystalization of the forces within, for the greater end of growth and maturation through strength. When Saturn returns by transit to its natal position in the chart, the individual is faced with the lessons of adulthood. Only when one is not ready to progress into this new world of responsibility will Saturn be experienced as a malefic. In an emotionally mature, integrated personality, Saturn's challenging events will be more energy-producing than painful. The greatest challenge of Saturn is expansion. Its greatest pitfalls are fear, restriction, and stagnation.

URANUS

Uranus is the planet of sudden disruption and surprise. It is associated with the qualities of originality, independence, genius, eccentricity, innovation, and sometimes insanity. Uranus is the bolt from the blue. By transit, it brings unexpected change, the specific nature of which is often difficult to predict. It can also bring about a state of startling excitement that is at once inspiring and electrifying.

When Uranus is prominent in the horoscope, an individual is freedom-loving, changeable, erratic, rebellious, and views the world in progressive ways. By profession, these people can be astrologers, occultists, scientists, psychics, psychiatrists, or inventors. Emotionally, there is great detachment, and when seriously afflicted, instability.

Uranus can indicate an extra-ordinary genius that comes in sudden mental flashes. In this type of chart, it gives rise to a kind of supernormal mental awareness that unfolds itself without any kind of study.

Uranians are unusual, magnetic, and self-expressive. Their desire is interaction with the world; their horror is constriction and stagnation.

NEPTUNE

Neptune is the planet of illusion, nebulousness, mysticism, deception, and escape. The energies of this planet are the most difficult to deal with in a productive way, since in the average personality they often create a state of psychic confusion. Neptune has a narcotic effect on the logical mind. Sometimes this feeling is euphoric; at other times it can produce a kind of wild despair. Occultists often refer to this emotional experience as "the dark night of the soul."

When Neptune aspects a significant point in the chart by transit, an individual will have one of several distinct experiences: romantic love and light-headed joy; intense loneliness, alienation, apathy, and futility; a desire for drugs and/or alcohol; overwhelming feelings of victimization; or spiritual bliss, mystical longing, and desire for union with the God state. The specific way in which the

Neptune transit will be felt will depend on the spiritual and psychological development of the individual. It can bring about a period either of self-regeneration through the adoption of new values and attitudes, or of self-destruction through overindulgence or even suicide.

On its highest levels, Neptune represents the principle of divine unity through self-sacrifice, empathy, intuition, psychism, the artistic imagination, mystical expansion, and communication with the higher states of consciousness.

On its lowest level, it can indicate confusion, deceit, drug addiction, alcoholism, suicide, daydreaming, and an inability to function productively with reality. Neptune is the planet of "unreality," and therefore is often seen to be prominent in charts of people who create a new world from the five senses, such as film, ballet, fiction, poetry. Neptune also is connected with such endeavors as Yoga, Buddhism, ceremonial magic, psychic healing. And in this capacity, it can elevate the consciousness to the level of the sixth sense.

Neptune's influence is inspirational. Its directions can be multiple and quite diffuse. On its highest level, Neptune's inspiration will be toward spiritual love; on its lowest, suicide. In between these extremes, every individual has a fundamental choice of either the self-sacrifice involved in sympathy toward others or the swamp of self-compassion. The domicile can be in either place. Neptune merely opens up the senses in preparation for the human choice.

PLUTO

Pluto is the slowest-moving planet in the zodiac, and since it was discovered only in 1930, there is still a great deal to be revealed about its nature. In general, Pluto has a generational influence and is the unfolding force of major social change and mass occurrences. Its principle is transformation, and the sign that it falls in shows in what way the world at large is slowly but sedulously transforming.

At the present time, Pluto is in Libra, the sign of relationships. Transiting through this sign, it has slowly brought about great change in the nature of love, marriage, and relationships in general. Old structures are dying off; new attitudes are evolving; sexual mores, commitments, and roles are being reevaluated.

In 1984 Pluto enters a sixteen-year transit into Scorpio. This transit will introduce an epoch of colossal world change, upheaval, growth, death, and transformation. Scorpio is the sign of death, and since Pluto naturally rules this sign, it is most powerfully placed in this position. It has been predicted that this will be a time of fires, floods, volcanoes, and wars that will challenge world consciousness toward universal love and spiritual growth, characterized by Pluto's later transit into Sagittarius, the sign of religion, peace, and expansion.

Because there are still so many scientific facts to be learned about Pluto, a task that can be accomplished only through years of research, this planet can be regarded as fascinating and mysterious. Pluto's essence is transformation, and its process is the dying-off that prepares for regeneration and growth.

When Pluto is placed on the ascendant in the horoscope, it indicates an intense individual who is fated to experience much personal change in a lifetime. Sometimes this change is ushered in through external events that bring about temporary upheaval; at other times, it comes through the individual's own personal need for expansion and growth. Such Plutonian people are often private, deep, and serious, liking to be alone a great deal. Interestingly enough, some astrologers refer to Pluto on the ascendants as the "Garbo aspect," since both the former actress's behavior and her chart are characteristic of the Plutonian need for solitude.

Pluto rules over all types of mass change and upheaval, such as war, uprisings, and holocausts. It is also associated with undercover groups such as the Mafia, the CIA, and the secret police. The changes Pluto seems to bring about so abruptly are actually processes that have been brewing under the surface for a long period of time. On a personal level, these processes are thought forms in the mind; on a mass level, they may be the rumblings that precede a war or an uprising.

The challenge of Pluto is the most consuming, for it is the challenge of nurturing new life from the processes of death. In order for this transformation to occur, negative situations must be brought to the surface, destroyed, purged, and the energy transmuted. Pluto represents energy in its most volcanic form, but also at its purest and most spiritual. Through working positively with the energies of this enigmatic planet, one is able to transcend the human limitations that are barriers to the higher nature. On this personal level, Pluto brings about the death of the ego, and concomitantly, the consciousness of the absolute.

II

YOUR
PERSONALITY
GUIDE

THE SIGNS
OF
THE ZODIAC

When the average person comes up to you at a party and asks "What's your sign?" most people do not realize that this question refers only to the sign or constellation placement of the sun in the heavens at the time you were born. The symbolic properties of the sun, astrologically speaking, refer to the actions of the outward ego, defined by the inward personality drives that tend to set you into the slot of Leo, Virgo, Libra, etc. However, often you may find that you just don't fall neatly into any of these preorganized categories, and indeed, your personality may even defy their quoted characteristics. That is because the sun is but one of eleven major categories working in your chart, which includes ten planets and an ascendant. Each of these eleven points in the chart falls into one of the twelve zodiacal signs. Further, the geometrical relationship between each of these points modifies the combined effect of a specific planet or ascendant falling in a specific sign. These relationships are referred to as the aspects. And still further, but only for the record, the exact point calculated to be equidistant from two planets in aspect, known as the planetary midpoint, is also significant and can reveal some fascinating details about an individual's personality.

For our purposes, we shall here delineate the characteristic properties of the signs. We have already considered the properties of each of the planets and the energy levels on which they most easily function. As each sign is described, we will refer to its influence on the sun.

However, the properties of each sign can also be considered in terms of influence on the other planets.

The romantic compatibility section of this book is not meant to be negative. On the contrary, it is meant to poke fun at the seriousness with which we take ourselves.

Its main objective is to try to make you look at yourself, your relationships, and your roles in them in a larger perspective and to realize that we all have faults, fears, and vulnerabilities that control us from time to time. However, the esoteric purpose for relationships is that they provide us with the opportunities for a specific kind of change, growth, and expansion that can be motivated only by love.

This love section is based on the sun sign, which, in itself, offers only the most general indication of emotional compatibility.

However, what I wish to stress is that there really is no right or wrong sign for anyone. Whether or not a relationship works depends totally on the individual's commitment to the working out of personal conflicts that is necessary for a mature experience of human loving.

The single most important factor in any situation of chart comparison is the individual's both conscious and unconscious will to love. If that desire is severely conflicted, the most congruent planetary placements occurring between two people are meaningless and cannot be counted on to cement the relationship.

Love, like astrology, is not a magical game to relieve the daily ennui. At best, it requires constant effort, commitment—during the difficult times as well as during the joyful ones—a certain amount of self-sacrifice, and a great deal of understanding.

The horoscope in its entirety is merely a tool for the sensitive astrologer to determine the individual's subconscious drives, his conscious action patterns, and any conflicts between the two. As such, it is like a floor plan for discovering destructive fears and desires that have been causing repeated relationship problems. In this way, astrology can be an aid toward the growth of a deeper personality integration, along with a greater harmony between the layers of the self as well as with significant others.

It is through a serious and thoughtful assessment of the horoscope that the astrologer is able to help the individual understand his responsibility in the experience of loving.

ARIES

Dates: March 21—April 20
Ruling planet: Mars
Element: Fire
Mode: Cardinal
Quality: Masculine, positive
Planetary principle: Action
Primal desire: Leadership
Color: Red
Jewels: Diamond, amethyst
Day: Sunday
Archangel: Samuel
Magical number 5
Material factor: Enterprise

ARIES OF
FAME AND FORTUNE

Henry Kissinger	Joan Crawford
Warren Beatty	Bette Davis
Julie Christie	J. P. Morgan
Marlon Brando	Joseph Pulitzer
Steve McQueen	Vincent van Gogh
Tennessee Williams	Nikita Khrushchev
Houdini	Erica Jong
Henry Luce	Linda Goodman

THE ARIES FEMALE

Favorable

You're like a light in the forest or a firecracker on the Fourth of July. Your extraordinary energy is a magnetic force that both dazzles people and draws them to you.

As a teenager, you were probably captain of the cheerleaders and president of your class as well as of the debating club. You are the classic superachiever and can't sit still because you're always seeking some new challenge.

You are highly effusive, enthusiastic, extroverted, and the kind of person to whom others gravitate. You are the fervent follower of a cause and often the spokesman. You are passionate, ebullient, honest, and imbued with great personal power.

You have a do-it-yourself attitude, and what you can do is often more than a multitude of people put together. You are leadership personified and could end up doing anything from producing and directing a successful movie to becoming a Nobel Prize physician.

When you get an idea in your head, there is no stopping you. You are so highly motivated that even if someone locked you up in jail, you would still find a way to get the job done.

You are nervous, intense, and committed to whatever you undertake. You like people who are direct, who get to the point quickly, and who don't take up your time with trivia. You're a chain-smoker, a compulsive gum-chewer, and you often drink coffee by the gallon.

In matters of love, you are a romantic idealist. You want to be swept away with a most dramatic display of feeling. But at the same time, you don't want to be drowned in sentimentality.

You are most attracted to a man who is the dynamic go-getter type, and the more successful, the better. Basically, you want the man you love to look good and to be able to enhance your self-esteem in the outside world. When it comes to marriage, you feel you have most in common with a truly accomplished person who shares your own success drives.

Once you are committed, you are completely faithful and likewise demand the same. Somewhere in the depths of your consciousness, you believe in unlimited loyalty, even if you leave the laws unspoken. You fully expect to get back what you give, plus a little more. Well, you're worth it.

You are very emotional, idealistic, and far more vulnerable than you look. You're basically uncomplicated and work very hard for what you value, whether it's a job, worldly success, or a relationship.

In the latter, you need someone who makes you feel special, since you're far more insecure than one would think. You are self-assured when you can hide behind the trappings of your own success. However, when it comes to loving, you have a hard time leaving your career behind you, even in the course of casual conversation.

Chances are, you talk about your work over dinner, over breakfast, and even in bed. You'll never allow yourself a naked moment when you're just a woman with a certain physique and a certain feeling. Instead, to keep yourself secure, you have to project your successful self-image everywhere. And, at times, it can all get a bit boring.

Because you're always on, and at times rather relentlessly so, you can give those around you a headache. You need constant approval and will go to any lengths to get it. However, there are moments when this can be a turn-off, especially to someone who just wants to sit back in silence and relax.

The hardest lesson you'll have to learn in this lifetime is that not everyone wants to listen to you. Keep your own space, but don't crowd others with your career matters. The less self-conscious you become, the more you will learn how to enjoy yourself *by yourself*, and without the gilded trappings with which you so identify. You put restrictions on your self-image that are harsh and demanding and need not be there. Remember that before you become a public figure, you first have to be a person. And in the long run, the more you become comfortable with that alone, the greater a public figure you will be.

Unfavorable

You're a barracuda with a Me complex. Your sentences begin with "I" and end with "me." You're bossy and controlling, self-centered, and committed to getting what you want, no matter whom you have to walk on to get it.

You have a personality that's like a storm in the night. You are pushy and impatient, arrogant and insensitive. You're interested in a subject only if it relates to you. Otherwise, you'll rudely interrupt to let everyone know that you don't want to listen.

You are power-driven and have a way of psychologically pummeling people for attention. You get it—even if you have to stand on their feet, shout in their ears, and push your elbow in their stomachs. Oh, yes, you definitely make your presence known!

As a child, you were a toughy who always had to have her way, and since then you haven't changed much. Even under your best manners you're still a child and a toughy.

You're also a fighter who doesn't know defeat. That's mostly because you have a way of exhausting those around you until they give in to anything just to shut you up. You are demanding, easily agitated, temperamental, and prone to throwing tantrums if you feel you aren't being taken seriously. Basically, your life philosophy is "What's yours is mine, but what's mine is my own." With this in mind, there's not much that you ever miss out on.

You are jealous, competitive, at times cruel, but never cunning; you're much too blunt and outspoken for that. Fundamentally, you are a narcissist who expects flattery, regardless of how badly you're behaving. However, that's something that you would never notice, because you create the most convenient blinders against anything that might be self-incriminating.

At best, you're a caricature of the "pushy broad." When you don't get your way, you are both petulant and painful to be around. Your underlying attitude is "Don't confuse me with the facts. It's only what's in front of me that counts."

In romance, you're a terror and a most capricious kind of flirt who lacks insight and discrimination. You're looking for a challenge. However, in a moment when no one of interest cares enough even to acknowledge you, you'll settle for anyone foolish enough to inflate your ego. Of course, you do have a way of leading a man along. Ask him sixty-five times a day if you're not really great, and after a while he'll get so tired of listening to you that he'll agree to anything.

Generally, you are unfaithful, because your ego is at the mercy of any flirtation that should come along. And in such moments, you are far more grabby than mysterious and subtle. At first, you make a man feel like you're doing target practice on the middle of his forehead. And then, when you move in, because you don't want to waste any time, you make him wonder if you might be a lady wrestler who just got off work and is still a little jumpy. However, there are times when you feel that, just to preserve your pathetic ego, you should get a little huffy at a stranger's approach. (This is your attempt to make him think he's really getting a hard-to-win prize, because you're the elusive, shy type who needs to be courted.) At this point, in a blind effort to call the shots, you grin and mutter, "Don't call me. I'll call you."

Those men who do have relationships with you come away feeling that they've been used like a toaster. This is because you consider men to be simple gadgets that you plug in, turn on, use, and forget. However, when you feel that you really need *them*, you'll agree to talk to them long enough to tell them what you want.

Quite conveniently, you don't have to consider their wishes, because you don't hear them and never realize that they have any. For you, ignorance is more than bliss. It gets you everything you want without having to give anything in return. And any way you look at it, that's more than a lot.

THE ARIES MALE

Favorable

You move more quickly than a coursing bullet and have thought waves faster than the speed of light. You are the principle of aggressive action personified and are the kind of charismatic man that every woman wants to meet.

You have a vitality that defies the laws of medical science and a courage that helps to carry you quickly past your darker moments. You are the man who rushes in where angels fear to tread and possess a toughness that can be truly intimidating.

Physically speaking, you are strong, athletic, energetic, and very restless. You have the spirit of the warrior and the eminence of the elder statesman. Power is your password and positive thinking the light along your path.

Usually, at an early age, success summons you to a more expansive realm of existence. But this is merely a precursor of even greater things to come. By middle age, you are the object of public attention almost every time you put your head outside the door, and in your later years, your name has probably become a household word.

Part of your prosperity is due to your high intelligence, another part to your hard work. When dedicated to a task, you are both inexhaustible and highly inspired. Defeat is something that has never been a consideration, and certainly never a reality.

In business you like things done immediately, if not sooner. And since you usually wield more power than the mayor you get what you want exactly when you want it. In the professional atmosphere, you get yourself so fired up that you're like a missile hurling through space. Your temper is quick and can fulminate into a fast but powerful explosion. However, you seldom bear a grudge, but rather let the whole thing blow over and then pass on quickly to something else.

You are always busy—at any given moment, at any time—and think that other people should be also. You love new projects, new people, new interests, and like especially to be physically active. You find relaxation in the kind of athletic activities that force your mind temporarily to take second place. Fundamentally, you are a centurion who never knows when to stop.

You intensely dislike pessimistic people, having to wait in line in the supermarket, employees who are slow and lazy, and people who talk too much and never get to the point. You love change and challenges, people who have achievement attitudes, being around powerful personalities, reading your name in the newspaper, and parties where more people know who you *are* than actually know you.

Romantically speaking, you are most attracted to spirited, dynamic women. You prefer them to be powerful, prestigious, highly motivated, energetic, vivacious, and very sexual.

In love, you are ardent, passionate, and aggressive. You have an all-or-nothing attitude and take your emotions to the extremes. You really want to be bewitched and overwhelmed, but if that doesn't happen, you'll turn your attention elsewhere and find someone new in record time.

Even when your heart is emotionally committed, you have a casual attitude toward sex that often spurs you on to have outside affairs. Your desire for new experience often leads you through so many people that it's a good thing that your body is strong and your vitality limitless.

Basically, you are on a quest for constant excitement, amusement, challenges, and total enthrallment. And because of your ardent enthusiasm, you always get what you go after, and often a little more.

Whether it's women, worldly success, or the power to be allowed to try something new, you have it. You are a self-propelled person who gets the supremacy he seeks and maintains it. Your incandescent approach blinds and exhausts all opposition, and your fortitude drives you past all obstacles. You wield the most potent kind of power, and the key to your force is that you believe in yourself far more than in anybody else. You have perfected the power of your own will to the point that it makes your wishes materialize. The world is yours for the taking, and not only do you know it, you also know what to do with it. You are the paradigm of influence, and you prevail with a magnetism that people can never forget.

Unfavorable

You're an *enfant terrible*, with the attention span of a two-year-old. You are temperamental and insensitive, quickly bored, and burning with the need for new experience.

You are motivated by self-interest, excitement, challenge, and the unconscious desire to create chaos. When you're in the running for something you want, you are ruthless, guiltless, and willing to sacrifice anything if it will help you get ahead.

When your anger is aroused, you are the kind of man who could kick little old ladies and not feel guilty. There are times when you are violent; other times, merely cruel. And after the storm is over, you're annoyed if people are still upset by the volcano that has just erupted.

You really want to be liked and can't understand why others dwell on the damage you do. You certainly don't.

There are too many other things to take up your interest, like riding your motorcycle through the living room and torturing the dog when you're sure that someone is looking. (You love attention and like to perform while you're getting it.)

The most intrinsic qualities of your character structure are belligerence, bossiness, and boastfulness. You don't necessarily want to love a woman, you just want to possess her, run her life, and have her around to make you look good. In turn, she is supposed to be grateful to you for putting her in her place.

Fundamentally, you have a chewing-gum attitude toward relationships: throw it away when the sweetness starts to wear off. It takes you little time to find another.

Casual sex is your favorite way of getting close to a woman. Your idea of intimacy is the quick removal of clothing. Your concept of love is merely the physical act that you know familiarly as a four-letter word.

One-night stands suit you best, but if the woman has a lot of sex appeal, charisma, beauty, and charm, you might let her stay around as long as she performs her services. However, the rule is she has to remember whom she has to answer to.

Although sex (in any form, with anyone or anything) is one of your greatest pleasures, first and foremost, you enjoy looking into the eyes of someone who is looking up to you. You are an egotist and as arrogant as they come. Flattery makes you feel fantastically alive, and next to decadence, it's your favorite thing.

Basically, you're a show-off who would like to think he has a lot of power. Some Aries are pushy and wouldn't mind committing murder to further a few career goals. Others are lazy but loud enough to let you know all the things they would like to *think* they've accomplished.

You are a petulant individual whenever you are blocked. Since your mind moves too fast to listen to reason, you would rather attack first and find out the details later.

You have a hair-trigger temper and love to intimidate people with it. It gives you a sense of power that in calmer moments you feel is missing. When you disrupt calm situations with a little abuse, you obtain the kind of larger-than-life drama to which you are so addicted.

Your particular forte is playing superiority games.

You are so self-righteously convinced that you have to bend down to communicate with the world that sometimes you have the more simple souls around you believing it's true. However, those who are more perceptive know that you are merely more selfish. Anyone who dedicates as much time as you do to his own self-satisfaction has to come out on top, regardless of his intelligence. In the end, it's not really a matter of personal power; it's a matter of how much pain you want to put others through. And your capacity happens to be limitless.

DECANS

Every sign in the zodiac can be broken down into three subdivisions, called decans. Each decan roughly corresponds to ten degrees—the first third, second third, and last third of the sun sign's time span, which is approximately thirty days.

As each of these periods has different subrulerships, the personality of a person is slightly modified by the specific decan it falls in. For instance, an Aries born in the second decan would be ruled by Mars, but subruled by the sun. Therefore, he would tend to display a greater sense of pride, boastfulness, egotism, and optimism than an Aries born in the third decan, which is subruled by Jupiter. This Aries would tend to be more freedom-loving, flighty, travel-oriented, and interested in subjects of a philosophical nature. An Aries born in the first decan would be the most aggressive, but not necessarily the most productive and accomplished.

Decans are important, since they do account for a more detailed assessment of an individual's personality characteristics. They also show how two people born under the same sun sign can be markedly different.

If you were born between March 21 and March 30, your sun falls in the Mars decan of Aries, and you most typify the qualities of your sign.

You are aggressive, enthusiastic, energetic, and demanding. You have a highly dominant personality and are a definite attention-getter.

Since you have a primal need to be number one in everything you do, your personality abounds in leadership qualities. You can't stand the idea of staying in second place. Therefore, you will drive yourself to the top, regardless of the personal cost either to yourself or to others.

You are impulsive, spontaneous, self-involved, and self-motivated. Your attitudes are positive, and your basic approach to life is action-oriented. You are the trailblazer and the restless initiator of new projects. You are self-assured, enthusiastic, adamant, and always alert to the opportunities around you.

Your overwhelming idealism is backed up by very strong convictions that carry you through even the bad times. No matter what negative circumstance befalls you, you're never down for long. You emerge from every situation dauntless and fully aroused for an even better beginning.

You can be so arrogant and cocksure that you are capable of walking on or over other people without offering even a mild apology. Your constant self-absorption can alienate you from others, especially when they get in the way of something you really want to do.

You move straight on a course and will not consider opposition; nor will you hear any advice. In everything you desire, you play from the position of boss, despite appearances that may seem to say otherwise.

Aries of this decan are the most impulsive, headstrong, accident-prone, and temperamental. You tend to love love affairs far more than the idea of marriage. There are always sideline temptations that can tear your heart out if you feel you have to refuse them. You are a clever opportunist and have more than enough success orientation and sex drive to carry you to another planet.

You are most ambitious, dynamic, a go-getter, and wherever you go, you seem to achieve a lot. That is because you're not afraid of asking for what you want, and never hesitate to lunge ahead and grab it. Then, when you've got it, you have a way of flaunting it so people want to give you more.

You're nervous, high-strung, and come on like a gangster out for a kill. And although you're blunt, basically you're honest. You're not always out to win friends, but you do influence people. And since that's really what you want, any way you look at it, you have to be considered a success.

* * *

If you were born between March 31 and April 10, your sun falls in the solar decan of Aries.

You are idealistic, ambitious, a classic superachiever, and the kind of person who always attains whatever he aspires to.

You have a dynamic, vital personality that takes you places, and a power drive that needs to be expressed in competitive situations.

You are warm, passionate, emotional, and you light up a room with your enthusiasm. You can be a constant inspiration to the more sedentary souls who surround you and an incandescent force to those who are already inspired.

You are willful, intense, creative, and lust for the accoutrements of success. You attach your sense of self-worth to the quality of your achievements and drive yourself past your limits to attain your goals.

You are an extremely hard worker and embrace a sense of organization that is lacking in the other Aries decans. Your inherent strength and persistence in the face of opposition are qualities for which you are most highly admired.

This decan is one that usually experiences a high degree of success in life, through the constant application of effort. However, at the same time, there is usually a strong sense of egotism. You need to be the center of attention and to share your achievements with others in a way that might be considered bragging. You are the most intense example of the Aries Me complex; often, in relationship with others, you cannot think past the limits of your own ego. You tend to be vain, proud, and headstrong in situations involving your self-image, and you usually see most situations as revolving around your self-image.

In love, you are romantic, impulsive, and so idealistic that you get hurt far more than one would ever think. Your greatest challenge in a love situation is to learn a little self-sacrifice and not to feel so incredibly compromised when you have to give in to someone else's desires.

There is an innocence to your ego problems that sometimes makes your selfish behavior more tolerable. However, only when you learn to give equal time to the demands of those significant others in your life will you be on the road to greater self-awareness and a more enriching love experience.

* * *

If you were born between April 11 and April 20, your sun falls in the Jupiter decan of Aries.

You are less achievement-oriented and more fun-loving than the previous two decans. In addition, you are more inclined to burn off your energies through a commitment to some kind of sport.

You also love to travel and like to take off impulsively. You see life as a kind of adventure that beckons you to try many things and visit many places.

Your attitudes are fresh, optimistic, daring, and sometimes lacking in conventionality. At times you are a proselytizer; at others, an inspired force engaging in your playtime activities.

You are not as ambitious as other Aries, but you are more philosophical. Chances are, your overactive mind will express itself through more intellectual forms, and you will become fervently committed to some kind of study, value, or ideal. You are a perpetual student, with a penchant for finding all experience educative. You have a special need to find meaning through a system of values, and you give expression to an idealism that can be fanatical.

You're probably the most well-liked native of all the Aries decans. That is because you have both a sense of humor and a spontaneous kind of ebullience that make you pleasant to be around.

You have an invincible charm that can often get you further than hard work. Your charisma quite naturally attracts love, friendship, and all the forces of good fortune.

When it comes to money, there are so many things you want to spend it on that you often feel frustrated. However, because of the beneficial power of Jupiter, it is not unlikely that your economic situation can improve quite unexpectedly.

You find romantic flirtations irresistible and sometimes have a hard time being completely faithful. The exuberance of your personality will provide many opportunities in this direction. Although you are kind, helpful, well-meaning, and generous in spirit, at times you are a trifle undependable and can be considered slightly capricious.

However, your basic honesty, individuality, and good

intentions are usually enough to overcome all your faults and make you a lovable person that others truly appreciate.

LOVE

You are romantic, dramatic, and daring. You adore the drama of the first glance, the smoldering flirtation, and the larger-than-life love.

You want to be swept off your feet by a bold, deliciously seductive soul who craves as much constant action as you do.

You need someone who will build up and fortify your ego, tell you you're extremely grand, and love you for your accomplishments. (You still haven't learned how to love yourself for simply what you are. That's why you boast so much.)

You want to hear bells ring, see cannons go off, and be blinded by all the excitement. However, when you wake up, and the champagne looks more like stale beer, then you quickly consider cutting out and seeking some action elsewhere.

You are far more attracted to the superficial aspects of falling in love than you are to the commitment for better or for worse. You want a love life that is hallucinatory and never stagnant, with a constant array of new faces that appear on the scene to prevent you from admitting that you're bored.

You don't believe that there is merely one love that proves itself to be perfection. Instead, you like to live for the moment and leave yourself open for anyone exciting who comes tearing along to get your attention.

Basically, you feel that variety is more than the spice of life; it's the electrifying principle of existence. Therefore, the more, the better, and you hope that they just keep coming, since you have the courage to handle very many.

You are a highly sexual animal who strives for the saisfaction of its needs—and its needs are really rapacious. You appreciate a lover who is as sexually uninhibited and as direct as you are. However, should you encounter someone to whom you are attracted, who doesn't exactly mainline a path to your feet, you have not the slightest hesitation in taking the initiative. This might mean grabbing an elbow, staring relentlessly, knocking someone down in the midst of your enthusiasm, or just bluntly blurting out what you really want. (You're not exactly the most subtle of people.)

You're attracted to the aggressive, flashy sort who boasts of so many accomplishments that you'll never have to worry about being associated with a loser. You would most like to be devastated by the drug of romantic excitement. However, lacking this, you'll settle for someone who will inflate your ego without being too obvious about it. In your book, subtlety is just a waste of time, and time is of the essence. If you have to constantly remind someone that you're still alive, it's better that you just forget the whole thing. You believe in making the most of every moment, and for every romantic moment of your life, you certainly have a lot to remember.

MARRIAGE

The basic problem here is that you are both loving and freedom-loving, and this does not make for the most stable marriage.

There is usually one special person to whom you devote your daily larger-than-life dramas. However, it's all those people on the side that usually pose the problem.

You want to be able to have your apricot mousse and eat it too. But regardless of what you want, there are a lot of people who don't appreciate being shared.

You are most generous with your affections, which means everyone gets a little. However, your relationships usually run into trouble when that special person of the moment feels discontented with only a little love. What is wanted is a lot. And really, it's not that peculiar a preference.

At times, Aries can be truly uncompromising. And only for this reason do marital relationships pose problems. You need constant excitement far more than you need a mate, but sometimes you take both just to try them out.

Those little affairs on the side that you seem to need are really a constant interference with the feelings you express toward a marriage partner. And although, like a grabby child, you feel you must have both, the fact is that you really can't handle either. Your ideal is to have a little action in every corner. However, when the lights go out, and you're left all alone, it's not exactly fun and games anymore.

You have a strong tendency to marry late or not at all. But if you marry early, you have an even stronger tendency to have affairs and to divorce.

You are so independent, self-sufficient, and self-serving that most often you would be far better off not married at all. Your career usually takes up so much of your time that there just isn't a whole lot left over, and on top of this, your quest for the peaks and your repugnance of the plains and the valleys is not the most mature basis on which to begin a marriage.

There are some Aries who, with a mate, live happily ever after. However, within these individuals are contained the highest characteristics of their sign. For the most part, Aries is not the best marriage bet. Until you learn how to give as much as you take, somebody always comes out losing.

MONEY

When it comes to money, you can be both a spendthrift and someone who enjoys the game of making it.

You are an impulsive shopper who often develops a love-at-first-sight yearning for a variety of things. And once you are emotionally impassioned, you can just say good-bye to the concept of economic sensibility.

If you are a certain kind of Aries, heavyweight bills can accrue that bring creditors pounding at your door. When it gets really bad, you have a way of refusing to confront the issue. Maybe you'll just make paper airplanes from the unopened bills and send them flying swiftly to the trash.

If you are the other kind of Aries, the principles of survival are cemented in your consciousness. Therefore, you pay your bills on time and drive yourself to acquire a savings account as well as some sound investments that ultimately bring you a nice profit.

Since you have Taurus in your second house, ideally you like the sense of security that money brings you. But unlike Taurus, you don't derive a great deal of satisfaction from collecting possessions.

Basically, money provides freedom to do what you want when you want it. You like to be able to think that at any moment you can just pick up and go if the mood strikes you, and this applies to everything from a job to a marriage to a change of home to the ability to take a trip.

Money enables you to feel more in control of your life. It also allows you those delicious moments of self-indulgence that you so enjoy and usually deserve because you work so hard.

By itself, sitting in a bank, it means nothing more than that it's waiting to do whatever you tell it. And you have a special way of commanding it to bring you the kind of magical moments of which you always make the most.

CAREER

If success is not important, you really don't know what is. What you want most is to be at the top of whatever you undertake. Anything less means a lot of hard work to improve your position.

Perhaps only Leo enjoys the superficial aspects of success as much as you do. And while Capricorn needs power, you simply need the assurance that you have it.

You like to think that power emanates from you far more than from your position. Aries creates the positions; other people fill them and take orders.

Worldly success is intrinsic to your sense of well-being. Regardless of your profession, you can't live without it and feel good about yourself. You are driven and relentless in the struggle toward achievement. In the process, you may drive yourself as well as everyone around you, crazy; however, you're always too busy even to notice.

You are the most natural of superachievers and need the sense of success that accompanies recognition—the more massive, of course, the better. You love to be boss and command others while you congratulate yourself on how you've created it all.

You are driven, competitive, and you love the challenges that you undertake. You formulate your goals quite early on and follow them even in the midst of a national disaster.

Likewise, you have no patience for unmotivated employees, people who don't know what they want to do, and people who have decided that they don't want to do anything.

There has never been a five-minute standstill even when you felt unmotivated. Your attitude is that there are so many things to do and too little time to do them. Therefore, you make the most of every minute and force the people around you to move at your own pace.

Intrinsic to being a success is being boss and gaining the privilege of telling other people what to do. You don't love this; you consider it due you. There can be no debating that you are number one. You gained that position because you are best. You demonstrate it aggressively because you aren't shy and don't have the patience to wait around for people to notice it themselves. Nothing about you is a mystery. And neither is your rise to the top, which is usually faster than the speed of light.

Because you've got hair-trigger reflexes and have more energy than a team of football players, you would make a great athlete. However, your sense of daring and your courageous qualities would also make you suited for police work.

Since you are a leader rather than a follower, and an initiator of projects, you work best in situations where you give orders rather than take them. You are a pioneer with a purpose, an idea person with a mind that never stops.

Because you like to lay the groundwork and dictate what has to be done from there on, you could make an excellent movie producer, publisher, or even president of a corporation, or an entire country! Your desire for leadership will drive you to the top in all your professional undertakings. You combine a titan mentality with the fantasies of a dictator. And because you demand immediate gratification in everything you desire, you have a most extraordinary way of making your fantasies real and your thoughts materialize into money.

You are innovative and ambitious enough to build an empire out of nothing, and you have the kind of wild enthusiasm that makes others eager to go along with you. Once you get inflamed enough, people will follow you anywhere. And naturally, you love it.

Your mind is so adaptable that you can be anything from a beautician to a brain surgeon, from a dentist to an optometrist, from an actor to a writer.

You are dynamic, creative, highly capable, and have a special way of capturing people's attention. Whatever you decide to do, you are always noticed, usually appreciated, and often respected. You have a strong power drive that has to be played out, regardless of the professional setting. Like no other sign, you have a way of fulfilling this and making yourself heard, no matter how hard you have to shout.

FRIENDS

Although you're gregarious and outgoing, you don't have as many friends as one might think. Because you're always on the move, many of your relationships are more friendly and superficial than consuming and committed.

You're the party person who knows everyone but has time for very few. Since you usually travel in two directions at once, people have to be both fast and versatile to keep up with you.

Basically, you have a greater attraction to people who are ambitious, agile, vibrant, and enthusiastic. You like to surround yourself with the more successful inhabitants of society, since you feel that they improve your self-image. You also feel that you have more in common with a superachiever than with an average person. You do. However, chances are that when you get together you'll both talk about nothing but your work.

You are very loyal to those long-term friends that you really care about. In return, you expect the same consideration, and sometimes a little more. You're one person who is not afraid to ask for a favor, or two, or three, even at times that are less than convenient.

You love to "offer" your advice, even when no one has asked or is really listening. At these times you have a rather enthusiastic approach that is guaranteed to get attention if not always agreement.

Like Leo, you want to feel proud of your friends, since you see them as a reflection of yourself. Because you are a very emotional person, you take this exchange of feeling seriously and put a high value on it.

HEALTH

You have the vitality of a long-distance runner and the body of an athlete. Your energy level seems to be superhuman. However, you use every bit of it, since you happen to be one of the busiest people going.

That's a problem, since you can easily outdo yourself. Because you hate to sleep, you keep your cardiac muscles working overtime.

Aries rules the head, and yours is like an overwound clock that sometimes pushes your body past its breaking point. The result can be either physical exhaustion or a heart attack.

In general, you hate to be sick. It makes you crabby and unbearable to be around. This is because you're afraid that you'll miss something. Therefore, the longer the sickness, the more beastly your behavior. Deep down, at heart, you're just a baby, wanting some wonderful new toys.

Most of the time, your health is excellent, although you do have your share of headaches. However, when your temper is aroused, even germs don't want to linger around you for long.

Since you are a self-propelled force operating perpetually in overdrive, you usually run rather than walk, which makes you one of the most accident-prone signs of the zodiac.

You're a maniac behind the wheel and drive according to the basic rules of your own impatience. Your car accidents are usually unnecessary and merely a testimonial of your tendency toward blind impulse. At the same time, your motorcycle spills show that you're a daredevil who can't resist speeding.

Chances are high that you'll survive to a ripe old age to drive yourself and everybody around you crazy. At eighty, you'll be shouting and pointing, and the entire world around you will still be taking orders.

HOME

When it comes to your home, you're hardly ever there. You're usually on your way out to your multitude of activities, from which you'll eventually return exhausted but happy.

Unlike Taurus or Cancer, you would rather spend an entire day playing tennis than staying at home to build bookshelves. Therefore, your abode strikes an outsider with its informal charm. It often looks like you've been up all night working or that you've just gotten home and haven't the slightest idea of where to start.

When you do decide to fool around and change things because it all suddenly looks very stale and is starting to get boring, you do so strictly on impulse. At this point, you are more than totally consumed and will push all your social impulses to one side, stay up all night drinking coffee, and mentally and physically move about in overdrive. In the indecent hours of the next morning, one tense, exhausted, but very elated Aries is standing back among the debris and looking at the space where a wall once was and gloating about what friends will say.

Later in life, your home comes to mean much more to you, especially if you have Pisces or Taurus prominent in your chart. There is a point when you start to get a headache from the social clamor and prefer a little solitude from the hectic hustle and bustle. (You usually find your own company preferable to indiscriminate socializing.)

At this point, you like to think of your home as a place of relaxation where you can sit back, sip some wine in peace, and either entertain close friends or devote the time to some ego-oriented project.

Basically you see your home as an extension of yourself, and you will do everything you can to make it look its best and to reflect your ego in the most favorable way. It is not unlikely that your own paintings hang on the walls and that a visitor will be startled by a group portrait of your lovers as they enter the bathroom. Here and there, one is sure to find stunning little objets d'art—gifts from rajas and Pulitzer Prize-winning novelists, or perhaps bought by you in some exotic place to enhance your aura of good taste.

But whatever your domestic proclivities, your home is a spontaneous and genuine reflection of your immediate desires. Whatever those may be, your home speaks them honestly, and in so doing, is a statement of the deepest part of you that aggressively meets the world day by day.

COSMIC CHALLENGE

Your greatest challenge in this lifetime is to develop an awareness that extends beyond yourself. Often you have a hard time operating beyond your own personal needs, and without thinking, you can be offensive to others.

Every Aries has a tendency to be too self-involved and to look at the world from a deeply subjective perspective. However, if you have the courage to try to see yourself from the outside, while you try to see others from the inside, you will greatly expand your sphere of personal interaction. Slowly, certain experiences will become more accessible to you; and others, far more pleasurable.

Stand back from yourself and give yourself a little room to look out. There is an entire world out there that is not composed of *you*, although you can certainly be a part of it.

However, the rule is that the more you want, the more you have to give. After a while, the act of taking doesn't get you very far if you fail to do some giving along with it.

Once you learn how to like giving (which means that it's not always at your convenience), then your character will have soared to the level of the enterprising and indomitable, rather than the self-serving and audacious. At this point, your consciousness has passed into the highest form of Aries, and the universe that surrounds you is thankful for your presence.

INSPIRATION

You are the creative spark of the universe. You make it all begin and get everyone around you excited before anything even happens. Your courage and charisma will take you everywhere, and everyone who meets you knows this.

You are so enterprising and energetic that you are the center of attention all the time. Everyone would like to know you, because you have a stellar power that is as overpowering as cosmic radiation.

You radiate a life force that permeates the darkest reaches of any room. You have a will that devastates your most daring opponent. You have a kind of energy that could bring the dead back to life. And you have an ability to bring yourself forward to reap the most of every situation.

You are Aries. You are admired for your force, aggression, self-assurance, and enthusiasm. Worldly power is merely a place within reach of your fingertips, while love always hovers around you.

You have all and know how to redeem it. Within this understanding lies your power.

WHAT HOLDS YOU BACK AND HOW TO OVERCOME IT

The only thing that holds you back from getting what you want is spending too much time thinking about it. Your ego needs are so large that they can, at times, make you appear predatory. You have a convenient way of forgetting that there are other people in the world when you get consumed by something you want. You would just as soon walk on a person as around him, and then you have the audacity to wonder why you leave such smoldering resentment behind you.

You think mostly of yourself. Your fundamental vocabulary consists of "me," "myself," and "I." Beyond that, everything is extraneous. Sometimes you are so self-centered that you don't even realize what you're saying and the effect it has on those around you. You can be totally tactless, blunt, and bogged down with your own momentary machinations.

You have a way of fitting other people into your life and making them work around you and your activities. And when you do give of yourself, it tends to be with restrictions and a strong undercurrent of impatience.

Your attitude is that in your world you are the most important being. Therefore, everyone else's needs come into your consideration only as a second alternative.

You are so self-seeking that you usually get everything you want and come out with a little more besides. However, from the depths of your heart, you could never consider sharing. It would just not occur to you to do anything but grab all that you can as fast as you can, and you can be pretty fast.

Until you rip open your consciousness to consider those around you, you will always create a vortex of hostile vibrations. You really want to be loved and appreciated for your good points. However, if, in every life situation, you would leave behind just a little bit of yourself, stop interrupting and superimposing your unsolicited opinion, you'll get a lot more attention than you ever anticipated. People will like you a lot more if you leave something to their imagination. Give credit to their intelligence and just assume that they know that you're great. However, when you tell them so persistently, you only turn them off. At that point, what they really think you are is merely bad-mannered, loud, and very pushy.

LOVE AND COMPATIBILITY GUIDE

Aries with Aries

This relationship can have tremendous possibilities if you both decide that you don't have to be boss at the same time. At first, you'll wow each other with more aggressive enthusiasm than is seen at a political convention. However, when he starts acting dictatorial, and she starts getting pugnacious because she's not being treated like she's president, these two hot tempers can easily melt steel.

Both of you are passionate, energetic, fulminating with new ideas, and romantic in a flighty kind of way. Together, you can stay up all night shouting, waving your hands in the air, and planning how to design a new tennis ball that bounces six feet higher. However, when five A.M. comes, and he settles back happily to announce that it was all his idea, she is not above setting fire to the couch he is sitting on.

Since a bad case of the Me complex pervades your consciousness, you sometimes have a hard time hearing the other person. You both love to confess how great you are, but sometimes forget to mention that the other is really pretty good too. However, it's not unlikely that an Aries would compliment his (or her) lover by commenting, "You have to be fantastic, extraordinary, and wonderful if you have me."

The gentle art of humility is not one of your fortes. As a matter of fact, you probably don't even know what "humility" means, since it's one of those words that is much too subtle for your vocabulary.

Between your souls there can be much sympathy, kindness, understanding, and compassion, and between your bodies a tremendous amount of passion and sensuality. He will love the way her mind moves. She will love the way he seems to wield his power single-handed.

Initially, you will gravitate to each other like two war ships meeting during peacetime. After that, the cannons just keep shooting off. And so do your mouths.

This relationship is bound to be both highly tempestuous and trying on the nerves. But you'll both find that it's worth it. Only Aries can stand this insane excitement and then stick around to create more.

Aries Woman with Taurus Man

He won't exactly appreciate the way you point when you want something. Likewise, you won't like the way he refuses to move when you point.

You are bossy and used to wrapping men around your little finger and squeezing hard. Although he would be willing to climb Mount Everest for some woman who asks him nicely, he doesn't at all appreciate the pushy touch.

You operate from the principle of the faster the better, while he can't see why anything is worth doing if he has to kill himself. You are impatience personified; he wouldn't mind waiting for the sun to turn green. You are the classic superachiever who can never get enough power. He is the first to sit back and settle for what he has.

Sexually, you are his match; however, he won't like it if you are other men's as well. Basically, you do not believe in Mr. Right, and therefore are always open to a casual affair. You are adventurous, while he loathes risk-taking. You are committed only to the moment; he is ready to sell his soul to satisfy his future needs.

Your energy will excite him, but his energy won't exactly send you soaring. You want to be challenged, but he wants to be made to feel secure. You have a hunger to be at the top, whereas he gets satisfaction from staying somewhere in the middle.

Together, you both seem to be moving in different directions, but only you seem to be going somewhere. It's probably out of his life, since his stability makes you anxiety-ridden. However, in the long run he is far better off with a woman who doesn't even know the time but who does know how to walk without running.

Aries Woman with Gemini Man

You are so powerful and controlling that if he wants to play your game, it's got to be by your rules.

Your healthy sexuality will be an encouragement for him to keep his mouth shut. His insane sense of humor will make you laugh at yourself for the first time in your life. He is enamored of your energy. You are galvanized by his enthusiasm. He loves your courage, while you love his sharp tongue. You are so fast that you truly intrigue him, while he is so changeable that you don't have time to lose interest.

Initially, this attraction is quite exciting. However, if he makes a commitment on which he doesn't carry through, you'll get him, but good.

You have a temper that will shake him out of his jocular senses, and, in addition, you probably have more strength than he does. If he tries to play games with you, he'll just get a cold seat on your doorstep, because you really don't have the time. There are too many men waiting for your attentions, and the world is waiting for your leadership.

Therefore, if he behaves capriciously, you'll forget his first name as you leave him somewhere in mid-sentence. The only way to win you back is to appeal to your passions. It's worth it. You're one exciting female he'll never forget.

Aries Woman with Cancer Man

He is a truly lovable person, but his love is not meant for you.

Your fiery outbursts will send him into a sullen withdrawal. And his sullen withdrawals will send you through more fiery outbursts. Together, you are so different that you seem to be coming from two foreign countries that have never known the other was even on the map.

Emotionally, he is supersensitive, though he hates to show it. And you have a way of hurting his feelings even by the way you ask him a polite question.

His feeble attempts to camouflage his vulnerability make you chew your cuticles. His moods make you more than impatient. And his apparent passivity makes you stamp your feet just to break the silence.

Basically, he would rather spend a quiet evening at home cooking while you would like to party until dawn. You like to think you're conquering the world, but he likes to comfortably occupy a very secure part of it. He works hard for his future comforts, and you work hard just to work. He is interested in having a family, while the closest you want to come to children is in knowing him. You crave continual excitement; he seeks security at all costs.

Just to be dramatic, you might tell him that you're leaving him, and calmly he will remind you to take your cold tablets and your credit cards. Then he will go into the shower (probably to cry). At least, you'd like to think he's crying. But at that point it's really too late to find out, because even if you're crazy enough to turn back and run toward the bathtub, he undoubtedly has locked the door.

If you want a lot of drama with Mr. Cancer, you'd better go to a movie. Otherwise, pick someone else to increase your blood pressure.

Aries Woman with Leo Man

If he gets in your way, you'll stand on his feet and ask him what he's doing there. He's always had a yen for aggressive women, and you are a dynamo. Your energy level exceeds that of a tribe of angry aborigines. And at times he has to jog just to keep up with you.

Because you love a challenge, he should inflame you with his flirtations. After you decide you want him, you'll take over and move in so fast he'll feel passive by comparison. You are most direct and always strike the shortest distance between two points. His sense of dignity might dissolve because of your candor. Yet, at the same time, he'll approve that you don't take up his time with trivia.

You are headstrong, independent, achievement-oriented, and dedicated to doing what you please. If he doesn't restrain you, your achievements will exalt him. Since your anger is like a blowtorch, he should try to be his supportive self rather than a bully who criticizes. Deep in your heart you know that you were born the best and won't listen for a second when he berates your boastfulness. You're living your life to enable the world to have the same understanding, and if he hints that you're not perfect, you'll just shout that he's mumbling.

Your *joie de vivre* will rejuvenate his brain cells, and your passion will ignite his senses. Together, you are the principle of passion personified, and when you sit side by side, the world seems to shrink away. When your egos are controlled, this attraction is alchemic. But when they collide, the result is self-defense. Your fights would make a sphinx blink. But if he can be less ego-oriented, you are his, along with a treasury of the most startling surface excitement.

Aries Woman with Virgo Man

He'll remind you to comb your hair as you dash madly out the door to a pressing appointment, and nag you when you throw your clothes all over the floor. He'll point out to you your trail of unfinished projects, and when you're late, lecture you on the necessity of discipline and duty.

His approach to life is so cool and logical that at times you wonder if he has something missing. On the other hand, he will wonder at your need for hysteria, and may lose sleep worrying about your smoking and drinking. The basic difference here is that you take everything to its extreme, while he structures himself into a safe middle ground.

He is cautious while you compulsively throw caution to the winds. He is frugal while you can be capricious with money. He has a personality that is reserved, and you have one that can't be held in abeyance. He likes quiet moments, whereas you seek the excitement of crowded places.

Needless to say, you two are not exactly compatible. However, you could learn a lot from this relationship if you are willing to listen. He will teach you how to file your tax records, structure your time so that it doesn't overwhelm you, and learn how to see the other side of a situation. He will listen to your problems, and offer rational advice but will remain unsympathetic when you adhere to the dictates of your ego. You may consider his constructive criticism to be a cruel attack, while he may find your temper tantrums a bit more than he can handle. Only with patience can you come to see each other's point of view. However, since patience is something you don't have a great deal of, the life of this relationship does not look promising. In the beginning, you are both coming from different places, and in the end, you return to separate tables with different views.

Aries Woman with Libra Man

He'll drive you to a point just short of sheer insanity, because he's so indecisive. And you'll make him both nervous and depressed as you injure his self-esteem.

Anyway you look at it, you are not an easy woman for him to contend with. You're blunt and outspoken, while he likes women who are subtle. You're so hot-tempered that you terrify him, and you're so commanding that he feels nauseated when he tries to say no.

At first, he was drawn to you—like a lamb scampering toward a butcher. However, after a few shaky scenes, when he decided you were worse than his mother, even the fact that you were famous could no longer hold him to you.

You want a man who will announce to the gods that he's never been so in love, but even if Mr. Libra tries this, chances are that the original feelings won't last long. It is far more likely that you will torment him to just say *something*, and what he will say is that he really doesn't know what to say. While you're waiting impatiently for him to scream that he would die for you, instead he will mutter that he has no idea what he feels, at which point you shout, "Speak up!" because you've suddenly convinced yourself you're hard of hearing.

Undoubtedly, the most romantic statement he'll make to you after the initial novelty wears off is that he doesn't *not* want you and that you're a really nice person. "Now, that's not true!" you shout, with enough force to kill him.

Besides, you hate being called "nice." It sounds too innocuous.

You and Mr. Libra are great for that blistering romance that lasts about five days, or as long as a package vacation to Puerto Rico. What happens after that time is a truly sobering experience that you never would want to face sober. So it might be best to just drink up as you travel fast in different directions.

Aries Woman with Scorpio Man

This combination is passion personified but one that involves a primitive kind of power struggle. Your egos will clash hard enough to bruise both of you.

He'll get miffed that you're talking about yourself rather than musing about what a mysterious man he is. And you'll get mildly outraged when he doesn't seem to be assenting to your self-laudatory comments.

You'll try to boss him around, and if he doesn't do as you say, you'll step on his foot. In turn, he'll snarl and throw out a few viciously sarcastic comments. However, you're so self-centered that you won't even be listening.

You charge around like a warrior, and although he admires your strength, he resents your lack of subtlety. He likes to be the aggressor, but somehow you always beat him to the punch.

You are strong, ambitious, and the prototype of the liberated woman. He respects your drive, your worldly accomplishments, your vitality, and your stamina. And you want him to, but do you respect his?

The first question is: Do you even notice him unless he trips you? In the long run, only your bruises will tell.

Aries Woman with Sagittarius Man

While this is definitely a delightful adventure, you may consider him too capricious to cope with.

Surely he is charming, exciting, and has the sense of humor that arrests your total attention. However, at the same time, he makes you feel so insecure that you may wish you had never met him.

You have to be first, and with this man, you always feel that you are merely one of many interests—women, activities, projects, crazy schemes. While you love the freedom to engage in impromptu flirtations, your ego in no way appreciates the man you call your lover doing the same.

He will bring on bouts of jealousy that will send you to bed—with another man, of course. (Somehow, even if he doesn't know about it and never will, you feel that you have avenged your mangled pride and inflicted enough pain to make him suffer a lifetime.)

Although he may take you skydiving, ballooning, and shooting the rapids, he will also tread on your ego so badly that it may need either a cast or time away from him in which to recuperate.

You like his outspokenness, but you hate the way he speaks the truth. You *know* you've gained five pounds during the past week, but there really must be something wrong with his eyes if he can see it. For your birthday he gave you a bottle of mouthwash, and for the day that you considered to be your "anniversary," he took out your best friend.

He does it all with such a smiling face and seemingly good intentions that for the first time in your life you feel like one of the most flawed individuals to walk the face of the earth. In solitary moments you always assured yourself that you were best, but he has the nerve to come along and make you feel merely okay.

You are both charmed and challenged by him. The worst part is that you've fallen in love, and every time you scream and point, you realize he's not there to hear you.

This man will put you out of control, because coercive tactics just leave him cold. Therefore, you have to put your ego in the corner, be your most charming, and call upon your complete supply of patience. You've always come to life with a little competition, but what you have here is a basic battle of your needs and wishes. And any way you look at it, to gain what you want, there's something you have to lose.

Aries Woman with Capricorn Man

He'll worry that you work so hard that you'll end up catching some bizarre disease that your body is too tired to combat. You will angrily retort that he is being overcautious. Deep down, Mr. Capricorn is a good soul who means well, but on the outside, you may at times find him to be a bit gloomy.

It's true that he could have written the original disaster movie. And at times you may consider him to be something of a sourpuss. However, if you disregard his propensity toward pessimism and concentrate on his sense of responsibility, you might find him a man worth meeting, knowing, and perhaps loving.

If he makes a commitment to you, you will remain uppermost in his mind, and he will never try to evade what he feels he has to do. However, he *is* controlling and chauvinistic, and he embraces a double standard, that you may have to break down before you go any further. He has advice to offer on every subject, which you might find somewhat irritating, since you're not used to listening to unsolicited opinion. However, often his insights are so deeply based in the little realities your ego can't find room for, that it would do you some good to listen.

He will find you exciting, stimulating, and provocative, but at the same time a little crazy. He'll admire you for your drive, determination, and ambition, but he'll question the way you go about getting what you want. You are headstrong, while he is stodgy. You are disorganized; he clings to his structures. You are blunt and temperamental, whereas he is defensive, supersensitive, and sometimes outspoken.

If you step on his feet, he'll be sure to let you know you're standing there and that he needs the space. And if he gets too bossy, you won't waste any time telling him to go find himself a geisha (which might not be a bad idea).

However, if you can both relinquish your individual needs to supervise and control, and put your energies instead into trying to understand the other person, this relationship could take you anyplace you might want to try going. It's worth the battles that will come about as a result of your efforts. Just keep in mind that it's not the fighting that matters, but the resolutions that really count.

Aries Woman with Aquarius Man

He is the ultimate challenge, and you hate to admit that he's got you. You think he has a beautiful mind, while he thinks you have a beautiful body. You feel you can't get enough of him, but unfortunately, he is not caught in the same vortex of emotion.

He likes women, men, dogs, cats. . . . He's not a snob; he'll speak to anybody. Naturally this bothers you, since you want to overwhelm him to the point where he'll beg to follow you anywhere. However, in this instance, you're the one who's doing the following, and, without planning it, he's the leader. Because his basic attitude is that he has nothing to lose, and because yours is that you stand to lose more than a lot, he holds the key to your heart.

Lose your temper, and he'll walk away; threaten to leave him, and he'll calmly say "go ahead." Try to make him jealous, and he'll mention that maybe you would be better off with another person. Try to coerce him, and he'll tune you out while he gives his attention to another woman.

The basic difference here is that he is detached from his ego, while you are too attached to yours. He is fascinated by many people, while you find yourself to be far more interesting. He is friendly but impersonal. You are friendly but very personal. Because of this, he won't appreciate your possessiveness or the vulnerability of your ego. To reassure you, he won't hold you to his heart and touch his lips to your temples. He'll give you something to think about and wander off in wonderment at why the earth tilts on its axis.

However, that is why he stimulates you; he is always caught between a bizarre set of questions and answers. If you can control your out-of-control feelings, this could be an exciting and rewarding love match. But if you feel his nondiscriminatory friendliness causes more pain than you're willing to confront, then it's better to be just his friend. This way, you're sure to have the best of both worlds.

Aries Woman with Pisces Man

Your temper may give him nightmares, but what you do to his daydreams is quite another matter. He is destined to fall flat on his face in love, but you won't want to hear it or see it.

He's too subjective for your sensitivities, and has a way of making you feel like you're working in a clinic for the emotionally disturbed. He tries your patience, never gets to the point, and drives you to a state of insanity with his moods.

You need a man who is strong enough to push you around after you step on his feet. However, Mr. Pisces will just let you stand there and play bus stop.

At the same time, you do need a lot of love and approval, and Mr. Pisces can truly drown you in devotion. However, when his sentimentality starts to ooze, and you suddenly feel more suffocated than aroused, you just know you're nearing the beginning of the end.

He sees you as a sadomasochistic kind of challenge. You see him as a noose around your neck that keeps getting tighter. At the end, through his tears, he'll wish you the worst. But you'll wish him the best, as you barrel your way out of his life forever, screaming.

Aries Man with Taurus Woman

You're pushy, while she's placid. You're impatient, but she just waits for change. You're flighty, and she never gets off the ground. But the very worst is that you're so bossy that sometimes she just wants to bribe you to shut up.

You see yourself as very exciting, and you'll tell her all about it. But what you won't tell her is that you have a temper that could make her swallow her bubble gum.

You live for challenges, but she seeks stability. You are freedom-loving, while she is fearful of moments spent alone. You are a many-woman man, whereas she is a one-man woman. Basically, you're looking for fireworks, and she's satisfied with just a little warmth.

Unless she has a lot of Aries in her horoscope, this relationship is better off left as an encounter. For a Taurus woman to lose her heart to an Aries man is like an orphan in a storm watching a wealthy family celebrate Christmas. All the lights belong to somebody else, and the closest she can get is to creep up and caress the glass.

Aries Man with Gemini Woman

She admires the way you connect your mind to your body. You respect the clever way she utilizes her mind. This is like a first-sight infatuation where you take each other places—everywhere from the tennis courts to the bedroom.

She'll get your total attention when she gives little killer jabs to your ego. You get her total attention when you don't call when you said you would. She tells herself she couldn't care less, but what's that tension wrenching apart her stomach? You tell yourself she's merely foolish when she fails to react to your sideline flirtations. However, does she realize that, due to her lack of attention, you're kicking the dog under the dinner table?

This is one relationship where the challenge never ceases. You get to each other on a very deep level, but neither wants to be the one to say it. Therefore, it is much more likely that you will communicate your love by smashing her such a hard tennis ball that it hits her in the head. And she will communicate her vulnerability by telling you to let your hair grow to hide your face.

If one of you can break through the verbal barrier and even mumble in your sleep, "I love you," chances are that you might both end up happily married.

However, that's not to say that you won't test each other the entire way to the church.

Aries Man with Cancer Woman

She'll fall in love with your dynamic enthusiasm, but undoubtedly get hurt by your lack of emotional understanding. She needs more nurturing than you know how to give and has more insecurities than you can handle.

You blunder your way through her life, and she holds back the tears when she sees you leaving (even for five minutes). You can't understand why she is so emotional, and sometimes you feel both closed in, and closed off.

On the other hand, she is that woman you can count on and the person who will hold your hand and listen to your problems. She will support you with a sincerity that you may find irresistible. She will love you with a loyalty that inspires your respect, and she will give you the kind of understanding that you can easily find addictive.

Her cooking will send you into another realm of sensual experience, and her sexual appetites can easily outdo your own.

She is one woman who will stick by you, for better or for worse. However, whether you will stick by her could be quite another story. Because you need to roam and run about, sedentary situations make you restless. Ms. Cancer can provide a kind of inner excitement, but until you are ready for it, you are better off remaining uncommitted.

Aries Man with Leo Woman

It's nothing less than love at first sight when you dash aggressively to her side to retrieve the appointment book she deliberately dropped. You're quick to pick up her cues. And complimentary—especially when she lets her eyes drift. You adore the challenge of winning her, and her many flirtations give you many challenges. The problem is that your flirtations give her indigestion. She can't imagine why you would even consider glancing at the bland-looking blond slinking by, when she is the grand lady of glamour. If you knew enough, you would be blinded. After all, when you're with her, it's theater, not a three-ring circus.

Between you there is warmth, passion, and much mutual admiration. You're one of the few men who can get away with telling her what to do. You know it, and this excites you even more. You are enthralled by her energy and enthusiasm. And you respect her independence and ambition. Her warmth and support spur you on to further far-reaching goals.

You both understand each other's fiery nature and tend to remain cool while the other is momentarily exploding. Grudges never pollute the air because you both feel free about your anger. That is fortunate, since most other signs would lock themselves in a closet at what you cheerfully refer to as a temper flare-up.

Sexually, you are highly compatible, except that you are more impulsive, while she is calculating. She won't want to be seen unless she looks her best, and if the scales should show an extra six ounces, there is no alternative but to pretend she has appendicitis. Admittedly, things can get pretty embarrassing if she winds up in the emergency room at 3 A.M. because you have carried her there. (You can be the most gallant crusader.)

You are honest, while she is a game-player. Most of the time, you never catch on to her maniacal manipulations. When you do, the first thing that you think is that she's crazy. Your inherent spontaneity will never allow you to understand why she compulsively calculates all consequences. You believe in the here and now, while she tends to white-frame the future. She doesn't want to play unless she has control; you want to play just to play.

You are a man who can make the muscles of her heart move, and she is a woman who can make yours stop dead. Between you there is much excitement, communication, and kisses, not to mention a few air-borne objects.

Aries Man with Virgo Woman

You'll teach her how to do Air Force exercises and preach to her the virtues of keeping fit. You'll have her mesmerized when she watches you eat steak for breakfast and play eight hours of tennis in the blistering sun. Yes, you get her attention, all right, and she admires your energy, respects your ambition, and feels a little wondrous at your constant enthusiasm.

But despite your ebullience, she has a hard time trusting you, especially when you call her at midnight to ask her out for four A.M. and then stand her up because something else catches your attention.

She finds you fun to be with, but a little flaky when it comes to romantic attentions and sensitivity. You are always late, never call her the day after, and have a peculiar way of forgetting your wallet at the most opportune times. If she invites you over for dinner, chances are you won't bring her wine but will drink all of hers, and won't bring her flowers but will inform her that the ones she's just bought for the occasion make the room look like a funeral parlor.

You need immediate gratification, while she is willing to wait awhile for something meaningful. You are looking for the challenge of your lifetime while she would just like a little love. You want to get drunk as you look into her eyes while she just wants to see some warmth in yours.

You tend to be selfish, and she tends to be selfless. And until you both hit a happy medium, this relationship is better off postponed for a later date, when you have grown up enough to really give her something.

Aries Man with Libra Woman

She will make your life a beautiful place to live in, and you will give her the romantic excitement she so needs. At a candlelight dinner, she'll drown you in the mellifluous tones of Mozart, as well as in her favorite vintage of Pouilly Fuissè. You will feel like a sultan as you sit in the lap of loving luxuries. In return you will sweep her off her feet and leave her feeling shaky but blissful. Sexually, you will take her by storm and give her strings of sleepless nights that she'll come to count on. Your unbridled passion will take her places she's never been before. However, it's where she feels she's going that she worries about.

All that startling surface romanticism is fantastic for a great beginning. But Ms. Libra needs much more than that, since she is not a one-night woman. Rather, she is the marrying kind. But that's all right, because she certainly can be a good one.

She has patience, sophistication, dignity, and graciousness. She is also sensitive, kind, and can see two sides of every issue. She can put up with your temper, even if she has to put her head under a pillow. And she can endure your selfishness if she knows that there really is some love underneath it. She will rationalize your shortcomings and the fact that you always seem to interrupt her when she's going to say something. And she will understand your ego needs, even if they make her leave the room and grind her teeth.

Her approach is more quiet than you normally like, since you appreciate the kind of woman who would have herself shot out of a cannon just to get your attention. You also like a woman who knows how to make demands, while Ms. Libra tends to be silent and accepting.

However, once you realize that your "challenges" are merely repetitive, and that each new face seems to look like the old one, then you will be ready to settle down with her. Don't be surprised when you see that you're starting to live for those quiet moments, when caring is far more meaningful than cavorting.

Aries Man with Scorpio Woman

You'll sweep her off her feet and carry her over the threshold. And for once, her mind will stop calculating whether she's going in the right direction. However, since you're both coming from such opposite places, this passion is short-lived, and in any prolonged involvement she'll start to think of you as both selfish and silly.

You're all energy, passion, vitality, and promises. You

run rather than walk. But often the direction is in circles.

Sexually, you'll take her by storm, and she'll love it, since deep down inside she's always wanted to be conquered. You'll lift up the bed with her in it, just to show off your physical force, and for about five days she'll think she's found her ideal. You'll dazzle her with your courage, vitality, and super-macho stamina. But when she notices that it's a much-repeated repertoire and that you're treating hers as one of a thousand faces, suddenly the starry passion dwindles.

Since you adore the idea of charging around to the tune of "My Hero," and so many women are waiting to be overcome, you are a busy man. However, a friend in need you definitely are not—unless you're going to get something out of it. And if she's looking for loyalty, she'd be a lot better off opening her pocket dictionary to L.

At first, your aggressive enthusiasm will win her over, but after she's seen you do your act a few times, you hold neither secrets nor rewards.

After a while your arrogance will weigh down the lighthearted tone of the relationship. And then she'll find herself listening to self-centered speeches that sicken her. From your perspective, the entire world is a private audience that has assembled just to admire you. As long as she remains quiet, admiring, sensuous, and supportive, she's in—along with anyone else who is also that stupid. However, should she hang on here too long, she should consider sending you a bill for her services.

Aries Man with Sagittarius Woman

She will consider your ego problems silly, and you will consider her behavior flighty. She has a lot of energy, but in the long run never seems to have very much to show for it. However, she can ruin your self-image on the tennis court and can outdo you in stamina on a bicycling trip.

Once you overcome your basic self-centeredness, the chemistry here can catalyze a very intense kind of love.

Both of you are freedom-loving, friendly, and optimistic. Her good-natured support will help you get your ideas off the ground. Your active sense of competition will spur her to do something with her life and not just talk about it.

She'll laugh at your bossy behavior and make you see yourself for the first time from the outside. At the same time, she will respect the power you get from being a superachiever, and you will admire the way her philosophical attitudes always seem to support her. You like the way she never lets anything get her down for long. And she likes the way your enthusiastic approach seems to get you everywhere.

You find her sense of humor contagious, and she finds that she likes to make you laugh. She loves the way you make decisions off the top of your head, and you love the way she makes you see only the sunny side of life.

You both like to engage in more activities than you have time for, and you share a sense of spontaneity that can take you to the most peculiar places.

She fascinates you on cozy nights with her endless tales of traveling adventures. And you fascinate her when she sees that you can have adventures without physically going places. In a very short period of time, you realize that you love being together far more than you like being apart. At this point, you will move in and ask her to marry you in a manner that's about as romantic as a holdup. She will be overwhelmed but not surprised. She's just too smart for that. If you really want to delve into things, you will notice that she's already packed half of her closet, and it's not because she's planned a prolonged voyage.

Aries Man with Capricorn Woman

On the surface, she is cool and steady, while on all levels you are a crazed madman who means well. Therefore, you'll be enthralled at the way she carves her way to greatness and in the process cuts out all the hysteria.

She will be a little overwhelmed as you come dashing into her life and along the way almost knock her door off its hinges. She'll think you're nice but maybe from another planet when you move about in her living room like a Mexican jumping bean and in the middle of a conversation start doing push-ups. You will excite her with the way you can get enthusiastic over a flavor of ice cream, and you will make yourself unforgettable in your repertoire of bedroom activities. However, if you want her to really warm to you, you have to exercise a little patience. Ms. Capricorn wants a man who is dependable. Unlike you, she doesn't seek a circus where the action in the main ring never ceases.

She doesn't believe in love at first sight, although she does believe in liking someone a lot. However, there has to be more than just surface activity to make her want to stick around. Since she is seeking a situation of substance and a human being who will not violate her trust, capricious behavior only leaves her cold, glacial, withdrawn, and looking elsewhere.

She is extremely ambitious, and unlike you, more concerned with perfecting her work than merely initiating new projects. You are attracted to her lists of accomplishments, but sometimes you might feel a little competitive if she works her way into too much of the limelight. She is driven, persevering, and probably spends more of her personal time at the office than you do. In terms of your work, she will be interested, supportive, and understanding. However, she really doesn't have time to polish your ego like an apple and stay up all night listening to you tell her how great you are.

If you want a woman who is real, then Ms. Capricorn is for you. However, if you are more interested in pursuing a challenge than in giving of yourself, go elsewhere. Ms. Capricorn has no tolerance of little boys who try to make the world believe they're men. She is too sensitive to live with only a facade.

Aries Man with Aquarius Woman

She awes you with her humanitarian idealism, and you overpower her with your lists of achievements. She is the kind of woman you love to talk to, and you are the kind of man to whom she likes to listen.

Beyond this, the basic difference is that you are a taker and she is a giver. You are absorbed by self-interest, while she has an interest in every person who crosses her path.

With you, chances are that she will end up giving far more than she's getting. Ms. Aquarius is so good-natured that she has a bad habit of sacrificing her own inclinations to other people's strong desires. You can be demanding, jealous, and possessive, although you fully expect the freedom to do as you please. You will scowl and play with your soup when you feel that she is being too friendly to the waiter. And when she leaves you in the middle of a sentence to go see a friend in need, you come closer to having temper tantrums. When the phone rings after midnight, and she murmurs in her amiable way, "Oh, hello, Harry," suddenly she has one phone that is no longer attached to the wall.

However, if you can give her the benefit of the doubt, you could have a fantastic thing going. She will give you the most extraordinary ideas for your new projects. She won't complain when you work so hard that you hardly see her. And if you have a little affair here and there, which, in a moment of gut-wrenching guilt, you have to confess, she'll tell you with a detached smile not to trouble yourself.

Any way you look at her, she is an unusual woman who is an experience unto herself. Consider yourself lucky to have found her.

Aries Man with Pisces Woman

For her, it's almost love at first sight, whether or not she wants to show it. But that's just for sexual starters. After the first few nights, you're still in the running for a total ravishment of her mind and body. However, after she witnesses how selfish you can be in the daytime, with the sun shining in your eyes, then it's quite another matter if the love continues.

She is still searching for that knight on his silly white horse to come and whisk her away. Superficially, you'll fulfill her fantasies, but underneath, not only will you not understand her, you won't even have the patience to try.

She has a way of getting her feelings hurt at the most inconvenient moments, and you have a way of treading on them without either realizing it or wanting to be aware. It inflames you when she withdraws and gets sad and sulky. At the same time, it makes her despair when she sees that you can be so insensitive.

You act first and think later, while she has a way of sitting still and just feeling. You need a woman who will challenge you, support you, and make you a little insecure. She needs a man you will love her, support her, and make her very secure.

You need a lot of time and attention. So does she. But you'll spare her very little time. In the end, this relationship is better off left to run its course without expectations. Yours or hers. Just play it as it lays, and you may find in the end that you have more than you both bargained for.

TAURUS

Dates: April 21—May 21
Ruling planet: Venus
Element: Earth
Mode: Fixed
Quality: Feminine, negative
Planetary principle: Production
Primal desire: Stability
Color: Green
Jewels: Emerald, moss agate
Plants: Daisy, moss, spinach
Day: Friday
Archangel: Auriel
Magical number: 6
Material factor: Prudence

TAUREANS OF
FAME AND FORTUNE

Barbra Streisand   Shirley Temple Black
Candice Bergen   Robespierre
Audrey Hepburn   Vladimir Nabokov
Fred Astaire   Gary Cooper
Sigmund Freud   Salvador Dali
Margot Fonteyn   William Randolph Hearst
William Shakespeare

THE TAURUS FEMALE

Favorable

You are the archetypal earth mother. You have the kind of strength, courage, and stamina that will take you anywhere. You know how to enrich what is around you and how to encourage conditions to expand and flourish. Even your plants and your pet rock have come to think of you as Mother.

In matters of love, you are monogamous, honest, forthright, and hate to be toyed with. Not only do you like to know where you stand in the present, you would also like to have guarantees for the future. Emotionally, you are much more sensitive than you appear and have a way of hiding your vulnerability behind a carefully controlled exterior. However, in seeking to keep things to yourself, you sometimes lose them, and your reluctance to reveal your deeper emotions can get in the way of your obtaining the kind of attention you crave.

There are moments when your strength undermines you, and to avoid the possibility of rejection, you try to avoid recognizing your own needs. At this point, you play at being cool, aloof, and noncaring. You find it easier to walk away in intense pain with your head held high than to confront the fact that this kind of caution is killing you. You're so enamored of the role of "strong woman" that you run the risk of overplaying the part.

In matters of the heart, that is the only risk you consider taking. And this is unfortunate, because it never takes you anywhere; it only keeps you in the same place.

You have a horror of being hurt that ties in with deep-seated security needs. To be abandoned by a lover whom you trusted is to feel you lose all. You sense the earth sinking away under your feet as you watch the world turn quickly colorless.

One way to avoid this sorrowful situation is to let your lover know what you are feeling in the present and what you expect to feel in the future. You must learn to set the limits in situations and not sit back while they are set for you.

You are a woman of many resources and have a do-it-yourself attitude. People close to you depend on you for your durability, stability, and stamina in the face of severe difficulties. You are respected for your tendency to remain unruffled, regardless of the severity of any storm. At the same time, you are very feminine, with a quiet, earthy kind of charm.

In terms of your work, you are organized, methodical, and pragmatic. You are dependable, hardworking, and practical in your approach to any new project. Since you have an uncanny ability to assess the value of what you're working with, you are excellent both as a negotiator and an appraiser.

You are a woman of substance who assesses the value of all experience. You see your relationships as durable investments that will bring you many rewards years into the future. You have a calm, resolute approach to your life that gives you a great deal of control that many of your zodiacal sisters are lacking.

Although you could easily find ways of enjoying wealth, it's not all that important to you. You're one woman who knows how to be well off with the rudiments of life. With the right amount of love, you are fortified against the world. You can go out and make things happen rather than waiting for them to be given to you. You are steady, sound, and efficient in all that you undertake. From being an outstanding epicure to managing monetary deals that would shatter someone else's sensitivities, you shine through the utilization of your own inner resources. You know how to hone out a place for yourself and make it last. With your combined creativity and sense of purpose, the world is yours. All you have to do is just convince yourself that you deserve it.

Unfavorable

You would never shout "Stop the world!" because you're not even aware that it's moving. You are a phlegmatic and faithful perpetuator of the status quo. You can be such a slave to your appetites that at times your body may look like a "Big Mac."

You're probably one of the few women in the world who can consume cold pasta, even when the sauce has started to congeal. At the age of twenty-two, you lost seven sets of house keys and didn't find them until your mother defrosted the freezer. When you're really hungry, you don't mess around with something as remote as the kitchen table. Instead, you pull up a chair to the refrigerator, open the door, and grab. When you binge and you're really desperate, you'll eat anything from sunflower seeds in a cup of mayonnaise to the leftovers meant for the cat.

You can be about as emotionally sensitive as a traffic cop in rush hour and as flexible as a slab of steel. Your lower jaw sets like concrete, and your attitudes are so ingrained that you have probably never even experienced what you blab about. You're a know-it-all in any situation, and stick stodgily to what you *think* you know.

When it comes to love, your attitude is "Take good care of yourself, you belong to me." You are so possessive that you're positively depersonalizing, and sometimes treat your lover as if he were your mattress. You're so security-oriented that you'll often trade off being badly treated to maintain the "stability" of a sorrowful situation.

You tie yourself up too easily to both men and jobs where you're getting close to nothing and going nowhere. In the face of friendly advice that might liberate you from your situation, you often remain obstinate and deaf to anything that you don't want to hear. You'll almost die in the bad place that you've put yourself in, and then cry out to the world that you're a victim. Your cowlike reluctance to take responsibility for your own life will ultimately leave you leaning on the weary shoulders of others if you're not careful.

At times you are like an object in space, overfed and immovable. However, if pushed past a certain point, your wrath hath no limits. You can bear a grudge past a human lifetime and would not consider giving anyone the benefit of the doubt. You love to nurse your wounds so long they start to fester, and you can remain unforgiving until your enemies are on their deathbeds.

You have a special habit of blaming others for your own worst faults, and often inflict on them the punishment of silence. If you walk into a chair, it's the chair's fault for standing there; and if you fall out a window, it's the window's fault for being open. If you insult a friend by your own selfishness, it's the friend's fault for not being more giving.

By nature you are habit-bound and probably have never tried any ice-cream flavor except vanilla. Your variety of nail polish consists of fifty-seven shades of red, and your clothes are variations on a theme of brown. Needless to say, you are not exactly daring. Change is one of the few things that sends you into a turmoil. Another is the trauma of remaining unmarried.

Unfortunately your sluggishness may not exactly make men moan with desire. In desperate straits you can be like a Venus's-flytrap: when a man strolls by, you are tempted to lean over and just grab him by the throat.

When it comes to marriage, you're far more interested in getting than in giving. He has to be able to pay for your possessions, or else his value will definitely depreciate, and you won't be shy about letting him know it.

He has to make the marital adjustments, because that's just not an area that involves you. You're sometimes so subjective and self-centered that after a while you forget there's another person in the marriage. However, you do remember when you wake up at noon to notice the accumulation of dirty dishes. At this point, you decide they must be all his, since now you don't eat that much. Last week, you cut down to three meals a day.

Should your lover decide he's had enough and try to escape your oppressive charms, he may find you attached to his ankle like a ball and chain. If that fails, you can always trip him as he goes out the door. You're a woman who likes to take injustice into your own hands. And you just better believe those hands can hold a lot.

THE TAURUS MALE

Favorable

You're a teddy bear with the traits of a tycoon. You know how to make money and how to keep it. You are strong, steadfast, sincere, and practical in your approach to all your undertakings. Those who are close to you know they can depend on you in any situation.

As a child you were so honest and obedient that you probably took the blame for things you never even did. Since then, you have grown up to both respect and expect the same integrity in others. And woe to those who disappoint you, since you can cut them out of your life almost as easily as you can include them.

You are stable and seek the foundation of all experience. You profit most highly from deeply committed love relationships that are warm and secure. In love, you tend to be a romantic, but not one that hovers in the clouds. You like to stay close to the ground and have the assurance that your dwelling is on terra firma. Since your attitude is that any woman you really want is well worth waiting for, you have been known to hang on to a situation much too long. As you stand in the shadows waiting for the object of your affection to get tired of her man of the moment, you sometimes let other females pass you by until the shadows become your domicile.

Although you know what you want, sometimes it's not always the best thing for you. Ultimately, you have to take responsibility for the situation you've created, and that isn't easy unless you work on yourself to be more aware.

As a husband, you are loyal, very loving, and have the kind of strength a woman can lean on. You love to give support, and gain tremendous satisfaction in offering succor in a stressful situation.

Since you love to cook and can conjure a truly dazzling epicurean feast, you can be a most seductive force in any domestic situation. You can sweep a woman's senses away with merely the aroma of your cooking, never mind the final product of your culinary expertise.

Any way you look at it, you are the insatiable sensualist who never tires of treating himself to the more supreme experience. Sexually, you tend to be demanding and probably have a subscription to *Playboy*, which you regularly peruse. However, your ideal woman is far more refined than the typical sex bunny, and quite soon you make her learn that she has to restrict her seductiveness to the most private settings. You are very possessive and just will not tolerate any man thinking that your woman might be public property. Too many flirtations on her part, and she'll soon find one very strong hand grabbing the back of her neck.

You tend to see the world in black and white, which can be very useful in business matters. Because your ideas are so grounded, they easily take form in a plodding, practical fashion. Your aptitude for all money matters surpasses most professionals in the economic mainstream. You have such an uncanny way of making your undertakings turn into the most lucrative ventures that you could do well working as a stockbroker. And because you are so organized, and have such a fine sense of priorities, you could easily run your own business.

At times, however, you have had problems with conjuring up a need for ambition, and get a deep satisfaction in sitting back and patiently accumulating your rewards. You don't have to be at the top as long as your material needs are met. And these are based less on wealth than on what you consider to be sound security.

Once you commit yourself to any situation, you tend to be prudent and persevering. In moments of crisis, you stand your ground stolidly, while your emotions remain unruffled. Your way of reckoning is with a resolute force that has been known to be stubborn. You utilize your talent in a steady, solid way, and in so doing, have a kind of stamina that defies logic.

Whatever your needs in this lifetime, they have nothing to do with excitement. A fairly plump savings account, a fine woman to come home to, a hearty meal, and some satisfactory sex, and you have what you feel is life's meaning. Your basic philosophy of life is that everything is simple, it's just people's minds that make it peculiar.

You have a special knack of reducing situations to their most elemental form, and from this making the decision of what is really worthwhile. Whatever your desires, your inner resources will point you in the right direction. And if you trust that there is something to be valued in all directions, then whatever way you move, you will see that there is some kind of gain.

Unfavorable

It has been said of Taureans that if they stand too long in one place, they'll start to grow roots. And you have been sprouting since the day you were born.

Your focus is so linear that you would miss a volcano erupting on either side of you. You have a slow, plodding intelligence that will take you to the most secure places, but you often move at such a leaden pace that it may take you a lifetime to get where you think you're going.

Your nature is "earthy" in the extreme, and at times you have the charm of a construction worker. Your manners sometimes indicate that you belong in a zoo, as you have been known to conspicuously slurp soup. You also have no reservations about digging into a meal with both hands.

Your love for food is obvious, because you sometimes wear it on your tie and under your fingernails. Your body is beefy, and you have a neck like a tree stump. Since your torso is a general repository for your appetites, your stomach can develop a bit of an overhang, if you don't watch yourself.

On general principle you tend to be grabby and will take anything you can get. Moneywise, you can be both greedy and selfish and wouldn't lend your best friend the money for bus fare. You're happy to live on black beans for a lifetime while you hoard away a fortune and let your friends feed you. You'll use one tea bag for six months, and consider water just as good as toothpaste. A little more attention to sartorial matters might be in order.

At your most flexible moment, you are somewhat obstinate. Your temperament ranges from phlegmatic to stubborn to violent when the animal in you is really aroused. At this point, watch out! You explode, wreaking havoc in all directions. However, not only would you have no regrets, you would never even notice! At times you exhibit the sensitivities of a gorilla, without the ambition.

You are also indolent and have as many interests as you have TV channels. A favorite evening: you drink beer and rub your stomach through soap operas, commercials, and quiz shows. When the test patterns finally appear, you think it's an avant-garde replacement for Johnny Carson.

You can get so far down in a rut you can barely see over the edge. Variety is the only thing that traumatizes you, and the concept of change has never ever been a consideration. You can play the same song on a record so many times that the needle gets stuck in the groove. You live a life of such routine that after a while you can stop thinking and just let the kinetic energy take over.

In matters of love, you want a woman to wash your dishes. But you'll be fortunate if you find someone who's willing to marry you for your money. At your worst, you can be so insensitive that a woman would have to shout in your ear and stick you with a fork to get your attention, if she wasn't at that moment feeding you. In no uncertain terms, you expect her to be grateful for all that she has to offer you. You'll offer her a life-style that is so sedentary that she'll have to occasionally plug a wet finger into an electric socket if she's looking for excitement. And when it comes to material comfort, she may have to murder you in your bed if she ever intends to touch your money.

In matters of career, you're especially good at plodding along and staying in the same place. If you're not careful, you could become as taken for granted as the office water cooler. But what's worse, you could even get to like it.

DECANS

Every sign in the zodiac can be broken down into three subdivisions called decans. Each decan roughly corresponds to 10 degrees—or the first third, second third, and last third of the sun sign's time span which is approximately thirty days.

As each of these periods have different subrulerships, the personality of a person is slightly modified by the specific decan it falls in. For instance, an Aries born in the second decan would be ruled by Mars, but subruled by the sun. Therefore, he would tend to display a greater sense of pride, boastfulness, egotism, and optimism than an Aries born in the third decan, which is subruled by Jupiter. This Aries would tend to be more freedom loving, flighty, travel oriented, and interested in subjects of a philosophical nature. An Aries born in the first decan would be the most aggressive, but not necessarily the most productive and accomplished.

Decans are important since they do account for a more detailed assessment of an individual's personality characteristics. They also show how two people born under the same sun sign can be markedly different.

If you were born between April 21 and May 1, your sun falls in the Venus decan of Taurus. Security is the keynote to your personality, and money is the foundation of your life.

You could never consider carrying on without a substantial savings account, and could even be accused of hoarding.

You're afraid of taking risks because you feel that you might lose something that you'll never see again. You tend to get in ruts, abhor change, and often make elaborate plans for new projects that never seem to get off the ground.

In matters of love, you're insanely jealous, possessive, and often treat your lover as an object. Someone who offers material security is most attractive to you. However, since you are fearful of a solitary existence, you can easily settle for someone on whom you can depend.

You tend to be stubborn, inflexible, and not particularly sensitive to those subtle feelings of others. You see people's behavior in black and white and tend to be highly judgmental. You are more likely to give practical advice than you are to empathize. However, at the same time, you have a passionate degree of loyalty that close friends are more than thankful for.

It is highly likely that you have some artistic talent. However, whether you use it or not is an entirely different matter. As this decan represents both a proclivity to laziness and a compulsion to act, either your talents will remain dormant or you will obsessionally drive yourself to express them.

The drawback of this decan is that life becomes a habit, and experience takes on an automatonlike quality. A greater receptivity to change should be cultivated, or else you may limit the fruits of your own growth.

If you were born between May 2 and May 11, your sign falls in the Mercury decan of Taurus. You are slightly more shy and aloof than Taureans born in the other decans. You are also more analytical and rely on your powers of reason to help you find answers to puzzling emotional situations.

In any deep involvement, you like to talk about things that may be bothering you or seem to be bothering the other person. However, if your partner is a Scorpio or Cancer, your feelings of frustration at his or her reticence may send you through many emotional gyrations.

Your attitude toward your daily life is intensely practical. In both your personal and public life you are highly organized, and an excellent planner with a great mind for details. You have a great head for numbers, and an uncanny ability to handle money and keep records. Chances are that your tax and expense records are every accountant's dream. Your inherent sense of order can make you somewhat compulsive concerning your earthly responsibilities.

Your career interests tend toward accounting and business, teaching, writing, and the field of communications. In the latter, chances are that you would find yourself in an administrative capacity rather than in a creative one.

You like to be around people, to share ideas, and to make elaborate plans for future activities. In all that you do, you seek precision. Because of this, photography may be a very productive avocation and afford you the kind of creative release in which you could find both excitement and relaxation.

If you were born between May 12 and May 21, your sun falls in the Saturn decan of Taurus. You are far more serious than other natives of your sign, and can, at times, incline to be pessimistic. You are dutiful, persevering, and tend to be successful in both teaching and executive positions.

You are extremely frugal and not particularly fun-loving. There is a high degree of anxiety in your personality, as well as fearful undercurrents that flow through the subconscious. Your personality is reserved and cautious, and you are not, by any means, easy to know. Strangers may consider you cold. However, the truth is that you are really shy and inhibited. Once the ice is broken and you have time to develop a deep sense of trust, you are a most steadfast and self-sacrificing friend.

Chances are that in your early years your father had a restricting effect on your life, and since then you have taken up where he left off. No matter what you do, there is a nagging sense that you're never good enough in the eyes of authority. These feelings are accompanied by deep-seated fears of insecurity. You have a hard time feeling the intensity of love that surrounds you; at the same time, you have a tremendous hunger for warmth and reassurance. It is not unlikely that you overcompensate for such feelings of vulnerability by a glacial exterior. There is no doubt about it: you are your own worst enemy.

Whatever task you take up, you usually carry it to the end. You are disciplined and devoted to whatever or whomever you commit yourself to. At times, you may battle feelings of loneliness, alienation, and depression. It is important for you to develop structures that help you through these periods. Sublimate your feelings into some creative activity and distance yourself from the situation that seems to be holding you down. If you make each day a creative reflection of your inner resources, then you will have much to show for your life.

LOVE

In love, you are an earthy romantic. You are emotional, sensual, pragmatic, and never feel totally complete without a partner. At times, you may get yourself into a funk longing for the perfect love and listening to sentimental mood music while you wait for the phone to ring.

Although you have a hard time showing it, you are highly vulnerable, and fear rejection to the point of obsession. If you have a lot of Aries in your chart, you may overcompensate with a cool attitude that keeps you on a safe footing with the outside world.

In any relationship you have to know where you stand; being put in an insecure position that is neither here nor there gives you a devastating amount of pain. Unlike the sign Gemini, which considers most interactions initially casual, you hope for the possibility of a relationship very early on in the game. In your younger years, dependencies develop that tie you into situations longer than you should be. It's hard for you to abandon the hope that you might be getting something in the future and that all the misery in the meantime is not in vain.

You are monogamous to the point of tying up your total being into one person. It's easy to sacrifice your own interests for your partner's or to put your own growth and development in the background while you spend your vital energies hoping, waiting, and wanting.

In general, professional success can never carry the same weight as an intimate relationship with much sharing.

However, if you have been burned just too many times, it is likely that you may seek to sublimate your emotions into career considerations. As you have a strong tendency to seek your value in the outside world rather than in yourself, you may find the approval and recognition from your career that are lacking in your love life.

Because you are so down-to-earth, you don't insist on being dazzled by a whirlwind romance. Instead, you prefer quiet evenings with homemade cooking and a flicker of candlelight. You like to prepare sybaritic repasts that are guaranteed to galvanize your lover's senses. A roaring fireplace will do wonders, but in lieu of a few logs and an air chute, you can easily supply the heat that will linger through the night.

You, more than any other sign, know how to transform your home into a love den. It's all calculated to make your lover never want to leave. However, sometimes your tendency to smother can snuff out a strong initial interest on the part of another. Try to remain tender, loving, and alluring without getting to the point where you're pushing your friend on the floor.

In any love scene, you are pleasure-loving, warm, and cuddly. However, at times you have a way of wrapping your arms around another body that can break ribs. Loosen up, let go of the jealous feelings you cling to, and in the long run you'll not only be a happier person, you'll also be a lot more loved.

MARRIAGE

Marriage is a must, whether you are male or female. You want to be tucked in at night. You also have the need to feel complete by having a partner. In the deepest part of you, you are on a security search for a lasting situation.

Life is not meaningful unless you have someone to come home to. In all that you do, you seek emotional foundations, and when they crumble, you'll settle for even the skeletal structure they once came in.

You'll hang on to a marriage long after it's over, and with patience and a mystifying sense of perseverance you'll struggle onward into an emotional mire. For a bad marriage to end, your husband or wife will have to leave you—and even then, you may kill your ex-partner trying to get back together.

You are highly monogamous, nurturing, and possessive. Often in a marriage you let yourself get into a deep, deep rut. However, should your wife or husband decide to seek excitement elsewhere, because living with you is like rereading last week's want ads, you'll suddenly develop the brute force of the bull. When your prime possession is challenged, you can rouse yourself into a rage that would make someone hide under the bed. Your stolid character quickly dissolves into steam heat, and you can be more dangerous than nitroglycerin.

From the time that you were pushed from the womb, you assumed that someday you too would be a parent. You consider a childless marriage a barren one and would probably adopt a child if biology prevented a birth. As a parent, you tend to live for and through your offspring. You would probably keep a notebook with a record of the first gurgle, and have one wallet that holds nothing but baby pictures.

Basically, what you seek in a marriage are the more practical pleasures of earthly existence. You need emotional support and material security, and you appreciate a splendid array of creature comforts. However, if you are lacking the latter, it's no problem as long as you feel loved and emotionally nourished.

You have such a hearty enjoyment of the little things in life, you can keep yourself stable and satisfied even in the most spartan existence. You are so strong and durable that you may attract a partner who marries you because of a need to lean a lot.

In marriage, you are extremely giving. However, when deeply committed, you sometimes forget to take. Quite naturally, you dazzle domestically, and your culinary forte would put a competitive French chef to shame. However, you need to know when to turn off and realize that you're not running a restaurant. What makes you most satisfied is nurturing the ones you love. This is fine. But remember that too much giving is just as bad as too much taking. The best move is to establish a balance in between. And that may be the challenge of your lifetime.

MONEY

Money is your middle name, and you are the sign who knows how to make it. You'll never starve, because however much you have, you know how to make it work for you.

From the time you were about ten, you probably had a secret savings account larger than your parents'! Your piggy-bank collection was the envy of every kid on the block.

You love money and know how to manage it. When you played Monopoly as a child, you were probably the banker, because you love to finger the bills. Since then you've managed to put away a tidy sum that gives you a special sense of security. You like to feel that you have something to fall back on for that rainy day that sometimes never comes.

You have a special horror of unpaid bills and charge accounts. You prefer to buy with cash so that there is nothing hanging over your head, and meticulously you file away every receipt so that you can deduct as much as possible from your taxes.

However, sometimes you are so economical that you forget to live and enjoy the little luxuries that are easily allowable. At this point, you are letting money victimize you. To conserve is being cautious, but to hoard is being foolhardy. When money becomes an excessive concern, it becomes a nemesis to your freedom, creativity, and expression. Just remember to look up from your bankbook and live.

CAREER

Success for you means security—in love, in money, and in status. Unlike Leo, you don't feel the need to stand out in front and put your finger to your chest to show the world you've got power. A comfy seat behind the scenes is more than adequate, especially if the salary skyrockets annually and the expense account allows you to write off toothpaste.

If it's love you're looking for rather than corporate power, it doesn't have to be a jet-set romance with the gift of an apartment house for your birthday (though it would be kind of nice). All you really crave is someone to come home to who will be around as long as your bed pillow.

Deep down in the dungeons of your consciousness,

success is dependence on someone who will not fall in love with someone else or tell you that you're fired.

For anything to be successful, it has to be lasting. Novelty doesn't thrill you; it's endurance that counts and gives you the impetus to carry on at all costs.

Since your ruler, Venus, imbues you with a great deal of creativity, and your sun is placed in the element of earth, there are vast numbers of professions that could suit you, and bring you success.

You shine in practical and business matters, and have a great head for details that others might consider drudgery. Since you are also highly organized, persevering, and have a strong aptitude in money matters, you could be anything from a corporate executive to a banker to an accountant. You have a very solid, committed approach to what you do, and like to feel that you're steadily building toward better opportunities.

Since Taurus rules the throat, many Taureans are singers. However, singing is not the only Venusian occupation that Taurus shines in. Sculpture and painting are also possibilities. At the same time, the teaching of crafts is another vocation from which you might find much internal satisfaction.

You have the inner ability to combine your mastery of mundane matters with a substantial artistic flair. Therefore, you have the potential of excelling in both a creative and an executive capacity in the arts. Producing films and plays or agenting high-strung actors may just be your special forte.

Since Taurus likes to build, architecture is another endeavor in which you may show off your creative acumen. However, let us not neglect mentioning those truly earthy occupations like landscaping, forestry, conservation, gardening, bricklaying, and civil engineering.

Whatever you do, you do it with patience, tenacity, and a sense of structure that is rich in purpose. You may not reach the heights as quickly as your friend Aries, but each stone you slowly turn over on the way, you will be sure to own. Your price is stability. And no matter where you're going, you know that you've got it.

FRIENDS

As a friend, you are both loyal and loving. As a child, you shared your one-eyed teddy bear with your best friend. As an adult, you might share your possessions and your secrets, though not your money.

Because there are relatively few people whom you trust, it is highly likely that your friends are few in number. Like your polar opposite, Scorpio, you are suspicious of those gregarious individuals who want to share their soul overnight. To get close to you, one has to go through levels of initiation. And anyone who tells too much too soon gets your haughty disapproval, along with a little of the cold shoulder.

At the same time, those privileged people you choose to take into your confidence probably consider you the best friend they ever had. They can trust you with their most outrageous secrets and know that at the price of torture, your lips will be sealed.

In any situation, you are the prototype of the friend in need. No service is too great if it means that someone dear to you will highly benefit. And no time is inconvenient if the person is in dire trouble.

Unless you are the selfish, unevolved sort, your greatest pleasure is in giving. You can take this to such an extreme that you can literally smother someone with your services.

At the same time, if the situation ever occurs where you are betrayed, you can be merciless, insensitive, and downright cruel. You can cut off your deeper feelings far easier than you can create them, and slide into a grudge that just carries you away. At this point, there is no reasoning with your Taurean obstinacy. You really don't care why your trust was betrayed. Just the fact that it was is enough to make you feel you want to kill the person off very slowly.

Your tendency to be jealous and possessive may often reach into the realm of friendship. Any friendship that is special has to be intense, with boundaries and limitations that are often circumscribed by your feelings. You're not happy sharing a best friend with many other people, and like to know that that sense of specialness is mutually acknowledged.

In general, your faithfulness is highly appreciated. However, your occasional inflexibility may sometimes be a problem. Once you develop a deeper understanding of the emotional needs and motivations of others, you will be more open to some rewarding personal experiences that somewhere you might have missed.

HEALTH

Weight has always been your problem, and when it comes to desserts, you have a hard time saying no. Unlike Capricorn and Leo, who have forgotten what the word dessert means, you tend to overindulge, and do it in a very committed fashion. If it came down to a choice between a piece of pecan pie and a dish of strawberries without whipped cream, the latter would not even be in the running.

In your framework, food is a panacea for all probable ailments, and at times you tend to binge your heart out. You have a special fondness for bread and other waist-expanding starches. And sugar just sends your senses soaring.

Dieting is difficult, since food is like a part of your personality. You can cook up a storm, and bake up a bundle of goodies, to the detriment of any diet. You love to hang out in the kitchen, and would rather receive a new wok than a television. Cooking and eating make you feel cozy, and so you like to plan your life around food.

If you don't watch it, excess pounds can be both physically and psychologically deleterious to a happy normal life-style. Too much weight can bring on varicose veins and even cause havoc with your heart. In addition, nobody is really attracted to a rotund body. Therefore, when your love life starts to deteriorate, and you get a bad case of the pitifuls, you may have to ask yourself why.

Since Taurus rules both the throat and neck, you may also be prone to sore throats and swollen glands. Take lots of vitamin C and suck on a garlic clove when you feel this discomfort.

In general, you are as strong as a bull and become ill infrequently. If you watch your diet and become less lazy about exercise, you'll only increase your chances for a happy, healthy life.

HOME

Your home is your foundation and your bastion against the world. You are naturally domestic, and delight in creating an abode with the most comfortable atmosphere.

You probably spend your Saturdays building bookshelves and cooking up a storm. On rainy days you especially like to bake, and on snowy ones, one can find you bingeing on your own cooking.

Your natural Venusian creativity shows off in your house in earthy but enviable ways. You adore your creature comforts. But you also know how to create them. From woodworking to building your own couch, your abilities shine and dazzle any nondomestic onlooker.

Your home is your private turf, where you like to play and relax. Often you prefer a cozy stay-at-home evening to a rowdy night on the town. That is because your furniture is not only comfortable, it's sensationally seductive. Your couch seems to enfold you in its curves, and your rug is soft, thick, luxurious, and a tantalizing tribute to lovemaking.

Your home is a showplace for your possessions, which are tasteful and thoughtfully chosen. A crystal carafe from your grandmother is a star attraction on any evening. And on a dining table of the most solid oak rests a Dionysian offering of wine, homemade bread, and fresh flowers.

If you had your dream kitchen, all the counters would be butcher block. A fireplace would roar its good tidings, and you would have a built-in oven that could feed a football team. One entire wall would be lined with enough gadgets and utensils to start a hardware store, and the kitchen table would extend for a half a block.

While your kitchen boasts the creative you, your bedroom would reveal the sentimental side of your soul.

A queen-size four-poster can do a lot for romantic dreaming, and big cushiony pillows along with a home-made quilt can make you feel more than cozy on a windy night. You adore spending Sundays in bed with your very special love, and have a talent at making breakfast last until supper.

Wherever you live, your home evokes a special lust for life—as well as for a lot of other things. Home entertaining is a most joyful pastime as well as an art. You know how to call upon your own resources to expand your domestic sphere. Your only problem is that your houseguests don't want to leave. But then, you can't really blame them. The minute they walk in the door, they're treated as if they've gotten in from a storm. Your nurturance is more than nice; it's habit-forming.

COSMIC CHALLENGE

Your cosmic challenge of this lifetime is to be able to assess objectively the value of what you possess. To do this, you must acquire both self-detachment and self-humor.

Try to project your mind onto a far wall and from this position look back at yourself. Do you see yourself clinging to a job, a person, or a situation of false security that is actually undermining you? Are you for the most part miserable, and because of a fear of the future, do you feel yourself entrenched and constricted?

Your special lesson in this lifetime is to be able to see clearly what you have to give up in order to be able to gain. When you play the game of life from a place of loss, it will come to you. And when you live in a place of fear, you abdicate the freedom that is yours. Once you accept the change that is an inherent law of the universe, you are in control of all the elements of your own life. Only at this point are you ready for a spontaneous existence that compensates the energies you put into it.

INSPIRATION

Your special lesson in this lifetime is to transmute your lower desires to your higher will, your self-centered actions to those that are self-sacrificing. You have tremendous strength, willpower, and perseverance. However, often you make these work against you by not realizing the needs of others.

Once you project your inner self into the being of another and look at the world through another's feelings, needs, and fears, you will have reached a kind of self-mastery that will bring you greater love and personal power. You must remember that your life is limitless. It is only the direction of your will that imposes restrictions. Egocentric behavior will ultimately only narrow your existence. Your key to deeper satisfactions comes through greater flexibility. The higher your emotional aspirations and the more expansive your personal universe, the greater the magnitude of your earthly joy and the less the intensity of your individual sorrow.

WHAT HOLDS YOU BACK AND HOW TO OVERCOME IT

What holds you back is yourself, but what inspires you is others. Although your desires are most demanding, you're often not willing to do what needs to be done in order to fulfill them.

You have a laziness and self-indulgence that are often self-defeating. And you tend to dig yourself a hole in the ground with your stubbornness and extreme rigidity.

You prefer the fruits of a situation to the growth that originally led to the harvest. However, the more passive you are to your own circumstances, the greater the chances that your life will begin to bottleneck.

You need to be pushed by some outside force if you are to avoid getting caught in situations with strangleholds. The greatest way to overcome yourself is to create a distance from yourself where you can see the specifics of your life in greater perspective.

Try to develop a sense of humor to help you see how ridiculous and funny you can be. Make an effort to get behind another person's mind so that through the prism of another's eyes you can watch your own behavior.

Don't become doggedly hostile when faced with constructive criticism. And above all, try to become less self-involved while you learn how to listen. Give the people around you the pleasure of your total attention without interrupting them with an "I."

The more you put yourself before others, the more they desire to leave you behind. Above all, the next time you fix yourself on a course, notice the direction you're turning in and be prepared to take responsibility for where it may take you. Your habits may harness you to the kind of experiences that are no longer needed for personal growth. If you perpetuate them through your own passivity, you pay a heavy price. It's called your life. While you keep pawing the ground from the same place, try to remember that it's passing you by. Either learn to move with it or don't blame the world when you're left behind.

LOVE AND
COMPATIBILITY GUIDE

Taurus with Taurus

It seems that the longer you stick together, the longer you stay in the same place. At first sight, this was the most secure situation. On second sight, it signified the worst kind of ennui. On third sight, it came to mean the most sedentary stagnation.

This is one relationship where nothing ever seems to happen, because both of you are patiently waiting for the word. After a while, life starts to get like a two-A.M. TV movie with too many commercials.

What really cements you together is the stability of inertia. However, only years later, at a point of jaundiced indifference, will you admit that the only stability is change.

This relationship can easily turn into marriage. However, chances are that if the marriage lasts, it's only because you have both become too indifferent to each other even to get a divorce. When the tedium gets past the point of being tiresome, and the rut the relationship is moving in becomes an excavation, then even explosives cannot shatter the "peace." Alas, what is left is the classic Taurean "stability." Nothing can rock this boat because this boat has rocks. And they're heavy!

Taurus Woman with Aries Man

He's pushy, but you're placid. He's impatient, but you just wait for change. He's flighty, and you never get off the ground. But the very worst is that he's so bossy that sometimes you just want to bribe him to shut up.

He sees himself as very exciting, and he'll tell you all about it. But what he won't tell you is that he has a temper that could make you swallow your bubblegum.

He lives for challenges, whereas you seek stability. He is freedom-loving, while you are fearful of moments spent alone. He's a many-woman man; you're a one-man woman. And basically, he's looking for fireworks, while you're satisfied with just a little warmth.

Unless you have a lot of Aries in your horoscope, this relationship is better off left as an encounter. For a Taurus woman to lose her heart to an Aries man is like an orphan in a storm watching a wealthy family celebrate Christmas. All the lights belong to somebody else, and the closest you can get is to creep up and caress the windowpane.

Taurus Woman with Gemini Man

You embrace stability; he can't exist without change. You gear your life toward future security, while he can't think past the present second. You gravitate toward a quiet kind of evening, but he prefers a New Year's celebration.

Needless to say, this combination is not the most compatible. You need someone steady, and he is maddeningly capricious. He wants a woman with a mind like a quiz show; you want to be loved for what you are.

He'll stand you up, forget your phone number and maybe even your first name. He'll talk you to death, tease you to the point of weeping, and then tear your ego to pieces. With him, there is only one thing you can depend on—the fact that he is utterly undependable.

A love affair with Mr. Gemini is like waiting in line in a rainstorm to board the Ferris wheel—only to find out that it's broken. If you're really smart, before you think of buying your ticket, you'll make sure first that you check out all the other rides.

Taurus Woman with Cancer Man

Much passion will definitely pass between you. But whether the relationship lasts depends on where you are both willing to take it.

He is loyal and loving, but the meaning of his moods will totally elude you. At one moment he is insecure and dependent; at another, he is totally withdrawn. His feelings have a way of tying you both up in knots. Together, you will satiate each other's security needs. However, you are the more practical one, he the more passionate. You are the earthly foundation; he is the ivory tower made from molten wax.

You tend to dwell in the fundamentals, while he lingers in the romantic overtones. He is carried away by softness and subtlety, whereas you are more entranced by some support.

However, you are both so jealous that you make each other feel sought-after when you trade suspicions. And you are both so domestic that together you can spend a weekend cooking up a storm.

In most respects, this relationship is highly compatible. When you combine your earth element with his water element, the result is fertility and sustained emotion. Once you pass through the emotional communication gap, where the silence is sometimes deafening, you will both realize that there is enough feeling here to last a lifetime.

Taurus Woman with Leo Man

You are most security-oriented—both materially and emotionally. So if he buys you daffodils, brings you to a French restaurant, and over the peach Melba, croons, "It had to be you," suddenly you're his and may even forget to eat the ice cream. However, he should join a health club immediately, since you're already planning your menus.

You love to nurture and to be nurtured. Hence, even your plants have come to think of you as Mother. The domestic duties that destroy him seem to delight you. However, before he should sit back and wonder when dinner will be ready, he should keep in mind a handy little fact: nothing in this world is free, and thus you also have a price. It's called marriage, and it's a highly motivating factor. Your life means nothing to you without it; but that's not *necessarily* how he feels about his. If his need to wander exceeds his ego need for approval, you may make him feel that he has as much freedom as your coffee grinder.

However, if he is at the point where his jaded soul has seen everything there is to see, you may just be *the* woman. Sexually, you spell animal, but can exhaust his senses if he's been working nights to prepare for the position of premier of the universe.

If he's up for the midnight marathons, the seven-course dinners, a loyal devoted wife, mother, and executive housekeeper, you're on! But a word of warning to him: next to Scorpio, you are the most jealous and possessive woman in the zodiac, and when he gets you angry, for whatever reason, a grudge is born that is never quite buried. Your silences can make him think he's living in a clinic for the hard of hearing. But at this point, he should just shut up and kiss you. Your view will remain unchanged till death. The question is, what's more important in the long run—winning a point or gaining love?

Taurus Woman with Virgo Man

Although he may nag you about the bathtub ring, you'll find this man most endearing. He is honest, vulnerable, giving, and loving. Because he tends to be a quiet stay-at-home, together you can share many cozy evenings. A flickering fire, some filet mignon, and a carafe of Beaujolais, and you're on your way to nirvana.

You will find him considerate, and he will find you warm and caring. He appreciates your practicality. You appreciate the competence with which he runs his life.

He tends to be shy, but you can melt his inhibitions with your animal sensuality. You tend to be insecure, but he has a way of reducing your fears. Basically he is kind, understanding, and someone you'll find easy to talk to. He is loyal, genuine, and the kind of man to whom you want to be committed.

This is a relationship based on a deep rapport, with a future of much feeling. Any way you look at it, you both have a lot to look forward to.

Taurus Woman with Libra Man

You'll really think you're "in" when he begins all his sentences with "we." However, do listen longer. There's a lot more for the hearing, like the little words "I love you." But don't be surprised if you find yourself smoking, eating, waiting, and listening. . . .

Basically, he wants to hear bells ring, while you're content to sacrifice the sound effects for some silence on solid ground. However, with Mr. Libra you'll only be treading in the cracks. He is not one to lean on; nor is he the one to allay your insecurities. On the contrary, he may both confirm and create them.

He is a ladies' man, while you are a one-woman show. You demand to know if he's going or coming, and he's never considered the question, since he's usually stuck in between.

He'll love the way you take care of him when he's sick, cook for him when he's hungry, and clean for him when he's lazy. However, when Saturday night comes and you find yourself alone and caressing the phone, just don't start telling yourself he's seeing his mother.

Invite him over for Sunday brunch (that you've stayed up all night to prepare) and ask him what he was doing on Saturday, and he'll smile in a friendly sort of way and tell you he took his fiancée to dinner.

One thing you can certainly say about Mr. Libra, he is honest. As a matter of fact, he has the kind of candor that kills. He'll inform you why he could never love you, and he'll share with you what it was that he was looking for and found in another woman. If you're smart, you'll tell him to look for the door. If it's cooking for another person that you're really into, you could get more appreciation from opening a catering service.

Taurus Woman with Scorpio Man

He'll take you in and make you travel places you've never been before. In one evening, you'll find him alluring, mysterious, magnetic, sexy, and dangerous. He is— and he's glad that you're smart enough to know it.

He'll find you warm, sensual, domestic, insecure, and very vulnerable. He can see through your spinach quiche straight into your soul, and what he'll see is a tremendous sense of need and a longing to be needed.

At first, this may scare him, and during dessert he may calculate how many giant steps it will take him to get beyond the front door. However, something besides the second cup of coffee and Grand Marnier will keep him seated. He has no idea what it really is, and that's because it really is a lot of things.

For you, this is a fatal attraction. Your heart will get caught up in his contradictions, and he'll enjoy the power he has just watching you try to get out. You are like a fly under the furry foot of a tarantula. And in whichever direction you choose to walk, you're going to get stepped on.

To your mind, he's a kind of three-ring circus without sound. You never know what show goes on next, and half the time you don't even know what you're watching. What he does and says and desires and wants and hates and needs is all beyond you. From your perspective, the mechanics of his mind are more obscure than the Bible translated into Arabic.

Your greatest desire is an honest relationship without games, and the kind of passion that comes without pain. He finds such scenes comforting only in the dark night of his soul, when he feels sad and lonely. At all other times, he wants his attention to be galvanized by some sort of challenge. And because of this, in the long run he may leave you feeling cold and hungry.

Therefore, the outcome of this encounter is most likely to be that of two people who pass in the night. If you're smart, the first thing you should do when you see him is just keep on walking. You'll save yourself a lot of heartache, and he'll save himself a few inches on his waistline from your cooking.

Taurus Woman with Sagittarius Man

He is a man of adventure, while you are a cozy stay-at-home. He likes to battle the elements, while you like to watch the world from your four-poster. You are controlled by your creature comforts, while he runs around and loves to rough it.

He is a fanatic for every kind of sport and has a hard time sitting still when he's eating. You prefer a sedentary life-style and keep all athletics restricted to the bedroom.

His sense of humor overshadows every situation, while yours takes twelfth place to your needs. His idea of romance is to arm-wrestle; yours is to sniff peonies and wear silk.

On a night when you'll want to lounge by the fire and cuddle, he'll want to play backgammon. At a time in the morning that's so early it seems like the middle of the night, he'll abandon you for a tennis date. And every time you go to kiss him, he'll tell you you need more exercise.

The outcome of this love affair is that he'll probably leave you for some girl who works in a gym. How can you compete with a woman weight lifter who jogs just to relax? Forget it and find someone who appreciates your home-ground coffee beans. Life is just too short to force yourself to be something that you're not.

Taurus Woman with Capricorn Man

He is the archetype of the ambitious breadwinner and the kind of man you would like to take command. You are the archetype of the fertile earth mother and the kind of woman he would like to serve.

Both of you share a sense of practicality and purpose that will truly draw you together. He is responsible, dutiful, loyal, and loving. You are solid, stable, devoted, and nurturing.

You admire his ambitious, hardworking nature. He respects your resourcefulness, and understands your security needs. Together, you could build a business, a marriage, a family, or a corporation.

He has a shrewd sense of money, and you have an uncanny way of making it multiply. He is dignified and fatherly; you are unassuming and motherly. While he may appear cool and aloof to others, you have a way of warming him up and getting his total attention in record time. You have a special way of fulfilling his needs, and he has a special way of fulfilling your expectations. Together, you enjoy a certain amount of material security along with a taste for those little luxuries that often make life worthwhile.

Much mutual support, understanding, and compatibility make this combination one that is especially meaningful. Together you could move mountains, or just a big place in each other's hearts.

Taurus Woman with Aquarius Man

He's far more interested in what's out in space than in what's right in front of him. And when it comes to those little sensual pleasures that make your life worth living, he has a way of reducing them all to a thought.

He'll torment your possessive proclivities and put your jealousy through a kind of trial by fire. Communication between the two of you is like an Arab eating pasta with a Russian. All that comes through are the strangest sounds.

His deepest desire is to have wings, while yours is to have an anchor. He is attached to nonattachment, while you have an infinite capacity to own. He sees love as only an idea, while you see it as the stuff that life is made of. He considers the connubial commitment an open marriage, while you would love a husband you can lock up.

Needless to say, this is not a compatible arrangement, but one you would be better off bypassing without expectation. Together, you are like two bumping cars going in different directions, except when you stop to crash into each other.

To your mind, he is strange, weird, most bizarre, and maybe even a little crazy. To his mind, you are confining, conventional, rigid, and foolishly willful. He is the grand humanitarian, while you believe that goodliness should begin at home. You are the servant of your own services; he is a man determined to do it himself.

There is only one thing to do in the face of this encounter: quit while you're still ahead, shake hands, slap each other on the back, and come out calling yourselves "friends" (a favorite Aquarian term).

This way, on lonely Sundays, you can call him up and tell him your love problems, and he'll leave his girlfriend and be over in five minutes to cheer you up.

Taurus Woman with Pisces Man

He's a fantasy addict, while you prefer facing the facts. Marry him and you take on the responsibility of a caretaker in a home for the convalescent.

He can't be bothered with day-to-day details, so you

have to assume what he shuns. He is overflowing with sympathy for the underprivileged. However, should you develop an acute case of bronchial pneumonia, he'll still expect you to bring in the car for the yearly checkup.

During bad times, he'll lean on you so hard you won't be able to stand up straight, but when you need him, he'll be so far into fantasyland that he won't even know that you're there. Marriage with him is a kind of do-it-yourself existence, except that you're doing for two and not one.

Undoubtedly, he will feel that you're a very fine person. The problem is that he thinks that about every woman on the street, as well as his affairs on the side.

In the divorce court, he'll tell his lawyer that you taught him a lot. What he taught you is that marriage is not really the wonder that you hoped it might be. Just reconsider your needs before you move on to the next.

Taurus Man with Aries Woman

You won't exactly appreciate the way she points when she wants something. She won't like the way you refuse to move when she points.

This woman is bossy and is used to wrapping men around her little finger and squeezing hard. Although you would be willing to climb Mount Everest for some lady who asks you nicely, you don't at all appreciate the pushy touch.

She operates from the principle of immediately, while you can't see why anything is worth doing if you have to kill yourself. She is impatience personified, while you wouldn't mind waiting for the sun to turn green. She is the classic superachiever who can never get enough. You are the first to sit back with a cigarette and settle.

Sexually, she is your match; however, she just may be other men's as well. Basically, she does not believe in Mr. Right, and therefore is always open to the most casual affair. She is adventurous, while you loathe risk-taking. She is committed to the moment; you are ready to sell your soul for the future.

Her energy will excite you, but your energy won't exactly send her soaring. She wants to be challenged, while you want to be made to feel secure. She has a hunger to be at the top, but you feel a satisfaction staying somewhere in the middle.

You both seem to be moving in different directions, but only she seems to be going somewhere. It's probably out of your life, since your stability makes her anxiety-ridden. Don't eat your heart out; in the long run you are far better off with a woman who doesn't even know the time but who does know how to walk without running.

Taurus Man with Gemini Woman

She is freedom-loving and flip; you are security-oriented and serious. She loves to test and tease and at any given moment has a thousand little games up her sleeve. As you can deal only with "down-home" women who lay their cards out face-up, she is enough to give you a psychosomatic case of lockjaw.

She has a convenient habit of forgetting that men are people. Therefore, if you move too slowly, she'll treat you as if you were a tree. She is compulsively capricious, and an irritant to your sense of stability. You are confining, and a suffocating force to her sense of freedom.

Other than that, you operate through your body, while she is imprisoned in her mind. Her emotions are merely momentary, while yours are entrenched in a limitless time span. She is glib and superficial, while you are groping and sedentary. You are deeply sensual, while she is deeply cerebral; you tend to be emotionally committed, but she tends to be emotionally detached.

At best, this relationship should be confined to a bank, where you get paid to tell her what to do. As you're helping her with her bounced checks *and* you see she hasn't balanced her checkbook in years *and* you notice her attention drifting to a point in the middle of your throat, the best thing to do is just kick her in the shins and be done with it. Her world is not your world, nor will it ever be. Therefore, the best thing to do after saying hello is to say good-bye before turning in separate directions.

Taurus Man with Cancer Woman

You are two truly stay-at-home creatures and can have a lovely evening just cooking a cabbage quiche. At times she will remind you of Mother on Thanksgiving morning. You will remind her of Daddy on days that he paid the rent.

In each other, you find your security fantasies satisfied, and for both of you that is a lot. She will find you to be someone solid to lean on, while you will find her a cushion of kindness.

You would both rather build bookcases together than go to the movies, and fantasize more about a family than about future successes. You are both supersensualists, with larger-than-life appetites. Therefore, your bedtime compatibility could bring you to exciting places.

She wants to be possessed forever and always. You want someone to treat you like a savings account. Deep down inside, you dream of a "little woman." And even if she is president of a multimillion-dollar corporation, she would be willing to take on that traditional role.

Although she can get caught in a vortex of emotion, you are so stable that she'll control her moods. You appeal to the practical side of her nature, while she appeals to your shadow sensitivities.

You were made for each other and could spend a lifetime loving. All that you have to do is meet.

Taurus Man with Leo Woman

This is definitely not a match made in heaven, as you both have a will that could splinter steel. You are stubborn and rigid. She is defiant and stubborn. Combined, these inharmonious qualities can spell a heartache.

You are Mr. Stay-at-home, while she walks holes in the floor if she can't get out. She likes the drama and excitement of life, while you are content with the ten-o'clock news.

It is not unlikely that you outdo her in the kitchen, a quality she awesomely appreciates, since she never considered it a divine right to have to cook. Yet, when you've slaved for hours over the stove to create a ten-course meal, and she dawdles over the asparagus because she's dieting, the "dinner" can become decidedly cold.

You tend to get into ruts, while she compulsively creates change. You can replay one record more frequently than a Buddhist meditating on a mantra while she yawns and wants to throw the whole thing away after the third time around.

You have a nervous strain dealing with her independence, and she delights in defying your reactions to her need for freedom. Her drive for power can make you feel impotent; your desire to possess her spirit can make her feel hostile. You sulk during and after her flirtations, while she's forgotten them the minute after she's fled. Days after, you are still not speaking. She shrugs her shoulders and seeks attention elsewhere, as you exit from your silence in a state of violence.

You delight in saving money, while she saves her sanity in spending it. You faint when you see that she's spent fifteen dollars on lip gloss, while she licks her lips and smiles because she loves to startle your conservative sensibilities. Mutually, there is passion, but after a while you find her a nemesis to your earthly nature. She considers sex an unnatural act if she doesn't look and smell like perfection and repeatedly, your animal sensuality is offended by her preoccupation with appearance.

Because of this, you see her as a mask of pretense, yet one that is undeniably seductive. You berate her because she'd rather be a *Vogue* cover girl than Jane of the Jungle. She berates you because your sense of sophistication is not startling, your sensuality so earthy she finds it degrading, and your stomach slowly creeping forward.

What even brings you two together? Her cover-girl appearance appeals to your ruler, Venus, while your sense of stability startles its way into her soul. You are a man she can depend on; she is a lady who makes you look good. Whether this spells love depends on how many times in one week you cook *boeuf à la bourguignonne*, each time serving it as if it were the first; how often she flirts with your friends, forgets to devour your cooking, and fights to reapply her lip gloss when you want to make love. As to the outcome of this strange and stormy combination, even the stars wearily abdicate all responsibility.

Taurus Man with Virgo Woman

She'll clean up after you make a mess. You'll cook for her when she's tired. Together you can build a bastion of love where you both gain the kind of nurturance you so need.

You admire her neatness and respect the way she respects her body. She admires your emotional strength and marvels at your stamina and endurance.

You are patient in areas where she is anxious; she is understanding in situations where you are befuddled. You'll find her thoughtful, kind, sensitive, and deeply caring. She'll find you to be the kind of loving, tender, and protective man she always wanted. This is clearly a case of two people living happily ever after.

In terms of marriage, you are a team that is marveled at, since your relationship seems to have the stability that looks too good to be true. That is because you are both so solid. Just remember to make the most of it.

Taurus Man with Libra Woman

This could be romance at second sight. She has the sense of beauty you so admire, and you have the money to buy the beauty she so desires.

Emotionally, she is so up and down that she'll fall in love with you just because you never get depressed. You are a force of stability, while she is wishy-washy. She is an ethereal romantic, and you are a practical idealist.

You'll take care of her moods by buying her trinkets and smothering her with love. She'll satisfy your sybaritic desires by cooking you a delectable dinner that sends you into a swoon.

You'll give her so much attention she'll stop sulking and whining. She'll conjure for you such creature comforts you'll never be the same.

She needs someone with strong arms, and you are just the person who can imprison her. At the same time, you need a woman who knows how to learn.

Your affair will have the romance of a 1940's movie, redone for color television. And your marriage will consist of those tender moments of which only advertising knows for sure.

Taurus Man with Scorpio Woman

Chances are, she won't find this chemistry a delight, unless you're cooking her dinner. And you're probably doing that only because you're too cheap to take her out. If she breaks a tooth on the bread, it's undoubtedly because you bought it on sale. And if the milk in her coffee separates, it's only because you wanted to use up last month's before you opened a new bottle. And should the steak have muscles stronger than hers after six months of jogging, she'll know that you bargained with a discount butcher.

She'll find your conversation great if she's been having insomnia problems. And she'll find your interests extremely varied if she likes to watch six TV channels in one evening.

She finds you terribly sensitive—when it comes to your own feelings. But should she desire you to comprehend a subtle emotional situation, she may have to lean over and shout in your ear. However, she shouldn't expect you to understand the first time around, or the fifth, or the tenth, or the sixteenth. . . .

For her mental framework to tolerate you, she needs enough patience to fill a time period called a lifetime. Yet you do have one distinctive attribute—you're faithful. However, that's because, in essence, you're too lazy even to move from one room to another.

You get into ruts more often than any other sign, so if she wants to get rid of you for good, she has to dig you another and give you a good push forward.

Taurus Man with Sagittarius Woman

Her idea of fun is lots of physical activity; your idea of physical activity is either sex or overeating.

She'll get up at dawn just to work on her backhand, while you would rather spend the day eating pasta than playing tennis. She loves to travel from country to country, while you rarely move from room to room. She prefers a spartan life-style to the lap of luxury. You prefer a sybaritic setting to one where you have to rough it.

She has a sense of adventure that leads her to exciting places. You have a sense of fear that entrenches you in the same spot. She is fascinated by Eastern philosophy; the only meditation you've ever done is on money.

You'll sulk when you don't understand her sense of humor, and she'll be impatient with your overwhelming possessiveness.

Needless to say, the chances are highly unlikely that

you will bring each other a lifetime of untarnished bliss. Instead, you would be much better off returning to your simmering pot of ragout and she to a solitary shopping spree for some new sweat bands.

Taurus Man with Capricorn Woman

She'll find you better than a Christmas present on a cold rainy morning. You'll find her to be the kind of competent career woman you've always gotten a crush on.

She is strong and dignified, yet has a lot of feeling underneath the cool surface. You are warm and cuddly, with an earthiness that makes her feel at ease.

She will inspire your career goals, while you will make her feel loved for herself rather than her title of vice-president. Her encouragement will help you drive yourself to greater places. However, in the end, your pace will help her to slow down and live a lot longer.

Together you will linger over your filet mignon in the candle glow. And you'll find her so stimulating that you may lose your appetite and not stop for an ice cream on the way home.

If anything, Ms. Capricorn will probably make you go on a diet. So clean out all your frozen pizzas, have a party, and announce to the world that you've fallen in love.

Taurus Man with Aquarius Woman

She tends toward humanitarian impulses, while your impulses are more self-seeking. She is independent and interested in everything around her, while you are more dependent and interested in what immediately concerns you. She likes to spread her time among a thousand people, while you prefer to concentrate on just a few.

Anyway you look at it, the two of you together are like strangers from two different planets. You eat different things, you see different things, and you need different things. Any interaction between you will probably be no more than in passing. Otherwise, the frustration can approach the level of paralysis.

She is inflamed by future issues, while your attention seems to get plastered in the present. She is dedicated to progressive ideals, while you are dedicated to immediate gratification. She has an eccentric mind that is ahead of its time; you have one that is conventional and confined to the moment.

You prefer either to hoard your money or to spend it self-indulgently. She likes to give hers away to needy people. She gets carried away by causes, while the greatest cause you embrace is personal gain. You gravitate toward the material, while her needs tend to be on the ethereal. It was someone just like you who created management, and it was someone just like her who created revolutionary uprisings.

The communication gap here is like a cosmic crack in the universe. If you hang around her too long, you may just fall in. However, who knows: what you may lose in the end may do you a world of good.

Taurus Man with Pisces Woman

You are like a big house that she can lean up against, and only a Taurus man can stand the weight.

She is a fragile, vulnerable creature with a mental makeup that you'll never understand. You are a stolid force with a matter-of-fact philosophy that totally eludes her because it's so simple.

The compatibility here is not exactly attention-getting; however, the underlying needs that are satisfied are something else. You both tend to be enslaved by the sensual pleasures that quicken the pulse and speed up the bloodstream. You both like to sleep in the sun and open your eyes to fresh orange juice spiked with a little vodka. You both could adore a marathon of sex from dawn till the daylight disappears. And you both prefer a body that is naked to one that is nicely dressed.

At this point, the similarities start to dwindle. She is emotional and weepy, while you are practical and put your emotions in a place where they don't show. Her sacred dwelling is in daydreams, while yours is in a material dynasty rooted in the earth. She is an ephemeral creature of the clouds, and you are a denizen of the practical business world.

You find her to be seductive, alluring, and at times more mysterious than your mind can take. She finds you to be solid, stubborn, sensual, and someone she can depend on. Her inherent creativity can bloom under your love and protection. Your sense of purpose can become inflamed under her support.

Together, you could become a worthwhile team effort, if your divergent approaches to life don't get seriously in the way.

GEMINI

Dates: May 22—June 21
Ruling planet: Mercury
Element: Air
Mode: Mutable
Quality: Masculine, positive
Planetary principle: Versatility
Primal desire: Communication
Color: Yellow
Jewels: Beryl, aquamarine
Plants: Honeysuckle, jasmine
Day: Wednesday
Archangel: Raphael
Magical number: 7
Material factor: Invention

GEMINIS OF
FAME AND FORTUNE

Bob Dylan
Judy Garland
Marilyn Monroe
Sir Arthur Conan Doyle

John F. Kennedy
Rudolph Valentino
Bob Hope
Ian Fleming

Joe Namath

THE GEMINI FEMALE

Favorable

As a child you were probably the smartest girl in your class, but you talked so much that you drove your teacher crazy. Chances are, you have never stopped driving people crazy. However, due to your high intelligence, the world is always willing to pay the price to take you on.

You are flip, quick, clever, and witty. You love games, abhor repetition, and sometimes are a slave to your sense of challenge. Your mind is restless and impatient, changeable and contradictory. You probably change your viewpoint every hour before you come to the final conclusion that you really don't know what you think. At best, you can make only a vague approximation.

You've never really understood yourself, although you've spent your life trying. There are people who would call you polymorphous-perverse, while others would sum it up by saying you're crazy. Your desires tend to take you in two different directions simultaneously, and then they change in midstream. You want to go to five parties at once, and at the point when you finally decide what you'll wear, you change your mind and stay home to read a book.

Everywhere you go, you're at least ten minutes late. Sometimes this is because you can't decide if you really want to be there. At other times it's because you change your clothes so many times before leaving. Quite often it's because you think only five minutes have elapsed when it's more like forty-five.

You are a blithe spirit with a mischievous streak that others sometimes fail to appreciate. You have a sharp tongue and a sense of humor that some find scintillating; while others find you too astringent for their sensibilities.

You are charming, verbal, spirited, but sometimes superficial in your assessment of others. You tend to be more deeply connected to your mind than to your body, and thrive on mental stimulation. However, often you get so deeply lost in your own logic that you suffer from insomnia and an aggravated case of overthinking.

You are nervous, energetic, and have a mind like

quicksilver. You have both a keen sense of order and a need for an underlying structure to support your experience. However, you tend to rely too heavily on superficial structures and expect them to provide the emotional security that you refuse to create yourself. You may stay in a job that is not satisfying if the rest of your life is unstable. You may get locked into a relationship in which very few of your needs are met, either because you subconsciously fear intimacy or because you lack faith in your own ability to create greater happiness.

In moments of severe stress, your stomach truly takes a beating. Any aggravated mental problem can make you lose your appetite, with a resulting weight loss that other women often envy. If they only knew the painful price you had to pay for your svelte appearance.

While, for the most part, you are well liked by others, you are your own worst enemy. You tend to play your life rather than live it, and view everything from the outside rather than feeling it from within. Your compulsive assessment of externals dissociates you from experiencing the kind of in-depth joy and sorrow that make a human being rich in wisdom. You tend to transform your feelings into thoughts that you reanalyze until you lose the original perspectives. At this point, you participate in life as if it were a game.

In matters of love, you are difficult, demanding, changeable, and critical. Your ideal is a highly competent man with a superb intelligence and a galvanizing sense of humor. Looks are strictly secondary and have less and less importance as you grow older. You like to be challenged verbally and can fall in love over a clever comment. You don't need candlelight, soft music, or incense. Rather, a scintillating mind in blinding daylight can send your emotions soaring.

Even when you *are* in love, you operate from a glib facade and have a horror of expressing deeper feelings. You are far more comfortable making a joke or uttering some absurd statement than you are in saying "I love you." Even if left swinging by your thumbs, it's debatable whether you would let yourself shout it.

It's understandable that men find you both maddening and emotionally detached. Quite often you are. There are few who get your total attention, and even those privileged ones are so often subject to your pride and your changing moods that they wonder if it's all really worth it.

One of your greatest attributes is your love of laughter and your wry ability to see life as comic. However, sometimes you take it all too far. You have to keep in mind that all the world is not a game, unless that's how you want to make it. Then take responsibility when people treat you like a Monopoly set that is superficially entertaining but neither meaningful nor memorable.

Unfavorable

You're a party girl who wants to be in several places simultaneously. You are restless, impatient, and seek your entertainment from the outside rather than from the inner you.

You hate to be alone because you're bored with your own company. Therefore, you'd rather hang out in a department store than discipline yourself to read a book.

You are clever, but compulsively capricious, shallow, and superficial. You are a people user and a dispassionate exploiter of the generous person. Since your mind is so mercurial and your needs so momentary, you never hang around long enough either to return a favor or to offer a hand. You display a kind of selfishness and can take advantage without the least anxiety or introspective awareness.

Although your mind is quick, you are so lacking in depth that it's difficult to spend time around you without earplugs. You chatter and babble, but often say very little. You love gossip, think in platitudes, and rely on mind games to give you a sense of personal power.

When people compliment you, what they say is that you're bright, not nice, understanding, warm, or compassionate. However, you *are* open about the fact that you're out for yourself, since your actions speak even louder than your words.

Although you consider yourself to be spontaneous, you're really compulsively capricious. You rarely follow through on promises, finish projects, or make an effort to keep your word. You live for the minute, and your memory rarely extends beyond this time span. Therefore, you usually lose recollection of what you've committed yourself to the minute before, and consequently take no responsibility.

You have a mind like an oscilloscope that communicates in non sequiturs. Your values are frivolous, and your priorities pleasure-oriented. You are dedicated to doing what you want to do, and anyone who expects otherwise will end up sadly disappointed.

In the area of love, you are highly critical and get your greatest pleasure in testing. You have a mischievous streak that borders on the sadistic and you get more satisfaction from tormenting a man than from trying to love him.

You have a tendency to think about an experience rather than feel it, and through your overworked intellect, you dispel all sensation. You tear down situations with your mind and then dwell on what you don't have. Underneath your easygoing facade, you are petulant, irritable, and a perfectionist in what you expect from other people.

You are also contrary, argumentative, impatient, and very fickle. You are a compulsive flirt, but underneath it all, you have very little feeling. You confuse men to the point that they consider you an enigma. However, you're really not that puzzling. You're ambivalent because you want everything but want to give nothing. Compromise is not part of your setup, since it involves feelings, and in this area there's a lot you seem to be missing. In life, you are the sauntering passerby who risks nothing and commits only to a momentary caprice. Passion and propinquity are not your desire. What you really want is a wealthy playmate who will indulge your fluttering fancies. And in return, it's likely you'll convey your gratitude by infidelity.

There is one thing that you have going for you that always seems to get you by. You're such a stereotype of the superficial that everyone assumes that there just has to be more.

THE GEMINI MALE

Favorable

You have a personality that could charm serpents, and a mind that is equal to any intellectual task. Your dynamic enthusiasm can take you anywhere, while your quiet sense of gaiety can easily create a crowd around you.

Mentally you move in overdrive and enjoy a great deal of success in the intellectual sphere. Your mind is restless and eager, your personality adaptable and interested in a multitude of subjects.

You have a high intelligence, a spontaneous kind of enthusiasm, and a definite way with words that is often the hallmark of your success. Because of your special fluency with language, you are noted for the kind of acute comments that can crack up an entire party of the most somber souls.

Your quick-witted mentality and versatile capabilities lead you to consume a variety of subjects. A great example of this specific kind of Gemini expression is Sir Arthur Conan Doyle, who, in addition to being a most successful writer, possessed degrees in both law and medicine and was an extremely devoted spokesman for the Spiritualist cause.

A keen sense of humor often makes you the center of attention, while your multifaceted mind makes you a most stimulating man to be around. You are an original thinker who is logical and reflective, analytical, and objective.

Women love to be around you because you're so fun-loving. Children like you because you make them laugh. Somewhere in you there is the personality of the playful little boy whose energies can occasionally overtax his audience.

Chances are, you've always been ridiculously popular, even if you didn't know it. You are the life-of-the-party type and the kind of man who can make a freedom-loving woman fall in love overnight. You'll make her sides split with your silly lines, and her life a lot happier, just by having you around.

Basically, people love you because you love people. You are gregarious, enthusiastic, curious, and comfortable with all types.

When it comes to affairs of the heart, you tend to be freedom-loving and seek to experience as many different kinds of women as possible. Your code is that variety is the spice of life as well as the gravitational factor that seems to keep you on the ground and running.

It is not until the thirties that the issue of marriage

becomes a serious consideration for the male Gemini. At this point you are mostly seeking a partner to share your exuberant life enthusiasm because you're getting a little weary of experiencing everything by yourself. In a wife you need a highly intelligent, spontaneous woman who likes to treat every day as if it were terribly different from the one before. A great sense of humor, intellectual depth, and a strong spirit of adventure would make her your "ideal woman." A classic superachiever is also the type that you are most attracted to. But then, the very act of marrying you could, in itself, be considered an achievement.

Unfavorable

You can be cold, detached, inconsiderate, and often lacking in compassion. You make far more promises than you ever keep, and repeatedly prove yourself to be totally undependable.

As a slave to the pleasure principle, you are self-centered, insensitive, verbose, and at your best, harmless though superficial. At your worst, you may be a liar, a cheat, a thief, and a guiltless vagabond. You will take anything you can get, but at the same time give up nothing in return.

You have the attention span of a 3-year-old and the memory of an amoeba. Your behavior is erratic, your feelings extremely flighty, and your company fatiguing.

Tedium distresses you to the point of fearing any kind of follow-through. You change your mind every minute of the day and then forget what it was that you finally wanted.

Your mind is quick, bright, but seldom put to good use. You tend to scatter your energies so much that you never stick to anything, including what you originally happened to be chatting about in the first place.

Often you are cruel, callous, conniving, and calculating, and your pithy comments have an astringency that can kill. You have an acid tongue that heartily enjoys tearing someone to pieces. But first you like to test and tease until your victim is well on the way to a demonical kind of dementia.

In the area of love, you are a rabid game-player who is seriously committed to noncommitment. You will stand a woman up without batting an eyelash, and if you're married, you'll probably have more affairs than someone single.

Because you're a snob, your shallow values will attract you to either a wealthy woman or to one who will make you think her name is written in the social register.

Basically, you love a challenge and a chase, but when it comes to winning the prize, you really don't know what to do with it. All that you desire from a woman is that she keep her distance so that you'll never have to experience the disappointment of getting too close.

It's very dangerous for you to fall in love, because after that there's nothing to look forward to. Your best bet probably is to marry for money and give so many parties that you hardly ever see your wife. This way, you'll keep yourself constantly entertained meeting a lot of new faces among the coats.

Despite what the world may think of you, you're really no enigma. You're simply ambivalent and very boring. You're lost so far down in yourself that your eyes can barely peep over the edge; they can only dart sideways without focusing.

Basically, you're looking for your own face in the faces of other people, but you can't stand still long enough to glimpse even your own reflection in a mirror. Loneliness is what keeps you moving to those mentally distant places. You're a runner, and you run fast since you're afraid of getting caught in someone's eyes. In other people you see your own emptiness staring back at you. And that is just as terrifying as openly admitting that you feel anxiety-ridden, fearful, and very alone.

DECANS

Every sign in the zodiac can be broken down into three subdivisions, called decans. Each decan roughly corresponds to 10 degrees—the first third, second third, and last third of the sun sign's time span, which is approximately thirty days.

As each of these periods has different subrulerships, the personality of a person is slightly modified by the specific decan it falls in. For instance, an Aries born in the second decan would be ruled by Mars, but subruled by the Sun. Therefore, he would tend to display a greater sense of pride, boastfulness, egotism, and optimism than an Aries born in the third decan, which is subruled by Jupiter. This Aries would tend to be more freedom-loving, flighty, travel-oriented, and interested in subjects of a philosophical nature. An Aries born in the first decan would be the most aggressive, but not necessarily the most productive and accomplished.

Decans are important, since they do account for a more detailed assessment of an individual's personality characteristics. They also show how two people born under the same sun sign can be markedly different.

If you were born between May 22 and May 31, your sun falls in the Mercury decan of Gemini. Your life is a battleground between your mind and your emotions, and too often your thoughts enslave you with a merciless force.

You are highly intelligent and possess verbal talents that could lead you to success in the fields of writing, teaching, and all forms of communications. Because of your quick-witted talents and the legerity of your mind, you have the personality of the proverbial life of the party or the TV commentator who truly commands an audience.

You are nervous, restless, talkative, and gregarious. You love to laugh, and have the kind of sparkling sense of humor that is definitely an attention getter.

Although you are friendly, you are also very fickle when it comes to your feelings. You are cautious and critical in regard to romantic matters, and usually never fall in love, but creep into your commitments sideways, all the time wondering if you're really doing the right thing.

You analyze situations to the point where you start to wish someone could help you shut off your mind and get on to something else. Because there is such a strong tendency toward perfectionism in your character, you have a habit of finding little faults in what could be your greatest joys, if you'd let them be.

Insomnia is a lifelong problem that has a tendency to torment you in the wee hours. Chronic anxiety, nervousness, and worry are also the pitfalls of a mind that works overtime. Chances are, you tend to read till dawn and then face the morning moaning that you will never make it through the day.

Physical activity is a must for a mind such as yours, and is probably something that you have always avoided like the plague. Deep down, you believe that everything that isn't mental is really a waste of time. However, once you overcome this limitation and experience the mental relaxation that accompanies strenuous exercise, you are destined to become a fun-seeking fiend of the physical. Once you learn to liberate yourself from your mind, and learn how to control it, rather than letting it control you, you will see how limitless your life is, and how simply joy can be achieved.

If you were born between June 1 and June 11, your sun falls in the Venus decan of Gemini.

You are charming, highly flirtatious, slyly romantic, and extremely creative. Your verbal abilities can bring you recognition in the areas of fiction as well as creative journalism. Since you are never at a loss for words, you can make a highly successful public speaker and have the invincible charm of a comedian who is at ease performing in front of the masses.

You have a truly contagious kind of enthusiasm that can be quite successfully utilized in the areas of both public relations and show business. Your rapid, logical mind, combined with your charisma, could give you the abilities to be anything from an entertainment or literary agent to a TV writer to a producer of both film and television.

However, whatever you do for a living, you undeniably have a wealth of creative talents, whether or not you actually use them. Painting and writing are possible outlets. At the same time, a very strong enthusiasm for serious music has always consumed you. Chances are, you are a frustrated musician who's never made a total commitment to the discipline of the study.

You are an elegant host or hostess, and since you tend to be something of a snob, your parties are always populated by the "right" people. You entertain with a true sense of elegance because you enjoy festivities and are perfectionist in your personal expression.

No one can deny that you are a delight to be around. You have a kind of stellar sense of humor and a joie de vivre that imbue you with a lot more personal power than you may give yourself credit for. If you allow your artistic sensitivity a disciplined expression, you may find that fame is really not that far away.

If you were born between June 12 and June 21, your sun falls in the Uranus decan of Gemini.

Of all Gemini natives, you are the most freedom-loving and unconventional in your attitudes. You prefer many ongoing relationships to a monogamous situation, and have a restless, erratic nature and often a brilliant and original mind.

You work best in a milieu of many people, and are particularly oriented to the areas of film and television, as well as computers. However, you also have the aptitude for becoming anything from an astrologer to a psychotherapist to an inventor.

You are extremely changeable, love anything new, lose interest in things and people quickly, and have a rather experimental attitude toward sex. In any marriage or love relationship you need a lot of room, have a paranoia about feeling confined, and delay making commitments until you are given an ultimatum.

Because you are such a people person and a party-lover, it is difficult for you to be faithful to one person until later in life—and even then you may experience many temptations. You like each day to promise something different and exciting, and if you can't find it around you, you'll do your best to create it.

You tend to be detached and interested in everything around you. You may easily stay up all night thinking of new ways to organize the universe, and heartily enjoy sharing your ideas with others and getting their opinions.

You are open-minded, quick-witted, but at times a trifle unstable in the way you live your life. You are definitely well-meaning, but often undependable until well into middle age. Of all of the Gemini natives, you are the most high-strung, nervous, and anxiety-ridden. You need to be very disciplined about how you use your energies, or else they may diffuse into many half-finished projects, conversations and good intentions that never seem to go very far.

LOVE

In love, you are maddening, madcap, and emotionally ambivalent. You either want everything at once, or you think you want nothing at all.

The most you give anyone who has a romantic interest in you is audition privileges. And if you feel the need to yawn too often during the first couple of acts, you just wave the person away and shout "Next!"

In relationships, you worry more about being entertained than you do about loving. You're more critical than a judge for the Miss Universe contest, because you're seeking that perfect package that carries with it the assurance that things *look* like what they should be.

However, if after a certain number of lonely years as an earthly inhabitant you realize bitterly that you have not found Mr. or Ms. Right, you may decide that you're willing to settle. At this point, since you're so flexible, you may reduce the qualifications you are seeking to sheer brilliance, a startling wit, and a most compelling charisma.

You are highly aroused by an intellect of prizewinning quality. And if someone inquired as to the personal qualities that made you fall blindly in love, your almost programmed response would be: "The mind." While a great body also helps, you are far more titillated by a pithy retort than by a little love pat in an erogenous zone.

One category, however, in which you are the least demanding is that of the "good person." This is because if you feel that you are soaring to the heights of all the mental pleasure your cerebrum can take, about the last thing you'll damage a relationship looking for is warmth.

For the Gemini mind, love is a dangerous thing. When you receive what you have analyzed as too much, you behave like an aging, fussy, and very obese gourmet whose chateaubriand for two is served more well done than suits his taste. At that point there is nothing to be done except to send it back to the kitchen, where it really belongs.

When it comes to receiving someone's emotions, you need just the right amount, like the perfect pinch of salt.

A little too much attention in your direction, and you feel more burdened than flattered.

It takes your mind a lifetime to understand what you *think* about feelings. Some Geminis die first, and some just live on, never even realizing that they have any. However, for this particular kind of Gemini, the lack of emotional awareness is so acute that loving is never even a matter of too late.

MARRIAGE

Since you are freedom-loving, critical, and something of a flirt, marriage is not exactly a rabid desire. Of all the activities that life has to offer, there are many other things that you would prefer to do rather than to commit yourself to a state of connubial bliss.

Basically, you like a lot of variety in your love life, and are not that inclined to settle down of your own accord. While this, by far, is more frequently seen in the Gemini male, it is also a trait of the Gemini female, but somewhat less so.

Up until the thirties, you still get your thrills far more from relationships with many people than a monogamous situation. Basically, you prefer a playmate to a marriage partner. But when you do feel you're ready to settle down, you seek most of all a stimulating partner with whom you feel you can share many mental interests.

It is extremely important that you feel respect for the person you marry, and you actually find it preferable to be intellectually overshadowed than to have to reeducate.

You prefer a highly adaptable situation that offers you a great deal of freedom to one where your time is heavily committed. You also appreciate a dynamic personality that can keep up with your pace and has the patience to cope with some of your inconsistent emotional needs.

If someone should ask you out of the blue what you're really looking for, you would throw back some quick quip, grin, frown, and admit that you really don't have a clue.

The fact is, you're waiting for your mind to be swept away, and the best advice is: Don't wait *too* long. You have only a lifetime, and the longer you spend flirting around, the less time there is for loving. On the other hand, Gemini is one sign that might prefer to get it from books rather than through a bodily experience.

MONEY

When it comes to spending, you're a fiend and should be locked up every time you flash your credit card. It doesn't matter how much you make, you never have the slightest idea where it went, and sometimes wonder if it just walked away by itself. Of course, you never think to check your wardrobe, which is so jam-packed that your clothes get wrinkled just hanging there. And you forgot that you just bought a vibrating waterbed to lull away your insomnia problems. (Of course, that *did* come last week, so now it's pretty old.) And you never considered checking your purse for the four lipsticks you bought at lunchtime. (Although they don't really count either, because you're already sick of the colors.)

Although there are always exceptions, generally speaking, when it comes to managing your money, you're a menace. You have more credit cards than a politician, and you regard them with the same kind of fondness a St. Bernard has for his food.

You are a madly impulsive spender who tends to grab at whatever catches your fancy, even if it's a hammock for your two-by-four bedroom or a grand piano for the foyer. Chances are, whatever you're buying will bore you to death in a shamefully small amount of time. Therefore, ever onward along the road of superconsumption. The department stores are waiting, and if they hear that you're coming, they may even stay open until dawn.

CAREER

In general, you don't desire staggering corporate power. You would much rather meet the power people at dazzling parties and be that popular person about town who gets invited everywhere.

When it comes to career, you spend much of your

life in confusion about what you really want to do and trying to decide if you're *really* happy doing it. Since you like to talk and be around people, you're not the type who is happy staying at home and being married to a millionaire you never see. Besides, you would probably give the maid an auditory hernia from your friendly chatter, and send her off to work happily in a hospital for the deaf, dumb, and blind.

Since you have a private horror that somewhere you're going to miss something, you would most like to be everywhere at once rather than sitting quietly in one place working by yourself. At work, you have a hard time behaving yourself for long stretches of time, and like to get up, walk around, and find out what everybody else is or isn't doing and why. You love gossip and have a tremendous need to be in the center of things to make sure that no tidbits get past your burning ears.

Your breezy personality, arresting sense of humor, and rapier-sharp tongue could bring you to the top of your field in teaching, writing, broadcasting, television, and all forms of communication.

Because you love to talk, you could be anything from a telephone operator to a TV commentator. And because you like to read, you could be anything from a magazine editor to a librarian to a book critic.

Since you are so gregarious, the field of public relations is also a definite possibility. And because you have such dexterity and are so independent, inventive, and creative, a profession as far-out as jewelry designing is an exciting consideration.

You have a rapid, logical mind that could bring you far in the field of law. You also have an aptitude for details that could make you a truly indispensable executive secretary.

However, whatever you decide to do, you have to remember that your versatile mind abhors being bored. You need to be stimulated, or else you turn your attention elsewhere and simply coast along on a day-to-day basis, trying to make some definite career decisions. One of the reasons you have such a hard time deciding what to do is that you actually can do so many different things.

And because of this, success is something that often comes naturally to you without staying up all night planning your next move. What really matters more to you than any title are such sideline accouterments as creative freedom and greater social accessibility.

In your mind, both power and success are very relative concepts. However, regardless of the rate of professional advancement or the achievement of a level of socioeconomic status, the need for freedom of communication is foremost. Without the satisfaction of this primal desire, the greatest sum of money will grow to lose its meaning for the Gemini mind.

FRIENDS

While you probably know more people than make up the state of Texas, you have very few friends. Despite the fact that you have the personality of a publicist, you are not really that easy to get close to.

You tend to keep most of your encounters limited to the superficial plane, and move quickly from place to place.

Although your laughter and gaiety would light up any room, you're a lot lonelier than most people think. Behind your compulsive chatter there is a person whose emotions have a hard time coming out in the situations you create.

What you need most in a friend is someone who stimulates your mind and shares your interests. You like to be mentally challenged, even in a friendship, and enjoy spending time with people whose minds are as curious, spontaneous, and mercurial as your own.

You heartily enjoy a congenial interchange, a good laugh, and love to fraternize with anyone you feel to be your mental equal. Since language has always had a special appeal, you are far more attracted to verbal people who express themselves with a certain élan. Your irresistible charm attracts many people to you, but those who remain in your life have to be what you consider special. They are usually lively, spirited, and imbued with an energy that often makes them a stellar attraction in any group.

Unless you're the unevolved sort, when committed to a friendship you are loyal, kind, and sympathetic. You give of your time freely and are generous, understanding, and capable of offering very sound advice. You don't dwell in maudlin emotions and you expect the same of others. What your friends come away with is a more optimistic and far less constricted outlook, and any way you look at it, that's a lot.

HEALTH

Your nerves are your nemesis, and nervous problems are something of a lifetime battle.

You have a fragile mind that moves in overdrive and sometimes stubbornly snubs your physical needs. Depression due to sleepless nights is not an uncommon Gemini problem. Equally nasty are those daytime bouts of anxiety when your pulsing stomach tells you it's tranquilizer time.

You have a definite problem trying to turn your mind off, and often you are a victim of those circular questions that never seem to have answers.

Try a diet that is rich in B vitamins, and supplement it with a brewer's-yeast concoction done up in a blender. As awful as the latter may sound, it really helps to diminish the jangles. Both of these remedies are panaceas for those peculiar places your mind can take you, as well as for the kind of nervous tension that ties you in knots.

For a mind that works all through the night as well as in the daytime, take up Transcendental Meditation and discipline yourself to do it twice a day. If you're really into spending money and would like a more exotic cure, visit a hypnotherapist to learn how to change the direction of your thoughts and thereby circumvent depression.

Mental breakdowns are far more prevalent in your sign than in most of the others; therefore, certain measures of prevention are not only more invaluable but also less costly than any cure.

As monotony can really bring you down, as well as a persistent lack of stimulation, make sure that you structure your life to obtain the most beneficial circumstances available. Since a need of change is basic to your existence, make sure you get it, even if you have to move around your furniture every other week.

On a physical level, you are prone to diseases of the lungs and bronchial tubes. Therefore, avoid cigarettes, try chewing gum, and occasionally keeping your mouth shut, since an overexertion of your vocal cords can bring on laryngitis.

HOME

You have two telephones in two different colors, and every time they ring, you forget where you put them. Your home is basically a kind of launching pad from which you take off for your other activities. And since you usually have no idea if you're coming or going, the physical arrangement can get in a bit of disarray.

Unless you have a lot of water in your chart, or Pluto prominent on the ascendant, you hate to be alone, and your home always looks it. There are either bodies or clothes or both draped about—unless, of course, you are the supertidy type of Gemini.

This Gemini is the compulsive who tends to lose control if even the TV antenna looks like it's leaning a little too much to the right. If your personality falls into this category, you have a tendency to file even your grocery receipts; your accountant sends you flowers at tax time, because of your records; and you are so neat that you spend your spare moments taking care of *imaginary* spots. Since order is intrinsic to your sense of psychic well-being, it might drive you mad if during an entire dinner a friend's napkin looks like it's fated for the floor but never quite seems to make it.

You have never been consumed by the need for a lavish abode. However, what you do need are bookshelves.

Since you are one of the few people foolish enough to go mountain climbing carrying your immediate library rather than your clothes, your books have a special place in your heart. You probably still have your first copy of *Winnie the Pooh,* as well as five different dictionaries and two copies of Roget's *Thesaurus,* not to mention a collection of Zulu aphorisms someone once gave you as a birthday present. Your books are perfectly ordered on the shelves, even if you were a bit distracted by the phone one day and began to alphabetize them starting with the letter P.

If you are the more "spontaneous" kind of Gemini, your bathtub ring probably looks like you could grow grass on it, you lose whatever was in your hand once you put it down, and you do your laundry only when you can find it. Your idea of home entertaining is your guests bringing their own food and just helping themselves. You like things casual, and therefore wouldn't think of interfering with the cooking, although you do excel in mud pies. Your laissez-faire attitude extends to your cleaning; anyone who wants to is welcome to go ahead without your interference. However, when there are no volunteers, things can get pretty challenging as you consult the *I Ching* to see if you might ever find your chairs again. If even the hexagram looks a little hesitant, there are always enough clothes around to keep a slender derriere cushioned while it's sitting on the floor. A Gemini's home has that invincibly creative touch that people can never forget—even if they try really hard.

COSMIC CHALLENGE

Your cosmic challenge in this lifetime is to overcome the limitations of your own logic. You have a tendency to treat the logical part of your mind as a kind of diety. However, there are places that logic cannot take you. And to be a slave to its laws is to restrict the scope of your total human experience.

You are like Rodin's *The Thinker*, brooding over a matter in your mind so many times that the situation starts to become abstract. At this point, your effort to think things out will no longer bring you any benefit.

The richer you become in terms of human experience, the more you will realize that there will be times when "why" no longer matters. What you have to deal with is what *is*. To probe for its cause will not alter a situation that has already happened. Nor will it alter the nature of your experience or the emotional adjustments through which your mind must ultimately evolve.

When you start to let your logic control you, you start to lose control altogether. Try to maintain a balance between logic and emotional understanding and you will be making the most of your life and gaining the most from it.

INSPIRATION

In Greek mythology, your ruler, Mercury, was associated with Hermes, the messenger of the gods. Hermes, also known as Thoth by the Egyptians, traveled back and forth from the world of darkness to the world of joy and light to carry out his tasks. Thus, after a time, he became known as the great transmitter of both knowledge and wisdom, the kind of wisdom that is gained from an experience of both kinds of worlds.

The Gemini intelligence, put to use on the highest plane, is a force that brings forth good feeling, joy, laughter, knowledge, and understanding. It carries the kind of illumination that opens minds and uplifts hearts.

The key to Gemini power is in the way it is used. As this is a mutable sign of duality, the mind is caught in a conflict between what it wants to build up and what it finds itself tearing down.

Once you can transcend the limits imposed by your own critical faculties, you will use your mind to discern rather than to destroy. A greater detachment from your own desires and a deeper sympathetic awareness of the desires of others will bring you the kind of freedom that allows you to make others happy. And in doing so, you will elevate your emotions to a state of divine balance with your mind.

WHAT HOLDS YOU BACK AND HOW TO OVERCOME IT

At any given time, you have a mind that moves in too many directions. To most people around you, this is maddening. However, you are the one who really suffers for it.

Until you become more grounded and centered, your undisciplined energies will fall into a state of entropy, your scattered attention span will control you, and you will leave behind you a most conspicuous trail of unfinished projects.

Those people who consider you so capricious that they would like to lock you up and set fire to your telephone don't realize that you are operating from a level of paralyzing anxiety and that the only way for you to stay moving is to keep moving. That is why you are so often seen dashing in or dashing out, or peeling the layers of your paper napkin, or cutting up the tablecloth with your fork. You really want to sit still like a calm adult who doesn't have to chain-smoke. But you feel you can't. For this reason, you could be a really dangerous dinner guest if you live in California. There you are, jiggling the table with your foot, and your host starts to think it's the beginning of an earthquake and prepares himself for the end.

For some people a course in meditation would help. However, for Gemini it's more like a crash course in the most basic concentration techniques. Only after that will a course in Transcendental Meditation help to tune your mind down.

It is necessary for you to slow down the frequency of your brain waves to achieve any kind of inner peace. Otherwise, your mind will have a tendency to tread the same circles like a demented track runner who just can't stop—until, of course, his body does it for him. Don't let yourself ever get to that point. In this incarnation your highly intelligent mind is a gift that you earned from a past life. Use it with love, but don't let it become a tyrannical monster. If you do, you will be treading the same painful path on the wheel of karma to relearn lessons that are easy once you allow yourself a few tools to help you along.

There is a basic code in the occult called the Law of Silence. This law means many things, depending on which level of initiation you happen to be operating. For the Gemini, it means learning to silence the mind to all forces, thus achieving a very high level of power that can be utilized in any direction of life. The silencing of the mind is the first step toward the perfection of thought.

The magician mentally presses his right forefinger firmly against his closed lips and says to himself: "To will, to know, to dare, and to keep silent. The only law is that of love."

Try it regularly, but don't be surprised if it changes your life.

LOVE AND COMPATIBILITY GUIDE

Gemini with Gemini

First it's on and then it's off and then it's on and then it's off and then it's *really on* after you break up and you're both seeing other people.

After some time together you will torment each other to a kind of bitter acquiescence. This is what a Gemini knows as love. As the emotional games get more daring and the mental forays leave you both with a fatigue that just enfeebles your senses, the time comes when you consider marriage. At this point there are no new games left. Therefore, even though it's dreadfully boring, you might as well play at commitment, because at least it's something new.

You don't really have to go through with the wedding, because just the planning will make you lose interest. Your attention span is not all that great. Therefore, the relatives should just pretend that they've already bought you wedding presents and put that money aside for Christmas.

You have no idea what you're feeling, because you always confuse it with what you're thinking and have always assumed that emotion is just a thought like "Now it's time to do the laundry." However, in what you *think* to be your emotional scheme of things, you value mental challenge over human consideration. This is exactly what this relationship gives you. You have a unique way of swallowing each other up and then thoughtfully spitting it all back with a grin. Although this activity is a bit draining, not to mention time-consuming to the average person, you just go ahead and have a lot of fun. After all, you're not going to get much else.

Gemini Woman with Aries Man

You admire the way he connects his mind to his body. He respects the clever way you utilize your mind. This is like a first-sight infatuation, and the two of you become very busy taking each other places—everywhere from the tennis courts to the bedroom.

You get his total attention when you give little killer jabs at his ego. He gets your total attention when he doesn't call when he said he would. You tell yourself you couldn't care less, but what's that tension wrenching apart your stomach? He tells himself you're merely foolish when you fail to react to his sideline flirtations. However, does he realize that, due to your lack of attention, he's kicking the dog under the dinner table?

This is one relationship in which the challenge never ceases. On a very deep level you get to each other, but neither wants to be the one to say it. Therefore, it is much more likely that he will communicate his love by smashing you such a hard tennis ball that it breaks your racket. And you will communicate your vulnerability by telling him he should just let his hair grow to hide his face.

If one of you can break through the verbal barrier and even mumble in your sleep, "I love you," chances are you might both end up happily married.

However, that's not to say that you won't test each other the entire way to the church.

Gemini Woman with Taurus Man

You are freedom-loving and flip; he is security-oriented and serious. You love to test and tease, and at any given moment you have a thousand little games up your sleeve. As he can deal only with "down-home" women who lay their cards out face-up, you are enough to give him a psychosomatic case of lockjaw.

You have a convenient habit of forgetting that men are people. Therefore, if he moves too slowly, you'll treat him as if he were a tree. You are compulsively capricious, and an irritant to his sense of stability. He is confining, and a suffocating force to your sense of freedom.

Other than that, he operates through his body, while you are imprisoned in your mind. Your emotions are merely momentary, while his are entrenched in a definite time span. You are glib and superficial, while he is groping and sedentary. He is sensual, while you are cerebral; he tends to be emotionally committed, while you tend to be emotionally detached.

At best, this relationship should be confined to a bank, where he gets paid to tell you what to do. As he's helping you with your bounced checks *and* sees that you haven't balanced your bank statement in years *and* notices your attention drifting to a point in the middle of his throat, the best thing for him to do is just kick you in the shins and be done with it. His world is not your world, nor will it ever be. Therefore, the best thing to do after saying hello is to say good-bye and then turn quite quickly in separate directions.

Gemini Woman with Cancer Man

He is emotional and vulnerable, while outwardly you are cool and controlled. He is often victimized by his feelings, while you are put out of control by your mind.

This is one relationship in which the communication is definitely going in different directions. He is so supersensitive that he considers your friendliness to other people purposely insulting. And when he sulks over his meal and refuses to tell you the time, you come to the conclusion that he would rather be with the waitress.

You both have a way of bringing out each other's insecurities that is more than painful; it's a kind of quiet emotional immolation. You have a way of laughing at the times he wants you to be serious; and he has a way of being glacial at the moment when you most need his warmth.

You can't fathom his feelings, while he feels that you just don't have any to begin with. He makes you bite your tongue when he gives those dark looks and his eyes travel off into the distance. You make him miserable when he reaches out to touch you and you hit him with your acid sense of humor.

When you're together, you need an interpreter who jumps in every five minutes, talks more than either of you, and points. Otherwise, the going can be so rough that you both fumble, stumble, get very bruised, and come out hurting yourselves.

Your only real hope is to stop chatting and start talking. Decide to be brave, put away your emotional masks and supports, and try leaning on each other. Even if you lose the relationship, in the end you could both stand to learn a lot about loving.

Gemini Woman with Leo Man

It's a challenge just trying to get you on the telephone; no doubt you have two. And after he's torn his out of the wall because he can't stand the incessant busy signal, and he charges out and up to your door, what he'll undoubtedly see as he's going in are two angry men who are coming out (and who don't seem at all to be together). Yes, you are a busy soul . . . and friendly. *Too* friendly!

You'll run his ego through the wringer and be very amiable while you're doing it. He'll never know where

you're coming from or where you're going. But that
shouldn't make him feel inferior, since neither do you. To
say you're fickle is a grand understatement. And while he
wants to grab you by the throat to get your total attention, at the same time he's amused because you're also
very funny.

If he has the energy to stay up all night to map out
his games for the next day, he's got you—for a little while.
Actually, you've got him, because he's never worked so
hard for anything.

You love novelty. Therefore, he should create his
own carnival. You loathe commitment, so he should be
debonair and casual. He should call you at the last
minute and make you laugh so hard you disconnect your
other phone. He should knock you dead with clever ideas,
projects, and peculiar little pastimes. Then he should wait
till you've stopped flirting with his best friend before he
commands you to become his life partner. You'll probably
say yes and tell him that you thought he'd never get
around to it. While he might want to retort that it was
because you always have more men around you than someone protected by the Secret Service, he should let it
pass. Instead, he should give you his Leo smile and say
that it took that long to count all your personalities. Then
you'll smile, because you know that he's not prepared for
a lifetime of new ones.

Gemini Woman with Virgo Man

This is like trying to combine cherries jubilee with a
dill pickle.

He thinks you are too crazy to be responsible for
even your own actions. You think he's too cautious even
to cross the street by himself.

He does his laundry at the same time on the same
day of every week, while you get yours done when either
you have a maid or all of your closets are full.

He considers your personal affairs a department of
chaos, while you think he runs his life with a kind of
bureaucratic control.

In your moments of "spontaneity" his mind moves
like a Univac computer when someone has fed it a rotten
banana. He can't comprehend why you no longer open
your mailbox just to avoid your bills, why after you've insisted on pizza, you decide you can't live without chicken

chop suey, and why after making a date with him for the movies, you suddenly change your mind to stay home with your dog.

He tries to deal with your behavior logically, uses his patience, offers his kindly advice, and you laugh in his face. You're enough to give him an incurable case of eczema that seems to get worse the more he takes you seriously. The communication here would be greater if he just stayed home alone and tried to talk to his TV dinner.

Gemini Woman with Libra Man

You adore the fact that he's romantic but not suffocating. He's intrigued with the fact that you're so clever you always seem to call his next move.

He'll bring you violets and drown you in champagne cocktails when you feel crabby. You'll make him laugh like a fool in those murky moments when he no longer loves himself. When he's around you, lots of nitty-gritty nonsense no longer seems to matter. When you're around him, tender little attentions start to get addictive.

You both love people, parties, the idea of the midnight rendezvous, and the kinds of amusements that have that incomparable luster of the first time.

He wants a woman who will be his soulmate. You've never considered such a thing, yet you're always willing to try something new.

Once he wants you, he'll go a-wooing with a book of double crostics, the best of H. L. Mencken, and a collection of the wit and wisdom of Oscar Wilde. And that is one package compelling enough to make you stop talking for at least five minutes.

No matter how sophisticated Mr. Libra is, there's a part of him that's like a shy, unsure little boy. At his best he's irresistible. At your best you're a one-woman show. You can give each other gaiety, laughter, inspiration, and the creative urge to go ahead and conquer the world. It's been waiting too long for such a talented teamwork. Even at dinner, you can be the greatest couple since Fred Astaire and Ginger Rogers. The only difference is that he'll play the violin and you'll supply the lines to make him look like a star.

Gemini Woman with Scorpio Man

You'll play havoc with his emotions, and when he acts moody and macabre just to scare you, you'll giggle in his face and chatter on as if you didn't see him.

There's no way he can control you, because you're a law unto yourself. Let him try to bombard you with his mysterious airs and you'll grin and call him "Operation Overkill." You are flip, funny, and always have the last word. If he attacks you with his savage sarcasm, you'll smile and get him back with an instantaneous retort. You are quick with the comebacks and can hold your own in any situation. And at moments, he may want to dismember you because he's jealous of your blithe detachment.

Neither of you is operating on even related wavelengths. You could give him an auditory hernia from your talking. At the same time, he could give you a suicidal sense of boredom because he seldom says anything. You are mental; he is emotional. You are a spendthrift, while is he a money-maker. You are motivated by casual flirtations; he is committed to intense encounters. You are detached and freedom-loving; he is serious and jealous. He'll dismiss you on the grounds that you're superficial. You'll dismiss him on the grounds that he's predatory.

At first he will find you refreshing, but after your energies have had a chance to blend, what you both need is a psychic purgation. Gemini with Scorpio is like trying to cross an Afghan hound with an irascible Chihuahua. It's better off for him just to buy a bloodhound.

Gemini Woman with Sagittarius Man

He makes everything an adventure that you want to be a part of. He is friendly and funny, at times silly and lacking in sense.

He can talk you into a hike through the Himalayas, where you have to go for days without reading matter, or an African safari, where the lions seem to act as if they've always known you.

With him, you come to expect the unexpected. Unfortunately, a good portion of this is his lack of followthrough. Mr. Sagittarius will heartily promise you the heavens, but when it comes down to it, you're lucky if you get a little moonlight.

You can depend on the fact that he is undependable. And it will probably never change in the course of his lifetime. However, one thing you might try is a kind of shock treatment; inform him that despite appearances, you do have feelings. And although it may set him back a minute to learn that you are more than the mask you project, certainly in the next hour he'll forget it. But it will all be for his own good.

He likes you best as a constant amusement, and when he has to stop and consider your emotions, the lively moments suddenly start to drag.

He considers himself extremely freedom-loving (which is code for the fact that he hates responsibility), so if any woman comes close too fast, he considers taking a trip.

Therefore, hold it all in, live off your laughter, and no doubt you'll have him—as long as he doesn't suddenly decide that he wants somebody else.

Gemini Woman with Capricorn Man

You'll think he's a terrible bore because he would rather work than go dancing. He'll think that you should be locked up when he sees the scattered way you run your life.

You are willful and defiant; he is commanding and bossy. He can dedicate his life to one sense of purpose, while you have no idea what that means, since you change your mind every other minute.

He seeks stability and security, while you would throw your life away for the right kind of excitement. He makes decisions slowly, while you agree to anything off the top of your head. He is possessive and wants to settle down, while you are freedom-loving and like to wander. He is controlling; you are like quicksilver running through a fork.

His personality is sober and often gloomy, while yours is lighthearted and full of laughter. You love a man who makes you laugh, but he can make the corners of your mouth turn down. He never knows if you're serious or if you're just trying to torment him. You never know how he can be happy when he always looks so sad.

You live for the moment; he plans his life past the point of old age. He is brilliant at conserving money, whereas you have a gleeful enthusiasm in spending it.

He will like you a lot, but you'll make him feel uneasy, since he's never met anybody quite as crazy. He may find you so foreign to his inherent sensibilities that he might ask you to marry him because he thinks you're more entertaining than going to the movies. Now, he's not exactly your definition of mind-shattering excitement, but he is warm, supportive, sincere, and willing to put up with all of your insane behavior. Besides loving you, he is the man to help you get your life together and give you a lot more than you could ever think to ask for. So don't be surprised if you find yourself giggling in his nervous face and saying "Maybe."

Gemini Woman with Aquarius Man

You'll stay up all night talking, and he'll unfold to you the secrets of the universe. He is on a perpetual quest of "why," and never ceases searching—even in the middle of making love.

You're intrigued by his genius and by how he seems to make the most simple things complex. He is curious about how you make the most complex things simple, and he thinks your sense of humor is a scream.

He will share with you his inventions, his universal theories, his friends, and his need for freedom. You offer him a superb sense of the ludicrous, and you teach him how to write down his theories so that he doesn't lose them somewhere in his head.

You share his enthusiasm at meeting new people, going to parties, and discussing the personal habits of the hostess for hours. He is smitten with your sensational mind, respects your independence, and thrives on your infinite repertoire of witty lines. In turn, you are intrigued by the fact that his unpredictable nature is almost as intense as yours and are relieved that he doesn't make you feel like you're suffocating.

While the sexual passion here is not likely to make either of you pass out, the ideas that are mutually inspired are enough to steam up the windows. This could either be a match made in heaven or a platonic love with the luminescence of the stars.

Gemini Woman with Pisces Man

This combination is so incongruous that the only qualities you have in common are that you are both human (hopefully) and that you are both alive (even more hopefully).

In a remarkably short period of time you will mutter to yourself that he is just a garbage pail of emotion. At the same time, he will think quite secretly that you are nothing but a chatterbox and an emotional void. What he won't admit is that even if he can't stand you, you're also such a challenge that he fears he loves you. Now, if you try to understand all this, it means that already you're spending too much time with him for your own good. (In that case, he must have a lot of money.)

He is like a damp blanket that makes your nostrils twitch. You are like a relentless buzzing sound zinging through his brain. He is mawkishly sentimental and regards his own melancholy as invincibly romantic. However, even when you're depressed, you're too detached to know you're sad.

He thinks your mind is a fascinating puzzle. You think his burgeoning emotions make him a self-obsessed bore. He feels that your personality is consumed by trivia, while you are convinced that he doesn't know the difference.

After a while, you wish he'd go off and drown himself in his own emotions. However, he daydreams that your glacial heart will still give him a chance. The only chance you're willing to consider is a peaceful parting. Your mind is just too restless to be forced to focus on such a sideshow of sentimentality. And to truly get your attention, he's not above weeping through a megaphone.

Gemini Man with Aries Woman

She is so powerful and controlling that if you want to play her game, it's got to be by her rules.

Her healthy sexuality will be an encouragement for you to keep your mouth shut. Your insane sense of humor will make her laugh at herself for the first time in her life. You are enamored of her energy. She is galvanized by your enthusiasm. You love her courage, while she loves your sharp tongue. She is so fast that she truly intrigues you, while you are so changeable that she never has time to lose interest.

Initially, this attraction is quite exciting. However, if you make a commitment on which you don't carry through, she'll get you, but good.

She has a temper that will shake you out of your jocular senses, and in addition, she probably also has more strength. Playing games with this woman will get you a cold seat on her doorstep, because she just doesn't have the time. There are too many men waiting for her attentions, while the world is waiting for her leadership.

If you behave capriciously, she'll forget your first name as she leaves you somewhere in mid-sentence. The only way to win her back is to appeal to her passion. It's worth it. She's one exciting female you'll never forget.

Gemini Man with Taurus Woman

She embraces stability, while you can't exist without change. She gears her life toward future security, while you can't think past the present. She gravitates toward a quiet kind of evening; you prefer a New Year's celebration.

Needless to say, this combination is not the most compatible. She needs someone steady, but you are maddeningly capricious. You want a woman with a mind like a quiz show, and she wants to be loved for the simplicity of herself.

You'll stand her up, forget her phone number and maybe even her first name. You'll talk her to death, tease her to the point of weeping, and then tear her ego to pieces. With you there is only one thing she can depend on—the fact that you are utterly undependable.

For her a love affair with you is like waiting in line in a rainstorm to board a Ferris wheel—only to find out that it's broken. If she's really smart, before she thinks of buying her ticket she'll first make sure that she checks out all the other rides.

Gemini Man with Cancer Woman

She is a stay-at-home, while you can't be in enough places at once. She is shy, deeply emotional, and very moody; you are detached, mental, and changeable.

You are a gnawing enigma to each other in the best moments and a murderous annoyance in the worst.

She craves emotional security, while you live for your freedom. She needs to be made secure; you need to be challenged.

She'll fatten you up with her cooking, nag you to take

your umbrella, and sulk when you leave her at a party you attend together. You will consider her confining, obsessive, dependent, and a definite threat to your capricious nature.

The things that she takes seriously, you laugh at; the things that you take seriously, she can't comprehend any more than a computer printout. She will think you're insensitive and superficial; you will think she's supersensitive and wastes her time worrying.

At the same time, you can't deny that you're attracted to her warmth; she can't deny that she's spellbound by your sense of humor. She envies the way you take life so lightly; and you find it curious the way she finds so many incidents to react to.

Emotionally, you are about the least compatible. However, for this very reason you could be very good for each other if you are both really willing to try. At the very least, you could realize that you really have feelings underneath that overworked mind. And at the very least, she might realize that she really has a sense of humor under all the layers of her obsessive fears and insecurities. Where you take it from there is entirely up to you.

Gemini Man with Leo Woman

You'll charm your way in and out of her life so fast she'll forget she ever knew you. Should you stick around, you won't woo her with romantic notions or be on time for the wedding. Your charisma comes from the fact that you're so clever. Your hang-up is that emotionally you're a fool.

You are friendly but very fickle. Your attention span is faster than a speeding bullet, and your thoughts like the second column on a digital clock. You're bored unless she beats you at being amusing, which can be a little depressing unless she was trained for the entertainment business. If she's fast enough, she might fascinate you for an hour. But she should be careful that you don't wander away while she still has her mouth open.

Her beauty may attract you but not detain you, since what you are most interested in is a multitude of personalities that flash across your attention span like a kaleidoscope. To keep you around, she has to game-play and switch roles so swiftly that even she can forget who she is if she's not careful. If she is the Academy Award kind of actress, she may have you around for a lifetime. The question is, does she really want you?

You must respect a woman's mind, since you've never realized that she has emotions. From the perspective of her ego needs, you are maddening, madcap, and monstrous to handle. When she loses her temper, you laugh; when she cries, you tell her she's not using her logic. What you casually consider early, even she calls unbearably late. In social situations you flirt enough for both of you, which makes her furious, since she's so busy watching you that she forgets there are other faces. When she flirts to get your attention, you never seem to notice. Or worse, if you do, you may mumble in her ear, "Not bad."

It may certainly seem to her that you have no feelings. The fact is that your feelings change so fast that you've forgotten you've had them. Unless she can also forget that she has hers, she should do herself a favor and instead forget you.

Gemini Man with Virgo Woman

You can't help but like her—she's so kind, warm, caring, and solicitous. But she has to be a committed masochist if she takes you too seriously, since you're about as stable as a strip of crabgrass blowing about in a holocaust.

She has an erroneous reputation of being cold and critical. On the contrary, she is too giving and understanding for her own good. With a critter like you, she will be both walked on and trampled, while you grab her little kindnesses, eat her cooking, and in repayment one night warmly confide to her how you wish you could find the perfect woman. At this point, unless she feels that it's time for some "Sympathy for the Devil," she'll just tell you to get lost and to take your picture of your last girlfriend with you that you somehow left lying on the living-room couch.

One thing she doesn't need is your self-created problems that you take more seriously than any woman. What you *do* need is a lot of razzle-dazzle, mind games, calculated insincerity, and sly up-the-sleeve tricks—laden, of course, with a cruel sense of humor, a lack of vulnerability, and a mentality that cuts you to pieces while it puts you back together again with a very sexy smile. In other words, you seek, not love, but the proverbial perverted challenge.

Until you grow up (and some Geminis never do, but there's always hope), this relationship is better off bypassed. Your false promises and foolish grin won't take her very far, or at least in the right direction.

So, when you are ready to center your energies on something other than your own selfish thoughts, maybe you'll be ready for a real woman. She is one, but to have her you have to be a man, not a mere overworked mentality.

Gemini Man with Libra Woman

Superficially, you seem to have the kind of love at which strangers marvel. However, what happens beneath the surface is something else altogether.

She needs loads of emotional support, and you're like a matchstick to lean on. She is basically so insecure that she marvels at why even her mother loves her, and you are a constant reinforcement to her lack of assurance. She is romantic, sentimental, and waiting for a Cary Grant to carry her away, while you are about as romantic as Joe Namath during a fall workout.

At first she is charmed by your sense of humor. However, when she realizes how much she suffers for it, it has a way of quickly losing its appeal.

You consider her gracious, charming, well-mannered, but on closer inspection so dependent that after a while you feel like you've been drafted. She'll love your quick lines; you'll appreciate her culinary expertise. You'll keep her laughing all the way to the church, but when you don't show up, suddenly everything ceases to be funny.

More than anything else, Ms. Libra is looking for a dependable kind of man who takes her seriously. So, unless you are either very highly evolved or have just had a prefrontal lobotomy, this relationship needs a lot of work before it can be considered a workable one in which much mutual satisfaction is fully enjoyed.

Gemini Man with Scorpio Woman

At its best, this combination is friendship. At its worst, it's a quiet but very painful kind of immolation.

Although you think you're very clever, she sometimes

sees you as simpleminded. You seem to be going in every direction but getting nowhere, while she stays in one place but seems to travel very far.

You get yourself exhausted seeking constant amusement, while she can find entertainment reading in solitude. You are indiscriminately friendly and freedom-loving, whereas she is cautious, unfriendly, jealous, and possessive. You chatter on about banal trivia; she wonders if you're really that superficial or just talking in code.

Your thoughts create a kind of theater, which she finds fun until it gets too obvious. On the other hand, you liken her mind to a French film with a very lengthy script but no subtitles.

Even if you took a course in Scorpio psychology, you could never understand her. And even wearing goggles and a pair of earplugs, she feels that your perceptions are merely gratuitous.

It is true that your sense of the ludicrous always keeps her laughing. However, your constant lateness just doesn't amuse her.

Your behavior is so erratic that it would be easier to depend upon the words of a man mumbling in a coma. At the same time, her sulking when you fail to understand what she's purposely not saying forces you to leave her for a quick date with a girl who giggles.

There is no doubt that she truly intrigues you far beyond any other woman. However, there are too many times when you find her fascinating but too much trouble. Like no other man, you can make her jealous, insecure, and close to suicidal. However, her tight emotional control never lets her get that far. When it starts to get heavy, she will inform you that she is too busy, madly in love (even if she's just spending evenings at home alone), or just wants to be friends. (That's if she's already too hooked to cut off.) Deep in her heart, she hopes to hear a stifled sob as a response from the other end. Instead, she hears a cheery voice that seems to be telling her goodbye. She puts down the phone, stares at the wall, and sadly admits that even in the end you got her.

Gemini Man with Sagittarius Woman

In this combination there is a magical kind of compatibility. You love her laughter, and she loves the way you always make her laugh. You both find everything funny, have a strong need for freedom, and share a basic enthusiasm that could lighten up any room.

You amuse her with your spectacular knowledge of trivia; she entertains you with her tales of voyages to peculiar places. She is the only person you ever met who can be later than you are. You are the only person she has ever met who can beat her at backgammon.

You are both restless, impatient, friendly, and fearful of getting too close too soon. You'll help her balance her checkbook and show her how to save her tax receipts. In turn, she will teach you Transcendental Meditation and how to dive seven feet off a springboard.

You are both adaptable, adventurous, good-natured, and a little crazy. Together you can make every act an affirmation of the best life has to offer. Your life knows no limits, and neither does your imagination.

Gemini Man with Capricorn Woman

This is definitely not a match made in heaven, but it just might bring you to that well-known place called hell.

Neither of you can really understand where the other is coming from, but even if someone told you, it wouldn't be much of a help. She needs assurance in a relationship, and the only assurance you can give her is that you're one person she'll never get it from. You heartily enjoy frolicking from one woman to another, while she is capable of sitting still if there is really something to sit for.

She appreciates the finer things in life, while you can live hand-to-mouth. She is hard-working and persevering, while you persevere at not working hard. She sees her life seriously; you see yours through an insipid sense of humor.

She has a deep sense of loyalty and commitment; you are capricious and undependable. Your witty comments have a way of winning her heart, but your kinetic avoidance of commitment cools her propensity for passion.

She may consider you fun, but certainly not her dream of the future. Once she gets past the persiflage, her deepest desires will direct her straight to a man who is a model of stability and graciousness. Her ideal is the sturdy epitome of accomplishment, while you are the fanatical free spirit whose vision of stability is change.

At best, this can be a friendship; at the very worst, it can be a marriage (but that's only if you marry her for her money). In general, Ms. Capricorn is too sane, stable, and successful for your tastes. You need a woman who, after you torment her with a grin, will still look up to you because you're so witty.

However, after a few of your choice performances, Ms. Capricorn will only give you the cold shoulder and inform you that what is really amusing about you is that one day your capricious antics will make you very sad.

Gemini Man with Aquarius Woman

You'll never meet a woman who's as easy to get along with. And she'll never meet a man who's quite as crazy.

She'll love the way you make her laugh until her sides hurt. However, she won't appreciate the fact that you're always late and sometimes don't show up at all.

Her secret is that although she is good-natured and will go along with a lot of insanity, she still has feelings. And although she won't mention it, being stood up is not her favorite way to spend an evening.

You'll respect her basic attitudes and the way she is committed to her sense of freedom. However, when you see that she's as nice to her mailman as she is to you, for the first time in your life you may sulk and feel a little slighted.

This is one woman who can teach you a lot if you shut your mouth for a while and just watch her. While you are critical, she is accepting. While you limit yourself to loving change, she benefits from both change and stability.

You'll respect the way her mind works and the fact that it operates in so many directions. And it's not unlikely that she'll capture some place in your heart that you never even knew you had. You may stay up all night trying to figure out what's really happening to you and why. However, if you just allow yourself to forget both time and reason, you'll figure out in the end that it's not really why that matters. It's only how you feel that counts.

Gemini Man with Pisces Woman

You are both enigmas; the difference is that she has depth. She is emotional, empathetic, compassionate, and moody. You are cerebral, self-centered, critical, and moody.

Despite the externals, deep down she is shy and unsure of herself. More often than not, she will find you uncaring, and you will find her confining.

She is sensual and winsome but doesn't exactly devastate you with the kind of comments that cut a space in your attention span. She is in touch with her feelings, while you hate to take the time even to think about the fact that you have any.

She remembers her commitments and honors them; you promise your life away but forget what you've said five minutes later.

Deep down inside, she seeks emotional security, while you seek the perfect state of freedom. While you can be callous and abrupt with her, at the same time you can be chummy with the world. Her feelings are badly bruised when you conspicuously ignore her at an intimate dinner party. But her feelings fly away when later you whisper clever love lines in her ear. In between, the peaks of misery make her feel that life's not worth living. It isn't, with you; she needs a man with a lot of warmth to offer. And the warmth that you've got just doesn't seem to go very far.

CANCER

Dates: June 22—July 23
Ruling planet: The moon
Element: Water
Mode: Cardinal
Quality: Feminine
Planetary principle: Love
Primal desire: Security
Color: Violet
Jewel: Emerald
Plant: Hazelnut tree
Day: Monday
Archangel: Gabriel
Magical number: 2
Material factor: Tenacity

CANCERS OF
FAME AND FORTUNE

Ernest Hemingway   Marc Chagall
Duke of Windsor   Henry VIII
Louis Armstrong   Pirandello
Rembrandt   Rubens
John D. Rockefeller   Pearl Buck
Nelson Rockefeller   Hermann Hesse
Marcel Proust   Nathaniel Hawthorne
Helen Keller   Degas
            Andrew Wyeth

THE CANCER FEMALE

Favorable

You're a moon child who wears her moods on her sleeve, along with a lot of longing. You are the original creature of desire and have more cravings than you or anybody else knows what to do with.

Basically, you are the kind of person whom everyone needs to know and experience. You have a way of anticipating someone's needs before they happen, and of offering your unsolicited services before anyone has a chance to ask. You are a perpetual Good Samaritan who never feels that she does enough. Even your beagle considers you his best friend.

Because of your supersensitive emotional response to the masses, you're a lot more vulnerable than the average person. Be careful where you place your empathies, as people may take your generous nature for granted and tread on you when you least expect it. Such an experience calls for an instant retreat to scrutinize your bruised and swollen sensitivities. It's more than difficult for you to detach yourself from offensive behavior aimed in your direction and to chalk it up to someone's acid indigestion or a bad day at the office. Usually you're so concerned about another's welfare you can't help wondering if *you* did anything wrong. Most of the time it's not your fault, no matter what your feelings seem to be saying.

You need a lot of love to keep you happy and are prepared to give back more than your share in return. You're a highly sentimental woman who is happiest when being thought of and catered to. In turn, you love to nurture to such a degree that you have probably never had a plant that died, drooped, or contracted a peculiar disease. However, sometimes, because of a deep-seated sense of insecurity, you feel your attentions are unappreciated. You need one very special person who knows the depths of love as you do.

One must always remember that you mean well, because everything that you do is in someone's best interest. When it comes to your own interest, you crave a constant reassurance that you are loved, needed, wanted, and appreciated, and that your presence is pleasure-producing. When you let yourself relax and enjoy your life, you have a wondrous way of making a lovely time lovelier.

You flourish in a committed relationship. After a short while, you find casual dating unsatisfying and hunger after the security of a husband. You need caring, not casual sex or a night to remember with a ne'er-do-well you'll never see again. You're a sweet old-fashioned woman who longs to have a family, not a half-dozen "friends" to sleep with.

You're usually the one to make an early commitment. After the fifth date, it's not beyond you to start worrying about whether you're going to wear a traditional veil at the wedding. At the same time, it's not always true that your newly found "friend" is making similar preparations. Remember that relationships work best when you bide your time.

In general, you're a romantic who cries at weddings, weeps over memorable moments, and sniffles at sentimental movies. The problems in your own life often assume the proportions of those on stage and screen.

You spend a great deal of time seeking roots in places and people outside yourself. Likewise, you allocate to others far more power than you ever allow yourself. However, the fact is that, despite your fears, you are a strong woman who can endure any storm. When responsible for someone else, you can be a formidable attention-getting force who fights hard for what she wants until she gets it. By fully understanding the force of your own will, you can give to yourself what you so easily give to others. Learn to give less attention to obstacles and more to the direction of your own desires, and in the long run you will have the love you've always wanted and you'll be the kind of person you've always yearned to be.

Unfavorable

You're your own worst enemy; there's no doubt about it. You're at the mercy of your moods, a slave to your sensitivities, and a miserable victim of the full moon. You're so insecure that you live your life from a place of defense, conjecture, and downright suspicion. You overcompensate, weave masochistic fantasies, and suffer in a self-created drama that pits you against the world. Your sympathies are exerted in your own direction because you feel you need them far more than anyone else.

Your emotions batter you about until there is nothing left but one weepy woman who wants to be left alone to choke and drown in her own tears. However, if it happens to be a day when you feel more irritable than melancholy, you might massacre someone else's feelings with one savagely sarcastic comment that comes down like a swift blow to the brain. Instantaneously, you can turn into a cold, critical barracuda. However, while one very innocent victim is left blubbering and berating himself for what he must have done to cause such a cruel comment, what he doesn't realize is that it's a displaced anger releasing itself. More than likely, you're really mad at your mother because she told you last week that your haircut was horrendous.

When really provoked, you can get hysterical and throw the kind of tantrum that tempts a bystander to give you anything that you want just to buy some peace. What often induces such behavior on your part is that you entertain the momentary belief that you can't cope. And what usually makes you feel you can't cope is the feeling that you are an alien in a world indifferent to your needs.

You may think you need someone to love you—but do you? Yes, but often you find the love far more exciting if it's "flown in." Think about Mr. Faithful climbing five flights of stairs every day just to spend the evening. After about seven times, all you can do is look at him and say to yourself, "So what?" Softly you inquire if he wouldn't like to relocate to Southern Australia. You've heard the job possibilities are great there.

You have a penchant for falling in love with the kind of man who can never make up his mind—about you. Usually, everything else is quite clear to him. He knows how he feels about his mother, his great-aunt, his job, his boss, his secretary, his ex-wife, his first girlfriend when he was twelve, and his dog. But you . . . The brow furrows, the ebullient enthusiasm drops off to a few dragged-out monosyllables, the corneas get cloudy, and the phrases become dangerously uncommitted. Suddenly you feel like an anxiety-ridden dinner guest with a dish of inedible food in front of you and no hungry dog sitting under the table. You stand there holding your breath as he bends over to tie his shoes, hoping fervently that when he stands up, he'll say something. He does. Good-bye.

To make up for this kind of scoundrel, who is not above absconding in the night while you go to the bathroom, you bitterly take your hostility out on some other poor innocent fellow trying his best to make a good impression but failing miserably. For instance: he talks too much (because you're making him a nervous wreck). Ultimate decision: He's a self-centered slob.

He asks what you would like to do (only because you seem to have such strong opinions). Ultimate decision: He's so wishy-washy, he's in danger of drowning you.

He has a library from floor to sky and is well informed about every subject from seventeenth-century metaphysical poetry to computer crime. Ultimate decision: Yawn. He's a desiccated intellectual who doesn't dare shut up and just kiss you.

He has a gold medal in Olympic swimming. For avocational activities he teaches tennis, skiing, and skydiving. In bed, he even makes you forget you're there because you want to get married. Ultimate decision: Yech, all brawn and no brains. He looks good, but you can't take him anyplace where people are expected to talk to each other.

He is a Rhodes scholar who smiles a lot. He cooks elegant dinners, has a superb sense of humor, a versatile intellect, a plethora of interests (all of which he excels in), is dangerously good-looking, and keeps *seeming* to be so nice. Ultimate decision: You hate him because you love him, and also because your best friend thought she saw him walking around last week with a beautiful girl. You purposely forget to change the water for the daffodils he sent you, sit back and sadly resolve the end of the affair. You really hate to do it, but you know you have to. At the same time, you comfort yourself that the decision is all for the best. After all, in the long run, how could you ever trust a great man like that to love a girl like you anyway? You'd only become a nervous wreck wondering when he was going to break your heart.

Such romantic matters are not always quite so cut and dried. There is still the relationship in which you are enslaved because you get mixed signals. At this point, the man would rather see less of you than his German shepherd. However, when you are together, he smiles a lot, is terribly amusing, and really makes it seem as if he wants to be there. The next morning, it always seems that he has a tennis match, most evenings he spends "working," on your birthday he always has a date (needless to say, it's not with you), and when he doesn't even call, never mind send a card, you tell your friends that he means well. He does—to himself.

Too often, you become enslaved in situations where the level of human warmth just barely exceeds that of an institution for the criminally insane. When you stubbornly clutch at what's worst for you, without considering what you're really doing to yourself, you create an unfortunate personal injustice that may take years to rectify in your own mind. Try to remember that, in the end, you have to be your own mother, father, husband, sister, brother, and best friend. When you give yourself the security you're seeking from other people, you're stronger and more successful in your demands, and less willing to settle for what you don't want, just to have something. Face your life with the calm assurance that it's all coming to you as quickly as you can learn how to take it.

THE CANCER MALE

Favorable

You're a softie who has sympathy for the underdog, the underprivileged, and the indecently deprived. Not only do you offer aid for a friend in need; you're the type to give a blind street beggar something extra for the sales tax.

You're a warm, sentimental, and vital man who lives through his intuitions and in spite of his emotions. Your mind is shrewd and thoughtful, your understanding thorough and far-reaching, and your intelligence attuned to an in-depth assessment of any situation.

You have a highly creative imagination that could bring you recognition in the arts or a great deal of pleasure in your spare time. Whatever you seriously undertake, you do it with an intensity that overtakes you.

This is especially true in regard to your career goals, which you tenaciously strive toward with a quiet passion. Nothing deters you when you become goal-oriented and driven to get what you want, no matter what the sacrifice.

In romantic matters, you're a sentimentalist who never feels secure enough in a love situation. Instead, you brood and dream and sometimes make yourself miserable with the possibilities of the outcome.

When your heart starts throbbing, your head goes out the window, and you're left bubbling over in bursts of emotion. You treat the woman of your affections as if she were a combination of the Queen of Sheba and Mata Hari. You melt at the sight of her, and as soon as she's out of your sight, dream about the next time you'll see her.

Because you're naturally generous and get a tremendous pleasure out of giving, you probably inundate her with presents. Although you're shy, you're also sensual, affectionate, and sensitive to the romantic touches that make a woman's heart flutter. You love to create those occasions when mood music, candlelight, and fine food and wine take you both to an emotional place not soon to be forgotten.

When you fall in love with a woman, you want her all to yourself and can easily resent the presence of friends, family, pets, plants, and, of course, competition. Even the milkman should keep his distance, and her male colleagues should immediately understand that her life is now different because you're in it.

In marriage, you're a loyal and devoted partner who gets a great deal of pleasure out of providing for the woman that you marry. You probably make the bed, help with the dishes, and cook the kind of meals that no one can compete with. You're the proverbial family man. You know how to make the most of the domestic scene and enjoy giving your children more attention than you probably got from your own mother. You are a concerned parent who takes an active part in his children's activities and gains satisfaction from guiding their lives in constructive directions.

You are happiest when secure in a marriage that fulfills your needs and nurtures your emotions. In turn, you have a magical way of maximizing the happiness of those you love, by openly giving of yourself from the deepest places in your heart. It is highly likely that those people whom you hold close to you value you as the precious and sympathetic being that you are. Your love light shines brightly and boasts of a person whose love power knows no limits. Your entire life is a statement of the personal success you have created through a selfless loving and a transcendence of ego needs.

Unfavorable

You're a man of many moods, and a mystery unto yourself. Your feelings are so subjective that you fear that the mailman has stopped liking you if you find your mailbox empty. Regardless of the matter at hand, your emotions make you suspicious, supersensitive, and very moody.

You crave love, and when you get it, you use it as a kind of mind control. If people love you, then they have to prove it through a constant devotion. In your own quiet way, you are so demanding that you can drown a person in your personal requirements, even when you're being your cool, aloof self. When you're sulking, you have a way of looking at someone as if he had contracted terminal leprosy and didn't know it. You also have a way of closing all doors to inform the accused that you've been offended.

Usually you communicate by the most indirect route. If you feel that someone has committed a minor crime against you, you withdraw, and every once in a while shoot out a few withering glances. Your eyes are like laser beams that with practice could probably turn human flesh into smoke. When the accused can't cope with the rays any longer, and blurts out in a moment of panic, "What in the devil is wrong with you?" he is answered by a carefully enunciated "Nothing." Why do something as obvious as tell him the crime, when he knows in his heart how he's wounded you?

One of the greatest offenses against Cancer is that of omission. To *not* be invited someplace by someone close whom you've trusted is a sin of the worst category. You live in anguish at the idea that your presence has been usurped. And that, even worse, nobody but you has noticed.

Another grave sin is indiscretion. At times, you may be even more secretive than a Scorpio with laryngitis, and cringe at the thought of someone letting your secrets loose to the world. Unfortunately, almost everything in your life is a secret that will violate your sense of self if it "gets out." You probably fib about your favorite foods, lie about your personal preferences, and refuse to discuss your emotional makeup with anyone but a hypnotist who puts you in a trance.

In your love life, you often get snagged on the impossible dream. Basically, you're looking for a kind of Shangri-la where some voluptuous woman with a flower in her hair will tastefully seduce you and then stand back to let you claim ownership. Because you have more than a slight masochistic streak in your personality, you usually lose in love, and sometimes believe you're losing even when you're winning.

You're most naturally attracted to the vivacious but detached woman who needs your sense of schoolboy drama like a load of cement poured in the living room. This analogy is not far off, since your ardent attentions are sometimes quite suffocating. Once you've decided that you've found the woman of your dreams, she really has little to say about the situation. You have bought your ticket to fantasy land, and you're zipping along on the express. Before long, you're planning your future together and see it all in a sentimental mist that successfully clouds the fact that she is frowning in the corner. Somehow, you're not listening to her, because you're so busy telling her how it's going to be. She knows how it's going to be. She has another date in a half-hour.

Once you've made up your mind that you're in love, you can't tolerate the idea that it might not be two-sided. You will hound the object of your affections with such a degree of merciless tenacity that in a more desperate moment she might consider having you murdered. It's just a matter of time, you tell yourself, until she comes around and realizes that your desires are her desires. In the meantime, her protests may dampen your enthusiasm, but they won't deter it. Obviously she's just a woman who doesn't know her mind as well as you do, and the problem is that she resists your showing her.

In matters of love, you can be as possessive as King Kong, but sulk rather than roar. Being a dependent person who panics when left to his own resources, you tend to treat your lover like a Siamese twin who doesn't have a chance of surviving an operation. Undoubtedly, any woman you really get close to has your fingerprints on her waist and a great deal of guilt in her heart. Like no other sign, you have a way of making a woman feel like a child beater if she rejects you. And if she loves you, you give her the freedom of a circus performer who has to do her act seven nights a week, with a few matinees in between.

When it comes to your feelings, you have the flexibility of a bronze statue. You live your life so preoccupied with your own sensitivities that you either forget about other people's or cursorily consider them invalid when they fail to fit into your preconceived scheme of things. Although you can work yourself up into a really weepy state over some suffered infraction, the fact is that you're as much a victim as a four-year-old who controls his parents, his grandparents, and his nursery-school teacher. When you play from total emotional control, there is no such thing as being a loser. There is only the *performance* of the loser who is always greedy for more love.

DECANS

Every sign in the zodiac can be broken down into three subdivisions, called decans. Each decan roughly corresponds to ten degrees—the first third, second third, and last third of the sun sign's time span, which is approximately thirty days.

As each of these periods has different subrulerships, the personality of a person is slightly modified by the specific decan it falls in. For instance, an Aries born in the second decan would be ruled by Mars, but subruled by the sun. Therefore, he would tend to display a greater sense of pride, boastfulness, egotism, and optimism than an Aries born in the third decan, which is subruled by Jupiter. This Aries would tend to be more freedom-loving, flighty, travel-oriented, and interested in subjects of a philosophical nature. An Aries born in the first decan would be the most aggressive, but not necessarily the most productive and accomplished.

Decans are important, since they do account for a more detailed assessment of an individual's personality characteristics. They also show how two people born under the same sun sign can be markedly different.

If you were born between June 22 and July 2, your sun falls in the lunar decan of Cancer.

You are highly emotional, impressionable, sensitive, and often psychic. Your personality is an affable, outgoing one, and your behavior is gregarious, good-natured, and quite often generous.

There is tremendous creativity in your character, which calls for expression. Chances are, on the domestic level you're a do-it-yourself kind of person who can create anything from a couch to a wall hanging to a wonderful four-course meal.

You have gourmet talents in the kitchen that put most people to shame. Even if you have slaved for seven hours over some impossible dish, you serve it with more effortless ease than someone who has ordered from the corner deli.

You are a highly intense person with an urgent need for love that effaces all other desires. At times, you tend to become a victim of your own sentimentalism and have a hard time looking at an emotional issue objectively. You often get carried away by your feelings, to the point that they control you and thereby distort the reality of the situation. Sometimes you feel slighted by a situation that has nothing to do with you, and you nurse grudges that would best be either consciously dealt with or dismissed altogether.

A profound sense of insecurity pervades the deepest reaches of your soul, and sometimes you overcompensate with defensive behavior. Sly remarks, sarcastic comments, and calculated cutting phrases all communicate their point, but in the worst way. Unless you learn to be direct, not only will you suffer from the consequences, but also you will become a victim of what you don't say.

It is important that you learn to objectify your feelings and to spend some time in thoughtful analysis of the other side of a situation. When you do, all issues look less intense from where you are sitting, and somehow seem less confining. To give the other person the benefit of the doubt is, in the end, only to release yourself from negative feelings that are unnecessary.

Once you become accustomed to confronting your own emotions with greater honesty, you will gain invaluable insights, understanding, and a far richer sense of well-being.

If you were born between July 3 and 12, your sun falls in the Pluto decan of Cancer.

You are extremely intense, secretive, often psychic,

and very private. You have a penetrating mind that is deeply compassionate and strongly intuitive. A tendency to be both analytical and emotional sometimes causes you to feel confused about your own feelings.

You have tremendous emotional needs. At the same time, you sometimes feel a great deal of anxiety about fulfilling them. This is because you tend to be attracted to situations and people that do little to enhance your life. In negative situations, you often hang on for too long.

It is highly likely that your mother has had a profound effect on your life and that your ties to her are deep and pervasive. This does not mean, though, that your relationship is entirely smooth. It may, in fact, be a stormy love-hate situation that at times clouds your consciousness. Chances are, you harbor strong subconscious feelings about your mother that are highly complex and diverse. This will affect your relationships with members of both sexes, as residue feelings rise to the surface.

In general, you are a loyal friend, lover, and marriage partner. Once you consciously make a commitment to a person or situation, you view it seriously and do your best to fulfill your part. In turn, you have strong expectations of others. In love relationships, you can be extremely jealous. However, you carefully conceal your feelings and suffer inside. Marital fidelity is crucial to your sense of well-being, for the pain you can suffer from such disillusionment is strong enough to endanger your emotional makeup for years to come, as you cling to those tormented feelings.

If you were born between July 13 and 23, your sun falls in the Neptune decan of Cancer.

You are tolerant, intuitive, optimistic, and strongly sympathetic. Your mind is impressionable, receptive, creative, and often artistic. You are less ambitious than Cancers born in the other decans, and spend more time thinking and dreaming than in engaging in some aggressive activity.

You have a strongly adaptable personality that sometimes tends toward unconventional interests. Spiritualism, the supernatural, the occult, and Eastern philosophies are all areas that you may find appealing. You like to look at the world in new ways, and delight in being overtaken by the unusual.

Emotionally, you are highly romantic and often have an unrealistic attitude to your love relationships. You prefer to think of life as a continual drama whose action never ceases, and your feelings about love are often an outgrowth of this attitude.

At times you tend to get caught in the past and to take a passive approach to the movement of your own life. You often enjoy moments spent in solitary reflecting over portions of your life.

Even at your most affable, you're an extremely secretive person who is often an enigma even to yourself. No one ever knows you completely, as your reserve is impossible to penetrate. Sometimes your moody behavior puzzles people and leads them to believe that you're a little peculiar. You're not. You're merely a mysterious Cancer who has a hard time understanding yourself.

LOVE

Love means everything, and without it you're a miserable person trying to make the best of things. Most likely, your greatest fear is growing old with no one to love you.

Love is a kind of nourishment that revitalizes your soul and gives you the energy to interact with the world with greater zest and vitality. You seek to insulate your deepest emotions in a tight bond of trust and sharing.

You are a highly emotional individual who often allows sentiment to saturate your romantic experiences. Therefore, it is not unlikely that you have suffered some bitter disappointments because of your relentless subjectivity.

As a defense against a tremendous vulnerability, you sometimes appear cool, aloof, and noncaring. Less intuitive individuals are perplexed by your enigmatic behavior and react defensively to it.

However, the fact is that you're not cold at all. You're merely being cautious, perhaps because you've been hurt too many times.

A difficult love life makes you moody, lackluster, and depressed. The intimate give-and-take of love is your deepest desire, and even when you try to sublimate your feelings rather than satisfy them, you often find life much harder to handle. You have tremendous security needs that seek an outlet in an intense love relationship. And until you find your partner, a subliminal kind of pain seems to sift through you.

The devotion of a vital partner probably means more to you than material things. However, to fulfill your desire you'll need to develop more positive attitudes and an objective outlook.

You have a way of looking at all your lovers as prospective marriage partners and mentally assuring yourself that it's just a matter of time. Meanwhile, the object of your intense affections could be telling you in little ways that the only possibility is a freer kind of love that does not and never will include marriage. However, chances are that you'll make yourself believe that this person is suffering from brain fever and will soon recover his or her senses.

The more your overworked mind moves you away from reality to temporarily satisfy your emotions, the more you suffer in the long run. A prerequisite for a successful love relationship is that you have to listen to what is going on around you. And if you don't like what you're hearing, tear your attention away to another person who may ultimately satisfy you more. Remember that the end of a relationship is not the end of the world. Rather, it may be the beginning of something better. Stop clinging to the past, open your mind and your heart, and let the future come to you.

MARRIAGE

Marriage means a lot, since you crave the kind of emotional security that lasts forever. One-night stands are not your idea of emotional satisfaction, even if you had a contingent of lovers lining up for your attentions. You heartily believe in "happily ever after" and would like to make it work for you. However, sometimes you try too hard and have difficulty admitting that a bad relationship is destined for failure. When it finally breaks apart— despite your gesticulations, tears, and entreating comments —you often become bitter and disillusioned, fearful and fretful that you'll never find love again.

Fundamentally, you want someone to come home to

and to wake up with, and this means more to you than a castle in Spain or a diamond from Cartier. You find your greatest excitement in people, and have a sentimental nature that longs for situations that evoke your deepest emotions. You desire an intimate, sensual contact based on trust and profound communication, and are an honest person who hates hide-and-seek games. But you can be so guarded with your feelings in more insecure moments that you appear to be creating distances rather than evoking intimacies.

Your defensiveness often proves an obstacle to what you want most, and people have a hard time getting through. Consequently, you suffer deeply. As you stumble through the anger that seems to imprison you, your aloof behavior can blight the marriage that you want so much to work.

Unless your moon falls in a cardinal sign, you are usually faithful in marriage, and can be quite devoted to your partner. However, you are also jealous, suspicious, and possessive, and can become excruciatingly crabby if your competitive feelings are aroused. Whenever your security is threatened, you compulsively create spaces to protect yourself. The unfortunate fact is that you're so subjective that sometimes your feelings are imaginary, and the spaces you create start to pry the relationship apart.

A childless marriage is seldom a consideration for Cancer, as matrimony is often a mere precursor to parenthood. The presence of children is extremely important to you, and is sometimes the reason why you want to get married in the first place. Whether male or female, your Cancerian nurturing instincts seek a primary satisfaction in the experiences that come through having a family.

Because the conditions of marriage satisfy so many of your urges, it's highly unlikely that you will remain single. However, it's important to give relationships time to develop before making final decisions. A nubile Cancer in an emotional frenzy over the status of being single sometimes takes on a supermarket attitude toward relationships. "Hmmn, I'll take that one, or that one . . ."

Whichever one you finally take, just make sure that it's for the right reasons. If you marry just to escape a situation, you usually end up creating a worse one. This is one area in which you should definitely separate your mind from your emotions and realize that there may be a lot more to marriage than meets your eye. Remember, a love that is blind is usually blighted, so never fail to have periodic checkups on your vision.

MONEY

Money is your security blanket when everything else in your life seems unsettled. You're a formidable saver, even if you make barely enough to pay the rent. Plenty of money is a means to greater independence, since you hate borrowing and indebtedness.

You're shrewd enough to be a financial wizard and are the kind of person most likely to get rich quick. You have a highly organized mind that thrives on economic details, combined with the tenacity to sacrifice a little of the present for those blue-chip investments that will pay off in the future.

Even if you accumulate a million, you still live with the fear that inflation will get you. Some Cancers are downright cheap; others are cautious. However, since all natives born in this sign are pleasure-loving people, you don't hold back about spending it on what makes you happy, although you may haggle with the neighborhood butcher over the price of pork chops.

You love little luxuries, without being self-indulgent. Good food, good wine, a beautiful home, and the pleasure of occasional outside entertainment are experiences that are highly appealing to you.

You spend money readily on fine possessions that will last you a lifetime, but you are never tempted to spend your last penny on petty amusements or a shopping spree that takes you by storm. You know how to put your mind where your money is, and you always come out making more. It's an attribute for which you are both envied and admired, especially by those people who never seem to know where their money goes.

You are far too emotional for money to ever bring you happiness. What it will bring is a good deal of satisfaction from the sense of security it imparts and the creature comforts it provides.

CAREER

You usually attain success because you have the tenacity that will take you anywhere. When you finally decide what you want to do, you devote your entire self to the perfection of the outcome, and feel uncomfortable with a lesser performance.

You're a hardworking, highly organized individual who knows how to make your shrewd sensibilities work best for you. Your trenchant assessment of any business situation often puts you far ahead of both associates and competitors. However, you still suffer the insecurity that maybe you're not as good as you'd like to be.

You're the type to bring the office home with you and to agonize in the middle of the night about a minor detail left undone. When emotionally involved in perfecting your professional performance, you work overtime and even on weekends. Nothing will persuade you to lessen the load once you've made a commitment to it.

Quite often you're the do-it-yourself type who doesn't trust anybody else to do the job as well. You make an exacting, critical boss, so devoted to high efficiency goals that you may overlook some lesser priorities—like the people's feelings who have to work with you.

You have a single-minded approach and let nothing interfere with your goals and schedules. Therefore, you often gain a high degree of professional accomplishment that brings you the respect you so desire.

Your specific career choice strongly depends on the sign in which your moon is placed, but something creative and consuming generally suits you.

The film world fascinates many Cancers, mostly because of its intensity, creativity, and sheer competition. However, to survive in such a bristling business, you first have to harden your feelings and desensitize your emotions.

You make an excellent executive because you are highly organized and extremely hardworking. Also, work with the public in politics or economics could be quite appealing.

Because you're as shrewd with other people's money

as your own, you could become a financial tycoon, a film producer, an art dealer, or a real-estate broker.

If you are the kind of Cancer who needs to nurture, teaching, nursing, or social work is more suitable to your personality.

Whatever profession you ultimately commit yourself to, you do it with a deep sense of responsibility and an all-or-nothing attitude. Serious involvement in your professional goals gives your life an additional meaning. As you mature in your profession, you take pride in the expertise that your tenacity, intelligence, and awareness have made available to you. Your mind is that of the specialist who is respected not only for knowledge but also for high performance standards. And because of this, a great degree of career security is yours. It is something you have won for yourself through the most devoted attitude toward your work. Because of your high degree of competence, your job is something that no highly energetic usurper could ever walk away with.

FRIENDS

Your friends are an important part of your life, and you live in service to them. You have no idea how to say no when asked for aid, regardless of the difficult situation it may place you in.

Your concern for the welfare of those close to you can put you in all sorts of uncomfortable positions, from playing psychiatrist to a weepy friend at four A.M., to lending your home to a stray German shepherd that somebody else has taken in—before taking a little trip.

In turn, you expect your friends to be there for you when those murky mood swings make life too hard to handle alone. You feel rejected if the company you desire isn't immediately forthcoming. In addition, you often have a hard time asking for what you want, and expect that the important people in your life should know your desires intuitively.

It is important to realize that you are not a victim in your friendships. Rather, you have placed yourself in these situations and have to take the responsibility for what happens. Chances are, you are more appreciated by other people than you would ever guess. However, the greater the amount of time you spend worrying about it, the more you will feel forsaken.

Your general attitude toward your friends is a highly emotional one that implies a deep sense of loyalty and trust. Close, intimate friendships give your life a profound meaning that makes the difference between a life that is enjoyed and one that is filled with longing. Living for yourself alone is never enough, since you find fulfillment in the give-and-take of shared experiences that are close and often consuming.

You are the proverbial "friend in need" who never thinks a no is appropriate. Nor is less than enthusiastic assistance an allowable response in your own behavior. Because of the degree of your kindness, sensitivity, and caring, you probably have more "best" friends than anybody else. Each individual undoubtedly feels a warm appreciation of you as a person and a thankfulness that you are a friend.

HEALTH

Your emotions are your stumbling block, and this can menace your health. Repressed anger, grudges, and painful remembrances can ultimately be reflected in a serious mental and emotional syndrome.

Emotional obsession, depression, severe anxiety, and a variety of gastrointestinal disorders can be deleterious to your well-being and bring you to a state of mere functioning.

Compulsive eating and escape-oriented drinking can also wreak havoc with your health and make you even more gloomy.

You love food, the richer the better, but sometimes your stomach is too sensitive to stand a heavy onslaught. Temperate eating is wisest, supplemented by regular exercise. This will make you want to eat less and will help disperse some of those morose emotions that weigh you down.

Stick to a low-starch diet that is high in protein and vegetables. When you feel the need to overindulge because you have a bad case of the drearies, stick to fresh fruit and you'll be doing your system a favor.

Take a class in yoga to help cool you out, and practice each posture diligently. You're one sign that could especially benefit from yogic breathing exercises, since they provide relief from the kind of stress that ties you in knots. Cancer women tend to suffer a period of premenstrual tension, and such a regime could provide a miraculous panacea.

HOME

Because your home is your haven, you like it to be as cozy and as colorful as possible.

For the living room, choose a plush L-shaped couch to curl up on when those murky moods overtake you. A majestic fireplace is also a must for those rainy nights when the wind makes your windows shudder and you're so thankful to be hanging out at home.

You're a special enthusiast of old-world charm, and have an eye for antiques and priceless *objets d'art*. Your living area is an eclectic ensemble of the very best of both worlds—the old and the new. Chances are, you prefer shutters to blinds, and a damask tablecloth to a linen one. A patrician pair of brass candlesticks adorns your coffee table; while the white cloisonné lamps lend the room a dignified luster.

A glass-top dining table supported by a chrome base is a more modern representative of your elegant furnishings. Cane chairs complement it in a very cheery way. Not only your dining area but also your kitchen possesses that Cancerian charm known only to enterprising souls who have mastered the more fanciful food dishes.

Your kitchen counter is adorned with everything from a juicer to an electric crepe maker to a ten-speed blender to a yogurt maker. And on the wall, let's not overlook cutting boards that come in every shape and size. You're still debating buying a microwave oven while you're waiting for a dishwasher to be invented that dries the dishes as it puts away the pots. You're a formidable cook who is the kind to create recipes rather than follow them. You love to entertain those close to you and those you wish would get a little closer.

However, in terms of that latter category, the bedroom is a far more crucial place for cavorting. Turn it into a love nest with potted palms, a fake fireplace, and,

of course, a four-poster! Drape tie-back curtains around
the bed for a touch of drama. An electric blanket may
not be necessary, but why not try some satin sheets, if only
for reading in bed. That supersensual part of you should
be prepared to make the most of *every* moment. Hang
ferns here and there to create a forest effect that is as
enticing as a midsummer night's dream. And in a white wicker étagère, do include a stereo speaker to sift forth sentimental love sounds through the long and wondrous night.
Whenever possible,. let your bedroom boast bouquets of
fresh flowers. And as you wake up to greet them, vow to
yourself that you will treat every day in the string of tomorrows as a celebration of the joyous life and love you
have always wanted and know you will someday have.

COSMIC CHALLENGE

Your cosmic challenge is to acquire a more universal
perspective on your life, and in doing so, to become more
emphatic. Your most highly evolved attributes are sympathy, patience, tolerance, and intuition. These develop
when you go beyond your own feelings, desires, and demands, to enter the experience of another, thus gaining
greater human understanding.

Too often you react to the world around you through
the narrow prism of your own feelings, and in doing so,
seem to filter out the feelings of others. Until you can forget yourself temporarily and try to understand another
person, your life will be severely restricted by your own
emotions.

As you develop a deeper compassion, you will shed
some of your supersensitivity and begin to live your life
without the painful restrictions your emotions impose.
More than anything else, in this lifetime you need to acquire freedom from yourself and to realize that in the
end it is really you who creates those unsatisfying situations you most want to avoid.

INSPIRATION

At your purest, you are master of your own emotions, and the law you observe is the highest universal
law, which unites you with higher beings. You are a per-

son of compassion and humanistic love and are committed to caring for your fellow beings.

You love all, yet you are nonattached in your loving. You are generous in your services, yet you ask nothing in return. Your emotion is expansive and impersonal. It transcends sentimentalism, and thus, the restrictions of the ego, to encompass a collectivity of souls.

Your love is the vehicle of the most pervasive unification, just as your will is for the betterment of human life. You have transcended the personal and the immediate to unveil a far more joyous experience. And each day, the light of the higher forces radiates through your mind, and what you know to be your life unfolds into an experience that is limitless.

WHAT HOLDS YOU BACK AND HOW TO OVERCOME IT

Your supersensitive feelings often get in the way of your personal progress and development. You have been known to take offense at comments, situations, and circumstances that were not even meant for your benefit. However, regardless of that fact, you harbor hard feelings that sometimes seek an outlet through sarcastic retorts. Often you can't peep outside of yourself to objectively see and hear the other side of the situation. And you have a difficult time viewing an intense personal interaction dispassionately.

The more you behave as a slighted human being, the more you put other people on the defense. Try to remember that they have feelings too and consequently can become very hurt and perplexed by your hostile remarks. It is best to practice bringing your feelings out in the open and confronting the accused in a warm, inquiring way that may, in the long run, bring you closer. The more you keep your emotions bottled up inside, the angrier they eventually become and the more they are likely to bring on some sort of psychosomatic problem.

As a general rule, you have a very difficult time being direct in your relationships. An excruciating schism exists between that which you feel and that which you are able to say. However, when this personality characteristic becomes so pronounced that both you and the people in your life are suffering for it, then it is time for change.

Both individual psychotherapy and group therapy could prove an invaluable investment toward greater self-expression and more satisfaction on the social scene. In addition, other areas of mind expansion could also prove highly rewarding experiences leading to greater emotional growth.

When your mind makes a cocoon of your emotions, your life becomes imprisoned by your feelings rather than expanded by them. Loosen up, take yourself a little less seriously, and resolve to analyze a situation rather than just react to it. What you ultimately gain through emotional growth never leaves you. And the people who love you only appreciate your presence all the more.

LOVE AND COMPATIBILITY GUIDE

Cancer with Cancer

You are a cozy couple who probably never leave the house when you don't absolutely have to. Both of you are domestics who would just as soon cook in than be taken out to the most elegant restaurant in town.

You share the same dreamy-eyed sentimentalism, shower each other with tender love tidings, and emotionally empathize in those moody moments that seem like they're never going to subside.

This is a relationship of deep understanding, a high degree of compatibility, and a plethora of physical passion. Because of the intense rapport and the feelings of selfless caring, it could easily last a lifetime.

Quiet nights with quiet talk could bring you both the kind of excitement that perhaps no one else understands, but for you represents the deepest loving and the greatest happiness.

Cancer Woman with Aries Man

You'll fall in love with his dynamic enthusiasm, but may get hurt by his lack of emotional understanding. You need more nurturing than he knows how to give, and have more insecurities than he knows how to handle.

He'll blunder his way through your life, and you'll hold back the tears when you see him leaving (even for five minutes). He can't understand why you are so emotional, and sometimes he feels closed in and closed off.

On the other hand, you are that woman he can count on and the person who will hold his hand and listen to his problems. You will support him with a sincerity that he may find irresistible. You will love him with a loyalty that inspires his respect, and you will give him the kind of understanding that he can easily find addictive.

Your cooking will send him into another realm of sensual experience, and your sexual appetites can easily keep up with his.

You are one woman who will stick by him, for better or for worse. However, whether he will stick by you is quite another story. Because he needs to roam and run about, sedentary situations make him restless. You can provide a kind of inner excitement, but until Mr. Aries is ready for it, he is better off remaining uncommitted.

Cancer Woman with Taurus Man

You are two stay-at-home creatures and can have a lovely evening just preparing a pot of stew. At times you will remind him of Mother on Thanksgiving morning. He will remind you of Daddy on days that he paid the rent.

In each other you find your security fantasies satisfied, and for both of you that is a lot. You will find him to be someone solid to lean on, while he will find you a cushion of kindness.

Together you would rather build bookcases than go to the movies, and fantasize more about a family than about future success. You are both supersensualists with larger-than-life appetites. Therefore, your bedtime compatibility could bring you to exciting places.

You want to be possessed forever and always. He wants someone to treat him like his savings account. Deep down inside, he dreams of a "little woman." And even if you are president of a multimillion-dollar corporation, you would be willing to take on that traditional role.

Although you can get caught in a vortex of emotion, he is so stable that you'll stop having moods. He appeals to the practical side of your nature; you appeal to his sensitivities.

You were made for each other and could spend a lifetime loving. All that you have to do is meet.

Cancer Woman with Gemini Man

You are a stay-at-home, but he can't be in enough places at once. You are shy, deeply emotional, and very moody; he is detached, mental, and very changeable.

You are a gnawing enigma to each other in the best moments and a murderous annoyance in the worst.

You crave emotional security, whereas he lives for his freedom. You need to be made secure, while he needs to be challenged.

You'll fatten him up with your cooking, nag him to take his umbrella, and sulk when he leaves you at a party you attend together. He will consider you confining, obsessive, dependent, and a definite threat to his capricious nature.

The things that you take seriously, he laughs at; the things that he takes seriously, you find as incomprehensible as a computer printout. You will think he's insensitive and superficial; he will think you're a supersensitive worrier.

He can't deny that he's attracted to your warmth; you can't deny that you're spellbound by his sense of humor. You envy the way he takes life so lightly; he finds it curious the way you find so many incidents to react to.

Emotionally, you are about the least compatible. However, for this very reason you could be very good for each other if you are both willing to try. At the very least, he could realize that he really has feelings underneath his overworked mind, and you might realize that you really have a sense of humor under all the obsessive fears and insecurities. Where you take it from there is entirely up to you.

Cancer Woman with Leo Man

It might seem that you want his plasma on a silver platter. You do. When it comes to affairs of the heart, you are the superconsumer. You crave Mr. Leo's total love, attention, affection, fantasies, thoughts, dreams. In other words, you want it *all*.

When you don't get your way, you are weepy. At first, this is effective. But after a few of the same performances, your repertoire reeks of repetition, and this man begins to cool off.

Your dependence will flatter him, but your demands will make him feel claustrophobic. On your first coffee date, you'll inquire where you stand in his future. If he is sufficiently vague to get to the second date, you'll ask him if he prefers the wedding in June or December.

You're a woman who revels in romanticism. One of your frequent sexual fantasies is hearing the words "I love you." However, your very favorite is "Marry me!" If he does, he'll find he has a very loyal and devoted wife. If he brings you daisies and kisses you a lot, he'll find a woman who will create a kingdom around him.

His blind spot is your emotions. He'll never understand why you're brooding and sulking. Just because he forgot your anniversary and then flirted with a gorgeous blond . . . He can't grasp the emotional connection, and besides, he just bought you a new refrigerator last week. What more do you want? You should just take another look at the freezer. Ice cubes in three seconds!

At moments, you'll be his mother; at other times, his little girl. It's very hard for you just to be his lover, because you never feel that much at ease with your emotions. You are so insecure that you often role-play to cut off being so vulnerable. Your deep-seated emotions have Mr. Leo mystified. Your words occasionally lose him. But your fears escape him altogether.

When you're secure, you're warm, lovable, sympathetic, and supportive. When you're insecure, you're cold and withdrawn, but in a way that's always verging on the weepy. You'll be his mother if he treats you like a child. His challenge is treating you like a woman, and letting you believe it. But that takes a very selfless kind of loving. No comment on whether Mr. Leo can do it.

Cancer Woman with Virgo Man

Although your moods often confuse him, your intense emotions provide the encouragement that gives him tremendous comfort. He is as insecure as you are, though he covers it up with his will and his acute sense of logic.

You will evoke his more vulnerable emotions, and he will help you to filter life through your head as well as your heart. However, at times he won't be as cuddly as your affectionate nature would like. He spends most of his time working, and when he's not working, he's worrying about whether he could have done a better job.

He doesn't understand your need for constant attention, and you don't understand the excruciating disciplines he puts his mind through.

He is an exceedingly mental individual, whereas you are exceedingly emotional. But if both of you can respect the other's perspectives, and can learn to work through them rather than around them, this could be a relationship of lasting value that results in a sound marriage.

Cancer Woman with Libra Man

Not only will you give him all the attentions of Mother, you'll throw in a few more. However, after you have poured yourself out to him endlessly, and all he has said to you is that he can't decide what he wants in a woman, it should be a running good-bye. Unfortunately, you'll just hang around for a few more of these tender emotional scenes.

Mr. Libra considers himself to be a person with feelings. He is, but they're all for himself. When he kisses you, he wants to hear *Rhapsody in Blue*, but instead, all he hears is your whistling teakettle. Just remind him that the tea is for him.

You need to be smothered in love, while he needs to sit back and think about it. Therefore, at times, when you barricade the door with your body, he feels a bit too confined. You'll send him little cards to remind him you're still living (as if he could forget, because you call him every day). Finally, the agonizing time will come when he must confront you with the truth: he has to hear bells ring. At this point, you'll get up and lean on your doorbell. Slowly he shakes his head. You offer to carry cymbals.

It takes a lot for you to realize that it's really over. But it takes even more for Mr. Libra to realize that it's even begun. The emotional timing here is so bad that it would probably take more than a lifetime for you to get together. First it might be helpful if you both die and get reborn into another sign.

Cancer Woman with Scorpio Man

You'll nurture all his needs, make him fat and happy on your cooking, and try to be understanding when he's being surly. You are kind, giving, compassionate, sympathetic, and more caring than a Red Cross nurse. You'll listen to his problems, pay him more attention than he desires or deserves, and make him feel like he's "the greatest show on earth."

All that you ask in return is love. You want to be smothered in it. You want to be drowned. You need to be possessed, cherished, and suffocated in order to feel secure. You want to hold him, consume him, devour him, and digest him. And what will remain, remains to be seen.

Mr. Scorpio appreciates your love and affection. However, something deep within him makes it difficult for him to totally accept it. He needs to keep his own space—not necessarily because he wants it, but perhaps because he has a fear that if any woman gets too close and he starts to need her, she just might be taken away.

He has a hard time trusting, and you have a hard time holding back. His moods may make you feel unloved, while your needs may make him feel he's in a prison.

On the other hand, he could find you very nice to come home to, as you are loyal, sensual, supportive, and a positive witch at conjuring creature comforts.

You'll fall in love practically at first sight, though you'll be too shy to say so. However, he'll be able to read it in your smile.

This could be a great match, should he be ready to settle for some connubial bliss. Should Mr. Scorpio have only a good fling in mind, after you tell him your sun sign he should just keep on walking.

Cancer Woman with Sagittarius Man

He'll see you as a drag to his defiant independence, and you'll see him as a threat to your tentative sense of security. You'll be hurt and hostile when he doesn't even finish his dessert because he has a twilight tennis game. And his patience will be provoked when you would rather sit by the fire than go skiing.

You want a one-woman man, but he's a restless roué who wants to sample as many pretty faces as time will permit. You need a lot of security, while he needs a lot of space. You want a man who is somewhat settled; while he has a vagabond nature that often turns him into a ne'er-do-well.

You seek a quiet kind of romance with someone who will provide an array of creature comforts. He seeks a short-lived affair that is more like an animal chase. His charm will probably rip right into your soul like a grenade going off in a sleeping village. And because you often want what you can't have, you will undoubtedly obsess, agonize, and drive yourself into a depression over the fact that he doesn't seem to want to settle down to a cozy existence.

Any way you look at it, the two of you are about as compatible as pickles and ice cream. Unless you both feel you want to become fast friends, forget it!

Cancer Woman with Capricorn Man

He is the security that you've always longed for, while you are the woman who can give him the warmth he so needs. Between you there is an undeniable attraction and a very basic understanding.

You need a strong man you can care for, and he needs a woman who knows how to care. Your vulnerable femininity will melt his cool veneer, and his competence and ambition will win your highest respect.

You are a woman who can be so nice to come home to. You will nurture his needs and never allow him to feel neglected. In return, he will be your bastion of material security and buy you the kind of creature comforts that make life worth living.

Together you can live a cozy existence, showering lots of love on each other and sharing many intense moments. Within the depths of your feelings he will be able to see the same insecurities that bring on his own melancholy moments. The more you allow your sensitivity to expand into the depths of each other, the more emotionally rich your life will ultimately be. And once you've had it, you can never deny that that is the greatest kind of wealth.

Cancer Woman with Aquarius Man

You live by your emotions, whereas he relies on his mind. This creates the kind of friction that may be more than either of you can handle.

You may think you have to knock him out with a swift karate chop and then hypnotize him with the right words just to get a little romance going. Otherwise, work up the courage to tell him you love him, and he'll respond that that's really quite fascinating. Then he'll ask you why.

Make him an ice-cream pie, and he'll take it apart, stare at it for a while, ask you what's in it, and then forget to eat it because he's too busy talking. Needless to say, Mr. Aquarius gets more pleasure in finding out how the whole thing works than he does in the actual experience.

The same goes for your relationship. He may spend agonizing hours analyzing your feelings and his thoughts, until finally you conclude that he's falling in love. Impatiently you propose, and cheerfully he informs you that all relationships are merely an illusion. At that point, you have another piece of ice-cream pie and savagely attack the crust. He smiles at you, sips his coffee, passes you the cream, and tells you that you're much too sentimental.

Although Mr. Aquarius is the good-hearted sort, he sometimes gets so entangled in his theories that he reminds you of a mad scientist who sleeps with test tubes under his pillow. If you want a man to hug you, make passionate love, and remind you how much you mean to him, start looking quickly in another direction. To show his affection, Mr. Aquarius is more likely to slap you on the back and hand you a slide rule to illustrate some recondite point to which you've only just pretended to listen. Although he means well, he is just not your type, and trying to adapt to his emotional level is like skinny-dipping in the middle of February.

Cancer Woman with Pisces Man

He will find you so nice to cuddle with. You will create a plethora of seductive creature comforts and provide the emotional backup that he needs to do his best. Not only are you warm and sensitive, you have the kind of womanly strength that reminds him of Mother. You will understand his moods, listen to his problems, and lend him a lot of loving assistance for those projects he knows he'll never finish.

In turn, he will write your love poems, send you daffodils in January, and bring you champagne to sip by the sea. With rapturous enthusiasm he'll make you feel like you're a combination of Wonder Woman and Aphrodite. He'll lavish praise on your femininity and provide you with the encouragement you so crave.

Sexually, you'll both send up smoke signals, drums will start to beat, bells will start to ring, and you may find out that you are deeply in love.

In essence, this combination could be a divine exploration into the deepest experience of loving. The communication here may carry you out to the farthest planes of feeling.

Cancer Man with Aries Woman

You are a truly lovable person, but your love is not meant for her.

Her fiery outbursts will send you into a sullen withdrawal. And your sullen withdrawals will send her through more fiery outbursts. The two of you are so different that you seem to be coming from two foreign countries that have never even known the other existed.

Emotionally, you are supersensitive, though you hate to show it. And she has a way of hurting your feelings even by the way she asks you a polite question.

Your feeble attempts to camouflage your vulnerability make her chew her cuticles. Your moods make her more than impatient. And your apparent passivity makes her stamp her feet just to break the silence.

You would like to spend a quiet evening at home cooking; she would like to party until dawn. She likes to think she's conquering the world, while you like to comfortably occupy a very secure part of it. You work hard for your future comforts; she works hard just to work. You are interested in having a family, but the closest she wants to come to children is the experience of knowing you. She craves continual excitement, whereas you seek security at all costs.

Just to be dramatic, she might tell you that she's leaving you; calmly you will remind her to take her Dristan and her credit cards. Then you will go into the shower (probably to cry). At least, she'd like to think you're crying. But at that point it's really too late to find out, because even if she's crazy enough to turn back and run toward the bathtub, you undoubtedly have the door locked.

If Ms. Aries wants a lot of drama, she'd better go to a movie. Or pick someone else to increase her blood pressure.

Cancer Man with Taurus Woman

Much passion will pass between you. But whether the relationship remains depends on where you are both willing to take it.

You are loyal and loving, but the meaning of your moods will totally elude her. At one moment you are insecure and dependent; at another, you are totally withdrawn. Your feelings have a way of tying you both up in knots. Together, you will satiate each other's security needs. However, she is the more practical, you the more passionate. She is the earthy foundation; you are the ivory tower made of molten wax.

She tends to dwell on the fundamentals, while you linger on the romantic overtones. You are carried away by softness and subtlety; she is more entranced by some support.

You are both so jealous that you make each other feel sought after when you trade suspicions. And you are both so domestic that together you can spend a weekend cooking up a storm.

In most respects, this relationship is highly compatible. When you combine her earth with your water, the result is fertility and sustained emotion. Once you pass through the emotional communication gap, where the silence is sometimes deafening, you will both realize that there is enough feeling here to last a lifetime.

Cancer Man with Gemini Woman

You are emotional and vulnerable, while outwardly she is cool and controlled. You are often victimized by your feelings; she is put out of control by her mind.

This is one relationship whose communication is definitely going in different directions. You are so supersensitive that you consider her friendliness to other people purposely insulting. And when you sulk over your filet mignon and refuse to tell her the time, she comes to the conclusion that you would rather be with the waitress.

You both have a way of bringing out the other's insecurities that is more than painful; it's a kind of quiet emotional immolation. She has a way of laughing at the times you want her to be serious, and you have a way of being glacial when she most needs your warmth.

She can't fathom your feelings; you feel that she doesn't have any to begin with. You make her bite her tongue when you give her those dark looks and your eyes travel off into the distance. She makes you miserable when you reach to touch her and she hits you with her insipid sense of humor.

When you're together, you need an interpreter who jumps in every five minutes, talks more than either of you, and points. Otherwise, the going can be so rough that you both fumble, stumble, get very bruised, and could come out hurting each other.

Your only real hope is to stop chatting and start talking. Decide to be brave, put away your emotional masks and supports, and try leaning on each other. Even if you lose the relationship, in the end you could both stand to learn a lot about loving.

Cancer Man with Leo Woman

Though you love romantic games, you are soon defiled by the reality of your emotions. You have called her twelve times a day for countless days, and she's always busy. On the first call, you are casually interested; by the sixth, you are morosely impassioned; by the ninth, you feverishly abandon all control; soon you can no longer think and mutter to yourself about suicide from overeating.

For even her Leo sensibilities, your histrionics are indecently excessive. At your most dramatic, you are dark and brooding. When your affections are unappeased, you melt into melancholy and defiant doldrums. You try to get her attention by not speaking or calling, and with relief Ms. Leo surmises that you've finally found some self-respect. With discipline, you prolong your dolorous confinement, since you want to make her suffer even more from the silence. When you find that you can no longer stand it, your clammy fingers feel their way to the phone. Assuming your cold, aloof, before-the-mirror look, you invite her to Acapulco for the weekend. She tells you that she has to wash her hair. Gulping with great dignity, you invite her to a play, midnight dancing, Sunday brunch, and a late-afternoon double feature, seven weekends from next Saturday. Graciously she claims that she's cleaning her closets. You ask if she's busy on the Saturday after Christmas. (At the moment, it happens to be July.) Yes, she replies, as a matter of fact, she's getting married.

Even if Ms. Leo's love life has been nonexistent, she won't cajole herself into considering you. She finds your moods a constant irritant and will vengefully frolic with your feelings. In turn, you find her cold, abrupt, bossy and intimidating.

Life *must* offer more than this, you crossly mumble. So would a sojourn in solitary confinement.

Cancer Man with Virgo Woman

You'll make her feel like a nineteenth-century femme fatale in a picture hat. You'll heartily respond to her shyness, her little insecurities, her warmth, and the way her face flushes when you compliment her on her mental powers.

She'll love the way you court her, she'll treasure your concern when she has a slight cold, and she'll be thankful for the way your affection makes her feel finally appreciated.

She'll plan consuming activities to divert your mood swings, throw surprise parties on your birthday, and remind you in a very matter-of-fact way how much everybody loves you.

For one of the first times in her life, she feels secure in her feelings, while you feel that this is the fantasy you've always hoped for. Together, you can take each other to many wondrous emotional places and enjoy the kind of emotional happiness you've never had before.

Cancer Man with Libra Woman

You'll give her all the attention she so craves, and delight in creating those cozy stay-at-home evenings she loves. For dinner parties, you'll help her cook and will probably originate a few gustatorial delights of your own.

However, you *will* question why she had to spend a thousand dollars on stemware and two hundred dollars for new boots when last year's still look perfectly new.

There will be moments when your moodiness will make her morose. But not enough to take away from the joy you can experience in being together.

You will tell her how attractive she is at least five times a week, lose a little sleep when she gets the sniffles, and help her rearrange the furniture on rainy Sundays. After a hard day, she won't have to ask you to hold her, and during one of her "down" days she can expect you to sympathize with her dreary emotions.

You are sensitive, kind, caring, and deeply feeling. Even if you have cut off from your emotions in an attempt to obviate vulnerability, Ms. Libra can help restore your emotional balance. Basically, you want a woman you can be secure with, and she wants the same, plus the pleasures of shared experience. Together, you could create a romance of which only dreams are made. And with all of your charm, it's an easy task to transform a dream into the most romantic kind of reality.

Cancer Man with Scorpio Woman

For her, you're a package deal—a man with the qualities of Mother. You'll understand her moods, kiss her on the temples, bake her an apple pie, and serve her tea with lemon.

This combination is highly compatible, especially if she was born in the last decan of Scorpio. As long as she respects your feelings, you are kind, caring, and love to be controlled by Ms. Scorpio's feminine power.

You'll feel flattered by her jealousy and return the feeling fourfold, which will make her feel all the more secure. She is your constant source of inspiration, and you are her constant bastion of support. Together, life can be a team effort offering many satisfactions and memorable experiences.

You are supersensitive and nurse your bruises. However, she's so adroit at handling fragile feelings that you never have the opportunity of rolling over and playing vulnerable. Since both of you communicate largely through what you *don't* say, conversation is never a problem. On full moons, you may resort to sign language, interspersed with periods of self-imposed solitude. However, as long as you both don't live together in one room, the situation is salvageable.

At times, your sexual passivity may provoke her. However, since she obtains a sense of power from being sexually controlling, this is not a major problem. And with you, Mr. Cancer, the most efficient way to control is just to command.

Once she makes you feel secure, you are loyal, loving, proud, and possessive. You'll romanticize her personality and give her total power. You'll let her take you wherever she wants to go, and make it known that she is the trip that you want to be taking.

You'll put her on a pedestal and seduce her with this new self-image. Any way you look at it, Ms. Scorpio has a lot of needs and you have a lot to offer most of them. She'll probably find you easy to love, and almost as easy to spend a lifetime with.

Cancer Man with Sagittarius Woman

You need her beside you, but she needs the space to be by herself. She'll undoubtedly inflict a mortal wound when she asks you why you're so dependent. But she'll bring you to the verge of suicide when you hand her a love poem and she laughs and shrieks, "You've got to be kidding!"

She'll never understand your sensitivities, and you'll never understand her need for freedom. You'll become so infatuated with her vitality and sense of humor that you'll want to follow her to the supermarket and spend time with her while she stands in line. You'll get emotional over the way she butters her English muffin, and when she's not looking, you'll fondle her tennis racket.

However, the more you candidly express your feelings, the more she mutters "Yech!" and asks you to shut up and pass the mustard. She's a swell person, but you need her like a hole in the head. She's a menace to your tenuous ego and a deflated balloon to your romantic reveries.

Much of the time you spend with her you'll spend

sulking in conspicuous silence, feverishly hoping that she's eating her heart out. However, when she cheerfully slaps you on the back and asks you if you have indigestion, all hope is lost and you suddenly decide you want to go home, even if you *are* home already.

She doesn't have to love you, and she probably won't, but she should try not to batter your ego. Otherwise, Ms. Saggitarius may suffer the punishment of becoming a Cancer in her next life.

Cancer Man with Capricorn Woman

She'll be touched by the way you seem to care for her welfare. But she'll have a hard time dealing with your moods.

You seem to create slights and then sulk in them. And no matter how she tries, she can never discover what she's done wrong.

You'll resent all the time she spends at the office, not to mention those cocktail parties that seem to enhance business. In turn, she'll resent your suspicions and the way you make her feel guilty when she tries to ignore you.

However, despite these minor considerations, she needs a lot of love, reassurance, praise, and support, and you're just the person to provide it. Although you may be impressed with the fact that she's president of a corporation, you'll love her for her total personality, not for her title. With you, she can strip away her soul and stop worrying that you will find her less worthy. You don't care if she gains five pounds, doesn't have time to wash her hair, and cooks you a dinner that self-destructs on the way to the table. You want the woman, not the gilded super-achiever.

Therefore, if she can manage to look at you from a less superficial standpoint, she may find a man who is very much worthy of her attentions. However, she'll have to pay in kind for your sympathy and services. The more she lets what happened at the afternoon's board meeting get in the way of her better moments, the more she will be prying apart a potentially happy union. In order to get, she has to give. The important decision is whether she wants to pay the price for a successful private life.

Cancer Man with Aquarius Woman

You crave closeness, but she feels more comfortable with distance. You prefer cozy tête-à-têtes, and she embraces crowded settings. You enjoy quiet evenings at home, while she prefers mass riots. The differences between you are distance-producing.

You need a woman who will nurture your strengths and overlook your insecurities. She needs a man who has fewer insecurities and a greater degree of emotional detachment.

She'll become impatient with your supersensitivities, your mood swings, and your possessiveness. At the same time, you'll feel morose and sulky when she treats some meaningless stranger with as much attention as she does you.

She is a freedom-loving, freethinking woman who creates her own spaces. You tend to close them off with your attempts at getting her total attention.

At first, she may respond enthusiastically to your romantic gestures. However, if you move in too far too fast, she may take a giant step backward for a quick breath and another look.

Since she is adaptable to most personalities, she could also come to love yours. However, if you drown her in a swamp of mawkish emotions and make too many demands, she'll leave you to your sentimental dreams and memories of an affair that *almost* made it.

Cancer Man with Pisces Woman

This psychic rapport will leave you starry-eyed. You will sympathize with her mood swings, cry along with her in teary grade-B movies, and remember what she wore on the day you first met her.

She will marvel that you are a better cook than she is, that you are equally as sensitive, and that you seem to know not only what she's thinking, but why.

You'll both find yourselves saying the same thing simultaneously; you'll finish each other's sentences and respect each other's ideas.

This relationship is one made for lazy weeekends at ocean retreats, evenings of champagne and candlelight, winter afternoons of Bach, quiet talk, and a snifter of brandy.

Prepare for a lifetime of love on the beach, under the stars, beside a bowl of roses, and near an open window that lets the moonlight peep in.

LEO

Dates: July 24 to August 23
Symbol: the lion
Ruling planet: the sun
Element: fire
Mode: fixed
Quality: masculine, positive
Planetary principle: creativity
Primal desire: power
Colors: red, orange, gold, yellow
Jewels: amber, ruby, chrysolite
Plants: anemone, anise, chrysanthemum
Tree: oak
Herbs: fennel, chamomile, mint, parsley
Day: Sunday
Archangel: Michael
Magical number: 19
Material factor: power through effort

LEOS OF
FAME AND FORTUNE

Jacqueline Kennedy Onassis   Princess Margaret Rose
Mae West   Alfred Hitchcock
Benito Mussolini   Carl Jung

George Bernard Shaw	Sir Walter Scott
Napoleon Bonaparte	Percy Bysshe Shelley
Helena Petrovna Blavatsky	Dustin Hoffman
Henry Ford	Robert Redford
Astrologer Alan Leo	Andy Warhol

THE LEO FEMALE

Favorable

You need a camel to cart around your charge cards, and a multimillionaire to pay them. You can exude glamour in a pair of jeans, but little does the world know that it took you two hours to coordinate three shades of blue. If there was a fire in your building, you'd be the only one who stops to put on your makeup. As a teenager you probably changed your clothes four times a day and twice for each meal. All the mirrors in your room were highly polished, and you were always late for school because you kept getting lost in your own reflection. You feel you always have to look your best, which could be dangerous, because you would knock down a German shepherd and two little old ladies in the supermarket to avoid your heartthrob if you felt that your hair didn't look up to par.

At dinner parties you're usually the center of attention—especially when everyone else is diving into a third helping of lasagna and you're making your celery stalk last the night. You subscribe to the belief that a woman can never be too thin—or too rich.

You love life, parties, people, and you usually see the world as a brilliant wide-screen movie. Because of your detached awareness of yourself, you have a fine sense of humor and usually laugh the hardest when your larger-than-life drama turns into a three-ring circus. You imbue life with a luster that others find so appealing that they often form a fan club. You never have to go looking for excitement, because you find it even at the launderette, and in the lengthy checkout line at the supermarket.

Your constant gaiety and enthusiasm dazzle the crowds of people moving through your life. Because of this, it seems to some people that you are impervious to pain. Actually your pride and need for privacy are so great that you do not easily show more deeply felt emotions.

Men most often confuse the strength of your personality with the strength of your passion, and often mistake impersonal warmth for seduction tactics. However what you enjoy most is the dramatic game, and the persuasive tactics that men use to conjure your presence. You adore love if it scintillates with glamour and reeks of the romance of a midnight movie. Otherwise, you are indifferent to Chinese dinners and ten-o'clock phone calls inquiring if you'd like company.

You are independent, ambitious, and highly goal-oriented. Your prime goal is leadership on a grand scale. Your difficulty is that you cannot appreciate your successes on a small scale. As you drive yourself up the ladder of success, try not to lose hold of your mental flexibility, or else when you finally do get to the top, you will find that you are queen of an empty kingdom.

Unfavorable

You are a snob. But unlike the Capricorn woman who discreetly drapes her body with a subdued Dior original, you wear St. Laurent on your sleeve. Your desire is for the appearance of power; if the substance is lacking, the facade will often do. This also applies to the men who move in and through your life. If you're really careful, you'll get a directory and ask them to sign in. Title first, of course.

Men are never certain what it is you really want, although sometimes they get the idea that it might have something to do with control, as you suddenly leap across the room shouting orders. Because you have a temper that could break glass, and a look in your eye that seems to threaten any self-assertive person, most men tend to be thoroughly intimidated by you. However, you really want to be treated like a little girl, you wail as they make a beeline for the nearest exit, mumbling nervously that they'll talk to you soon.

As far as love goes, you gravitate toward men who make you look good. Because appearances must be kept at all costs, you have no time for a man who may be devoted but minus money, power, status and good looks. You assign an inordinate importance not only to what your friends think but also to what your neighbors, chic acquaintances, co-workers, and the general public think. Although you may believe that you want love, you really want romance, and unfortunately, you've never grown up enough to consider that there may be a difference. Therefore, you occupy your time with superficial values, superficial encounters, and superficial expectations of an unfolding future.

No one ever has enough power or money to suit you, so you often have to settle. Usually the man is passive and more than content to trail behind in your larger-than-life luster. You adore crowds—especially if they're populated with famous faces. Then, with undisguised abandon you quickly dash about and make yourself known to the truly celebrated. You are a skilled and enthusiastic manipulator, and because of this, you must be careful about what you really want, principally because you always seem to get it.

Basically, you have a queen complex that makes you self-centered, egotistical, childish, and outrageously haughty. Every act is well-thought-out to bring you the maximum advantage. And any person who is allowed to come close enough almost withers from your control.

If someone daring could relieve you of your expensive furs, fine jewelry, and flawless makeup, what he would find would be a little girl with soft eyes who yearns to be cherished. But if he should be so intrepid as to try to tenderly kiss your fingertips, your nails would greet his nose. Then you would meet his eyes and smile before slowly walking away. You want a man to adore and adorn you, not to love you. Life's so much safer when the softness comes in furs.

THE LEO MALE

Favorable

Deep down, you're a pussycat, but you'd rather growl around a lot than let the world know it. You are proud, ambitious, and driven, and view your achievements as an extension of your personal power. Therefore, it is not at all surprising that you work faster than five steam engines in overdrive. Your overwhelming ego is a facade that protects your tender emotions. Because your needs for self-glorification are so strong, you are easily captured by insincere flattery.

Romance can rivet you to a fantasy realm that has

very little to do with real love. Your chosen lady is merely an embodiment of the ideal qualities with which you would like to be associated. Beauty, charm, a scintillating intellect, and a modicum of wealth are always comfortable starters. Because you cling to such towering standards, you are easily disillusioned. After the initial incandescence has dimmed, nothing is ever as grand or glamorous as it once seemed. Too many soul-consuming love experiences will leave you empty and searching—your blood rushing from red to jade green.

Because your nature is basically generous and protective, you are an easy prey to the femme fatale feigning helplessness and vulnerability. The practiced bat of an eyelash can send you scurrying to so many flower shops that your heartthrob's house could easily end up looking like a funeral parlor.

Despite your occasional clouds of temper, you are basically good-natured and life-loving. But to you "life" is only an assemblage of the very best. Why drink beer when you can pay more for a Pouilly Fuissé that is worth its price just in its syllables? Why settle for a VW when you can have a Mercedes—even if you do have to use your food money for the next six months for the down payment. After all, fasting can only improve your physique, and you're going to have to look your best for your exit from the front seat.

Somewhere inside, you've always preferred to see yourself as a luminous figure attracting a crowd of admiring faces. At the same time, you need one partner to play back to you the drama of your own life, and to constantly assure you that you're truly lovable. Whereas the more unevolved Leo would love to languish in a den populated by beautiful bodies, you know that while that would be fun for a while, it still wouldn't satisfy your deeper emotional needs. Although you may be loath to admit it, your favorite life experience is love, and the more intense, scintillating, and romantic, the better. Years of hard work, high salaries, and powerful titles really don't seem to be worth it in the end if you have nothing more than a beautiful but empty apartment to come home to.

You are definitely the marrying kind, and you'll probably try to father your wife as well as your future children. You're the strong, honest, dependable kind of man that women often feel is their answer to the knight on a white charger. Warmth, tenderness, and passion flow from you freely along with advice on how to do everything better, from brushing one's teeth to taking out the garbage. Even if you appear to be a shy and far more reserved Leo socially, chances are in private quarters you're more overbearing than a bull who knows he's got someone cornered. Although you might never consider yourself controlling, other people would bear witness to your daily demands, requests, and suggestions for betterment.

In terms of marriage, you're most likely to find happiness with a woman who is as challenging and aggressive as you are. The woman you finally choose to marry has to make you look good. At the same time, she has to provide an emotional foundation that makes you feel secure, needed, deeply loved, wanted, and definitely admired. Your ideal wife also has a firm shoulder you can lean on and knows how to make you feel comfortable with the more vulnerable side of yourself.

Any woman who has all these qualities need never worry that you will stray from the luxurious Leo love nest. Once you are satisfied that you have found "the one," you are Mr. Faithful personified. However, that doesn't mean you don't flirt a little, now and then—even if you don't realize you're doing it. You love the attentions of women as well as their company, and probably have more female friends than any other sign except Aquarius.

At the same time, those women who start to take your attentions a little too seriously and begin to fantasize about the beginning of an affair will undoubtedly be stopped dead when you flash a smile and start talking about how much you respect your wife. As with the female Leo, your warmth and friendliness do not imply a need for a closer familiarity. You're just a charming person who likes to be around people. If that's called flirting, well, that's not your problem. People can think what they like. As for you, you're usually too busy superachieving to worry about it.

Unfavorable

When you lose your temper, you tend to fire people from your life. Then, sometime later, while they are morosely packing their baggage, you politely tap them on the shoulder and ask them where they might be going. Your pride will send you mountain climbing, and your determination and energy are so expansive that you'll probably arrive at the top before a helicopter. Your lack of patience with the less-fiery souls around you will send you stalking away fuming and twitching. The least you demand is that your associates be psychic, because it takes too much time to answer their questions.

Unless you're the lazy Leo type, you like people in your life to move at the reasonable pace of immediately-if-not-sooner. If you do happen to resemble the more lazy lion, then you like to sink your body into a velvet armchair while you daydream about the activities at your health club, and how your energies could easily consume the phlegmatic world. You can be bombastic, bossy, and boastful. Not only were you made for the "good life," you created it. Your secretary, wife, and faithful Fido call you master and create a constant current of air by running to attend to your every need.

While your secretary mutters that you're a chauvinist as she is frantically scrubbing your dessert from your tie, you are bellowing because she's not in your office taking dictation. But even she is aware that your basic credo is that all the world's your servant. It has nothing to do specifically with women. As a matter of fact, who are they? Oh, that's right, they're the people you spend time with when you're not with your wife.

It's a given that you're compulsively unfaithful. After all, you need intense action from every angle, and for a person who is as romantically active as you, your marriage could never offer enough.

Your favorite types are the more flashy females who fall somewhere between a grinning beauty queen and an overdressed call girl. It is extremely important that these ladies look good, because, after all, your reputation is at stake. It is likely that you can wear yourself out in this role of Lothario. All that rich food and liquor that goes with the role can slowly dissipate and age a once-athletic body.

However, being conveniently myopic, you excel at overlooking your stomach, which is slowly creeping forward. Instead, you would rather spend your time informing one of your many women that she is sadly getting out of shape. Diplomacy was never one of your virtues; nor is concern for the dignity of another human being. Your attitude is that someone who can't take the truth should just remain stupid and suffer. Strange how someone so enamored of the "truth" builds his life on so many lies and is so totally intimidating to anyone who ventures an honest opinion.

However, any really intelligent human being is aware that your intimidating temper is merely another form of your control that signifies that you are totally out of control. Underneath the furious glance is merely a frustrated child who wishes he knew what to do next. And this is not an easy situation for a man who condescendingly acts as if he has all the answers. Because you loudly establish yourself as a "know-it-all," you create little cushion room for mistakes. And because you're so smug and have never learned how to say "I'm sorry," you operate your life through the pressures of having to show other people where their thinking is in error.

The kindest comment that might be made about you is that you wear your insensitivity like egg on your tie. More than annoying, it's terribly embarrassing. It indicates a person one should feel sorry for, but never fear. Your egotistical outbursts are nothing more than a show to prove to yourself that you really have power. However, the fact is that it's only a matter of time until everyone around you gets tired of your repetitive performances. In the end, your emotional immaturity will always betray you, and the people who will remain in your life will be the ones you need but never really want. However, your strength is that you can quickly come up with more lies to obliterate the loneliness. It's not bad for a person who suffers from such misplaced talent. After all, it gets you from day to day and has you convinced that in the end you're really going somewhere.

DECANS

Every sign in the zodiac can be broken down into three subdivisions, called decans. Each decan roughly corresponds to 10 degrees—the first third, second third, and last third of the sun sign's time span, which is approximately thirty days.

As each of these periods has different subrulerships,

the personality of a person is slightly modified by the specific decan it falls in. For instance, an Aries born in the second decan would be ruled by Mars, but subruled by the sun. Therefore, he would tend to display a greater sense of pride, boastfulness, egotism, and optimism than an Aries born in the third decan, which is subruled by Jupiter. This Aries would tend to be more freedom-loving, flighty, travel-oriented, and interested in subjects of a philosophical nature. An Aries born in the first decan would be the most aggressive, but not necessarily the most productive and accomplished.

Decans are important, since they do account for a more detailed assessment of an individual's personality characteristics. They also show how two people born under the same sun sign can be markedly different.

If you were born between July 24 and August 4, your sun sign is in the solar decan of Leo. Here your ego needs are somewhat stronger than those of the Leos born in the rest of the month. Pride pushes you into goal-oriented situations in which you gain the recognition you hunger for. Driven on by ego dreams, you are like a machine out of control, and can't stop until you've run your course. Since all playtime is a waste of time—unless it's a means to meeting the "right" people—you never consider vacations unless they revolve around work. That is the closest you can come to being idle without breaking out in boils from boredom. Since you were about six, people begged you to relax, but being a tense extrovert, you've worked your way to adulthood in spasms of energy that often ended in exhaustion.

You are enthusiastic, optimistic and interested in everything around you. Already you have activities set aside for when you're eighty-three, since you can't seem to fit them in any sooner. You are positive, idealistic, and very aggressive. You know how to transform ideals into realities, and your mind sets the stage with the right attitudes. You get what you want because you can't even consider failure; the only factor you reflect on is time. One day you'll want to stop the world, and you will, but when you do you won't get off.

If you were born between August 5 and August 15, your sun sign is in the Jupiter decan of Leo. You are jovial, good-natured, and have an especially fine sense of humor. You love to make others laugh, and tend to look upon the brighter side of a situation. Optimism pervades your soul, even when difficulties seem to loom larger than life.

You seek a greater meaning to your existence than you can find in the material sphere. Philosophy, religion, metaphysics, and the occult are areas to which you would naturally turn to find important answers. As you grow older, education has an ever greater personal significance. Studies of all kinds become more appealing, and the excitement you gain from them can provide substantial support during periods of adversity.

There is a strong inspirational side to your personality, which others both admire and envy. You have a solid sense of purpose combined with a faith that always sees you through. Not infrequently do you find yourself listening to people's problems and offering thoughtful advice. Your inherent strength strongly attracts the more flappable souls, who often assume that you find everything in life easy.

Deep within your soul, you have a robust enjoyment of life, which seldom deserts you. But unlike the Leo born in the first decan, you also derive a profound sense of pleasure from life's *little* treasures, and although you both share an abundance of nervous energy, you seek to balance the time dedicated to work demands. Yoga, tennis, and T'ai Chi are activities to which you would most naturally turn to gain release from inner tensions. Travel has a very important place in your heart, and each trip is a special learning experience.

If you were born between August 16 and August 23, your sun sign is in the Mars decan of Leo. You are a dynamo running at full speed, and heaven help those poor fools who get in your way. This decan has the connotations of both Leo and Aries. It is aggression directed by the most potent power of will. You live on a treadmill of push, push, go, go—and you love it, though your friends faint with exhaustion at the very thought of the tasks you casually take on. This both irritates and puzzles you, because you know that the harder you work, the greater your energy. Unlike the first-decan Leo, who works for the ego, you work for the pleasure of working.

You're not easy to be with, since your high energy, operating overtime, leaves others with half-finished sentences and three blocks behind, jogging just to keep up. You are abrupt, quick-tempered, and loathe people who yawn. Since your mind moves at the speed of light, those poor souls who talk slowly and repeat their point make you twitch. You do your best to avoid telephones, garrulous people, unenergetic individuals, and clocks. For you, hell is being sequestered with a lazy, whining, obsessive soul who repeats each sentence three times. Your only fear is of illness, because it slows you down and forces you to get at least three hours' sleep.

You're a maniac for challenges. Situations that would put others to bed get your mind and body dancing. With the greatest of ease, you can deal with each crisis, upheaval, and tragedy. What really gets you down is a period when nothing is happening, but with your courage, faith, drive, will, and tenacity, you're never down for long. You are resilience personified, merely regenerating for the next supercycle of challenges.

LOVE

At its best, it's sheer romance: the impassioned glances, the breathless interchanges; the feeling of first love; the feeling of last love; the daily, dramatic phantasms. You love love; but even more, you love romance.

Even for the most supercharged Leos moving in overdrive, life really isn't worth living without loving. This is not merely a matter of loneliness, but something more complex. While Virgos claim that you are what you eat, you believe that you are what you attract. And if it happens that you're not attracting . . . You are a most idealistic sign, and often create a dream world to shield you from what you don't want to see. Eventually, disillusionment dawns, and the sun suddenly retreats. What is left is a cold, grim kind of person shuffling through a myriad of new projects in an effort to scatter the pain. The most unfortunate fact is that it usually works. In these matters, you are the cowardly lion, and your lack of courage in confronting all the factors in a love situation keeps you from learning, changing, and growing.

In matters of love, the Leo male is most vulnerable.

He has the largest ego problems in the zodiac, and to get what he wants, he's got to put it all on the line. It becomes a make-it-or-break-it situation, and the only way he knows how to survive the savage insecurity is to boast abominably, to overcompensate by a conspicuous "non-caring" attitude, or to sulk. Take away his toys and tools of worldly career attainment, and what you have is the most vulnerable of human beings, cowering under two stiff lips and a lot of self-righteous attitudes. He needs love desperately, but he'll never say it. It's infinitely more masculine to scream, shout orders, and throw around the power that society has lent him. "Big" men don't cry, they certainly don't talk about pain, and if they're fast and fortunate enough, they're much too busy even to remember they have feelings. Is it a wonder that so many Leo men really "make it"?

The Leo female is far more flexible, because her ego needs are easily gratified and her emotions are ambivalent. This is certainly the most flirtatious sign. But while Mr. Leo can heartily indulge in the sport only if there's someone securely waiting in the background, Ms. Leo can live from one flirtation to the next without the personal props. Certainly, she would like *love,* but unlike the Leo male, a life attachment is far from her first priority.

It's power that makes her pulse race and often leads her down the wrong path. This girl thinks in superlatives, and because she's so sly, self-possessed, and sexually magnetic, she gets what she wants, but only on the surface. Somehow, there's always something missing: she has the chinchilla, but no communication; the president of General Motors has just proposed, but he's an unbearable bore; she's involved in a mutual intoxication with an international intellect, but he has no emotions. In spite of herself, she finds the kind of consuming love that will last a lifetime, but his income won't last even a month. So it's back to the halfhearted flirtations with famous faces.

With the most dazzling lovers, the Leo lady is lonely —so she keeps moving, is often promiscuous, and has a deep-seated fear of settling down. Like the Leo man, she sublimates her emotional dissatisfactions by driving herself toward public prominence. Until this is attained, she is strong enough to survive on superficial encounters. The key to her strength is in knowing that she is her own mother—that all love proceeds from what she gives herself. Her weakness comes when she can't cut the cord and see that she is too self-dependent.

In general, Leo is a loving sign, with generous, warm, and paternalistic qualities. When both sexes work to transcend their self imposed limitations, there is a great potential for many joyful love experiences. There is also an expansion of the creative drives that tend to dry up during each emotional malaise. When a Leo is in love, everything is easy. But when a Leo seeks to deceive the emotional self, the price is that life somehow becomes even more than hard.

MARRIAGE

Your need for love, approval, and affection will push you in the direction of marriage. However, whatever happens after the moment of the vows can be quite another matter.

If you are the lower Leo type, at some point you will yearn for greater freedom; if you are the higher Leo, your goal will be self-expansion, and the right union is a continual source of inspiration. Your ultimate benefit from marriage depends on where you want it to take you.

In general, the Leo need for partnership is far more urgent than most people realize, because there is a profound desire to define the ego through another. First, a partner provides the audience needed to play back the drama of personal experience. Second, the ideal characteristics of the chosen partner exalt the Leo's concept of himself. On the higher level, this ideal is based on what the person is; on the lower, what the person has and does. Third, a partner is needed to feed the rapacious ego with acts of love, approval, and affection.

The schism in the Leo personality comes from the desire to be as autonomous as the Aquarian, confused by a longing for personal loving, which obliterates the desire to live a lifetime alone. Confusion arises only because of an immature ego whose tendency is to *have* rather than to *give*.

If your mind is clear concerning your concept of loving, marriage can be a merry meeting of the minds and hearts. But if you enter into it only because you are lovelorn, seeking gratification rather than growth, marriage can be a bitter mistake. Grow up first and consider your goals. The life you may save could, at the very least, be your own.

MONEY

Money is a flash of green through the thumb and the forefinger, but you rarely see it because you write checks and are quick with your credit cards. You definitely prefer convenience buying, which means not knowing how much you've spent until you get the stamina to synchronize your checkbook with your charge receipts.

As an infant, your first words probably were "I want it." Since then, they've changed to "I'll have it." Spending money is your panacea for every ailment: a common cold calls for a seventy-five-dollar bracelet; a bad cough can be cured by purchasing a bottle of vintage champagne; fatigue will be banished with a pair of purple suede boots; but hysteria, anxiety, and depression run too high even to mention. It might be noted that this cure may last only until your checkbook is balanced, but this is only one of its dangers. Needless to say, the emotional satisfactions are so great that it can also be habit-forming.

At least there is one thing to be said for Leo: You're not one of those people who whine that they don't know where their money goes. With you, it's never a mystery —it's on your back (just read the labels) or in your home (who could miss that chandelier in the bathroom?).

Money is merely a means to an end. Sitting by itself in a savings account, it's simply not taking you anywhere, and when there's never any time, how can you be expected to wait for the interest? Waiting is anxiety-producing, and the mere thought of anxiety makes you fondle your credit cards. Needless to say, you've just decided that you have to be somewhere. Could it begin with B for "boutique"?

CAREER

Success is your astro name and you've always known it. You feel you were born to sit on a throne and tell others what to do. Mediocrity drives you to despair, but it's not a word that applies to you, nor will it ever.

From the time you were an infant you had a sense of power. You would enter the world only to be president, prime minister, chief of surgery, or chairman of the board. On Oscar night, you could see yourself bowing to the glittering audience.

You think in superlatives, so material success means *all*—the more flashy and showy, the better. You reign from supremacy and only a Scorpio would dare contest it. The one thing to remember as you watch your minions file forth is that you're more vulnerable than you would like to let yourself think. Since you need far more than the average human being, not only do you have to work a lot harder, but also you can stand to lose a lot more.

Basically, you want to rule the world, not just a cozy corner. Fame, power, and fortune have beckoned since you were about four. Most difficult for you are your destiny decisions, since there are so many directions in which you would like to turn.

But wherever your goals lead you, the gateway to fame will surely give way at your arrival. Both acting and directing are definite considerations, since you've always loved the limelight. Public relations is also a possibility, since you tend to be rather people-oriented. With your sense of luxury, you could be supercreative at seducing the consumer. Your sense of beauty and color can put you in high places, in positions ranging from writing vacation brochures to fashion designing, from interior decorating to selling orchids in December. Then, there's always painting, preparing new kinds of perfume, literary consultation, and, of course, teaching, since you excel in telling people what to do.

If you can't run the company, chances are you'll own it. You've always been a boss, and love giving orders as much as you love working. On-the-job idleness irritates your nerve endings, since your own success gears are far from static.

In essence, you are a workhorse and loudly let the world know it. You can drive more placid souls past their point of sanity quite easily. Your public assumes that you've undoubtedly lost yours, along with any realistic sense of timing.

When you know what you want, you have to have it quickly. One day, your name will be in lights to illuminate the dreary world.,

FRIENDS

You seem to have more friends than the population of China. You don't really know how they all got there, but somehow the numbers keep getting out of control. You need a secretary just for your social invitations—and even then often find that somehow you're committed to three different dinners all going on at the same time.

You're so warm, charming, and friendly that strangers want to adopt you. But instead, they seem to arrange it that *you* adopt *them*. At times it may seem that you're a people collector, but the fact is that you're just agreeable and slightly confused when it comes to people priorities. When your degree of social interaction starts to sabotage your professional plans, you panic, shut off the phone, and lock your door, opening it only for the dry cleaner. You feel that people are funny, exciting, and wonderful, but when they move into your life too intensely, it can be draining and far closer to pain than pleasure.

Peace and privacy are requirements you must satisfy periodically, and when you've gone too long without them, you can become a cranky, irascible creature that no ones likes to be around.

In your more intimate friendships, you are loyal, giving, sincere, and faithful in all moments of need. Since you're often closer to your friends than your family, these ties can last a lifetime. Such friendships fill your life with great meaning, and because of your large capacity for love, the ties that bind you are seldom broken.

HEALTH

Here, your strength is your vulnerability, since you are prone to push yourself too far. While solar energy floods your being with an awesome vitality, the frenetic rate at which you live your life can bring you to the brink of both sickness and exhaustion.

Since Leo rules the heart, this organ is particularly vulnerable to long periods of sustained stress. In middle age, heart attacks and other coronary ailments are the Leo's danger area, so exercise caution.

Learn the gentle art of relaxation. You'll never slow down, but do observe regular rest periods. Twenty minutes a day of deep breathing and/or Transcendental Meditation will depress the heart and pulse rate sufficiently for rest and revitalization. Consider it, and be careful to avoid strain.

In general, you are healthy, robust, and have a horror of sickness. Being caged up and physically incapacitated gets you into a panic. Since everything you require and desire is dependent on your ability to move about, life is not worth living if you have to spend it in bed alone.

However, your inordinate impatience will not let any illness linger. Your mind projects so many positive thought forms that sickness is seldom a problem. It's not even a consideration. That's why it rarely even occurs.

HOME

Your home is your castle, even if you live in a cottage. You love luxury, so chances are your couch is nine feet long and covered with crushed velvet. Your ceiling seems to reach toward the sun—so high that one stares at the walls. Scattered humbly among the Picassos are some of your own paintings. Your Leo fifth-house creativity imparts color to your canvases in a splendor of splashes. Green, orange, yellow, and magenta dance off the wall and dazzle the eye.

Like the sunflower, you need light to flourish. While some people collect sculpture, you collect lamps that light up even your sleeping hours—which are never very long anyway!

In your rooms, mirrors are evident in such subtle settings as the linen closet, the kitchen cabinets, and across from the bathtub. You have five color televisions you never watch because your reflection is so fascinating. Your maid is in a perpetual state of madness because you finger the mirrors, forget to buy Drano, and frantically implore her to find your favorite shoes. Strange how they always end up in the closet.

When you get truly bored, you turn up your album of cobra love calls, don a safari hat, and with a stuffed picnic basket forage through your fur coats. When the going gets heavy because of too many big animals, you stop to have an early lunch. Intimate friends suggest you build a stage within the privacy of your boudoir, but you explain that when you act, it has to be an adventure. Of course, you've considered moving to a medieval castle, but decided that apartments are more of a creative challenge.

Because you have always fancied wild animals and ivory, a five-foot elephant's tusk points at your refrigerator from the opposite wall. When you originally bought it, it had seemed highly original, but since then you've lost too many drunken party guests seeking ice.

When you think back upon your childhood, home was never like this. No wonder you were always bored, and staging desperate battles with your brother over the shredded wheat. And when he began to whine because he hated milk and sugar in his hair, the only good thing that home offered was the knowledge that one day you would leave.

Now that your life is like a three-ring circus, boredom begins only when you tire of your treasures. But your superexotic houseguests usually pick you up in time. Especially when you forget who they are and have to politely inquire their country of origin.

COSMIC CHALLENGE

Boredom is the blight of your existence, and so you are always busy. Highly charged solar energy intensifies a sense of restlessness and enthusiasm that makes it difficult to deal with all situations. You crave constant stimulation, and when you are not totally immersed in projects, people, and activities, your agitation is overwhelming. You are painfully impatient with tedious details, colorless people, slow thinkers, slow talkers, slow walkers, and often you are abrupt and finish others' sentences without being aware of what you are doing. You prefer responses in two words or less since there's never enough time and you're tearing off to an appointment, and are probably already late.

Like all the fire signs, you demand immediate gratification, as time lapses threaten and slow cycles depress. You are driven to live a life filled with action and excitement, and when the pace slows down, you panic. You lust for a life of peaks, but what you don't realize is that too many peaks become a plain. You demand new thrills from each day, and when you feel that they're missing, you'll exhaust yourself trying to create them, but when all attempts fail, you fall into gloom. Your most profound horror is the sense of having nothing to look forward to.

Pain and panic need not consume you in these moments if you deal more creatively with static situations. Try to accept without sorrow that maybe only 90% of your life will have the fevered pulse of a paperback novel, and the other 10% of the time need not be discarded. Take up activities that are focused inward and formulate personal excitement through creative self expression. Writing, painting, music, sculpture, crafts, and courses to expand awareness should all be considered. Develop the self-detachment of your Aquarian counterpart and learn that every man and woman is a star and has something worthwhile to offer—but to hear it, you must learn how to listen. Think about the word "slow" and make a list of all the positive states and conditions it has to offer. If you get to this point, you may realize that it's not your slow periods that confine you, it is the constrictions of your own mind. Learn how to free it from imprisoning perspectives and you will see that you are the sole power in your private universe. If you are ready to accept this challenge, you will also be ready to relinquish all the restlessness.

INSPIRATION

You are optimistic, cheerful, generous, witty, and generally good-natured. Remember, you create your own clouds—so think constant thoughts of sunshine. You have a noble nature and the strength of the lion. No task is too small. You are the leader personified and exalted in your creations. Your solar life-force can penetrate the most protective panoply. Share it with the world in a loving way, and power will pervade you forever.

WHAT HOLDS YOU BACK
AND HOW TO OVERCOME IT

Your ego and your pride are two shackles that will chain you for a lifetime if you let them. You have a will that could make Mt. Everest crumble, so use it to expand your feeling of power from within. When you open yourself up to your intrinsic power, you will no longer need to hide behind the status-conscious trappings you favor. Enjoy your toys and trinkets, but don't let them control you, and try to be ever conscious of the difference. You have an inner strength and lordly nature that others deeply admire. Learn to be silent and flexible, and your life will be a reign of unquestionable glory. Finally, stop shouting your own reviews, or you will cease to have an audience. If you try too hard to tell the world that you're a prince, everyone will drift away muttering that you're a frog. Let humility be a coat of arms emblazoned on your robes, and your royalty will forever inspire your followers and silence the claims of all impostors.

LOVE AND COMPATIBILITY GUIDE

Leo with Leo

A Leo with a Leo spells either love or hate—and sometimes both. Competition can trail off to the truly absurd, as he explains to her the principle of nuclear fission, while she, a doctor of physics, fulminates into a fiery explosion. He is horrified that she can't appreciate his helpfulness, and lets her know that she belongs in a zoo.

To him, she is willful, temperamental, and bossy. To her, he is the most foolish kind of egoist. She sees him again only to make him suffer. He sees her again only to let her know that he really didn't want to see her. It's not unlikely that on the second date, after the first exchange of the first fifteen sentences, he'll find that he's morosely munching his chateaubriand by candlelight—but alone.

Should the smoke be dispersed by sheer chemistry, this combination has the potential of the ideal duo. Both share the same value system, sense of romance, and materialistic attitudes. When she invites him to dinner, he gasps at the salmon mousse, sighs at the year of the Pouilly Fuissé, and moans with delight over the baked Alaska. In turn, he nourishes her femininity with fresh flowers and remembers to tell her that she looks beautiful by candlelight. She is enraptured by his romantic anachronisms, and he is in love because she is enraptured. If, at some point, both manage to annihilate their ego problems before each other, Leo and Leo could easily share a most happy marriage.

Her glamour makes him look good, so he grins good-naturedly when she displays her third new fur (and it's only September). As a husband, he is strong, successful, and supportive. And aside from her eighteen hours at the office (where she runs a million-dollar corporation), she devotes her entire time to him. Apart from his more dolorous moments alone with a half-frozen TV dinner and the notes for his new novel, called *Divorce*, he is truly happy. It has taken him a long time to penetrate her veneer, and what he has found are his own frailties. Now when they fight about who knows more about the art of gravestone rubbing, he is sly enough to change the subject before the chandelier breaks.

Leo Woman with Aries Man

It's nothing less than love at first sight when he dashes aggressively to your side to retrieve the appointment book you deliberately dropped. He's quick to pick up your cues. And complimentary—especially when you let your eyes drift. He adores the challenge of winning you, and your flirtations give him many challenges. The problem is that *his* flirtations give you indigestion. You can't imagine why he would even consider glancing at that blond slinking by, when *you* are right there. If he knew enough, he would be blinded. After all, when he's with you, it's theater, not a circus.

Between you there is warmth, passion, and much mutual admiration. He's one of the few men who can get away with telling you what to do. He knows it, and this excites him even more. He is enthralled by your energy and enthusiasm, and respects your independence and ambition. Your warmth and support spur him on to further far-reaching goals.

You both understand each other's fiery nature and tend to remain cool while the other is momentarily combusting. Grudges never pollute the air, because you both feel free about your anger. That is fortunate, since most other signs would lock themselves in a closet at what you cheerfully refer to as a temper flareup.

Sexually, you are highly compatible, except that he is

impulsive, while you are calculating. Everything must be canceled when you don't look your best; if the scales should show an extra pound, there is no alternative but to tell him you've contracted mononucleosis. Admittedly, things can get pretty embarrassing if he shows up with a dozen daffodils—and his doctor. Aries can be most gallant crusaders.

He is honest, whereas you are a game-player. Most of the time he never catches on to your manipulations. If he did, he would probably think you're crazy. His inherent spontaneity will never allow him to understand why you compulsively calculate consequences. He believes in the here and now, while you tend to focus on the future. You don't want to play unless you have control; he wants to play just to play.

This is a man who can make the muscles of your heart move, and you are a woman who can make his stop dead. Between you there is much excitement, communication, and kisses, not to mention a few airborne objects. My suggestion is: for these tender disagreements, stock up on paper plates.

Leo Woman with Taurus Man

This is definitely not a match made in heaven, as you both have a will that could topple a redwood tree. He is stubborn and rigid; you are defiant and stubborn. Combined, these inharmonious qualities can spell explosion.

He is Mr. Stay-at-home, while you walk holes in the floor if you can't get out. You like the drama and excitement of life; he is content with the eleven-o'clock news.

It is not unlikely that he outdoes you in the kitchen, a quality you appreciate, since you never considered it a divine privilege to have to cook. Yet, when he's slaved for hours over the stove to create a ten-course meal, and you dawdle over the asparagus because you're dieting, the "dinner" can become decidedly cold.

He tends to get into ruts, while you compulsively create change. He can replay one record more frequently than a Buddhist meditating on a mantra while you yawn and want to throw the thing away after the third time.

He has a nervous strain dealing with your independence, and you delight in ignoring his reactions to your need for freedom. Your drive for power can make him feel impotent; his desire to possess your spirit can make you feel hostile. He sulks during and after your flirtations, and you've forgotten them the minute after you've fled. Days after, he is still not speaking. You shrug your shoulders and seek attention elsewhere, as he exits in a state of violence.

He delights in saving money, while you save your sanity by spending it. He faints when he sees that you've spent fifteen dollars on lip gloss, while you lick your lips and smile because you love to startle his conservative sensibilities. Mutually, there is passion, but after a while he finds you a nemesis to his earthly nature. You consider sex an unnatural act if you don't look and smell like perfection. His animal sensuality is offended by your preoccupation with appearance. Your inner attitude is that love is not worth living if you have to reveal your "naked" self.

Because of this, he sees you as a mask of pretense, yet one that is undeniably seductive. He berates you because you'd rather be a *Vogue* cover girl than Jane of the Jungle. You berate him because his sense of sophistication is not startling, his sensuality is so earthy that it's degrading, and his stomach is slowly creeping over his belt.

What even brings you two together? Your glamorous appearance appeals to his ruler, Venus, while his sense of stability insinuates its way into your soul. He is a man you can depend on; you are a woman who makes him look good. Whether this spells love depends on how many times in one week he cooks *boeuf à la bourguignonne*, serving it each time as if it were the first, and how often you flirt with his friends, forget to devour his cooking, and fight to reapply your blusher when he wants to make love. As to the outcome of this strange and stormy combination, even the stars wearily abdicate all responsibility.

Leo Woman with Gemini Man

He'll charm his way in and out of your life so fast you'll forget you ever knew him. Should he stick around, he won't woo you with romantic notions, be on time for the wedding, or remember your first name. His charisma comes from the fact that he's so clever. His hang-up is that emotionally he's a fool.

This man is friendly but very fickle. His attention goes faster than a speeding bullet, and his thoughts move

like the second column on a digital clock. He's bored
unless you beat him at being amusing, which can be a little exhausting unless you were trained for the entertainment business. If you're fast enough, you might fascinate
him for an hour. But be careful that he doesn't wander
away while you still have your mouth open.

Your beauty may attract him but not detain him.
What he is most interested in is a plethora of personalities that flash across his attention span like a kaleidoscope. To keep him around, you have to game-play and
switch roles so swiftly that even you may forget who you
are. If you are an Academy Award–caliber actress, you
may have him around for a lifetime. The question is, do
you really want him?

This man must respect your mind, since he never
realizes you have emotions. From the perspective of your
ego needs, he is maddening, madcap, and monstrous to
handle. When you lose your temper, he laughs, and when
you cry, he tells you you're not using your logic. What
he casually considers early, even *you* call unbearably late.
In social situations he flirts enough for the two of you,
which makes you furious, because you're so busy watching
him that you forget about the other men. When you flirt
to get his attention, he never seems to notice. Or worse, if
he does, he *may* mumble in your ear, "Not bad."

It may certainly seem that this man has no feelings.
The fact is that his feelings change so fast that he's forgotten he's had them. Unless you can also forget that you
have yours, do yourself a favor, and instead, forget him.

Leo Woman with Cancer Man

Though he loves romantic games, Mr. Cancer is soon a
victim of his own emotions. He has called you twelve
times a day for 12 days and you're always busy. On the
first call, he's casually interested; by the sixth he is merely
impassioned; by the ninth, he feverishly abandons all
control; but by the thirteenth, he can no longer think and
mutters to himself about suicide from overeating.

For even your Leo sensibilities, his histrionics are indecently excessive. At his most dramatic, Cancer is dark,
brooding, and could easily upstage Hamlet. But when his
affections are unappeased, he melts into melancholy and
the defiant doldrums. He tries to get your attention by not
speaking or calling, and with relief, you surmise that he's

finally found some self-respect. With discipline, he prolongs his confinement long past a decent convalescence, since he wants to make you suffer even more from his silence. And when he finds that he can no longer stand it, his clammy fingers feel their way to the phone. Assuming his man-in-complete-control look, Cancer casually invites you to Acapulco for the weekend. Cheerfully, you tell him you have to wash your hair. Gulping to keep his voice from cracking, he invites you to a play, midnight dancing, Sunday brunch, and a late-afternoon double feature seven weekends from next Saturday. Graciously, you claim that you're cleaning your closets. Hyperventilating, and fingering his lower lip, he queries if you're busy on the Saturday after Christmas. (At the moment, it happens to be July.) Yes, you reply, as a matter of fact, you're getting married.

Only if your love life has been less exciting than Sunday morning at a convent can you cajole yourself into considering Mr. Cancer. Chances are that during the weeks of sedulous wooing, his supersensitivity will start to strangle your nerve endings. He finds you cold, abrupt, bossy, and intimidating. You find his moods a constant irritant, and vengefully frolic with his feelings.

However, at the same time, his cloying attentions energize your rapacious ego, and your lack of attention energizes his need to suffer. But when the high drama gets so tedious that you beg him to write a new script, the mind's light flashes that this poor excuse for love is not even a solution to isolation. Life *must* offer more than this, you crossly mumble. So does a sojourn in solitary confinement.

Leo Woman with Virgo Man

Despite his bad press as a nit-picking crab who brushes dandruff off your back collar, the Virgo man is really not as bad as he sounds. If he was born between eight and nine o'clock or between four and five o'clock in the morning, there is a good chance that you might find this relationship a stimulating one. However, if he was born between six and seven A.M. and has Virgo rising, this association will not register even long enough for you to forget it.

If you are the more Aquarian kind of Leo, being more cerebral, detached, intellectual, and interested in your surroundings as much as in yourself, this will be a distinct advantage in any relationship with a Virgo man.

He is shy, studious, cautious, introverted, and analytical. He loves order and has more systems than an overwrought accountant. His underwear drawer looks like it just came back from the dry cleaner; his desk, as if he never worked there; and the contents of his freezer, like a pop-art exhibition. He is mystified at what you consider organization, while you silently lapse into shock at his tedious ceremonies.

You live in a social flurry of dinners, parties, theater, brunches, and ballet. He would rather read about them than live them. The cold constrictions of his logic elude you; the lack of feeling in your histrionics leaves him distraught. Chances are, the night before the maid comes, he pulls an all-nighter to clean his apartment. You stay up to dirty yours. He makes you nervous when he checks the dust in the corners, looks under your bed, and stares intently at a hangnail you were trying to conceal by keeping your hands in your pockets. On a day when you feel your most attractive, he'll lean over and whisper in your ear. You anticipate the words "I love you. I need you. I can't live without you. Come away with me or I'll kill myself." Wrong script. He's telling you your coat should be cleaned.

You share springtime as your favorite season. To you it means sunshine, romance, suntans, and sensuous nights of scandalous pleasure. To him it means spring cleaning.

Of all the signs in the zodiac, you are least likely to be an inspiration to his mental health. Your temper makes his stomach twinge and his nerves shudder. Too often, he angrily acquiesces with your wishes to spare himself the tortures of your silences. But since you instantaneously lose respect for any man you can bully, his high-priced agreements only leave you cold and dissatisfied. Alas! While he is the one reputed to be critical, you are the one who can never be pleased. Whatever he does, it barely passes your standards. And no matter how you try to meet his mind, there is always something missing. It's called excitement.

Yet Mr. Virgo is kind, loyal, and faithful. But unless

he has Libra or Leo rising and shares your sense of drama and extravagance, intervals of ennui may be the price you have to pay for such stability.

His routines may bring you to a state of terminal boredom, but his consideration creeps into your heart. Mad and mindless passion is not a likely outcome from this coupling. More than likely this is because he spends all his time in the bathroom. However, if you should be creative enough to hide the toothpaste at bedtime, who knows what can come of it?

Leo Woman with Libra Man

He'll compliment your clothing, send you seventeen valentines, and learn to make love without smudging your makeup. This is the man who invented romance, so don't be surprised when you receive tender telegrams at ten P.M. and roses with champagne at midnight.

You share his love for the ballet, Baroque music, and books that no one else has heard of. You both love luxury, have a strong sense of beauty, and take Sweet 'n' Low on your grapefruit.

On gauzy evenings you dine amid the splendor of fine crystal, piano strains, and peonies. And on cold winter nights it's a roaring fire, fine brandy, and quiet talk.

Yes, life with Mr. Libra can be more than lovely. But only if you hold your breath and smile a lot. To say the least, he is terrified of your temper, and those stormy scenes startle his soul right out of his body. To maintain peace at all costs is his pastime. Never before have you considered it yours. Suddenly, there may be a lot you have to reconsider. Mr. Libra does not at all like to suffer, and in the heat of your temper can easily disappear as quickly as he came in.

If you behave, and he is the mature type, this could be a lasting union. However, the more youthful Libran is often a slave to his sense of beauty, and incapable of any monogamous commitment. It is true that he feels most fulfilled with a partner, but in a lifetime he is capable of having even more than many.

Here jealousy is your obvious nemesis, and agonizing insecurity falls on its footsteps. You feel like you're a contestant in the Miss America contest and wonder if you'll make the finals or be coldly eliminated as "Miss

Talent." This kind of competition was never your forte, and this kind of man is never worth the waiting. Go home and think it over. Do you want it to be excitement through sharing, or are you willing to settle for a bathing-suit contest? Remember that your choice is nothing more than what you'll get.

Leo Woman with Scorpio Man

If your ascendant, the moon, or Venus is in water, and even better, in Scorpio, this combination spells sexual Sturm und Drang. Here, my dear, is the drama that you dreamed of, but the question is, how long can you stand it?

This vibration is passion personified. Exciting, yes. But as the emotions condense into steam heat, just stand back and watch your sanity go up in smoke.

If there are no water signs prominent in your chart, this encounter will start off like a lusty Italian movie and terminate like a French film where nothing really happens and even the characters are so bored that they walk away.

He is an enigma, even to himself. But if you have Scorpio strong in your chart, emotionally you'll understand him, because you'll be starting from the same place —total obscurity. The key to this man is that he talks in code: "I like your ambition; there's a great project I think we could collaborate on." Meaning: "I know you don't want to waste any time either, so let's roll down the sheets." Code: "I'm really angry!" Meaning: "I'm hurt, but won't realize it until two weeks from next Sunday." Code: "I'm really hurt." Meaning: *"Now* I've got you!" Code: Silence. Meaning: 1. What did she *really* mean by that, and why? 2. In ten seconds, two hands will be wrapped around your throat. 9, 8, 7, 6 . . .

His code is not something he consciously creates every midnight for the next day of communication. Mr. Scorpio is *complex,* and as strange, bizarre, and peculiar as it may be, that's the way his mind works. In college, he probably failed all of his multiple-choice tests because he tried to read three answers to each of the questions, and after a while got so dizzy that he passed out. In his mind, nothing is simple: black is a darker shade of gray; a murderer is a saint who forgot his good intentions; a schizophrenic is a psychiatrist who asserts his insanity.

Comedies make him want to cry. Melodramas make him chuckle, since an awareness of the absurd saturates his soul. At his most entertaining, he has a trenchant sense of humor that causes you to smile unexpectedly as you shudder. At his most boring, he ventures nothing, stares at a point beyond your head, and retreats within the conversational framework of yes or no. Alas, you have caught him in a murky little mood. Although he still doesn't know it, it will pass. And perhaps, at this point, so should you.

Mr. Scorpio is not an easy one to love. Since he communicates in convolutions of thought and feeling, feeling through thought, feeling plus feeling, then thinking plus thinking, because it's easier than feeling, he gets himself hopelessly confused about what is really what.

At your most powerful, you're only playing with a few parts of him—until he decides that he desires *all*. Then watch out for the Old Inscrutable. His sense of power tells him he must be impervious to pain. Since he knows he never is, he has you under constant surveillance with ubiquitous eyes that see around corners.

Mr. Scorpio is wildly jealous, so you can just forget all your little flirtations. But alas! your consuming sense of drama will probably drive him until he's in the wrong direction. Then watch out! This man is a mold of emotional extremes, and aimless anger is not his style. He can go from cold control to violence, and back again in ten seconds. That's when it's over and you're out. It doesn't take him three strikes to see what he can't trust.

Sexually, he is a turn-on, but emotionally he can appear turned off. Old friends swear that he is of the most intense sort, yet he's often so self-absorbed that you'd rather find someone shallow. Chances are, he'll demand your total attention, dominate you with your own frailties, compliment you only on special occasions, and possess you in a kind of steaming sensuality. He is a pro at the game of power, and in this one you have no hope of winning. His rule is control at all costs. You know it well; because it's also yours—but this time you're the slave. You've always fantasized about someone strong enough to fearlessly force you about. Congratulations, you've got him. And now that that's over, you think you'll be going.

Leo Woman with Sagittarius Man

You are like putty in his hands, and he can't help but know it. From your face, the smiles and laughter never stop—even when he's not saying anything.

His is a world where humor frames an underlying philosophy: optimism. You cherish it and want to put him in a golden box for rainy days. The problem is that he must keep moving—and sorrowfully, sometimes the movement is out of your life.

He is the traveler of the zodiac, an adventurer ad infinitum, and his terrain usually transcends your control. But for once, you choose not to make this a problem. In his presence, you are delighted past your wildest probabilities. *This* is excitement, so a little sacrifice of the ego needs can easily slip past your control tower.

He is so good-natured that you accuse him of being from another planet. You are so glamorous that at first he thinks you're a gift from the gods. From there—if you can make it camping in hurricane country in the middle of a midsummer rush of rattlesnakes—you're on the way. At that point, when the brute forces of nature intercede and make marshmallow of your granite will, you're more than glad that one of you can still summon a sense of humor. And any deaf, dumb, and blind intruder could swear it isn't you.

You've always wanted to rub twigs together in forty degrees of wind, rain, and sleet, wearing clothes fit for ninety degrees in the shade. And as you grind your teeth in time with the saturated sticks, you wonder aloud if even ballooning in New Jersey over a field of burning matches might not be better. Then, just as you're reinstated in your cherished creature comforts, having wrenched all of the pine cones out of your hair and having found a makeup to mask the mosquito bites on your nose, it's ever onward to shoot the rapids. And on the way, a little skydiving to send the blood back to the brain.

On and on—but that's not the worst. Mr. Sagittarius is a flighty individual who blanches and balks at the sheer idea of even suggested restrictions. It's freedom that encompasses the most fortunate of men, he preaches, before jaunting to a tropical island with an Olympic swimming star who looks more like a Swedish sex goddess.

He told you that he'd be back on Sunday. He arrives three Fridays later—suntanned and smiling. Should you tell him to kiss off because you'd rather clean your apartment?

It all depends on your degree of control. With enough strength and stamina, anyone who's drifted higher than the heights should be able to acclimate to the sendentary side of daily living. Well, most anyone—but not you, Leo. Good luck in the Himalayas.

Leo Woman with Capricorn Man

This man takes everything in life seriously, so if you really want him, tread lightly with your temper. If you smile sweetly and speak softly, he'll walk the dog, take out the garbage, and forget there are other people in the world called women.

His price for such supreme fidelity is *control*. Like Mr. Leo, this man loves telling you what to do at every waking moment. He was the original model for male chauvinism, and since the term was originally coined, his ideas haven't changed very much.

Due to his Saturn influence, he tends to be rigid, cautious, and occasionally cold. Actually, it's all a front for a pervasive sense of insecurity. And the more you bring this out through emotional manipulation, the less likely he'll be to stick around.

You'll admire his ambition, drive, and tenacity. His goals are highly focused and his target is power. The more he has, the more you want *him*.

Together you share an appreciation for the very best. He can be a snob, a materialist, and an idolater of objects. But unlike you, who basically view your trinkets as your toys, he views his objects as a measure of self-worth. You can't really blame him, since he's probably killed himself to get them, and they represent a tenacious drive past the most unendurable limits.

His pace will never be as fast as you would like it, but his durability outdoes all. He is strong, sincere, honest, and loving. If you're smart, you'll shut your mouth, exert your warming influence, and you might even get him to support the vagaries of militant women.

Leo Woman with Aquarius Man

He is the detached humanitarian, and you are the emotional narcissist. His desire is to be friends with the world; your desire is to make sure that "the world" doesn't include women.

At parties, he thoughtfully observes, while you slink about to see *what* he's observing. You just may find that you're pouring your drink over someone's sleeve when his bright-eyed curiosity brings him over to the stunning blond towering over the celery tray. With one (you pray) unobtrusive giant step forward, you move in to smilingly distract his attention to an atrocious wall hanging that a century ago should have been recycled. "Isn't that unusual!" you gasp, pointing your empty wineglass.

"No," he cheerfully replies, "but did you notice that man in the corner with the balloon tie? Isn't it interesting that he's wearing two different-colored socks?"

Aquarius is a people-watcher, while Leo is a sign used to being watched. You cannot understand why he cannot be content watching you. But according to him, the blond's stellar attraction was only a split earlobe.

"This man is crazy!" you mumble as you turn your back to think out your next plan of operation. But as you decide to calm down and forgive him, turning around, you notice him talking to a gorgeous brunette. As you toss on your coat, twist your lower lip, and crisply inform him that you're leaving, he looks at you wide-eyed. She was only some electrical engineer with whom he was arguing about the polar state of the universe, he exclaims. But have you noticed that peculiar man gazing peacefully at the petunias in the corner? Did you observe that his spectacle frames frame only the air? With this revelation, he smugly smiles at you as you're sweating in your silver fox. Your makeup is beginning to smear, and you're finding nothing amusing. As you've already forgotten the bizarre man in the corner, you assume he is referring to your makeup, which is now moving down over your upper lip.

Swiftly you move for the door. But as you reach the sidewalk, your heart sinks toward the pavement. He didn't even run after you to beg you to return, you sputter to yourself. He must think you're grotesque, and he's glad that you're gone. But even worse, you can't even cry, since you're not wearing tearproof mascara.

At the party, Mr. Aquarius sinks slowly into the nearest sofa. "She certainly is a strange one," he mumbles.

And when he thinks enough about it, he decides you might even be the weirdest one there! Tomorrow, he'll have to remember to invite you to that lecture on the state of altered consciousness after the end of the world. Strange—before, he always preferred to go to his favorite things alone. This *must* be love! How very peculiar. Somehow, he had an inkling this might happen when he found himself focusing on your fire-engine-red fingernails. It might even be marriage. He chuckles as he realizes that while your fingernails enthralled him, he can't even recall the color of your eyes.

In women, Mr. Aquarius is not bedazzled by beauty. His ideal is a three-ring circus, and so far, you've come the closest. However, the salient question arises: will he have the energy to be a lion tamer?

Leo Woman with Pisces Man

He falls in love fast and sends you skyward with the verbal splendors of the midnight movie. Unfortunately, it's usually a double feature, beginning with something like *Love Story* and ending with *Gone with the Wind*.

The younger you are, the better this duo, since you'll find that all Pisces men seem to use the same emotional orchestration. If you've known a few in your lifetime, you'll be wary, impatient, and tell him that you have time for only one side of the record.

At sixty, Mr. Pisces still seeks a romance more fabulous than his fantasies. Needless to say, he rarely finds it, and the sad part is that he never stops looking.

Last week, to attest his love, he vowed his life away. This week, you catch him clandestinely kissing Miss Colorado. You might tell yourself he was just giving her an award, and then dare yourself to believe it, but more likely you'll settle into a state of anger and silent sorrow. Then, swiftly, the mood music changes from "La Vie en Rose" to *Rhapsody in Blue*.

Unlike your tenacious sister Ms. Taurus, one scene with a deceitful man and you're out the door, your lover wishing he was dead, if he isn't already. With Mr. Pisces, you might as well keep all exits open.

Although Mr. Pisces means well, he is held back by an underdeveloped superego. In his fantasy world of gilded ideals, guilt has no place. Although he is capable of being honest with you, *self*-truthfulness tends to tarnish his reflection. He embraces an infantile ideal of romance and dwells in the memories of his most divine love. He is addicted to your larger-than-life luster. The problem is that he can't tell the difference between love and addiction. The burden is on you, the blame on him. So if you choose to get involved in his game of emotional monopoly, just make sure that you're the banker.

Leo Man with Aries Woman

If you get in her way, she'll stand on your feet and ask what you're doing there. You've always had a yen for an aggressive woman, and this one is a dynamo. Her energy level exceeds that of a tribe of angry aborigines. At times you have to jog just to keep up with her.

She loves a challenge, so inflame her with your flirtations. After she decides she wants you, she'll take over and move in so fast that you'll feel passive by comparison. This woman is direct, and strides the shortest distance between two points. There are moments your sense of dignity might dissolve due to her candor, yet at the same time you'll be pleased that she doesn't take up your time with trivia.

She is headstrong, independent, achievement-oriented, and dedicated to doing what she pleases. Don't restrain her, and *her* achievements will exalt *you*. Since her anger is like a blowtorch, be your supportive self rather than a bully, and *don't criticize*. Deep in her heart she knows that she was born for the best, and she won't listen for a second when you berate her for her boastfulness. She's living her life to enable the world to have the same understanding, so if you hint that she's not perfect, she'll simply ignore you.

Her *joie de vivre* will rejuvenate you better than ginseng, while her passion will ignite your senses. Together you are the principle of passion personified, and when you sit side-by-side, the world seems to shrink away. When your egos are controlled, this relationship is magical. But when they collide, your fights would make the sphinx blink. Be less ego-oriented, and Ms. Aries is yours, along with a treasure of excitement.

Leo Man with Taurus Woman

Ms. Taurus is most security-oriented—both materially and emotionally. So buy her daffodils, bring her to a French restaurant, and over the peach melba, croon "It Had to Be You." Suddenly, she's yours, and may even forget to eat the ice cream. Join a health club immediately, since she's already started to plan her menus.

This woman loves to nurture and to be nurtured. Even her plants have come to think of her as Mother. The domestic duties that depress you seem to delight her. However, before you decide to sit back and wonder when dinner will be ready, you might keep in mind a handy little fact: nothing in this world is free, and this girl also has a price. It's called marriage, and it's a highly motivating factor. Her life means nothing to her without it, but that's not *necessarily* how you feel about yours. If your need to wander exceeds your need for approval, Ms. Taurus may make you feel that you have as much freedom as her coffee grinder. Even if she became the first woman president to lead the first exploration of Mars, she would feel a sense of failure if she were not also a wife and mother.

However, if you are at the point where your jaded soul has seen it *all* already, she may just be the woman. Sexually, she's a sensuous animal, but can exhaust your senses if you've been working nights to prepare for the position of chairman of the board.

If you're up for the midnight marathons, the seven-course dinners, a loyal, devoted wife, mother, and executive housekeeper, you're on! But two words of warning: watch your temper *and* your flirtations. Next to Scorpio, this woman is the most jealous and possessive of the signs, and when you get her angry, for whatever reason, a grudge is born that will never quite be buried. Her silences can make you think you're living in a Trappist monastery. But at this point, don't try to argue, just kiss her, since nothing will make her change her mind. But what's more important—winning a point or winning her love?

Leo Man with Gemini Woman

It's a challenge just trying to get her on the telephone; no doubt she has two. After you've torn *yours* out of the wall because you can't stand the incessant busy signal on *hers,* and you charge out and up to her door, what you'll undoubtedly see are two angry men who are coming out (and who don't seem at all to be together). Yes, Ms. Gemini is a busy soul . . . and friendly. *Too* friendly!

She'll run your ego through the wringer and be very amiable while she's doing it. You'll never know where she's coming from or where she's going, but don't let that make you feel inferior. Neither does she. To say she's fickle is an understatement. While you want to grab her by the throat to get her total attention, you're also laughing because she's constantly entertaining.

If you have the energy to stay up all night to map out your games for the next day, you've got her—for a little while. Actually, she's got you, because you've never worked so hard for anything. Not even your Ph.D.

She loves novelty, so create your own carnival. She loathes commitment, so be debonair and casual. Call her at the last minute, and make her laugh. She may even disconnect her other phone. Knock her dead with clever ideas, projects, and peculiar little pastimes. Then, wait till she's stopped flirting with your best friend before you command her to become your life partner. She'll probably say yes and tell you that she thought you'd never get around to it. You might want to retort that it was because she always had more men around her than somebody protected by the Secret Service, but don't. Just give her your Leo smile and say that it took that long to count all her personalities. Then *she'll* smile, because she knows you're not quite prepared for a lifetime of new ones.

Leo Man with Cancer Woman

It might seem that she wants your plasma in a silver pitcher. She does. When it comes to affairs of the heart, this woman is the superconsumer. She craves your total love, attention, affection, fantasies, thoughts, dreams. In other words, she wants it *all,* and there won't be leftovers.

When she doesn't get her way, this woman is weepy. At first, this is effective, but after a few of the same performances, her repertoire begins to bore you, and at this point you begin to cool off.

Her dependence will flatter you, but her demands

will make you feel claustrophobic. On your first date, she'll inquire where she stands in your future. If you are sufficiently vague to get to the second date, she'll ask you if you prefer the wedding in June or December.

Ms. Cancer revels in romanticism. One of her frequent sexual fantasies is hearing the words "I love you." However, her very favorite is "Marry me!" If you do, you'll find you have a very loyal and devoted wife. Bring her daisies and kiss her a lot, and you'll find a woman who will create a kingdom around you.

Your blind spot is her emotions. You'll never understand why she's brooding and sulking, and sulking and brooding. Just because you forgot her anniversary and then flirted with that blond at the party . . . You really can't grasp the emotional connection, and besides, you just bought her a new refrigerator last week. What more does she want—she should just take another look at the freezer. Ice cubes in three seconds!

At moments she'll be your mother; at other times, your little girl. It's very hard for her to be just your lover, because she never feels that much at ease with her emotions. She is so insecure that she often role-plays to cut off being so vulnerable. Her deep-seated emotions have you mystified. Her words occasionally lose you. But her fears escape you altogether.

When she's secure, she's warm, lovable, sympathetic, and supportive. When she's insecure, she's cold and withdrawn, but in a way that's always verging on tears. She'll be your mother if you treat her like a child. The challenge is treating her like a woman and letting her believe she is one. But that takes a very selfless kind of loving. No comment on whether you can do it.

Leo Man with Virgo Woman

Her idea of fun is to clean the refrigerator. Yours is to eat what's in it. She needs an extra room for her vitamins, aspirin, and nasal spray. You need a nutrition course just to understand the pills she's taking. She abhors dust, dirt, grime, and greasy pots. Because you're not particularly fond of it all either, you're grateful that you've found someone who will finally do something about it.

When courting her, bring her carrot juice, and from there you're really in. She'll worry about your blood sugar, reunite your mateless socks, and reorder your tax receipts, so for the first time in your life you might find them before April 1.

Graciously she bestows more services than the Red Cross. But when it comes to flattery, her time is limited. She is too busy working overtime to please her boss and spending weekends sorting out the bills you didn't know you had.

She is ruled by her head, while you are at the mercy of your heart. While this combination can be complementary, it can also produce a kind of circular trap. She likes to take care, while you like to be taken care of. She needs someone to need her, while you need someone who wants to be needed.

She'll sew on the missing buttons in the closet full of clothes you've snubbed for months due to their buttonless condition. In gratitude at seeing your old friends back, you go out and buy her a sewing machine. When the check bounces, she calls the bank and covers it with her own money, which she had stashed away for a little treasure like a vacuum cleaner. (The last one self-destructed when it swallowed the dog.)

When she has an anxiety attack about whether she shut off her electric typewriter, you're most supportive and reassuring; and when she gets an upset stomach after finding her cat won't eat her chopped liver, you gallantly dash to the drugstore. But should you, on arriving, forget what you came for and return with a full-length mirror, she'll just smile through her tears.

Despite the fact that she nags you about taking desiccated liver, this woman could very well be close to your ideal. She will mother you, nurse you, and serve you like a cleaning lady who's also studying accounting at night school. And because she's so nervous, anxious, and driven, she'll always be fashiohably thin through bouts of stomach trouble from thinking too much.

She'll be forever supportive, dutiful, and faithful. She finds affairs much too anxiety-producing, so don't worry if you catch her in an animated conversation in a dimly lit corner with a devastatingly handsome man. Undoubtedly he's a doctor, and she's discussing her protein metabolism level.

The only thing to be concerned about is whether all

her "health" concoctions will one day kill you. But if you feel that insecure, just break her blender, and when you do it, don't forget to smile.

Leo Man with Libra Woman

She wants a companion; you want a face that belongs on a couturier's runway. If she has either Libra or Venus on the ascendant, nice going—for *you*. You'll get the beauty of which you can boast. She'll get enough baubles to keep her mouth shut and make her think she's getting a lover.

She's always wanted a caretaker, and you've always wanted the power you feel from taking care. She is submissive, smiles a lot, and settles for whatever makes you happy. And since it's exactly this kind of behavior that makes you happy, she could be the woman of your dreams —if only you were stimulated by her temperament.

But since you can't have everything, and you know you've got to grab what you need, you'll marry her at twenty, and at forty you'll daydream a lot. She'll still be smiling—and wearing so much jewelry she won't be able to walk. All the better, since you see her as your possession, which means she had just better hang out close to "home," or else your temper will make her break out in hives.

She is so terrified of your anger that she watches your eyes for the early signals. Although these episodes have given her a trauma, they also keep her in good physical shape, since she does a lot of room to room running.

This woman is truly invaluable to you, since she has never learned she can make demands. She tenderly negotiates and usually settles for what she had before she began negotiating. Therefore, if someone would meet her at forty and ask her if she's happy, she'll stare back blankly and murmur that you work a lot. You do. She's not getting any younger, and you've got to keep her in plastic surgeons.

Beyond a doubt, this is the most pleasant woman with whom you could spend a lifetime. She does what she's told, enhances your self-image, and considers it a treat when she gets to share your time. The only bad part is that she bores you past the point of death. But then, life and death are so relative and philosophic. What really matters are the basics—constant compliments. And with her, they keep coming. So carry a cassette and fantasize about the rest of your needs.

Leo Man with Scorpio Woman

You wonder if she's speaking a foreign language that sounds like English. As long as she opens her mouth, you're always foolish enough to think you actually have a chance at understanding her. But when she closes it and stares at your lower lip, forget it! All hope is lost, and so is a fleeting sense of your sanity.

In her most lucid moments, this woman is an enigma, but if you're trained in palmistry, face reading, and phrenology (interpreting the bumps on her head), you might have a higher success ratio, provided you're not already too emotionally exhausted to notice. Ms. Scorpio does not verbalize; instead, she expects you to read her eyebrows (through the sunglasses). She is intense, intuitive, and intelligent in ways you never dreamed of. She is aloof, while you overwhelm people with your very presence. She lives in the realm of the internal, while you involve yourself hogging center stage. She is secretive, while you give your loyal listeners auditory hernias.

Needless to say, the attraction here is not compelling. And in terms of rapport, it would be easier to just mumble to your pet iguana. Ask her what's on her mind, and after a ten-minute pause, in which you wonder if she's gone into a trance, she'll reply, "Nothing." And that, of course, means everything.

Don't even think about it. This is one game where you never even get up at bat (or notice that there is one), because you're so dizzy wandering around the outfield.

At first your pulse raced at this woman of mystery, but after you realized that you didn't even know the plot, the drama got a little confused. When you try to intimidate her, she just drifts away. When you try to make her laugh, she looks at you, puzzled. After you "seduce" her, you realize that it's you who's been seduced. And when you try to make her jealous, she devastates you with a look that makes you run for the center of any crowd, wondering nervously if she's carrying a concealed weapon.

There is no doubt about it; this woman has a lot of power. With both eyes closed, she can see right into your soul, but with both your eyes open, and Superman's X-ray vision, her mind still remains a mystery. If you're so bored that you're lusting after the ultimate challenge, you've got it here. But if it's only mystery you're really after, do yourself a favor and settle for Alfred Hitchcock. In the long run, it's a lot safer.

Leo Man with Sagittarius Woman

You'll meet her in an airport, where she seems to be going in both directions. She's coming from South America, and she's headed for Egypt, a little boat trip down the Nile, and then a night flight to the Azores. Ms. Sagittarius spends more time in the air than a pilot for Pan Am.

To hold her attention you might have to become a travel agent, a traveling tycoon, or a multimillionaire with a fleet of private planes. You'll need them all just to keep up with her.

This woman loves the lure of adventure far more than romance. Take her on an African safari and watch her play with the boa constrictors. Take her to a desert island, and she'll swim with the sharks. She is a terror to take traveling, because you never know if it's the last time you'll ever see her. Undeniably, she gives you all the excitement you can stand—and you can stand a lot.

This woman is an athlete par excellence, and at times her physical prowess can overwhelm you. She'll beat you at tennis, badminton, and bicycling. On the ski slopes, she'll race past you; in the water, she'll swim circles around you; and at the end of a twenty-mile hiking trail, she'll wonder why you're tired. One thing you realize is that if you're wise, you don't try to outdo her or else you might wind up with a case of terminal exhaustion.

You'll find her conversation witty, her behavior flighty, and her mind strangely philosophical. She faces each day with a smile and a basic credo that everything is ultimately for the best. Her laughter uplifts you, while her ideas inspire you. Suddenly you find yourself fasting, reading Ram Dass, and attending weekend Yoga retreats.

Like never before, you feel fantastic and full of love. Ms. Sagittarius has a primitive power called vitality. It's guaranteed to capture your soul and to seduce your sensibilities. Go with it all, and you'll never be the same. That's because you'll never want to be.

Leo Man with Capricorn Woman

You'll meet her at a tennis club. She won't be playing, she'll be standing, but her outfit will be more smashing than your backhand. During ski season, check the sun decks. She'll have cultivated her tan, but don't even ask to see her stem christie; for all she knows, it's a piece of pastry.

To all appearances, this girl has class. If she didn't originally have it, she's paid a lot to get it, and what she's seeking is a reward—the bigger, the better.

She's guaranteed to love you the minute she sees you put down that hundred-dollar bill. And to keep her eyelashes aflutter, you'll keep producing more, even if you have to politely excuse yourself to do a little counterfeiting.

Together you could make an awesome twosome. At a party, the two of you look as if you were hired for appearance's sake. Between your smile and her jewels, you could light up the room.

This girl always looks good, so never worry that you'll catch her with acne. With divine discretion, she'll sneak off to have her face peeled. But when she returns, she'll spare you the sordid details and just murmur about a quiet sojourn with Mother.

You can charm her quite easily, but if you want to keep her, cut out the casual flirtations. Since this girl seeks control, in her mind nothing is casual. So when she cuts you cold, she's just being cautious. Your narcissism has made her very nervous, so if you don't want to be abandoned, you'd better behave.

She is serious, supportive, faithful, and trusting. In addition, she is usually successful. Her credentials will exalt you, and her concern will overwhelm you. Give her enough Leo love, and she'll forget she ever wanted a sable.

Leo Man with Aquarius Woman

Marry her, and you'll have your private social worker, psychotherapist, and recreational director. But that's only if you ever get the chance to see her.

Chances are, she knows more people than a politician—and they all occupy a special place in her heart. When it comes to people, she has an inexhaustible attention span and a penchant for helping lost souls. The phone probably rings till dawn and the doorbell till at least twelve-thirty. At ten o'clock you find her lavishing warmth on the lovelorn, while at two A.M. she deserts you to aid a "friend" just jailed for inciting a protest riot in a geriatric clinic. Sometimes you feel that you're sleeping in a social-welfare unit. At such moments, you yell, frown, grumble a lot, and sometimes kick the sofa. On her way out the door, she'll inquire if you're not feeling well, and you've got sixty seconds to answer before you hear it slam.

Her mind is so far-out that you stop going to the movies. What you would call a human zoo, she refers to as the basis of utopia. Her thoughts are in the future, while your heart is in the present, but with patience you can combine them into one loving and totally madcap time span. However, if you insist on using force, you'll only drive her away.

Despite her universal friendliness, this woman is frightened of emotional intimacy. She is at once loving and kind, freedom-loving, and impersonal. Don't try to figure her out, just love her. Through your love and encouragement, she will gain a sense of self, and through her infinite patience and understanding, your feelings may unfold into universal love.

Unlike many of your habitual heartthrobs, this woman generally doesn't bother with the superficials. She has little or no interest in her appearance and usually coordinates her clothes as though she has been awakened by a fire. She is different, but so genuine that even you can occasionally overlook the fact that she's wearing an embroidered work shirt to a dress-up dinner party, with a yellow button on the collar that says "Higher Wages for Banana Pickers!"

Leo Man with Pisces Woman

She'll mope around a lot, which can get pretty boring, but what she does in bed is something else altogether. This woman is the supersensualist. She talks through her body, and what she has to say has your undivided attention. Naturally, you'll like to have her around, but because you're the restless sort, it's a question of how long.

For a while you feed each other on dreams, and the air will reek of romance. In this relationship, neither of you cherishes the light of day. It's candlelight and *love*—all the way to the wedding. But after that point it can be loneliness if you start emerging from the emotional fog unprepared.

In the long run, she is too passive for your patience level, and you are too self-centered for her sensitivities. She'll smother you with love, but she won't stimulate you, and you'll clutter up her life with trinkets to make her momentarily forget her hurt feelings. She'll mope about and lose her sparkle. You'll become abrupt and increasingly busy. She'll take a lover, and you'll spend evenings at the office. One day you might collide in the kitchen, and each of you will see a stranger and not know how they got there. Neither will ask, but both will wonder—all the way to the divorce court.

Keep in mind that this woman is capable of very deep feeling. If you ignore her, she will wither, but if you expect her to confront you, you'll spend a lifetime waiting. She'll never challenge you with strength of will or stimulate you with a dynamic independence. She'll lean on you if she loves you, and cry rather than command. Her sensitivity will be your shackle unless you alleviate her insecurity, and this must come from tenderness, not trinkets.

Ms. Pisces represents one of the few signs that can let the feelings flow. And while she may not be outwardly indestructible, she has strength through vulnerability. You acknowledge strength only in a "stiff upper lip," so until you open your head and your heart and learn how to tie them together, this woman is better off bypassed.

VIRGO

Dates: August 24—September 23
Ruling planet: Mercury
Element: Earth
Mode: Mutable
Quality: Feminine, negative
Planetary principle: Purity
Primal desire: Crystallization
Color: Brown
Jewels: Jasper, cobblestone, emerald
Plants: Sandalwood, grains, apple tree
Day: Wednesday
Archangel: Raphael
Magical number: 7
Material factor: Service

VIRGOS OF
FAME AND FORTUNE

Aubrey Beardsley	Peter Falk
Peter Sellers	Agnes De Mille
Lauren Bacall	Samuel Johnson
Grandma Moses	Ingrid Bergman
Sophia Loren	Greta Garbo
J. P. Morgan	H. L. Mencken
Ken Kesey	Elia Kazan
H. G. Wells	Leonard Bernstein

Goethe

THE VIRGO FEMALE

Favorable

Without realizing it, at times you can be an intimidating lady. What appears to be your cool self-possession can often be off-putting to someone who is insecure. However, the fact is that you are friendly, somewhat shy, and very diffident. You're not the type to bare your soul by the water cooler. Your basic attitude is that there is a time and a place for everything. Therefore, indiscriminate chatter with someone you barely know is not only considered foolish but also time-consuming.

Basically, you're an old-fashioned person who believes in moral principles and privacy. You loathe public displays of affection, people who talk while they're eating, and people who never know when to shut up. You are prudent, intelligent, cautious, analytical, and very understanding. Simultaneously, you're as strong as a pioneer woman and as fragile as a Southern belle.

Your mind is so organized that you could probably run a multimillion-dollar corporation from behind the scenes. However, your emotions are so vulnerable that at times you feel like a teenager with that first blight of killer acne. Given half a chance, you're capable of finding fault with every aspect of yourself, and to come out wishing you could trade identities with any random passerby on the street.

Your feelings are very delicate, and so are your emotional demands. You're probably the last person to give an ultimatum, and the first to try to accept something even if you can't understand it.

In terms of love, you're really more cautious than critical. You can't stand a man who comes on to you too aggressively. At the same time, that smooth fellow with the shining teeth tends to bring out your latent feelings of inferiority. Basically, you prefer the down-to-earth type who reminds you of your former physics professor. A swift mind, a considerate soul, and an undefinable aura of competence make you melt. The candlelight really isn't necessary.

Many astrology books give you the reputation of being a frigid woman, but this is far from the truth.

You're a highly sensual being who is merely discriminate. Although a man's mind may be the first thing to turn you on, you'd never go so far as to say that it's the sexiest part of him. You have a distinct earthiness all your own, and no man who really knows you can deny it.

However, romance is only one of the many things that exhilarate you. Other excitements are a tennis court at dawn, a tricky ski slope, a sun-drenched sailboat whipping its way to sea, and, of course, riding like the wind on the sleekest horse across the lushest pasture.

When you are feeling doubtful, miserable, mentally anxious, or insecure, immersing yourself in nature seems to have a protective, purifying effect. Since you're not the type to cry on people's shoulders and dirty their handkerchiefs, you have to let your anguish out somehow, and physical activities are often the most inconspicuous release.

Although you'd probably be the last person to realize it, you are viewed with the highest respect by your acquaintances and with love and admiration by your friends. You're one woman who has her life so much under control that at times you take it all for granted. What other people consider gargantuan tasks, you attack perfunctorily with calm and composure. And when everything is accomplished, you have the most amazing way of looking around for more to do.

You are very real, kind, warm, and deeply caring. You have a quiet, tasteful way of inspiring the greatest efforts in other people, and a loyalty that invincibly brings out the better part of their nature. One walks away from you with the fervent hope that you will always stay as good as you are.

Unfavorable

If someone offered you a million dollars, you'd sit down and worry about what you'd do after you'd spent it. You take life as spontaneously as a heart surgeon who is married to his schedule and his scalpel.

You are a creature of habit who has about as much creativity as a rat in a maze. Your imagination is almost nonexistent and your mind invincibly narrow.

You have the kind of bureaucratic intellect that wears a person down as it wears him out. Your thought process operates on preconceived facts and narrow opinions that seldom have anything to do with insight. Your mind is biased and mechanical, your attitudes computer-like. Needless to say, your personality is as off-putting as your prim self-righteousness.

Passing time in your company is an exercise in tedium. You're a garrulous worrywart who nervously looks for the worst to complain over. You are compulsive, talk too much, eat too much, think too much, and sadly never come to any happy conclusions. Your rigid thinking and restrictive opinions (usually about something of which you know nothing) depress you so much that you compensate by bursts of self-indulgence.

In general, your idea of conversation is someone who listens to your endless monologues. However, outside your living room, you deal with life in a far different manner. Your boss probably makes you stay late to clean his typewriter and even on sick days you humbly apologize for staying in bed. You've spent eight years of your life working overtime, even on Fridays, and you still haven't gotten a raise or thought of looking for another job. This is because basically you don't want your boss to think you're unloyal.

You care what other people think of you far more than what you think of yourself, and spend your life striving to coordinate your actions with public opinion. You spend so much of your life taking cues that you could be a great actress if you weren't so panicky at the thought of a little attention. In general, you are totally intimidated by any person you respect. Feelings of worthlessness overwhelm you and in turn you put the person on a dehumanizing pedestal that leaves no room for imperfections.

In general, your world is black and white, with no space for gray in between. As you drag yourself down with such a shallow outlook you even try to impose it on other people who already understand that there are more important things in life than killing yourself trying to be perfect.

When you get in a rut, no resistance short of death will make you stray from your course. However, the cruelest thing about your judgment is that you never feel an impetus to investigate the other side. You are frightened of change, your own life, the opposite sex and your power as a woman.

Since you strictly adhere to a framework of good

and bad and usually find life to contain more bad things than good, you have everything worked out to the point that you no longer have to think. All you have to do is worry, and all your fears come to you. At this point you savagely discard what looks like freedom, and cling to what ties you down. You're like a drowning body clinging to a sinking boat when all the time you could swim to shore if you'd just pick up your head and look toward the horizon.

THE VIRGO MALE

Favorable

Undoubtedly your first toy was a file cabinet and your second a typewriter. Even at the age of six you had no idea what children meant when they talked about playing. You spent your time practicing your violin, thinking up the plot for your first novel, and learning the alphabet for a second language.

Today you are an even more industrious individual. You probably get up at dawn to begin work, and finish the far side of midnight. Now you hear people mumble about recreation, and you figure that it must be an enjoyable kind of work.

Work is your source of excitement, even when you're so exhausted that you start walking into walls. However, even more exhilarating than work is the feeling of accomplishment you get from doing it. You have a highly disciplined mind that seldom conceives of a task as too great. The more difficult a job, the more you will see it as a challenge, and become consumed with the idea of mastering it.

Only rarely do you give your body a rest. When you're not working, you can be found batting around tennis balls, and when you're not batting around tennis balls, you can be caught thinking about some new kind of work. There's no doubt about it, you're a busy man who makes the most of both his time and his life.

You're so organized that not one moment is ever wasted. You hate waste and consider efficiency the closest thing to godliness. You have more systems for getting through your daily tasks than the Federal Reserve has money. And each day you cheerfully plod on to greatness, going one slow, careful step at a time.

Unlike the Aries who loudly revs up and zooms in with one ferocious burst of energy, only to abandon a task when it starts to become something of a bore, you calmly keep going like a roll of tapes from Muzak. Neither lightning, nor thunder, nor earthquake, nor tidal wave will deter you from finishing your last piece of work for the day.

The most exciting moment of your life, next to falling in love, was the day that your lateral file cabinets were delivered. Naturally, they went in the bedroom, where you could watch them from under your lids when you only pretended to sleep. However, by three A.M. you knew you had to bring in your electric typewriter, and then at four o'clock it was your desk lamp, and at four-thirty your dictionary, followed by your thesaurus, until finally it was seven o'clock and time for you to get up and go to work—with circles under your eyes.

However, there is really more to your life than non-stop work. There is also love, and that is quite important. In general, you want to get married so that you no longer have to take the time away from your work to worry about your love life. Obviously, the most efficient way is just to have it waiting at home.

Although you do tend to be a perfectionist, you are also kind, noble, and beneficent. For instance, you would marry a woman who had several annoying habits if she were also a good soul who respected your systems. Marrying you, she would be getting a first-rate self-improvement course without the expense of registration. If she doesn't mind your telling her how to comb her hair and how to clean the kitchen counters, then in the long run she may benefit far more than she would believe at first sight. You're loyal, honest, caring, and consumed with the idea of being a good husband. Even if you run to the bathroom to brush your teeth before you kiss her, this is only an example of your consideration. After all, there are worse things in life than a germicidal mouth to blow kisses to.

Unfavorable

You are as relentless as a plowhorse who has only just begun his day of work. Your attitude toward the world is totally idiosyncratic. You make a vociferous fuss about how much you help other people, but the fact is that you could give lessons on how to be self-serving. You're the most deadly kind of chauvinist, for you disregard what you don't believe, and you believe in only what you want to.

You are small-minded, totally subjective, and destructively critical. However, what you tear down, interestingly enough, is never a work of your own. To justify your effete yet laborious life-style, you need all the compliments you can get, and if they're not forthcoming, you'll sit down and simply supply them yourself.

Because you are petty, argumentative, and at the same time rapacious for approval, you're as irritating as a persistent fly that keeps cleverly eluding his eventual demise. Your mind is cunning and manipulative, and you are so determined to be well thought of that you try to make everyone else look wretched by comparison. Unfortunately, like all people who take themselves much too seriously, often your efforts boomerang and you come out looking like a defenseless fool lost in his own confusion.

You have an extremely swift tongue and a sharp mind that you waste on sarcastic comments and meaningless chatter. You embrace an attitude of superiority as tenaciously as an infant its baby bottle. When you speak, your listeners should feel grateful to get your criticism about what is wrong with them and why.

You're a person who always has an eye for improvement—except when it comes to your own conduct. Then you retreat behind your pious attitude as either the dispenser of justice, or the victim who never had the benefit of knowing it. You put such a great deal of energy into blaming others for your own failures that it's a shame you're never convincing. Because your personality is so unadaptable, altercations are not infrequent. Therefore, you tread a heavy path in life, your resentment rising much more often than it ever seems to settle down.

When it comes to bearing grudges and nursing wounds, you become exhilarated with a kind of demoniacal pleasure. Because your basic value system is that you want as much as you can get without having to give in on any points, you stick to your resentment with remarkable tenacity. In keeping with your basic life code, you feel that if you don't deserve something, you might as well begrudge it to the next person. After all, seething jealousy is an emotion that can motivate you to get a lot accomplished.

When it comes to love, you demand someone who will meet all your requirements. It would truly delight you if the woman were a millionaire who made you look good. However, first she must be willing to submit to your entire control. After all, you know what's best for her far better than she does, since what's best is merely a matter of your own mind. In the long run, extreme selfishness probably works pretty well for you. It may not make you happy, but it does get you what you want, even if you're discontented when you get it.

DECANS

Every sign in the zodiac can be broken down into three subdivisions, called decans. Each decan roughly corresponds to ten degrees—the first third, second third, and last third of the sun sign's time span, which is approximately thirty days.

As each of these periods has different subrulerships, the personality of a person is slightly modified by the specific decan it falls in. For instance, an Aries born in the second decan would be ruled by Mars, but subruled by the sun. Therefore, he would tend to display a greater sense of pride, boastfulness, egotism, and optimism than an Aries born in the third decan, which is subruled by Jupiter. This Aries would tend to be more freedom-loving, flighty, travel-oriented, and interested in subjects of a philosophical nature. An Aries born in the first decan would be the most aggressive, but not necessarily the most productive and accomplished.

Decans are important, since they do account for a more detailed assessment of an individual's personality characteristics. They also show how two people born under the same sun sign can be markedly different.

If you were born between August 24 and September 1, your sun falls in the Mercury decan of Virgo.

On the positive side, you are intelligent, discriminating, logical, pragmatic, and prepared to do more than your share when it comes to a work situation. You are disciplined, highly dependable, and extremely trustworthy. Deep in your soul there is a desire to be of service. This finds expression in a personality that is warm, sympathetic, and generous. You have a methodical mind, an inherent sense of order, and a penchant for details. You are most often not only a highly efficient worker but also an indispensable one.

On the negative side, you can be more critical than discriminating, and you have a tendency to tear down without considering the idea of building up. Often you impose perfectionistic standards on people whom you respect, and should they fall short of your expectations, you're not above coldly canceling them out of your life. You nurse slights, bear grudges, and waste time worrying about trivial matters. Your greatest difficulty is losing perspective and seeing a situation only from your own viewpoint. Then you can be exceedingly judgmental, self-righteous, and emotionally restrictive.

A good lesson to learn is patience, dispassion, and sympathetic understanding. The less you live your life through the fear of being victimized by other people, the more you will be alive enough to enjoy it. Otherwise, you may just watch it pass you by, and all you'll have to show for it is that you got a lot of work done.

If you were born between September 2 and 11, your sun falls in the Saturn decan of Virgo.

On the positive side, you have tremendous discipline. Your will is so strong that with a sufficient amount of tenacity you can make all your dreams come true. The most highly evolved natives of this decan dedicate their lives to self-improvement plans and activities, and usually bring themselves a long way in the desired direction.

Other members of this decan have a tendency to work in steamy fits and starts. Several days of total dedication to a project may be followed by an equal amount of time lazing around thinking about all the work that was done.

Sometimes this decan is associated with wealth or material prosperity, often gained through marriage or inheritance. It is highly likely that the family has had some supernormal significance in your life that will probably shadow you to your last days. To overcompensate for negative family influences, you have probably sought a stable and comfortable marriage that would allay many of your insecurities.

In most instances, you are charming, pleasant, and often socially gracious. You make an excellent host or hostess and often get satisfaction from entertaining.

On the negative side, there is often a tendency to be status-conscious, social-climbing, and acquisitive. There is a need to associate with the "right" people, have the "right" material possessions, and be invited to the "right" places.

Virgos of this decan often display a negative, self-indulgent propensity to dwell on what they don't have while they take for granted their advantages. There is also a tendency toward intense dissatisfaction, accompanied by an overconcern with improving everything. Sometimes the personality creates a narrow box that filters everything until it comes out looking smaller.

If you were born between September 12 and 23, your sun falls in the Venus decan of Virgo.

On the positive side, you have a creativity and superficial charm that attract many people to you. This is an especially fine decan for a career in the arts as performer, agent, producer, or director.

Your greatest conflict in life arises from the battle between your mind and your emotions. At times, you would like to think that a satisfying love life doesn't matter as much as personal achievement. However, in the long run, some consuming love usually gets you, and suddenly your mind has a hard time dealing with the matter at hand. Simultaneously, you have a need for both love and emotional control. You'd like to think that your intellect can get you anywhere. However, more and more, there are times when its formidable force crumbles under the weight of your emotions.

You tend to be industrious and to drive yourself hard after a sought-after goal. You are anxious, analytical, and often quite tense because you impose such perfectionistic standards on your own performance.

On the negative side, you can be selfish, self-indulgent, and ruthless. You often place materialistic goals before human considerations. Sometimes you have a tendency to be sloppy, self-serving, lazy, and supersensitive.

The unevolved Virgo of this decan frequently brings himself down along with everyone else around him. Complaints, criticism, pessimism, and self-obsession lead the individual down a long, hard dusty path he chooses to think of as life.

LOVE

When it comes to your love life, you're a critical and fussy perfectionist who could probably even find something wrong with something perfect. However, should someone's mind be scintillating enough to attract your total attention, then you're willing to overlook some minor flaws.

Basically, you want love more than anything else you can think of. However, there are a lot of other things that you don't want along with it. First impressions are crucial, therefore crude, immature behavior or game playing can close your mind to granting a second chance.

Although you can appear cold, aloof, and unduly critical, you are, in fact, shy and supersensitive. "Nothing ventured, nothing gained" would never be your motto, since you are so protective of your self-image that you would rather withdraw altogether than stand the chance of surrendering your self-respect.

A fine mind is the first thing to attract you, and after that, warmth and human consideration rate very high on the list. What you desire most is to feel cherished and needed. In return, you are willing to devote yourself to the welfare of the one you love.

Your love life has a very important place in your daily existence, and when it is lacking, you tend to compensate through overwork. However, there is no denying that although intellectual accomplishments can pick up your spirits like a dry martini, there is nothing like coming home to someone you love to give your life a vibrant luster. You seek expansion through love, and ironically, you find it when you least expect it, since it's one area of your life you can't plan, order, or organize.

MARRIAGE

Unless Uranus is very strongly placed in your horoscope, marriage is a definite expectation. In general, you're a person of serious intentions who finds superficial encounters unsatisfying.

In your mind, marriage is a symbol of the emotional security you seek. And within its framework, you look forward to a profound emotional and intellectual rapport as well as calm and order.

Your ideal partner is a person with an intelligence you respect. Shared interests and a high degree of emotional compatibility are in the long run more important requirements than physical passion. However, there is a very strong likelihood that your heart was once broken by a romance whose sexual chemistry took you by storm, leaving little time for you to think, plan, or prepare for what was happening next.

More than anything else, you hate games and the feeling of being enslaved in a situation. Therefore, in marriage, trust is of utmost importance. Your own behavior is loyal, honest, loving, and often devoted. In turn, you expect, at the very least, both truth and trust from your partner.

Faced with your partner's infidelity, you may experience feelings of bitterness so intense as to haunt you for years afterward. Rejection in any form is a horror to your delicate psyche, which often prolongs emotional pain by obsessing about it. However, should you yourself decide that a relationship is over, you can be remarkably cool and cerebral about the entire matter.

Virgo is a sign that has a fairly high divorce rate, only because natives born in this sign are often too set in their ways to make the necessary adjustments required in marriage. Flexibility is a lesson that must be wisely learned by those who want to make truly successful marriages.

MONEY

You're both cautious and conservative with money and would never be the kind of person who is owned by credit cards. Because you're a record keeper to end all record keepers, you seldom get stranded by a lack of cash flow. Every fifty cents that's gone out can be accounted for and soon replaced by fifty cents coming in.

You're mystified by people who are victimized by their own money and whose checkbooks look like Russian-language primers. Basically, you believe in budgeted, controlled spending and view money as sound security. Vacations are saved for, as are those other little luxuries that someone else might buy on credit in a more impulsive moment.

When success results in your having a great deal of excess cash, you're more likely to sink it into a wise investment than to squander it on a custom-built swimming pool. Unless you have Libra or Leo strongly placed in your horoscope, your need for luxury is less than your need for the stable life-style that money can bring.

Wealth is not your foremost desire in life, but security is. Therefore, your prudence pays off when you can comfortably pay your bills and then make the most of the money left over. One thing you hate to worry about is basics, and money is about as basic as you can get. You structure your life so well that you make your money work for you, no matter how much or how little you have. Consequently, in the long run, you often acquire a good supply of it.

CAREER

You're a workaholic who never knows when to stop. Since perfection is your goal, mere efficiency makes you feel like an underachiever.

You are highly disciplined, organized, and a wizard at the most obscure kind of details. You're the kind of person who walks around with a file system in his head and who thinks of the lunch as an opportunity to catch up on more work.

You have more systems than a computer programmer and take a delight in always creating more. However, sometimes you get so bogged down in details that you don't find the time to collect the credit that you deserve.

Although you're a most reliable worker and spend

sleepless nights worrying about what wasn't done, you're also unfortunately the first to sell yourself short. You're more likely to ask for more work than for a raise, because your shyness overtakes you and you begin to worry that you're simply not worthy. Therefore, you sometimes stand by sadly in silence as others sprint ahead to grab all the glory—their offices filled with half-finished work.

Your logical, systematic mind, combined with a shy unsure personality, often places you in a behind-the-scenes position that could furnish the power behind the throne.

Because you have an eye for detail and a gift for organization, you could be anything from an administrator to an attorney, from an executive secretary to an accountant, from an editor to an engineer. However, due to your perfectionistic proclivities, you could shine as an efficiency expert and get paid to tell people how they can improve.

Since Virgo is the sign of service, such professions as nursing, social work, medicine, and chiropractic can prove to be satisfying choices. However, because this sign is especially associated with small animals, veterinary medicine can also be a most meaningful occupation.

Because Virgos are frequently sympathetic advisers, vocational and psychological counseling are still other areas to be considered. Interestingly enough, Virgo is also an excellent sign for the practice of astrology, since it often combines a studious personality with a penchant for detail.

Whatever you decide on, there is no doubt that you will do it well. You're a selfless worker dedicated to doing the best job possible. Anything less than your best effort makes you so guilty that you hate to get up the next morning.

You don't need the roar of applause and footlights to make you feel like a success. Rather, your practical mind requires a commensurate pay along with a little quiet appreciation.

You're the kind of person who could have more fun building an empire than presiding over it. However, even at such a peak of success, what would matter to you more than prestige would be maximum efficiency heralding a close-to-perfect output.

FRIENDS

Although you prefer only a handful of friends to be close to, you're the kind of person who can be depended on by mere acquaintances in moments of sickness, crisis, self-doubt, and self-indulgence.

You're the person who provides the broom for some disorderly friend to sweep the floor, who gift-wraps a bottle of roach spray for someone who has too many "little friends," and who provides a bottle of aspirin to the chronically hung over.

In general, you're a well-wisher who would go a long way for a good friend. However, you hate to be taken advantage of and sometimes purposely withhold your services if you sense that they are getting to be expected.

When you feel betrayed, used, or simply unappreciated, your resentment seethes away inside like an air mattress punctured by a hat pin. However, because you are basically insecure, you often have a hard time confronting the person who is causing you all the pain.

There is sometimes a tendency to turn yourself into a doormat to please a person you are terribly fond of. At the same time, you have a definite difficulty asking for and taking what should rightfully be yours.

Your friends mean a great deal to you, and you to them, especially in the middle of the night, when anyone else would probably hang up the phone and go back to sleep. However, once you learn to balance your giving with your own needs, you'll be a better friend to yourself, and a lot happier in the long run.

HEALTH

You're a health-food freak who sometimes tends toward hypochondria. You probably swallow vitamins like a child gobbling candy, and supplement them with spinach juice when things start to get really bad. It's likely that you play a lot of tennis, jog, do yoga, belong to a health club, and treat your body as if it were your temple. As far as food goes, you're probably a vegetarian, would rather have some carrot juice spiked with ginseng than a dry martini, and take massive doses of niacin rather than coffee whenever you feel your energy ebbing. In more extreme cases, you take one thousand milligrams of vitamin C every hour, won't walk near anybody holding a cigarette, and stay awake all night worrying about viral infections.

Yes, you care about your health. However, sometimes you care so much that you end up with a case of colitis from worrying. Actually, your nerves are your nemesis, and they exercise their power on your digestive system. You are prone to ailments involving the stomach, intestines, and bowels. Acid indigestion, ulcers, spastic colon, and diarrhea are common outgrowths of an overactive Virgo mind that never seems to settle anything. This is difficult not only because of the physical discomfort but also because, being Virgo, you hate to think that you too have waste products. Undoubtedly, you'd prefer to believe that this happens only to your neighbors.

Allergies and skin disorders are other health problems common to Virgos. Everything from hay feever and asthma to eczema and psoriasis is indicative of the extreme nervous tension often typical of this sign.

Those Virgos who resort to tranquilizers to quell the tension that seems to constrict the entire visceral area, might be well-advised to try instead doses of calcium-magnesium combined with vitamin B complex.

However, the real clue to your body is your mind. Once you overcome your tendency to worry, you may find that physical problems disappear rather quickly. Regular meditation and yoga combined with supervised deep breathing can be assets to your mental and emotional health and will provide the self-detachment and relaxation essential to a happy, healthy life.

HOME

If you're a typical Virgo, you like your home clean, orderly, and well-organized.

In your sleep, you could probably locate your ski socks, last year's receipts for mouthwash, and your appointment calendar for 1972. You have a file system that makes the IRS seem unorganized and a desk whose paper clips appear to be lined up for military combat.

However, if you're the maddened, active type of Virgo, your mind finds order within confines of chaos, and you can dispense with the external organization. Chances are, your living quarters look like a battlefield after a five-year war, and you're unfortunately on the losing side.

In terms of decor, the typical Virgo taste is more often traditional than modern. A few French antiques, a velvet sofa, and perhaps a few priceless Oriental pieces could make an ideal living room to come home to. A fireplace always adds a comforting touch on those quiet, rainy days when you just want to curl up with a book and not be bothered.

Ideally, your studious mind craves the luxury of a spacious turn-of-the-century study. Your desk would be oakwood, your floor-to-ceiling windows French, and your long couch a comfortable brown corduroy. The four walls would, of course, be covered with books interspersed with fine paintings.

In the bedroom, more books are a must, along with a lot of greenery. Hanging plants, trees, fresh flowers, and a geranium by the bedside all help to make your mind more fertile and your general attitude more alive.

In the bathroom, hang some colorful prints to wake you up on those mornings when you have to go to the office early. Put up a brilliant yellow shower curtain and place a tiny vase of dried flowers on a glass shelf above your sink.

Your entire living arrangement is probably a tribute to your ability to plan ahead and make a little luxury go a long way.

COSMIC CHALLENGE

Your cosmic challenge is to rise above the dictates of a selfish ego to serve your fellow man from the heart. You are the sign of service and therefore are meant to reach beyond your mental and emotional restrictions for the attainment of a loving communion with man and the spirit that is called God. When you are no longer a slave to the pettiness that pervades the lower self, you are already reaching toward a more deeply fulfilling reality that is everlasting and ever-changing.

INSPIRATION

You are the sign of perfection. At the highest, this perfection is a state of purity of the soul. To arrive there has taken years of discipline, discard, and sacrifice.

Your assiduous search for self-improvement has brought you along the path of holiness. You have lived only to build good habits and a greater awareness. Each step of your life, you symbolically pass through baptismal waters. You travel ever onward to enter into the service of the Master, to be released from the restrictions of self that are binding your joy.

WHAT HOLDS YOU BACK
AND HOW TO OVERCOME IT

Your own restrictive attitudes are your stopping point when it comes to having a rich and happy life. Guilt, narrow-mindedness, pettiness, undue criticism, excessive worry, emotional obsession, and fear are all factors that efface your sense of freedom and spontaneity.

To fully enjoy yourself, you have to learn to get beyond yourself, by developing a more expansive awareness. Negative thinking is not only anxiety-producing, it can be dangerous, since it sometimes brings on that which you most want to avoid. Believe it or not, the reality around you is merely a reflection of your mind and thought forms. Although you're probably not aware of it, you created it, and you can also control it.

Set aside some time each day to monitor your thoughts, and carefully examine their content. Are they positive, optimistic, vital, or are they obsessively fearful, angry, sad? If the latter is the case, transmute them by making each negative thought disperse. Then displace it with a mental picture of a pleasant situation or of something you want very badly to happen. Do this consistently, and you will see the atmosphere of your life slowly begin to change.

It is extremely important to be always in control of your thoughts, because once they come to control you, your life is in a sorry state. The power of the magician comes not from his robes or his altar or his candles. It comes from what he brings to all of these—his mind. Without a fully developed and controlled mind, magic is never forthcoming. What is forthcoming is the force generated by the thought. Magic implies the controlled use of that force through the mastery of the will. The first blockage to self-mastery is self-ignorance. You must first know yourself before you can control yourself. And even if it takes you a lifetime, there is nothing you will ever do that is more worthy of such assiduous effort. For even an act of kindness performed in an angry state is more beneficial than no act at all.

LOVE AND COMPATIBILITY GUIDE

Virgo with Virgo

Although you may find a definite compatibility in this combination, you could also come to the conclusion that daily togetherness is too close for comfort.

You'll undoubtedly agree on the same brand of sinus spray, as well as the importance of having your sheets hand-laundered. However, when it comes to being mutually spontaneous, fun-loving, lighthearted, and heady, you'll probably look each other in the eye and mutter "Boring!"

That is not to say that either of you is boring apart from the other. It is to say that, together, it is likely that the chemistry won't exactly make you lose your appetite, although it may motivate you to go home and wash your windows.

However, there are worse things than house cleaning. For instance, just think of Bonnie and Clyde and where their love affair led them.

Therefore, it is far safer to trade secrets of filing systems by candlelight than to plan bank robberies over brunch. Virgo with Virgo is like a beagle and a basset hound trying to share the same flea collar. Forget it. Before it gets to the point of fighting over who left the fingerprints on the bathroom mirror, get a little daring and try someone who put the toothpaste in the oven because in the dark it looked like the medicine cabinet. Inflicting a little order on a wild and willful soul will do you a world of good and may save your Virgo-Virgo friendship in the long run.

Virgo Woman with Aries Man

He'll teach you Air Force exercises and preach to you the virtues of keeping fit. He'll mesmerize you by eating steak for breakfast and playing eight hours of tennis in the blistering sun. Yes, he gets your attention, all right, and you admire his energy, respect his ambition, and feel a little wondrous at his constant enthusiasm.

But despite his ebullience, you have a hard time trusting him, especially when he calls you at midnight to ask you out for four A.M. and then stands you up because something else catches his attention.

You definitely find him fun to be with but a little flaky when it comes to some romantic attentions and sensitivity. He is always late, never calls you the day after you've cooked for him, and has a peculiar way of forgetting his wallet at the most opportune times. If you invite him over for dinner, chances are he won't bring you wine but will drink all of yours, and won't bring you flowers but will inform you that the ones you've just bought for the occasion make the room look like a funeral parlor.

He needs immediate gratification, but you are willing to wait awhile for something meaningful. He is looking for the challenge of his lifetime, while you would just like a little love. He wants to get drunk as he looks into your eyes, and you just want to see some warmth in his.

Quite basically, he tends to be selfish, whereas you tend to be selfless. And until you both hit a happy medium, this relationship is better off postponed for a later date when he has grown up enough to give you something worth having.

Virgo Woman with Taurus Man

You'll clean up after he makes a mess. He'll cook for you when you're tired. Together you can build a bastion of love and gain the kind of nurturing you so need.

He appreciates your neatness and admires the way you respect your body. You value his emotional strength and marvel at his stamina and overall endurance.

He is patient in areas where you are anxious. You

are understanding in situations where he is befuddled. He'll find you thoughtful, kind, sensitive, and deeply caring. You'll find him to be the kind of loving, tender, and protective man you've always wanted. This is clearly a case of two people living happily ever after.

In terms of marriage, you are a team that is marveled at, since your relationship seems to have the stability that looks too good to be true. That is because you are both so solid. Just remember to make the most of it.

Virgo Woman with Gemini Man

He can't help but like you—you're so kind, warm, caring, and solicitous. But you have to be a committed masochist if you take him too seriously, since he's about as stable as a strip of crabgrass blowing about in a holocaust.

You have an erroneous reputation of being cold and critical. On the contrary, you are too giving and understanding for your own good. With a critter like him, you will be both walked on and trampled, while he grabs your little kindnesses, eats your cooking, and in repayment warmly confides to you how he wishes he could find the perfect woman. At this point, unless you feel that it's time to play "Sympathy for the Devil," tell him to get lost and to take his picture of his last girlfriend with him, which he somehow left lying on the living-room couch.

One thing you don't need is his self-created problems that he takes more seriously than any woman. What he does need is a lot of razzle-dazzle, mind games, calculated insincerity, sly up-the-sleeve tricks prompted by a cruel sense of humor, a lack of vulnerability, and a mentality that cuts him to pieces while it puts him back together again with a very sexy smile. In other words, he seeks, not love, but a perverted challenge.

Until he grows up (and some Geminis never do), this relationship is better off bypassed. His false promises and foolish grin won't take you very far, or at least not in the right direction.

So when Mr. Gemini is ready to center his energies on something other than his own selfish thoughts, maybe he'll be ready for a real woman—you.

Virgo Woman with Cancer Man

He'll make you feel like a nineteenth-century femme fatale. He'll heartily respond to your shyness, your little insecurities, your warmth, and the way your face flushes when he compliments you on your mind power.

You'll love the way he courts you, you'll treasure his concern when you catch a cold, and you'll be thankful for the way his affection makes you feel finally appreciated.

You'll plan consuming activities to divert his mood swings, throw surprise parties on his birthday, and remind him in a very matter-of-fact way how much everybody loves him.

For one of the first times in your life, you feel secure in your feelings, while he feels that this is the fantasy he's always hoped for. Together, you can take each other to many wondrous emotional places where everything urges you to enjoy the kind of happiness you've never had before.

Virgo Woman with Leo Man

Your idea of fun is to clean the refrigerator. His is to eat what's in it. You need an extra room for your vitamins, aspirin, and nasal spray. He needs a nutrition course just to understand what you're taking. You abhor dust, dirt, grime, and greasy pots. Because he's not particularly fond of it all either, he's grateful that he's found someone who will finally do something about it.

When courting you, Mr. Leo should bring you carrot juice, and from there on, he's really in. You'll worry about his blood sugar, reunite his mateless socks, and reorder his tax receipts (so that for the first time in his life he might find them before April 15).

Graciously you bestow more services than the Red Cross. But when it comes to flattery, your time is limited. You are too busy working overtime to please your boss and spending weekends sorting out the bills he didn't know he had.

You are ruled by your head, while he is at the mercy of his heart. This combination can be complementary, but it can also produce a kind of primitive parental trap. You like to take care, while he likes to be taken care of. You need someone to need you, and he needs someone who wants to be needed.

You'll sew on the missing buttons in the closet full of clothes he's snubbed for months because of their buttonless condition. In wild relief at seeing his old friends back, he goes out and buys you a sewing machine. When the check bounces, you call the bank and cover it with money you had stashed away for yourself.

When you have a nervous attack about whether you shut off your electric typewriter, Mr. Leo is most supportive and reassuring; when you get bleeding ulcers after finding your nefarious boss perusing your trash basket, he gallantly dashes to the drugstore. But should he forget what he went out for and return with a full-length mirror, you'll just smile through your tears like Clara Barton.

Despite the fact that you nag him about taking desiccated liver, you could very well be close to ideal for him. You will mother him, nurse him, and serve him like a cleaning lady who's studying accounting at night school. Because you're so nervous, guilt-ridden, and anxiety-driven, you'll always be fashionably thin from thinking too much.

You'll be forever supportive, dutiful, and faithful. You find affairs much too anxiety-producing, so he shouldn't worry if he catches you in a little animated conversation in a dimly lit corner with a devastating man. Undoubtedly it's a doctor, and you're discussing your protein-metabolism level.

The only thing to be concerned about is whether all your "health" concoctions will one day kill him. But if he feels that insecure about your compulsiveness, he'll just break your blender—smiling as he does it.

Virgo Woman with Libra Man

You have a terrible habit of taking him at his word. Therefore, when he mumbles the word "marriage" in a drunken moment after you have cooked him a delectable dinner, don't expect him to remember.

You are earthy, shy, and exacting, while he is airy, indiscriminate, and convivial. He likes a good time and often overlooks how he gets it.

You are faithful, kind, caring, and very serious. Mr. Libra is often unfaithful, cruel without realizing it, and sensitive only to his own needs. He can cover up the necessity for responsibility by bemoaning his own confusion, and has a very clever way, at the same time, of trying to extract your sympathy. Too often it works, because you are so empathic, self-effacing, and delighted to be able to do something for someone else.

Basically, you are a woman who needs to be needed, and he is a man who has just too many needs. But if you are so dedicated to the idea of service that you prefer to play nursemaid to a person who will hardly appreciate it, then that's your problem. But in the long run, if you allow your brain to socialize with your emotions, you might get the message that it would be best for you to just move on. Some men are demanding, but Mr. Libra requires a romantic dream that personifies Woman. So, for whatever it's worth, perhaps he should make his own movie, pick his own actresses, and then sit back and watch his veins pulse.

Virgo Woman with Scorpio Man

He will appreciate your mind, your stability, and your services and together, you could have a companionship that is quiet and comfortable. The problem is that he desires one that is noisy and intense.

Here there is a lot of talk but very little action, and the passion just does not reign supreme. Together, you can analyze your feelings until you both fall asleep with your mouths open. However, it is highly unlikely that you can achieve a state of mind over matter.

You have an aspect to your personality that is highly healing. At the same time, there is a portion of his personality that needs to be healed. However, there is another that needs a consummate kind of passion and because of this, he is willing to take what you offer but to let the relationship pass him by.

Basically, he's attracted to a woman who calls the shots and galvanizes him with one passionate glance. However, you tend to follow the shots in an effort to be kind and pleasing. In his life, women have forced him to passivity through sheer sensual impact, and niceness was never a consideration. That is why rather than putting your hopes on him, you might be better off with a pet Pekinese. Mr. Scorpio will be looking for what isn't there but the Pekinese will know he has a good deal.

Virgo Woman with Sagittarius Man

You may fall madly in love with his spontaneity and invincible charisma. However, you won't appreciate his capriciousness or the way he treats you like a combination cook and Red Cross nurse.

His charm is like a cheap cosmetic that doesn't hold up under closer scrutiny. Therefore, at first, you'll be blown away when he brings you to the airline ticket office and tells you that he's taking you on a trip to Fiji. However, when the time comes and he's forgotten his original promise and ends up inviting your best friend, then somehow he loses first place on your list of lovers.

Mr. Sagittarius wants challenges and excitement to take him to the clouds, while you seek an earthbound kind of love. He prefers quantity to quality, while you seek plain and simple consideration.

In your most profound place you need to be needed, while he is so self-sufficient that he could survive being stranded in the desert. Any way you look at it, you both seem to be going in opposite directions. In the long run, he is far better off with a woman who is so flighty that she acts like she has wings rather than feet. You are too deeply entrenched in the earth to ever meet him in the clouds.

Virgo Woman with Capricorn Man

On the outside, he is probably president of five different corporations; on the inside, he's just a little boy who wants to be taken care of. Because you basically need to be needed, appreciated, and applauded, this combination could work out very well.

You'll handle him when he gets bossy, and in turn he will make your life better by his constant care and concern.

On the job, he is the most aggressive kind of go-getter. However, at home he is just a happy man who likes to spend time with the woman he loves. You appreciate his feelings, offer him a kind and sympathetic shoulder, and have an almost magical way of allaying his insecurities.

On dreary days, you'll cook him a beautiful dinner and then offer him your critical advice for the problems that seem so pressing. You are considerate, warm, and the kind of woman he always wanted to know. Your intelligence will stimulate him, your affection will open him up, and your fidelity will give him a sound strength in trying moments.

This combination has the components of happiness, mutual trust, and shared responsibility that can create a mature marriage.

Virgo Woman with Aquarius Man

When you tell him your deepest problems, he'll ask you a lot of questions and then offer you a diet root beer. He's far more curious than sympathetic, and somehow it doesn't sit well.

You are sensitive, supervulnerable, and need someone who will make you feel more secure. He loves your mind but has no patience with your emotions. It's his opinion that you worry too much. It's yours that he doesn't worry half as much as he should.

You'll never understand how he can get more involved with foreign aid than with balancing his own checkbook. He'll never understand why you worry because you have two cents in your bank statement that you can't account for.

Your penchant for order sometimes irritates and distracts him. Mr. Aquarius' compatibility with chaos can send your mind reeling. He loves to party with as many people as possible, while you are a shy stay-at-home who would rather have him all to yourself than lose him to a group.

Because you take everybody's feelings to heart, you have a hard time understanding how he can be so detached. At the same time, your obsession with your cat's sinus problems makes him impatient, restless, and ready to take a walk.

Mentally, there is much mutual stimulation; sexually, there is a lot of talk. Any way you look at it, this relationship is best left on a simple friendship basis.

Virgo Woman with Pisces Man

You are quiet, shy, and very sensible. He is chaotic, dreamy-eyed, and consumed by farfetched fantasies.

He has a mind that seems to be traveling in too

many time zones. On the other hand, you think straight ahead and don't get distracted by emotional side trips.

You may find his daydreams fascinating. However, you'll probably choke and sputter over the constant confusion he seems to live in. You love to have your time organized, but he can't commit himself seven seconds into the future. You feel secure when you can create a premeditated order, whereas he takes spontaneity to the most peculiar extremes.

You need a warm, stable, enduring kind of love, while he seeks the drama of a Russian rhapsody and a woman who is more a daring dance partner than a human being who may make demands.

After a time, you will probably watch your patience attenuate as you start to realize how easily he can turn the romance into a kind of riot. Meanwhile, his attention span has probably wandered past his sixth martini and he's wondering how he'll ever get to meet this year's Miss America.

Mr. Pisces is a man whose mind melts into a kind of bubble before breaking, while you're the kind of woman who prefers immediate action to a lot of ethereal thinking. The differences here are entirely too awesome for a smooth-running relationship. And the sensitivities are disparate enough for the kind of divorce that seems to deny there ever was a love.

Virgo Man with Aries Woman

You'll remind her to comb her hair as she dashes madly out the door for a pressing appointment, and nag her when she throws her clothes all over the floor. You'll point out her trail of unfinished projects, and when she's late, lecture her on the necessity of discipline and duty.

Your approach to life is so cool and logical that at times she'll wonder if you've ever mislaid anything. On the other hand, you will wonder at her hysteria and lose sleep worrying about her smoking and drinking. The basic difference here is that she takes everything to its extreme, and you structure yourself into a much safer middle ground.

You are cautious, while she compulsively throws caution to the winds. You are frugal while she can be capricious with money. You have a personality that is reserved, but she has one that can't be held in abeyance. You like quiet moments while she seeks the excitement of crowded places.

Needless to say, the two of you are not exactly compatible. However, she could learn a lot from this relationship if she is willing to listen. You will teach her how to file her tax receipts, structure her time so that it doesn't overwhelm her, and learn how to see the other side of a situation. You will listen to her problems, offer rational advice, but will remain unsympathetic when she adheres to the dictates of her ego. She may consider your constructive criticism to be a cruel attack, and you may find her temper tantrums a bit more than you can handle. Only with patience can you come to see each other's point of view. However, since patience is something she doesn't have a great deal of, the life span of this relationship does not look promising. In the beginning, you are both coming from different places; and in the end, you return to separate tables that view two disparate worlds.

Virgo Man with Taurus Woman

Although you may nag her about the bathtub ring, this woman will find you most endearing. You are honest, vulnerable, giving, and loving. Because she tends to be a quiet stay-at-home, together you can share many cozy evenings. A flickering fire, some cold chicken in aspic, and a bottle of Chablis, and you're on your way to nirvana.

She will find you considerate, and you will find her warm and caring. You appreciate her practicality. She appreciates the competence with which you run your life.

You tend to be shy, but she can melt your inhibitions with her animal sensuality. She tends to be insecure, but you have a way of reducing her fears. Basically, she is kind, understanding, and someone easy to talk to. You are loyal, genuine, and the kind of man to whom she wants to be committed.

This is a relationship based on a deep rapport, with a future of much feeling. You both have a lot to look forward to together.

Virgo Man with Gemini Woman

This is like trying to combine ice cream with a dill pickle.

You think she is too crazy to be responsible for her own actions. She thinks you're too cautious to cross the street by yourself.

You do your laundry at the same time on the same day of every week; she gets hers done when she either hires a maid or has nothing left to wear.

You consider her personal affairs a department of chaos, while she thinks you run your life with a kind of bureaucratic control.

You can't comprehend why she no longer opens her mailbox just to avoid her bills, why, after she's insisted on pizza, she decides she can't live without chicken chop suey, or why, after making a date with you for the movies, she suddenly changes her mind and stays home with her dog.

You try to deal with her behavior logically, use your patience, offer kindly advice, and she laughs in your face. She's enough to give you an incurable case of eczema that seems to get worse the more seriously you take her. The communication here would be greater if you just stayed home alone and tried to talk to your TV dinner.

Virgo Man with Cancer Woman

Although her moods often confuse you, her intense emotions provide the encouragement that gives you tremendous comfort. You are as insecure as she is, though you cover it up with your will and your acute logic.

She will evoke your more vulnerable emotions, and you will help her to filter life through her head as well as her heart. However, at times, you won't be as cuddly as her affectionate nature feels it needs. You spend most of your time working, and when you're not working, you're worrying about whether you could have done a better job.

You don't understand her need for constant attention, and she doesn't understand the excruciating disciplines you put your mind through.

Basically, you're an exceedingly mental individual, and she's exceedingly emotional. However, if both of you can come to respect the other's perspectives and can learn to work through them rather than around them, this could be a relationship of such lasting value that you may find you want to marry.

Virgo Man with Leo Woman

Despite your bad reputation as a nit-picking crab who flicks dandruff off her collar, you are really not as bad as you sound. If you were born between either eight and nine P.M. or between four and five o'clock in the morning, there is a good chance that this relationship could work. However, if you were born between six and seven A.M. and have Virgo rising, this association will not register even long enough for you to forget it.

If she is the more Aquarian kind of Leo, being more cerebral, detached, intellectual, and interested in her surroundings as much as in herself, this will be a distinct advantage in any relationship with you.

You are shy, studious, cautious, introverted, and analytical. You love order and have more systems than an overwrought accountant. Your underwear drawer looks like it was sent from the dry cleaner; your desk, like it was just delivered; the contents of your freezer, like a pop-art exhibition. Therefore, you are mystified at what Ms. Leo considers organization. At the same time, she silently lapses into shock at your ritualized ceremonies.

She lives in a social flurry of dinners, parties, theater, brunches, and ballet. In general, you would rather read about them than live them. The cold constrictions of your logic elude her. Likewise, the lack of feeling in her histrionics leaves you distraught. Chances are, the night before the maid comes, you pull an all-nighter to clean your apartment. She stays up to dirty hers. You make her nervous when you check the dust in the corners, look under her bed, and stare intently at a hangnail she was trying to conceal by keeping her hands in her pockets. On a day when she feels her most attractive, you'll lean over and whisper in her ear. She anticipates the words "I love you. I need you. I can't live without you. Come away with me or I'll kill myself." Wrong script. You're telling her that her coat needs cleaning.

You share springtime as your favorite season. To her it means ubiquitous sunshine, romance, suntans, and sensuous nights of pleasure. To you it means spring cleaning.

Of all the signs of the zodiac, she is one of the least inspiring to your mental health. Her temper makes your stomach twinge and your nerves shudder. Too often, you angrily acquiesce to her wishes so as to spare yourself the tortures of her rigid silences. But since she instantaneously loses respect for any man she can bully, your high-priced agreements only leave her cold and dissatisfied. Alas, the inevitable irony! While you're the one reputed to be critical, she's the one who can never be pleased. Whatever you do, it only barely passes muster. And no matter how she tries to meet your mind, there is always something missing. It's called excitement.

Yet you are kind, loyal, and faithful. And unless you have Libra or Leo rising and share her sense of drama and extravagance, the intervals of ennui may be the price she has to pay for your stability.

Your routines may bring her to a premature state of rigor mortis, but your consideration can creep into her heart. Mad, mindless passion is not a likely outcome of this coupling. Most likely this is because you spend all your time in the bathroom. However, if she should be creative enough to steal the toothpaste at bedtime, who knows what might come of it?

Virgo Man with Libra Woman

There is a kind of substance to you that she finds truly attractive. She will admire the way you never agonize over decisions but see every issue as rather cut-and-dried. She will be overwhelmed by your discipline in the face of distracting influences. And she will have respect for the way you do what you feel you have to do, without making a big deal of it.

However, should you start nagging her about the way she washes the dishes, or start giving her a dissertation about how she should improve her dental habits, suddenly she finds that she can barely stifle a yawn.

In general, you will enjoy Ms. Libra's *savoir faire*, her domestic graciousness, and her sophisticated appreciation of beautiful things. However, you'll let her know that her spending habits are monstrous and that she has to be demented to pay three hundred dollars for a simple linen tablecloth, even if it was imported.

You will have a hard time acclimating to her love of luxury and will never comprehend why, when she's depressed, she has to pay thirty dollars to get her legs waxed. Instead, you'll tell her to take a course in mental and emotional discipline that is offered on television at 5:30 A.M.

Despite any compatibility that can be achieved here, there will always be communication gaps that have to be carefully worked out. However, since she can see both sides of any question, and your understanding is a bit more restricted, the responsibility is really on her shoulders. In the long run, she may find that a little work invested in this relationship is well worth it. You are not a game player. You are kind, loving, and considerate. However, it's up to her to determine whether you are also receptive and willing to change.

Virgo Man with Scorpio Woman

You are attracted to her depth, intensity, and sensuality. She appreciates your stability, earthly sexuality, and sense of purpose. You may not understand her, and perhaps think her emotions silly, but you'll stay up all night listening to her problems. Even if she's obsessing a lot, repeats her point sixty-five times, and says the same sentence every hour, you will try your best to listen. However, at the same time, you may drown yourself drinking gallons of water because she's made you so nervous.

The basic difference between you is that she feels the world through her emotions and you see it through your logic. And you both overanalyze until the original point no longer matters.

Ms. Scorpio's moods make you shake your head in wonder. Your sense of logic on the subject of her moods makes her sulk. She feels you don't see the forest for the trees. At the same time, you think that she'll only get lost in the forest.

Despite the verbal banter, you are kind and nurturing, have the best intentions, but sometimes seem to ruin it all by being so critical. Should she suddenly get sick, you'll have a ready supply of nasal spray. But while she's coughing, sneezing, and spraying, you'll nag her for leaving the cap off the toothpaste. She'll share with you her greatest lifetime accomplishment, and you'll find the fatal flaw. If she asks if you like her new haircut, you'll tell her she should do something about the split ends.

Quite unintentionally, you invite the most trenchant sarcasm. At the same time, you feel that she invites a most constant restructuring of her life. Although, initially, this relationship may kindle a few favorable sparks, for the most part, consider it to be one that you are just passing through.

Virgo Man with Sagittarius Woman

You are overwhelmed by the fact that her bedroom looks like the aftermath of a great jewel robbery. She is fascinated by the fact that you record in a pocket notebook the number of soda crackers you eat.

She is like a cyclone to your sensitivities. She seems to be both coming and going simultaneously, whereas you move with caution from place to place.

You have never seen a human being who is so unorganized, and she has never met a man who is so ineffably ordered. Your idea of fun is to go shopping for file cabinets; hers is to sign up for a safari on the spur of the moment. Your idea of a pleasant evening is to sit in silence reading. Hers is to try to take three trips at once.

Ms. Sagittarius lives her life without any conception of limitation. You live yours with restrictions that you struggle to rise above.

If there is any meeting of the minds here, it will probably be one in passing. Your life-styles are so incongruent that the chemistry is the kind that can strangle you. Therefore, it's best to keep all your commitments on a less intense and more friendly basis.

Virgo Man with Capricorn Woman

Since neither of you knows how to sit still, you'll indulge each other's tendency toward workaholism. You will applaud the discipline, tenacity, and drive that take her straight to the top. She, in turn, will approve of your Sundays spent at the office to make your projects perfect.

She will find you to be a man with two feet on the ground but with a heart that is always happy to be of service. You are shy but loving, at times fearful, but always faithful. You're the fellow she can depend on when her friends' lives are filled up with their own misfortunes.

She will be touched by your shyness and terribly impressed with your strong resolve. You have the discipline to get up at six A.M. to take a self-improvement course. That is because, every day, in every way, you somehow try to be a little better.

You will offer realistic suggestions for solving her problems, and will know how to bring up her mood level when she gets the gloomies. Living with you is like an exercise in organization, but one that she welcomes heartily.

Ms. Capricorn likes a man who has his life under control. You like a woman with drive and ambition. Together, you have the kind of rapport and compatibility that can bring you both a lot of happiness. This could be a marriage that lasts a lifetime.

Virgo Man with Aquarius Woman

When you look at her life, you feel you should take care of her. However, the hardest part comes in trying to convince her that she needs someone. She's a free spirit who feels claustrophobic when caged. You're an orderly, controlling type who means well but may not always have the best ideas.

You may love her mind but resent her detachment. You will get cross when she forgets to do the dishes (even though there's only one fork). However, when she wakes you up in the middle of the night with a theory on the movement of electron particles, you'll sit up in bed and give her your full attention.

Ms. Aquarius appreciates the fact that you're a good soul who tries hard. At the same time, you make her feel like a cork on a corkscrew. You are willful and imposing; she is universal and used to doing what she wants.

No matter what she does or how she does it, you have a suggestion to improve the overall efficiency. Since Ms. Aquarius cares more about the experience than the outcome, your ideas will fall on deaf ears. She really doesn't want to hear your opinions or to do things your way. But when she tells you, you don't hear her. You merely make a new suggestion.

Your expectations have a way of taking up her space and making it cluttered and confining. On the other hand, she has a way of making you feel like a third sock that has less than an even chance of finding its mate. The way you live your life, by a thousand systems, is not the way she wants to live hers. The last thing she needs is someone to follow her around and tell her what to do. The first thing she needs is freedom. As this is not something she'll find forthcoming from you, it might be best to look elsewhere and to keep this relationship on a just-friends basis.

Virgo Man with Pisces Woman

She finds comfort in chaos; you crave order as a kind of control. She longs for a life of emotional excitement. You prefer the kind of stability that could give her sleeping sickness.

She is emotionally moved by grade-B movies, glamorous nights on the town, ghost stories, and getting what she wants when she never even thought of asking for it. You are moved by the mechanics of your mind and the number of shelves in your new file cabinet.

Basically, the two of you are so different that if you manage to get past the first five dates, then you may decide you have something. However, there will never be a strong compatibility, nor the kind of emotional rapport that obviates verbal communication.

You don't see the value of poetry, because it can't be proved. Ms. Pisces, on the other hand, can't see the importance of your structures, because they leave no room for spontaneity. On a spring night, you'll want to stay home and put your tax receipts in order, but she'll prefer to go out and paint the town purple. She'll occasionally overdo the brandy alexanders while you fidget with your skim milk.

You both may grumble at the other's way of doing things, but you are both cognizant of the mutual good intentions. Although you may be critical and at times fussy, you'll try to take care of her to the best of your ability. And because of her sympathetic and intuitive nature, she'll be able to see through your systems and straight into your heart. Your mind shies away from the supersensitive emotions that you fear will be your undoing. However, her sensuality could easily turn you into a cuddly creature. You may wear your heart on your sleeve and just keep begging for more.

LIBRA

Dates: September 24—October 23
Ruling planet: Venus
Element: Air
Mode: Cardinal
Quality: Masculine
Planetary principle: Balance
Primal desire: Union
Color: Indigo
Jewels: Diamond, opal
Plant: Rose
Day: Friday
Archangel: Anael
Magical number: 3
Material factor: Creation

LIBRAS OF
FAME AND FORTUNE

Aleister Crowley	Arthur Miller
Barbara Walters	Rimbaud
Gore Vidal	Rita Hayworth
John Lennon	P. G. Wodehouse
Thelonius Monk	F. Scott Fitzgerald
Cervantes	William Faulkner
Nietzsche	Graham Greene
Oscar Wilde	Brigitte Bardot

T. S. Eliot   George Gershwin
Mahatma Gandhi   Les McCann
Jimmy Carter

THE LIBRA FEMALE

Favorable

You love Fred Astaire and Ginger Rogers movies, 1930's love songs, and larger-than-life romances. Your favorite days are St. Valentine's and Christmas, and your moment to remember is the last time your lover told you that he loved you.

You hate being taken for granted, begging for affection, and men with very bad manners. You come alive with little loving attentions, and positively thrive on being appreciated.

You have a lot of needs, and one of them is that you need to be needed. Since you were born under the sign of Venus, love is intrinsic to your well-being. You're a vulnerable version of the femme fatale, and gentle flirting is your unconscious forte.

You are the kind of woman that men like to be around because you are so warm and womanly. In a diaphanous gown, you're a dream come true. Even in a tailored suit, you're fantastically feminine and make the kind of appearance that is attention-getting.

The surrounding world seems to jump alive through your creative efforts, whether it's a delectable culinary delight, a painting, a writing project, or a newly composed piece of music. Your artistic talent is totally consuming. To walk through your living room is to experience a decorator's genius.

Giving parties is one of your favorite pastimes, and attending them is a particular treat for your guests. You can create the most memorable galas that seduce one's senses with a very unaffordable kind of elegance.

You are truly dedicated to the good life, and enjoy all kinds of little pleasures, like candlelight baths with fresh flowers, blackberries with cream, vintage champagne, the kind of chandeliers that make a room scintillate, and the kind of fur coats that seem to embrace you.

You are a classic sensualist and a pleasure seeker but at the same time have the kind of perseverance to perform anything you put your mind to. You can accomplish a multitude of far-reaching goals in your career. However, each of them has to be a labor of love.

After a while you find it difficult to drive yourself during the day if there is no one to come home to in the evening. The deepest part of you seeks a meaningful love in which you can share all your life experience. You are a highly social being who doesn't like living alone, any more than you enjoy cleaning house. Somewhere in your heart you are still waiting for a prince on a white charger to come along and swoop you away to a castle in the sky, where you'll be showered with love and a lot of trinkets. Needless to say, your idealism has been disillusioned more than once. However, somehow you still can't give up hoping.

In any committed love relationship you are patience personified, and you can rationalize away more faults than most men have. However, in return you expect to be both indulged and highly appreciated. Unfortunately, it often doesn't work that way, and the person who is the object of your affections starts to settle back and take you for granted.

One of your most persistent faults is that you have a hard time asking for what you need, and an even harder time realizing that you have a right to.

While you smile most graciously and voice a "that's okay" attitude, often inside you're both miserable and angry. However, until you make the decision to take responsibility for your own life and to stop waiting for someone else to do it, your repressed emotions will tear you to pieces.

Your basic problem is that while you have no problems making big decisions, the little day-to-day ones make you both nervous and dreary. You agonize over whether you want a tuna-fish sandwich or a hamburger, whether you want to wear a pink blouse or a blue sweater, and whether you should tell your lover to take a long walk over a short cliff or just ask him to please pass the string beans.

In any social setting you are calm, poised, self-possessed, and very dignified. However, by yourself you probably cry into your pillow and throw your mood music against the walls. It takes years for you to understand that people still love you even when you lose your mannequin manners that are programmed to give the right response. However, until you learn to like yourself for what you are in the most spontaneous situations, what kind of response can you expect from other people? When you stop worrying about what others think of you and commit yourself to caring only about your own opinion, your abandonment fears will fly away along with your insecurities, only to be replaced by the feeling of a lot of love.

Unfavorable

Should a male passerby ask you the time, you're already beginning to assess the future of the affair. You are one woman with a lot of needs. Therefore, let no man be wasted.

Since you began to talk (and that was at an unfortunately early age), you wanted to get married. Because you are so passive, unassertive, and ineffectual with your own life, somewhere you figured that maybe a man might do better. You especially love big men with muscles, who make you feel even more helpless and "feminine." And if you happen to be blessed by a little beauty from the gods, you get all the mileage you can manage from playing Aphrodite to your Herculean defenders.

As men love to boss you around and watch you bounce back for more, and as you love being told what to do, before long you usually find yourself a "secure" place in a couple.

Security is probably your favorite thing, next to being totally taken care of. And once you find even a facsimile, you stick to the man like a barnacle. And no measure of rude, selfish, or bestial behavior will make you consider leaving. To get rid of you, a man has to come close to having you killed off, or, as a less drastic measure, he could just fix you up with one of his enemies.

No one has ever told you that you are a thinking being. Likewise, no one has ever told you that you have choices, and since you're so dependent on what you're told to do, you live your life patiently waiting. Needless to say, many things pass you by, but sometimes you're much better off for it.

Because living with you is like cohabiting with an electronic Barbie doll, after a while your lover is bound

to get bored and wander. Even if you look like the goddess Diana, your personality would never win you the
title of Ms. Magnetism. At your best, you are pleasant and
a little drippy; at your worst, you are whiny and a compulsive complainer. Therefore, the time comes when your
lover's nights at the office start to run into the next
day and his mental interests suddenly expand in multi-
farious directions. However, when he informs you that he's
also taken up tennis and would rather just play with the
machine, then you know that the time has come that you
have to do some heavy confronting.

Underneath the guise of your feminine helplessness,
you are something of a spoiled child. To get a "daddy,"
you'll play the role of "woman." However, despite your
success at evoking the negative anima, your attempt to be
a woman never transcends the role.

That is because a real woman is not afraid to ask
for what she wants, and has enough self-love to make sure
that she gets it. However making demands endangers
your sense of security. And it probably is a precarious act
with the kind of man you have purposely chosen. Every
action to which you commit yourself has a negative circular effect that enhances your feeling of total frustration.
However, the problem is that since you have no self-respect to begin with, you don't even have enough awareness to know the human rights that you are ignoring.

The result of these churning anxieties is that you
develop an oral fixation, and life becomes a matter of
compulsive dieting or compulsive eating, drug taking and/
or liquor, and a lot of incessant talking. Your need for
immediate gratification in a life that you feel isn't giving
you much could eventually lead you to a psychological cul-
de-sac that only therapy can help you get out of.

Quite often your talking turns to babble while you
digress and never get to the point. Your train of thought
takes so many side trips and twists into trivialities that
your audience's attention span becomes frozen. At this
point, you have become one self-obsessed Libra whose
communication flow has slowly dwindled to a disaster
area.

At such times, people find it painful to be around
you, for you never seem to reciprocate and listen to what
they might be saying. And certainly if someone's hair
caught on fire in the middle of a point you had been

trying to make (for the past half-hour), the person would just have to search silently for some water. For not even bloody screams will deter you from your own digressions.

Because your perspectives are so shallow, you often lose sight of larger issues. You lack a rich inner life that will support you in periods of aloneness, and consequently look upon your own company with fear and loathing. However, until you reach the point where you are willing to develop dimensions within yourself, other people can't fill those spaces for you by accompanying you to the movies. You have to learn how to take responsibility for your own life, for your own choices, for your own pain, and for your own joys. And even harder, you have to learn how to like it. Otherwise, you're creating your own vacuums, and you can't blame other people when they start to vacate those airless, empty spaces.

THE LIBRA MALE

Favorable

You are a life-of-the-party personality and have the kind of charm and sense of humor that bring people flocking around you. You love to socialize, be surrounded by people, and seek strongly interactive situations that enhance your sense of group fun.

Your attitude toward life is a rather robust one. You crave your creature comforts and like to overindulge whenever possible. Strongly hedonistic tendencies and an intense appreciation of good food can often transform you into a galloping gourmet. At your most natural moment, you are a confirmed sensualist and a fervent supporter of the good life. And because of this, you're usually a lot of fun to spend time with.

Often you enjoy a strong degree of success in your professional undertakings. That is because you are highly intelligent, creative in your approach to most issues, and have the foresight to envision the impersonal side of any situation. Your concentration is intense and your sense of timing almost uncanny. Likewise, your ability to synthesize many divergent factors at once is an asset that is much admired, along with your verbal faculties, which reflect a very distinctive articulateness.

You have a highly adaptive logical intelligence combined with an irresistible kind of charisma that makes you one person whose popularity could never be in dispute. Because you're so lively, people of all ages and both sexes heartily enjoy your company and put your name at the top of every invitation list. You have the personality of the entertainer, and whether you perform onstage or merely in your living room, you will never be lacking an eager audience.

Because of your personal power, women are highly attracted to you, and you, of course, to them. There is nothing like a pretty face to elevate your mood and put you in more sanguine spirits. More than anything else, you appreciate all manifestations of beauty.

When it comes to love, you're an invincible romantic who often enjoys the idea far more than the emotion. Basically, you're an odd combination of the sentimental and the cerebral, which means that at times you tend to overanalyze your feelings.

Because you're very idealistic, you live out your youth in search of a dream and often let your mind get seduced by a brief encounter with some devastating beauty. However, after some experience and a lot of thinking, you're usually ready to relinquish the superficials for a more mature love situation.

You're definitely the marrying kind, and seek a warm, stable compatibility with strong communication and a lot of shared activities. Once you fall in love, you are warm, affectionate, kind, loyal, and sympathetic. At first you seek to put your woman on a pedestal. However, after some time together, you start to see her more as a soulmate and less as a distant figure. There are times when love can be a painful experience for you because of deep-seated insecurities and fears of abandonment. However, with time, continual communication, and trust you can slowly replace your fears with more secure feelings.

In general, Libra is a sign that tends to be highly musical. Therefore, whether you play an instrument or not, you should get a lot of relaxation from simply listening to music. Your talents can take you from the literary world to law, from music to business, and even into medicine. However, whatever you do, you have a way of bringing a tremendous amount of talent to it.

You are greatly admired for the way you can make your creative visions materialize into far-reaching truths. You easily discern what is important to you and what isn't. Within this framework, you make every significant act an act of love. And your personal, emotional, and professional success results from it.

Unfavorable

You are the prince of the playboys, even at the age of sixty. Behind you there is a legend of love that you live just to exceed.

However, the fact is that you are a most fickle and inconstant lover and you care far more about yourself than any other person you could possibly meet. At your most charming you are a friendly and promiscuous panderer who takes far more than you ever leave behind.

At best, you are clever, witty, charismatic, and careful never to get into a compromising position. You are the kind of man who would leave a woman sitting in a train station if you were suddenly assailed by a prettier face. You are shallow, superficial, and highly self-serving. At one moment your histrionics could take you to the point of pledging your life away for the love of a woman. However, in the next hour you might abandon her for her best friend because "she no longer makes bells ring."

Your idea of love is to be overtaken and drugged by the passing emotion. However, usually your feelings are so ephemeral that you've forgotten them by the next day. Therefore, in your scheme of things the experience of a lasting love could take less time than it takes you to shave. Then you're on to some new infatuation, since what you love best is beginnings.

Chances are that you would marry a woman for her cheekbones and after the day of the wedding, start having affairs. You're a very busy man when it comes to your romantic activities.

Despite the fact that you behave like a flaky Rudolph Valentino, you're not as cool as you would like to think. Underneath all your cavorting lies a very dependent creature who runs when he has to confront his deeper feelings. Basically, you tend to be both insecure and depressed, passive and ineffectual, confused and indecisive. You would rather talk for hours about your feelings than let yourself feel them. And you would rather fantasize that you're making love to Ms. America than let yourself get involved with a real woman.

The terrible thing about a relationship is that the initial drug wears off, the fun starts to fade, and the woman starts making demands. And all of this can have an effect on you that is close to devastating.

You want to exist in a constant daydream that leaves no room for logic. However, when your reasoning process starts to intrude, you figure that you're losing that "loving feeling."

In any personal situation you're as dependable as a broken chair whose seat has fallen through the middle. You've never realized what it's like to be responsible, and you start to get depressed at the very thought of it.

However, with your high intelligence, you usually rationalize an entire thought system to justify your self-indulgence and the fact that you can't cope with another person whose needs are as great as your own. Basically, your value system embraces a double standard that never stops getting you what you think you want, no matter what the cost to others. When it comes to living, you are committed to the divine highs, without any kind of compromise considered, and whoever should get in your way will be most coldly disregarded. You really don't have time to worry about the world. You have to pursue a dream, and it seems like you're always just getting started.

DECANS

Every sign in the zodiac can be broken down into three subdivisions, called decans. Each decan roughly corresponds to ten degrees—the first third, second third, and last third of the sun sign's time span, which is approximately thirty days.

As each of these periods has different subrulerships, the personality of a person is slightly modified by the specific decan it falls in. For instance, an Aries born in the second decan would be ruled by Mars, but subruled by the sun. Therefore, he would tend to display a greater sense of pride, boastfulness, egotism, and optimism than an Aries born in the third decan, which is subruled by Jupiter. This Aries would tend to be more freedom-loving, flighty, travel-oriented, and interested in subjects of a philosophical nature. An Aries born in the first decan would be the most aggressive, but not necessarily the most productive and accomplished.

Decans are important, since they do account for a more detailed assessment of an individual's personality charactierstics. They also show how two people born under the same sun sign can be markedly different.

If you were born between September 24 and October 3, your sun falls in the Venus decan of Libra.

You are both highly creative and a classic romantic. Because your imagination is so active, your talents can often find an outlet in the arts.

You have the personality of the natural peacemaker and feel extremely uneasy if trapped at the location of an angry dispute. Because of your ability to see both sides of a question, you could have a successful career in law, working as the dispenser of justice.

Mentally, you are flexible, understanding, and sympathetic. You go to great efforts to try to experience the other side of a situation, and try to adapt your point of view accordingly. However, at the same time, you can be exceedingly vacillating and indecisive. In the face of an influence from a strong personality, you can be most easily swayed.

Emotionally, you are rather impressionable and tend to fluctuate strongly in your feelings. There are moments in your life when you might be accused of being fickle; at other times, stubborn and inflexible.

Basically, you are an idealist and a romantic in the full sense of the word. You seek the perfect love that is intense, consuming, and looks good to the outside world. Because you fall in love with the idea of love far more than with the depths of the experience, you would probably be more successful writing about love than patiently going through it. In this area, you lack a specific lucidity when it comes to understanding both the work and the responsibility involved in the life of a mature love relationship. You want the beauty and seek to discard the hardship involved in maintaining it. When an emotional relationship is not working, you would rather throw it out and find a new one than stick with it and objectively analyze your part.

Because of the Venus rulership of this decan, love

and partnerships are your most troublesome areas. You have a tremendous need for shared experience, but often have a problem in finding the right person. In early life, many aborted love affairs are not uncommon, but these are due only to the fact that you let yourself be ruled by your own unrealistic desires.

Libras born in this decan often suffer from intense depressions because they have a difficult time integrating the various aspects of their personalities. Often, at the deepest part of them, there is an ambivalence that blocks a more complete sense of satisfaction and happiness.

Remember that self-indulgence is the swiftest pathway to your demise. You need a tremendous amount of discipline to rise above your own sense of discontent. It is crucial to know yourself well and to let no emotion or inclination be a mystery. If you do not control your own feelings, they will definitely control you. And as a result, the sensations of feeling and thinking will be dangerously intertwined and lead only, in the long run, to more confusion.

If you were born between October 4 and 13, your sun falls in the Saturn-Uranus decan of Libra.

Of the three Libra decans, you have the most serious personality. You have a strong social consciousness, a proclivity to humanitarianism, and a sense of perseverance. Science and medicine are distinct possibilities for you, while occultism could be a strong back-up interest.

For those Libras most interested in the arts, this is the decan strongly favoring either film or photography. Natives born during this time of the month are often involved professionally in either acting or modeling. However, this is also a decan favoring music.

A salient trait in your personality is a deep feeling of responsibility for those you love. However, sometimes you take this trait to the extreme and become fussy and possessive.

You tend to be very insecure, and are at times overwhelmed by feelings of inferiority. However, you must realize that you create your own obstacles to the fulfillment of your desires.

It is important for you to develop a strong sense of humor to overcome those gloomy moments when you take yourself too seriously. A little levity will take you anywhere, but your persistent fear of limitation only creates more fear.

If you were born between October 14 and 23, your sun falls in the Mercury decan of Libra.

You have a logical mind, a strong sense of justice, and a tendency to analyze and reanalyze experience.

Like natives born in the first decan, you have an extremely sociable personality. However, you are even more gregarious and sometimes prone to garrulousness and idle chatter.

Your need to communicate could bring you recognition in the area of writing. Since languages are also your special forte, linguistics, translations, and teaching are strong possible professional choices. In the practice of law, your verbal abilities would outshine those of your opponents and counterparts. This, combined with your fast logical mind, can potentially bring you outstanding success. However, should you be the more lazy kind of Libra, the influence of this decan would probably lead you to choose a clerical position, so as to have less time tied up in working.

By nature you are orderly and have a strong sense of duty. As a friend you are loyal and well-liked. You have a good sense of humor, which always adds to your popularity.

On your darker days you can be irritable, sharp, nervous, and agitated. You may snap at someone who cheerfully wishes you good morning and growl at your co-workers in a moment of impatience.

Libras born in this decan must work toward a greater mental stability. Although on a good day you can be an awesome force as you coolly wheel and deal millions of dollars, there is always a tendency in your more private moments to let your own thoughts torment you. There is an irrational turbulent force that runs through you that can temporarily destroy and disrupt your sense of balance. If you abandon yourself to a mind run wild, emotional havoc will result that may take a long time to repair.

It is best always to know your limits and to proceed with full consciousness and a sense of responsibility into each undertaking. You are too gifted to allow negative emotions to overcome you. However, your challenge comes in knowing your own worth and making every act an act of love—first to yourself and then to others.

LOVE

Falling in love with love is one of your favorite pastimes. The history of the Libra personality is *"L'amour, l'amour toujours . . ."*

At the deepest part of you, you seek the beatitudes of romantic bliss. However, it often appears that you are far more in love with the idea of love than with the actuality.

You have a refined, idealistic nature that holds stock in the myth of "happily ever after." And this is not to say that two people can't be. However, it always takes at least a little work and many confrontations to come about. Especially in your early years, you cling to the fantasy of being swept away by an uncontrollable force that just starts to accommodate itself to your life. If, from this point, things start to go wrong, you either lose interest or feel hopeless, depressed, and overcome by the pain.

Basically, you want to hear bells ring. You also wouldn't mind a few lights going on at the same time. Anyone who can create this situation for you can occupy a secure place in your life for as long as the bells and lights last. You are attracted to a strong, forceful personality that reeks of both stability and charisma. However, when Cupid calls, you come running, and sometimes the situation is far from ideal.

The deepest part of you seeks to complete yourself in a union with another person, and until you find that missing link, you never feel totally fulfilled. Because your emotional needs are tremendous, you have a hard time making it through life all alone. When one partnership ends, it's a relatively short time before you find another one, and sometimes you treat your lovers like replaceable parts.

You tend to have strong feelings of dependence that you project onto the person with whom you become involved, and then you start to see life a matter of "we" instead of "I." However, until you are ready to exist in a relationship more as a complete person than as a clinging vine, your satisfaction will always be constricted by your anxiety.

When you put all of your energies into one person, you stand to lose a lot if it doesn't work. Therefore, you tend to get stuck in painful spaces that only you have created.

Try to remember that the more you expand your inner resources, rather than waiting for it all to come to you, the more you will gain in the long run. Also, the more you develop yourself, the less you have to lose in any relationship. Until you learn the lesson of selfreliance, the experience of love will be more of a compulsion than a creative emotional situation. Open your awareness to the limitless universe you live in, and try to transcend your frail ego to get to a place of peace you need never relinquish.

MARRIAGE

At some point or another, marriage is a must, since you nurture a profound need for shared experience. However, because you also seek an abstract ideal, in the long run you may emerge disillusioned.

It is not uncommon for Libras to have more than one marriage, because the feelings in the first one "mysteriously" attenuate. However, whether or not any marriage will be lasting really depends on your realistic assessment of your own values.

In addition, many Libras have a severe problem when it comes to give-and-take. They either give far too much or not at all. And this imbalance ultimately creates anger on at least one side of the relationship.

Deep down, you're searching for a soulmate. However on your quest you often get distracted by a superficial quality that you find terribly attractive. And then you abandon your inner need for a mature love to satisfy your outer need for either luxury or physical beauty. Consequently, you find yourself years later saddened and lonely.

In your ideal scheme of things, you would never live your life alone. However, it is precisely this rigid idea that sometimes makes you desperate, dependent, and closed off to more varied life experiences.

Many Libra women want to get married at the earliest age possible. Libra men are more cavalier and less overtly consumed by this need. Quite happily they can survey the field and make the most of the experience while they're doing it.

However, when a Libra represents a high degree of evolvement, marriage can be a most joyous and emotionally rewarding situation. For within the union is a close to perfect love attained through sympathetic understanding, emotional maturity, and a desire to give for the sake of giving. This Libra knows how to bridge the gap between the sexes until it no longer exists. Rather, there come to be two souls joined together in one exalted union that grows more solid as the years grow on.

MONEY

Since you love luxury, you can spend more money in one day than most people do in a year. You have sybaritic sensibilities, and an eye for the very best. After a particularly dreary day, a twenty-dollar bottle of wine helps bring up those saddened spirits. Five new pairs of designer pants worth five hundred dollars can also do wonders. And of course a simply devastating dinner at the most resplendent restaurant in town can take you to an emotional place that you feel is really worth paying for.

Since you are a confirmed adherent to the principle of immediate gratification, a peculiar little mood can ravage your pocketbook worse than a robbery. However should someone confront you with the undeniable fact that you spend more money than the interior decorator at the White House, you would probably stop and face the person with a perplexed expression. You really aren't at all extravagant, you protest. That's because you've already forgotten about the swimming pool, the oriental rug, the Mercedes, the six-thousand-dollar sofa, and last week's bottle of rare wine that cost more than many a small wine cellar. In your mind, these are life's little necessities. You really live a very simple life. After all, even your gilded china is getting chipped, and you haven't even considered a replacement.

It might be said in your defense that, unlike some signs, you are capable of keeping a budget. However, as is seen far more often, the budget has a sneaky way of keeping you.

CAREER

Although Libra often experiences a large degree of success due to an inherent creative capacity, this is not the most important factor of your satisfaction and happiness. When your love life is nonexistent, even a five-million-dollar salary and your face plastered on every magazine cover are not enough to raise you from the doldrums.

You need lots of love, affection, friendliness, and warmth—in a very personal way. Otherwise, after you leave the splendor of the public fanfare and go home alone to your lovely abode, the happy feelings of the day slip away and you are suddenly sad and very gloomy.

However, if you have someone behind you to act as a sounding board and to help you decide whether you should eat tuna fish or filet mignon (the big decisions, you carry off with an enviable élan; it's the little ones that get you cornered), then you feel far more equipped to deal with success issues.

You have talent, creativity, and charisma coming out your ears. And its only a matter of time until you are recognized and duly rewarded for your endeavors. However, even when that magical time comes, there is often a horrible sense of disbelief and a feeling of dread that maybe this materialization of your fantasies will just evaporate and go back to being a dream. Although to the outside world you represent poise, calm, and self-containment, inside you are far more shaky and unsure than your public would ever imagine. You have a most unfortunate way of putting yourself down for everything you do that is less than perfect, until you've lived long enough to realize that other people aren't perfect either. After a few years, when their flaws start becoming conspicuous and your successes start overtaking your self-criticism, you may get to the point where you'll admit to your best friend that you are pretty good after all (although it may give you an anxiety attack to acknowledge it openly).

To gain success in life, most people have to overcome a lack of talent. However, all you have to overcome is yourself. Once you decide that success is important to you, what you have to do is: (1) stop worrying about other people, (2) don't let what's happening or not happening with your love life interfere, (3) exercise plenty of self-discipline, and (4) give yourself a daily dose of praise for all your *little* accomplishments.

However, since you have more talent and creativity up your sleeve than most people witness in a lifetime, the choice of your profession could be a problem. But that's only because there are almost too many things you can do.

The entire field of the arts is open to you, and within this framework, music and writing have very high possibilities. However, fashion could also be an area in which your creativity and your shrewd mind blend energies to bring you to the top.

But if you are the more homespun type, a career in handicrafts—making them, marketing them, and perhaps teaching how to construct them—could bring you much satisfaction.

Many Libras choose acting as a profession because they not only need the outlet for their romanticism but also desire the attention that comes from being in front of an audience. And since Libra is the sign of the beautiful, many natives find themselves following a career in modeling that subsequently opens doors for them to pursue their artistic endeavors.

Because Libra has an extraordinary eye for exactitude, a career in either architecture or interior decorating could prove fulfilling.

For those Libras who prefer to unleash their creativity on Sunday afternoons rather than five days a week, the area of law could lead to a most challenging and rewarding career and should definitely be considered. Since Libra is a formidable negotiator, agenting in the entertainment field could both fulfill the need for a business framework and provide an outlet for those creative sensibilities.

But whatever career is chosen, a need for self-expression must be satisfied. Otherwise, frustrations will build to a point where new decisions must be considered and the appropriate action taken.

FRIENDS

Friends are a definite prerequisite for your total emotional happiness. Without them, you feel lonely, dissatisfied, and saddened.

You love to socialize and give lavish parties that people remember for months afterward, including dinners that simply defy one's gustatorial imagination.

You like to talk on the telephone for hours on end and to know you have special people in your life waiting to share meaningful moments. And since you are loath to go for a walk or even to a movie alone, you deeply appreciate a most constant companionship. As a friend you are warm and generous, and usually are appreciated for all your good qualities. When you entertain, you turn your entire home over to your guests. And when you are called upon in a moment of need, your good intentions and sound advice go very far to further the welfare of others.

At the very least, you're lots of fun to be with, and that's because you're full of life and love to have a good time. Because you have a way of making even the most prosaic moments seem like special occasions, people love to be around you. Likewise, you love to be around them. But, more important, in the very nicest ways, you know how to show it.

HEALTH

Because you have a delicate nervous system, it is more than wise to try not to overextend yourself. Too many nights on the town can leave you crabby and irritable the next day.

Libras love to overindulge, and food, alcohol, and occasionally drugs offer problem areas leading to a less than salubrious existence. You especially adore the divine high of drugs and drinking, because the tedium of everyday life slips away and suddenly leaves you in a joyous phantasm. However, Libras who have come to rely on the joys of their own creativity can get the same effect from the experience of fiction, a piece of music, a painting, or some highly charged poetry.

Since your kidneys are a vulnerable part of your body, any drug and alcohol use that starts to become an addiction can bring you more physical ailments than it's worth. Try to observe a balance in your pleasure-seeking behavior, and you will have a much better time for a much longer time.

Basically, there are two types of Libras: those who are obsessed with dieting and those who are dallying in obesity. Always, two versions of the extreme. The first type can suffer from malnutrition and vitamin deficiency in the desire to stay fashionably thin. The latter type can ultimately suffer from diabetes, low blood sugar, and the battle of the bulge in the desire to stay physically satisfied. This Libra has a sweet tooth that could consume a city of sugar. And while the first type eats just to live, this second type lives just to eat. Remember that not only will too much gourmandizing lead to a greater expanse of waistline, but also too little eating of the wrong foods can leave you feeling gloomy and lackluster.

Depression and a nonspecific "down" feeling are fairly common with Libras. It's due not only to an acute nervous sensitivity that is being ignored but also to a lack of decisiveness that sometimes causes you to endure a situation that at the same time you resist. Seek psychotherapy if you feel persistently out of accord with yourself. And if you are nervous and high-strung after a hard day at work, swallow some high-potency B-complex vitamins, put on some soothing music, close your eyes, and relax. Tomorrow is another day. Try to look forward to it without fear of failure, disappointment, or abandonment. Life is really what you make it. However, first you have to decide what you want it to be.

HOME

Since Libras love luxury, your home is always a reflection of your tastes.

You are very much a dinner-party person and hand a glass to everyone who enters your domicile. You are also the most gracious of people, and your home has a special way of exuding your aesthetic sensitivities.

You dine off imported china and sip libations from the sheerest crystal—so delicate that a mere fingernail might make it shatter. Mauve candles and voluptuous peonies (out of season and flown in for the occasion) set the stage for the most sybaritic kind of repast.

It's a special treat to be invited to one of your dinners (almost as exciting as Christmas). Your need for perfection pervades your cooking, which makes your guests sigh and close their eyes in a reverent kind of silence. As they open them, they are served the most memorable wine—chilled and frosty, dry, and so aromatic that one tries to delay the swallowing.

In the living room, a roaring fire awaits you with, of course, a snifter of cognac. A lavender chaise beckons from beside the crisp white fireplace. And how can you resist sinking into it?

On lazy evenings, you read by the fire—delicious romances that lend a touch of melodrama to your emotions. At times, your dreamy eyes drift off, to focus on a color in your oriental carpet. Far-off places come to mind, luring you along through imaginary voyages.

In domestic decor you are nothing less than an inspired artist continually bursting with new ideas. You bring the outside into the inner you with a spreading fig tree that helps you recall springtime. However, for the bedroom it's definitely palm trees to stretch majestically over your pillows, along with purple bed linen to give you those X-rated dreams.

You love a lot of space in which to wander. However, even if you have to live in less, you inherently know how to make it work for you. You don't need riches (although they never hurt). All you do need is the impetus to rise above yourself to confront your own creativity. Once you do that, you can turn a one-bedroom apartment into a palace.

INSPIRATION

You are the creative force of the universe, and your energies are felt by all. You are the messenger of love, art, and inspiration. Your energies flow through your soul out into the ethers, where they illuminate the consciousness of humanity. Contained within your self-expression is all the drama of existence, filtered through a prism of divine beauty. You carry within you the splendors of balanced force, and unleash them with a sense of justice and understanding that elevates the collective unconscious. You represent truth and timeless aesthetics in their most exalted state. You are Libra, the sign of universal love and beauty.

COSMIC CHALLENGE

Your cosmic challenge is to learn how to be alone and like it. Intrinsic to this is learning how to love yourself for yourself.

Relationships are a wonderful and necessary part of existence. However, when you use them as an excuse for not confronting your inner being, then they can become a hazard to your total functioning.

When you love, you must love as a consciously complete being, not as an appendage that clings and has claws that dig in. A husband or wife cannot give you what you feel you are lacking in yourself. He or she can only form the kind of emotional support that will allow you to find it.

As an excuse for not making your own decisions, you have a way of creating a love situation in which the partner controls you. However, in this kind of situation you can only postpone what you ultimately have to face— taking total responsibility for your own existence. The longer you postpone it, the more deeply painful it will become and the more anxiety you will feel in relation to the person you love.

Probably the hardest lesson you will ever face in your life is learning that there is a self and discovering what that means once you've found it. If you can abandon your fears and learn to like yourself, there will be no other joy in this lifetime than can be greater. And finally, the love you give will be equal to the love you take.

WHAT HOLDS YOU BACK
AND HOW TO OVERCOME IT

Your principal pitfall is your sense of insecurity. This is the demon that evokes your indecisiveness, depression, worry, and fearfulness. You have a mind that tends to work overtime, but in the wrong direction.

Like no other sign, you obsess about what other people think of you and brood about rejection before it even happens. At moments you are defensive and hostile. At others, morose and whiny.

Some very basic and sound advice: the less time you spend thinking about yourself, the better. Make sure that your time is well planned, and keep yourself too busy to begin brooding.

Another suggestion: involve yourself more with other people. Get yourself into the position of being the support to others that you so seek for yourself, and a deep sense of well-being will come back to you. Libras are notorious for being self-obsessed. However, when you live your life from this perspective, every little problem becomes a major issue and takes on a dimension of importance that is totally out of proportion.

The quickest way to strengthen yourself is to gain distance from yourself. When you gain a perspective from which you can watch your thoughts and your actions objectively, then you will be less passive to your own life and more willing to take responsibility for what occurs within it.

Finally, on those gloomy days when nothing seems to work and you start to feel like you're the only person in the world who has problems, try to remember this ancient Chinese aphorism: "While I pitied myself because I had no shoes, I met a man who had no feet."

LOVE AND
COMPATIBILITY GUIDE

Libra with Libra

Together you are a dreamy-eyed pair in love with love and each other. You are the creators of the coziest love nest, replete with those sybaritic luxuries that make life more than divine.

On blustery winter evenings you snuggle up in front of a brilliant fire and murmur love secrets.

Lazy summer afternoons see you sleeping in the sun —of course, together! Later, you sit, sun-baked but blissful, holding hands through the waning dusk, slowly sipping Singapore Slings, and getting high on each other.

Every sentence begins with "we" and trails off into mid-fantasy. Your dreams nurture you during the daytime when you have to be apart. Your thoughts are like drugs that you depend on. They take you anywhere you want to go. And you want to go a lot of places.

Libra with Libra means no limits on romanticism. You have a ticket for the heavens, and they reach out to you as you make love. However, it may take months for the marriage to be consummated, since neither of you enjoys making that first move.

Libra Woman with Aries Man

You will make his life a beautiful place to live in, and he will give you the romantic excitement you so need. At dinner, you'll drown him in the mellifluous tones of Mozart, as well as in his favorite vintage of Pouilly Fuissé.

He will feel like a sultan as he sits in the lap of loving luxuries. He will sweep you off your feet and leave you feeling shaky but blissful. Sexually, he will take you by storm and give you strings of sleepless nights that you'll come to count on, and his unbridled passions will take you places you've never been before. However, it's where you feel you're going that you worry about.

All that startling surface romanticism is fantastic for a great beginning. But you need much more than that, since you are not a one-night woman. Rather, you are the prototype of the marrying kind. But that's all right, because you certainly can be a good one.

You have patience, sophistication, dignity, and graciousness. You are also sensitive, kind, and can see two sides of every issue. You can put up with his temper, even if you have to put your head under a pillow. And you can endure his selfishness if you know that there really is some love underneath it. You will rationalize his shortcomings and the fact that he always seems to interrupt you when you're going to say something. And you will understand his ego needs even if they make you grind your teeth in another room.

Your approach is more quiet than he normally likes, since he appreciates the kind of woman who will have herself shot out of a cannon just to get his attention. He also likes a woman who knows how to make demands, while you tend to be silent and accepting.

Once he realizes that his "challenges" are getting repetitive and that each new face seems to look like the old one, then he may be ready to settle down. However, he will definitely shock himself when he sees that he's starting to live for those quiet moments, when caring is far more meaningful than cavorting.

Libra Woman with Taurus Man

This could be romance at second sight. You have the sense of beauty he so admires, and he has the money to buy the beauty you so desire.

Emotionally, you are so up and down that you'll fall in love with him mostly because he never gets depressed. He is a force of stability, while you are wishy-washy. You are an ethereal romantic, and he is a practical idealist.

He'll take care of your moods by buying you trinkets and smothering you with love. You'll satisfy his sybaritic desires by cooking him such a delectable dinner that it sends him into a swoon.

He'll give you so much attention that you'll stop sulking and whining. You'll conjure such creature comforts for him that he'll never be the same.

You need someone with strong arms, and he is just the person who can imprison you. At the same time, he needs a woman who knows how to lean.

Your affair together will have the romance of a 1940's movie, redone for color television. And your marriage will consist of those tender moments of which only advertising knows for sure.

Libra Woman with Gemini Man

Superficially, you seem to have the kind of love at which strangers marvel. However, what happens beneath the surface is something else altogether.

You need loads of emotional support, and he's like a matchstick to lean on. You are basically so insecure that you marvel at how your own mother loves you, and he is a constant reinforcement to your lack of assurance. You are romantic, sentimental, and are waiting for a kind of Cary Grant to just carry you away, while he is about as romantic as Joe Namath during an autumn workout.

At first, you are charmed by his sense of humor. However, when you realize how much you suffer for it, it has a way of losing its appeal.

He considers you gracious, charming, and well-mannered, but, on closer inspection, so dependent that after a while he feels like he's been drafted. You'll love his quick lines; he'll appreciate your creativity. He'll keep you laughing all the way to the church, but when he doesn't show up, suddenly everything ceases to be funny.

More than anything else, you are looking for a dependable kind of man who takes you seriously. So, unless he is either very highly evolved or has just had a prefrontal lobotomy, this relationship needs a lot of work before it can be considered a workable one.

Libra Woman with Cancer Man

He'll give you all the attention you so crave and delight in creating those cozy stay-at-home evenings you truly love. During dinner parties he'll definitely help you cook and will probably originate a few gustatorial delights of his own.

However, he *will* question why you had to spend close to a thousand dollars on stemware, and why you needed a new pair of two-hundred-dollar boots when last year's still look perfectly new.

There will be moments when his moodiness will make you morose. But not enough to take away from the general experience of joy you can have just being together.

He will tell you how attractive you are at least five times a week, lose a little sleep when you get the sniffles, and help you rearrange the furniture on rainy Sundays. After a hard day, you won't have to ask him to hold you, and during one of your "down" days you can expect him to sympathize with your dreary emotions.

He is sensitive, kind, caring, and deeply feeling. Even if he has cut off from his emotions in an attempt to obviate vulnerability, you can help restore his emotional balance. Basically, he wants a woman he can be secure with, and you want the same, plus the pleasures of shared experience. Together, you could create a romance of which only dreams are made. And with all of your Libra charm, it's an easy task to transform a dream into the most romantic kind of reality.

Libra Woman with Leo Man

You want a companion; he wants a face that belongs in a couturier's catalog. If you have Venus on the ascendant, nice going—for him. He'll get the beauty of which he can boast. You'll get enough baubles to keep your mouth shut and make you think you're getting a lover.

You've always wanted a caretaker, and he's always wanted the power he feels from taking care. You are submissive, you smile a lot, and you settle for whatever makes him happy. And since it's exactly this kind of behavior that makes him happy, you could be *the* woman of his dreams—if only he were stimulated by your temperament.

But since he can't have everything and knows he's got to grab what he needs, he'll marry you at twenty, and then at forty he'll daydream a lot. You'll still be smiling—and wearing so much jewelry you won't be able to walk. All the better, since you're his possession, which means you had just better hang out close to home or else his temper will make you break out in acne.

You are so terrified of his anger fits that you shudder a lot and watch his eyes for the early signals. Although these periods have given you a phobia, they also keep you in good physical shape, since you do a lot of room-to-room running.

You are truly invaluable, since you have never learned you can make demands. In a mewling tone, you tenderly negotiate and usually settle for what you had before you began negotiating. Therefore, if one meets you at forty and asks you if you're happy, you'll stare back blankly and murmur that he works a lot. He does. You're not getting any younger, and he's got to keep you in plastic surgeons.

Beyond a doubt, you are the most pleasant woman with whom he could spend a lifetime. You do what you're told, you enhance his self-image, and you consider it a treat when you get to share his spare time. The only bad part is that you bore him past the point of death. But then, life and death are so relative and philosophic. What really matters to him is the fundamentals—constant compliments. Because of you, they keep coming. So perhaps he should carry a cassette and just fantasize for the rest of his needs.

Libra Woman with Virgo Man

There is a kind of substance to this man that is truly attractive. You will admire the way he never agonizes over decisions, but sees every issue as cut-and-dried. You will be overwhelmed by his discipline in the face of distracting influences. And you will have respect for the way he does what he feels he has to do, without making a big deal about it.

However, should he start nagging you about the way you wash the dishes, and start giving you a dissertation about how you should improve your dental habits, suddenly you find that you can barely stifle a yawn.

In general, he will enjoy your *savoir faire,* your domestic graciousness, and your sophisticated appreciation of beautiful things. However, he'll let you know that the way you handle your money is monstrous and that you have to be demented to pay three hundred dollars for a simple linen tablecloth, even if it was imported.

He will have a hard time getting into accord with your love of luxury and will never comprehend why, when you're depressed, you have to pay thirty dollars to get your legs waxed. Instead, he'll tell you to take a course in mental and emotional discipline that is offered on television at 5:30 A.M.

Despite any kind of compatibility that can be achieved here, there will always be communication gaps that have to be carefully worked out. However, since you can see both sides of any question, and his understanding is a bit more restricted, the responsibility is really on your shoulders. In the long run, you may find that a little work time invested in this relationship could be well worth it. Mr. Virgo is not a game player. He is kind, loving, and considerate. However, it's up to you whether he is also receptive to change.

Libra Woman with Scorpio Man

You'll give him a sense of balance, and in return he'll give you a taste of intense love. You have a special sense of the beautiful and can create a setting of the most seductive creature comforts.

He'll appreciate your good sense of humor and the fact that you are airy and easy to be with. You'll detoxify his murky moods and fill his life with the little loving acts that take his heart away.

You are sentimental and romantic. However, with him you'll have time to die and be reborn waiting for a little love murmur. You fantasize about the day when he'll bring you flowers, but if you search his pockets for a trinket, all you'll find is a corporate financial statement.

You are so dependent that you hate to even go to the bathroom alone. And he is so independent that he can't understand your dependency. You are open and want to share every part of your life. He is closed and wants to share only selected moments.

You are sensual and loving, while he is sexual and possessive. Despite your faults, you are everything he wants and needs.

The question is whether he is everything you want and need. But since your needs overtake your desires, you'll be able to settle and make yourself enjoy it.

Libra Woman with Sagittarius Man

He is truly cute, charming, witty, and lovable. However, how long you can tolerate his terrible table manners is quite another matter.

He's like Dennis the Menace breaking into adolescence. And that's a heavy load for a lady who favors maturity, sophistication, and graciousness. He has about as much *savoir faire* as a forest ranger. He burps in public, makes animal noises when he swallows, and wears a T-shirt and combat boots to your most elegant dinner party.

Mr. Sagittarius is a most spontaneous guy who likes to be left alone to do his thing and to tread about *au naturel*. He is a law unto himself, and written into that law is a clause that forbids a deep sense of responsibility. He has the most adventurous ideas, but when it comes to carrying them out, he is like a child looking at his first

Christmas tree, and the next moment, all the toys under it are broken.

If you take him at his word, you may find that you'll be waiting a lifetime. His memory is conveniently short, and so are his relationships. He sees women as a kind of entertainment that is almost as good as a great western. He'll give you his entire attention for the part that's fun. But if you need a man who's willing to be a responsible friend as well as a lover, Mr. Sagittarius is not to be considered even in your most desperate flights of fancy. Instead, think of him as an outlandish escort who is truly amusing, but certainly not a romantic stopping place.

Libra Woman with Capricorn Man

Deep down inside, both of you are insecure. However, he has a much stronger personality and a tendency to be controlling. At first, you may feel it's splendid to be so loved; however, later on, you have to admit that he is truly bossy.

He is that tree you can lean on, but the harder you lean, the greater the price. At his most primitive self, he is the outrageous kind of male chauvinist who will tell you what to eat, when to cross the street, and what to cook to keep him happy. He'll reorganize your life, inform you how to live it, and pat you warmly on the head while he points out your feminine foolishness.

The price he exacts for being so nurturing is total subservience and filial devotion. Fundamentally, he likes to play Daddy and have you be the giggling little girl. That means you must obey him, because he knows what's right for you better than you know it, and of course, that's what's right for himself. (However, don't expect to understand this part, because he'll tell you that it's all beyond you.)

If you do as he says and don't give him any lip, he'll refer to you as a "good woman." But then, with him breathing over your shoulder, when would you get the opportunity to be bad?

Whatever he does, Mr. Capricorn means well. However, his level of awareness is as advanced as that of the gorilla who grunts and beats his chest to get the female to favor his wishes. He is typically the kind of person to exit from a self-awareness seminar feeling sorry for those other people with the problems.

If you happen to favor a man who is seeking to transform a woman into a Jane of the Jungle with a severe speech impediment to prevent any back talk, this is most definitely the man for you. What you will get in return for such subjugation is the security that he loves you. But with love like this, you might as well work in a geriatric clinic. There, at least, after a hard day on your feet, you know the people will go to bed early. However, Mr. Capricorn likes to stay up late to tell you how much you need him, and to give you midnight reminders of your orders for the next day. After all, he doesn't want you to forget what you're supposed to do, because then he'll have to gentle berate you for your bad memory. And you're just too good a woman for him to make you feel bad.

Libra Woman with Aquarius Man

Any way you look at it, he's a little strange and eccentric, but also kind and very understanding. However, the difference here is that he hangs out in his head, while you tend to get stuck in your heart.

You'll meet him at a party, where he seems to be talking to everyone at once and then drifts off into a corner to observe for a while. He is a people person, and in a small amount of time loves to touch as many lives as possible.

He comes alive in a crowd, while you are tantalized by an intimate tête-à-tête. He is detached and warmly impersonal, while you are terribly attached and personalize the world with which you come in contact.

This man is definitely loving, but not necessarily in the way you *think* you need it. He can be loyal, devoted, and most delightful; however, he needs his space. At the same time, you have a way of feeling insecure when the person you love would rather be by himself than with you. And you tend to need the kind of attentions that Mr. Aquarius might not always be around to give.

You feel a need for shared experience, but Mr. Aquarius needs the feeling of being free. That does not mean that he will abandon you because he's found someone better. Rather, he needs to spend a day in solitude, falling in love with his astronomy equipment, or he wants to attend a seminar on quadraphonic amplifiers—alone.

If you can discipline yourself to enjoy your own company, there need not be a problem. Mr. Aquarius needs a woman he feels is an equal in terms of developed individuality. He'll be your best friend, and help you with all your problems, but when you start treating him like a pillow, then suddenly the fun ends. Mr. Aquarius is a man who is warm, human, but also self-reliant and eager for new experience. If you can develop the same attitude, there are no limits to this relationship. But if you want a man who is more a cushion than a thinking being, you'd be better off walking on by him without any expectations.

Libra Woman with Pisces Man

He's a sentimentalist who will send you soaring past the limits of your logic. He will make you feel like you're the first woman he's ever wooed, and the only one he ever wants to. Together you will enter into a dreamlike existence where love becomes a drug more debilitating than the fruits of the poppy.

However, one day you may wake up from your romantic interlude to note that you are lying next to a man who is weaker than you are. At this point, you may slowly break out in an aggravated case of acne as you try to decide what to do for the next lively episode.

You are an open person who loves to communicate about feelings. However, except for a few effusive rhapsodies about the way he feels when the light shines on your pupils, Mr. Pisces is for the most part closed. You have a reverent attitude toward your own emotions; he would rather keep his in the closet. You love shared experience, but there are only limited portions of himself he is willing to share. He exists pretty much in the vault of his subconscious fantasies, while you can spend a lifetime trying to make your daydreams become real.

Emotionally, you both might be coming from similar places. However, how you approach life is different enough to create frictions of the minor sort. You want a man you can lean on. Mr. Pisces wants the same, but in a woman. Lean on him, and the two of you will topple over. However, if you feel you are willing to bypass the emotional brace to get to the companionship, and you don't mind enduring a regular assortment of murky moods, give it a try. You may end up with a bad back, because he can really be a heavy load, but whatever makes you happy is worth a little physical sacrifice.

Libra Man with Aries Woman

You'll drive her to a point just short of sheer insanity, because you're so indecisive. And she'll make you both nervous and depressed as she injures your self-esteem.

She is not an easy woman for you to contend with. She's so hot-tempered that at times she terrifies you, while you're so subtle that you make her lose her patience.

At first you were drawn to her—like a lamb scampering toward a butcher. However, after a few shaky scenes, when you decided she was even worse than your mother, even the fact that she was famous could no longer hold her to you.

She wants a man who will announce to the gods that he's never been so in love. If you attempt this, though, the original feelings probably won't last long. It is far more likely that she will torment you to just say *something*, and what you will say is that you really don't know what to say. While she's waiting impatiently for you to scream that you would die for her, instead you will mutter morosely that you have no idea what you feel. At which point she shouts, "Speak up!" because she's suddenly convinced herself she's hard of hearing.

Undoubtedly, the most romantic statement you'll make to her after the initial novelty wears off is that you don't *not* want her and that she's a really nice person. "Now, that's not true!" she shouts, with enough force to kill you. She hates being called "nice." It sounds as innocuous as being crippled.

Together, you are great for that blistering romance that lasts about five days, or as long as a package vacation to Puerto Rico. What happens after that time is a truly uprooting experience that you never would want to face sober. So it might be best to just drink up as you travel fast in totally divergent directions.

Libra Man with Taurus Woman

She'll think she's "in" when you begin all your sentences with "we." However, she should listen longer. There's a lot more for the hearing, like the little words "I love you." But she should not be surprised if she finds herself smoking, eating, waiting, and listening. . . .

Basically, you want to hear bells ring, while she's content to sacrifice the sound effects for some silence on solid ground. However, with you she'll only be treading in the cracks. You are not the one to lean on; nor are you the one to allay her insecurities. On the contrary, you may both confirm and create them.

You are a ladies' man, while she is a one-man lady. She'll demand to know if you're coming or going, and you've never considered the question, since you're usually stuck in between.

You'll love the way she takes care of you when you're sick, cooks for you when you're hungry, and cleans for you when you're lazy. However, when Saturday night comes and she finds herself alone and caressing the phone, she shouldn't start telling herself you're seeing your mother.

If she invites you over for Sunday brunch (that she's stayed up all night to prepare) and asks you what you were doing on Saturday, you'll smile in a friendly sort of way and tell her you took your fiancée to dinner.

One thing that can certainly be said about you is that you are honest. As a matter of fact, you have the kind of candor that kills. You'll inform her why you could never love her and share with her what it was that you were looking for and found in another woman. If she's smart, she'll tell you to look for the door. If it's cooking for another person that she's really into, she could get more ultimate appreciation from opening a catering service.

Libra Man with Gemini Woman

She'll adore the fact that you're romantic but not suffocating. You're intrigued with the fact that she's so clever that she always seems to call your next move.

You'll bring her violets and drown her in champagne cocktails when she feels crabby. She'll make you laugh like a fool in those murky moments when you no longer love yourself. When you're around her, lots of nitty-gritty nonsense no longer seems to matter. When she's around you, your tender little attentions start to get addictive.

You both love people, parties, the idea of midnight rendezvous, and the kinds of amusements that have the invincible luster of the first time.

You want a woman who will be your soulmate. She's

never considered such a thing, yet she's always willing to try something new.

Once you know you want her, you'll go a-wooing with a book of double crostics, the best of H. L. Mencken, and a collection of the wit and wisdom of Oscar Wilde. And that is one package compelling enough to make her stop talking for at least five minutes.

No matter how sophisticated you are, there's a part of you that's like a shy, unsure little boy. At your best, you're irresistible. At her best, she's a one-woman show. You can give each other gaiety, laughter, inspiration, and the creative urge to go ahead and conquer the world. It's been waiting too long for such talented teamwork. Even at dinner, you can be the greatest couple since Fred Astaire and Ginger Rogers. The only difference is that you'll play the violin and she'll supply the lines to make you look like Liberace.

Libra Man with Cancer Woman

Not only will she give you all the attentions of Mother, she'll throw in a few more. However, after she has poured herself out to you endlessly, and all you have said to her is that you can't decide what you want in a woman, it should be a running good-bye. But, unfortunately, she'll just hang around for a few more of these tender emotional scenes.

You consider yourself to be a person with feelings. You are, but unfortunately they're mostly for yourself. When you kiss her, you want to hear *Rhapsody in Blue*, but instead, all you hear is her whistling tea kettle. But please don't get too put out. Stop and realize that the tea is for you.

She needs to be smothered in love, while you need to sit back and think about it. Therefore, at times, when she barricades the door with her body, you feel a bit too confined for your liking. She'll send you little cards to remind you she's still living (as if you could forget, because she calls you every day). Finally, the agonizing time will come when you must confront her with the truth: you have to hear bells ring. At this point, she'll get up and lean on her doorbell. Slowly, you shake your head. She offers to carry cymbals.

It takes a lot for this woman to realize that it's really

over. But it takes even more for you to realize that it's
even begun. The emotional timing here is so bad that it
would probably take more than a lifetime for both of you
to get it together. First, it might be helpful if you both die
and get reborn into another sign.

Libra Man with Leo Woman

You'll compliment her clothing, send her seventeen
valentines, and learn to make love without smudging her
lip gloss. She'll consider you the man who invented
romance. Therefore, she won't be surprised when she
receives tender telegrams at ten P.M. and roses with
champagne at midnight.

She will share your love for the ballet, baroque music, and books that no one else has heard of. You both
love luxury, have a strong sense of beauty, and take Sweet
'n' Low on your grapefruit.

On gauzy evenings you dine in the splendor of fine
crystal, piano strains, and flowers. And on cold winter
nights, it's a roaring fire, cognac, and quiet talk.

Yes, life with you can be more than lovely. But only
if she holds her breath and smiles a lot. To say the least,
you are terrified of her temper, and those stormy scenes
startle your soul right out of your body. To maintain
peace at all costs is your pastime. Never before has she
considered it hers. So, suddenly, there may be a lot she
has to reconsider. You do not at all like to suffer, and
in the heat of her temper, can easily disappear as quickly
as you came in.

If she behaves, and you are the mature type, this
could be a lasting union. However, the more youthful
Libra is often a slave to his sense of beauty, and incapable
of any monogamous commitment. It is true that you feel
most fulfilled with a partner, but in a lifetime you are
capable of having even more than many.

Her jealousy is her obvious nemesis. And agonizing
insecurity falls on its footsteps. She feels like she's a contestant in the Miss America contest and wonders if she'll
make the finals or be coldly eliminated as "Miss Talent."
This kind of competition was never her forte, but also the
kind of man you are may not be worth the waiting. It
would be best for her to go home, think it over, and ask
herself if she wants it to be excitement through sharing,
or whether she is willing to settle for a bathing-suit con-

test. Her ultimate choice will be nothing more than what she'll get.

Libra Man with Virgo Woman

She has a terrible habit of taking you at your word. Therefore, when you mumble the word "marriage" in a drunken moment after she has cooked you a devastating dinner, don't expect her to forget it as fast as you do.

She is earthy, shy, and exacting, while you are airy, indiscriminate, and convivial. You like a good time and often overlook how you get it. However, she appreciates a man she can trust, and there is no way she can forget his feelings.

She is faithful, kind, caring, and very serious. You are often unfaithful, cruel without realizing it, and sensitive only to your own needs. You can cover up the necessity for responsibility by bemoaning your own confusion, and have a very clever way, at the same time, of trying to extract her sympathy. Too often it works, because she is so empathic, self-effacing, and delighted to be able to do something for someone else.

Basically, she is a woman who needs to be needed, while you are a man who has just too many needs. But if she is so dedicated to the idea of service that she likes to play Clara Barton to a person who will hardly appreciate it, then that's her problem. But in the long run, if she allows her brains to socialize with her emotions, she might get the message that it would be best for her to just move on. Some men are demanding, but you require a romantic dream that personifies Woman. So, for whatever it's worth, perhaps you should make your own movie, pick your own actresses, and then sit back and watch your veins pulse.

Libra Man with Scorpio Woman

One look, and she'll have you, but it will be quite some time before you feel that you have her.

You are a charmer, but she sees through you. At times, she'll think you're superficial and lacking in substance. At others, she will appreciate your sense of romance and the fact that you prefer Bach's organ music to a chorus by the Rolling Stones.

You'll try to woo her with lilacs, champagne, and perfume, and if she prepares dinner, you'll bring her fresh basil for the salad. But when you win her, it's only with an offer of a lasting relationship.

Should you take forever to make the commitment, and she finds you flirting on the side, you might as well bring over a wicker basket and take back your trinkets. Suddenly she doesn't want you, any more than she desires a sudden case of kidney poisoning.

Although a highly evolved Libra is surely a lovable creature, the daily garden variety tends to daydream a lot about whom they don't have. You are taken in by the superficials, while she probes and patiently waits for the substance. You fly around to do the Mr. Friendly routine, but only with the beautiful faces. At the same time, she stays in one place, looks aloof, and ponders what you could be saying that's taking so long. But should she notice that you're leaning over some lovely who's writing down numbers, it's curtains for you, and more time with her own company for her.

Give you a lifetime, and you'll never understand her. However, you may desperately fall in love, moan over her cooking, and keep referring to a future of connubial bliss. However, she should make sure that that future is with *you* before her obsessional heart gets carried away. You may already be a newlywed whose wife is visiting her mother. You hate to be alone, and at such times can be mawkishly sentimental. So when the spout turns on, she should check to see that the water is flowing in her direction. Otherwise, she should leave her picture on your pillow, have her phone number changed, and let you suffer.

Libra Man with Sagittarius Woman

Her exuberant enthusiasm has a magical way of conjuring up your wildest romantic feelings. Her sunny personality will sweep you off your feet, and her philosophical attitudes will inspire your deepest admiration.

When you're with her, it seems that there's action in every corner. She'll take you tramping in the woods to look for wildflowers, and you'll teach her the difference between rococo and baroque music.

She's a panacea for your loneliness, and you're an electric awakening to the sentiments she never knew she had. Her jovial sense of humor will incite you to throw all caution to the winds and come on as the impetuous romantic who has lost his mind and doesn't even want to get it back.

You'll tell her you love her twenty times a day, and she'll giggle good-naturedly and wonder if you've gone a little crazy. But don't expect her to bat her lashes and read you the poems of Elizabeth Barrett Browning. Her way of saying "I love you" is to laugh uproariously and inform you that you're a hysterically funny character.

There are simply no limits to where this love could take you. Life with Ms. Sagittarius is a life that is constantly on the move—up and down rivers, over mountaintops, and sometimes around in the air. However, although you may develop frostbite and get sore feet, you're guaranteed to love every minute of it. A bicycle trip in a blizzard is more fun with her than a dinner party with a hundred people, and that's because she is a party unto herself.

Libra Man with Capricorn Woman

She will appreciate your approach to aesthetics, and the way you can play your grand piano. However, when she wants somebody to just grab her, being with you is like sitting in front of the air-conditioner in mid-October.

While she is perfectly capable of appearing frigid, it's all a big show, and what she really wants is simply a lot of love. So do you, but you have a hard time doling it out or initiating any action in that direction.

You are endlessly impressed by her superachievements, enamored of her appearance, and attracted to her warmth. However, there is something about her sense of stability that is a little overwhelming.

It takes you half an hour to order three courses on a menu, while she makes up her mind with just one glance. You let your insecurities overcome you, while she keeps hers coolly under cover. You are amazed at her consistent self-reliance, and she marvels at how you need assurance on what part of the room to hang your spider plant.

She will hold your hand on gloomy days, tell you ten times in one hour that she approves of your latest ski boots, and give you her solicited opinion on your most recent career conflict.

However, when she needs a shoulder to lean hard on, she'll have to look elsewhere, because you'll be worrying about something else. She is the kind of woman who is solid, enduring, and devoted. You are the kind of man who is ephemeral, fickle, and self-indulgent. If you can overcome these traits, this relationship could become a close one. If not, consider it another Libra rhapsody that ends up battered and blue. And consider yourself the loser, because Ms. Capricorn is one of the few women who could bring you down to earth and make you like it.

Libra Man with Aquarius Woman

She will understand your ego needs and listen to all your problems (even with other women). You've never gotten such a degree of undivided attention, and, naturally, it can be habit-forming.

She doesn't make bells ring, lights go on, or your candles go out. However, she does make you feel like you've never felt before. It's a lot deeper than starry-eyed; it's more like devastated.

One day, you come to understand that you need her a lot more than she needs you. For months she has been a sturdy sounding board, but what have you been besides an amiable escort? Suddenly, panic sets in, and you become possessive. But it doesn't work, because she is everybody's person, but not one person's plaything.

Ms. Aquarius has an unlimited capacity for being selfless, while you have an unlimited capacity for being selfish. She can give a lot and doesn't ask much, while you can take a lot without offering anything in return. However, because there is this peculiar congruency that comes between you, you both could be quite compatible.

She will bring you to lectures on meditation and numerology, and you will teach her how to play the guitar. And because she has a million interests and knows a million people, you'll rarely see her, never have a chance to get sick of her, and will remain sufficiently insecure to maintain a consuming interest.

Besides security, you also seek the excitement of a challenge. And Ms. Aquarius, just being her honest, natural, everyday self, is one you'll never be able to overcome.

Libra Man with Pisces Woman

You will probably never understand her moods, her chaotic emotions, or the fact that she needs far more reassurance than you are probably giving her.

She is fearful of her feelings, while you have a way of enjoying yours. You rely on reasoning to gather insights, while she knows her intuition will get her anywhere. You see the world as a sharply defined puzzle; she sees it in pastel hues.

Sexually, she will sweep you off your feet, but emotionally you may feel that she brings you down. She has a way of seeing all the sorrow in the world, while you see only what gives you pleasure. She has a side that bubbles with a serious intensity while you prefer joviality to sobriety.

She is selfless; you take without saying thank you. She will listen to your complaints and will understand your problems. On difficult days, she will nurture your needs and smother you with love. The problem is, can you do the same for her?

Unless you have a very high sense of awareness, this relationship is not an equal one. However, it can be happy, peaceful, and very calm. Ms. Pisces has never learned that she deserves very much. And until she reaches that moment of reckoning, it's not fair to expect you to give her what she won't even ask for.

SCORPIO

Dates: October 24—November 22
Symbol: The Scorpion and the Eagle
Ruling planets: Pluto and Mars
Element: Water
Mode: Fixed
Quality: Feminine
Planetary principle: Power
Primal desire: Control
Colors: Black, purple
Jewels: Amethyst, topaz, cinnabar
Plants: Brambleberry, heather
Day: Tuesday
Archangel: Azrael
Magical number: 4
Materal factor: To rise above

SCORPIOS OF
FAME AND FORTUNE

Johnny Carson	Billy Graham
Katharine Hepburn	Dr. Jonas Salk
Marie Antoinette	Grace Kelly
Richard Burton	Chiang Kai-shek
Indira Gandhi	Prince Charles
Pablo Picasso	Robert Kennedy
Theodore Roosevelt	Margaret Mead

Martin Luther	Madame Curie
Daniel Boone	Dostoevski
	Edith Piaf

THE SCORPIO FEMALE

Favorable

You are kind, compassionate, psychic, intuitive, and you will never say no to a friend in need. Your vision is total truth, and with one penetrating glance you can see all. At a party, you can feel the pain of a laughing stranger and can understand the fears behind the smirk of his best friend.

Instead of chatting at the punch bowl, you probably sit in a corner listening to someone's problems. You have an emotional power over people that leads them to tell all their secrets in the first five minutes, and because the intensity of your eyes is so hypnotic, it isn't until you've glided away that they realize they don't even know your first name.

You tend to be secretive, somewhat shy, and consider your privacy extremely sacred. Because you reveal so little of yourself in a social situation, you sometimes gain the reputation of being both aloof and inscrutable. The fact is that you are cautious in all your interactions because you're so emotionally vulnerable. You feel so intensely that you erect safeguards to make sure your feelings don't undermine you.

Often there is a sternness to your character and a do-it-yourself attitude that sometimes drives those who love you crazy. It is rare that you ask for help, and when it is offered, it is equally hard for you to accept it. Unlike your Libran sisters, you tend to be a loner, and of all the signs, you are probably the most self-sufficient, a quality in which you take great pride.

On a daily basis, you battle with a darker side where the mood swings seem to swallow you. However, with enviable determination you usually overcome them to do what you have to do and do it well. Deep inside there is a hunger that has made you search for activities with greater meaning. You are highly intelligent and have a keen memory and a probing mind that restlessly seeks a broader understanding of the universe, and certainly of yourself. For this reason, as well as for your extraordinary insight, you can be a formidable psychotherapist as well as a psychic healer.

Unlike any other sign, you express a profound desire to rise above yourself and your limitations. Psychology greatly attracts you, as do certain areas of the occult. Both subjects amplify your interest in growth and expansion, bringing you more deeply in touch with your inner power.

The problems that would make another person fall apart and throw up his hands, you face with calm, poise, dignity, and a sense of self-possession. Any self-doubts, you keep on the inside, while on the outside you are willful, tenacious, and exert a formidable influence in all of your undertakings. Your unusual qualities of endurance and perseverance and your strength of mind can take you through any crisis and help you grow in the unfolding of new emotional situations.

When it comes to love, you can be deeply loving, loyal, highly trustworthy, and at times self-sacrificing. However, before you ever get to this point, you feel you have to first determine how much you can trust. Once you are involved in an intense and monogamous love situation, your deepest fear is abandonment. It is not unlikely that in confronting your feelings about the most important person in your life, you have simultaneously experienced a shiver down your spine as you've considered the question of what you'd ever do without this person. Because the depths of your feelings can frighten you more than a little, you are loath to confront that vulnerable part of you. Rather, you prefer to spend your time reminding yourself that you're simply a strong survivor in a very challenging world. And the fact is, you are.

However, should you find yourself in a romantic situation where you feel the affection is attenuating and you're beginning to lose more than you're getting, at a certain point of frustration your feelings cut off while your mind drifts to the possibility of a new lover. You never feel that you are compromising your fidelity if your frustrations tell you that you can only find what you need elsewhere. And so you ease yourself out of a decaying situation. Or by purposely easing yourself out, you bring on a confrontation that only makes the relationship stronger in the long run. It is highly likely that hope was always part of your motivation.

Because your mind is so shrewd and insightful, you never act without having a profound discernment of all possible outcomes. Your intuitive understanding, combined with your strong resolve and emotional strength, makes you one woman not easily forgotten. Not only are people intrigued with your personal power, they'd probably pay to have it. However, even if someone informed you of your effect on other human beings, your sense of self-effacement would never allow you to believe it. A sincere sense of humility is part of your charm, as well as your wisdom. It's also part of the reason why people consider you so difficult to understand.

Unfavorable

Your mind is power personified; your body a lethal weapon. You have the head of Mata Hari, the emotions of Mussolini, and the air of mystery of a Garbo. Men see you as a sort of sorceress, and *you* see them as tantalizing tinkertoys. As long as they remain within the confinement of your structures, they have your stamp of approval, but, should they dare to stray from your domain, they just might feel your fangs in their jugular.

You are the craftiest of connivers—the inscrutable sex siren whose tool is total mind control. Your modest goal is their complete surrender, and as any man who has crossed your path can verify, you're just not used to losing.

In sexual games, you are the cool, elusive gambler who sometimes enjoys the play even more than the prize. People are like actors so you set the stage, sit back, and watch the improvisation. You have a way of looking a man in the eyes that can make him tremble and talk too much. This especially delights you, because you know that he doesn't know *what* it is you are doing, never mind why.

Men never know where you are coming from, and there are many times when you're not quite sure yourself. All you're aware of is what you want and where you have to go to get it. It might take you a lifetime to come up with a reason.

You are extremely complex, moody, and often sullen during those moments when you feel powerless. You tend to obsess, connive, manipulate, and stay up all night reading something very complex into something very simple. No wonder it takes you so long to come to your final conclusion! That kind of convoluted analysis you put your mind through is enough to send Freud running back to his couch for a rest.

You need a man in your life to make you feel like a woman, but once he's there, your mental machinations only multiply. If you hold on to him merely for sex and the emotional security, but feel that materially he doesn't suit you, you'll do your best to tear him down. You'll never risk total involvement with a man of no wealth, unless he has some kind of sensational power. Only you can control your feelings to suit any need, and you have so many needs that your mind is always working overtime.

When it comes to getting power, you are cagy and ruthless, and rely upon your sex appeal to take you places. You can detach your mind from your feelings quicker than you can bat an eyelash, and you can jump into a stranger's bed faster than it takes to pull down the top sheet.

Since sex is like breathing for you, you speak through your body. Although there are many men who prefer this kind of communication to the kind called "talking," other, more sensitive souls find it frustrating trying to decipher what you're feeling from what you *seem* to be saying.

You communicate in code and use eye signals, sex, sullenness, and total withdrawal to get your point across. One withering glance, and your target may fear for his life. One smile, and he forgets what he was saying. One yawn, and he is dying with sexual desire. But just one blank stare, and he wonders if you're still the same woman.

Even at your most open and accessible, you're an enigma. But when you're closed, you're more cut off than a catatonic schizophrenic. The one thing that is *always* communicated is that you are never crossed—without the perpetrator paying a heavy price.

Which brings us to your greatest problem: anger. Since you've never learned what to do with it, it tends to torment you in the shadowy hours. At such moments, depressions can be devastating and immobilizing if your feelings have really had time to fester.

Unless you take to punching pillows or wearing poison rings that tend to conveniently open over a victim's martini, your anger will ultimately strike back at you, like a snake. Then you become the sad, embittered, suicidal Scorpio.

Death is always a part of you, and you can court it in subtle ways. Too much alcohol, too many pills, too many superficial scenes, and both death and life become one game that has only vague points of distinction.

Your real problem is that you are one woman with too much power and not enough self-awareness. You can see into the souls of others so easily and so far that you come out the other side. But when it comes to yourself, you get caught in your own emotional catacombs, and the danger comes in forgetting the exit and deciding to live there.

The real secret of the Scorpio is that at any time you can travel in two emotional directions. One is expansive and one is restrictive. The power comes in taking conscious responsibility for either choice, and then realizing that everything you really want is waiting for you.

THE SCORPIO MALE

Favorable

At the very least, you're a charmer who knows when to speak and when to keep silent. With that certain look in your eye, you could seduce a nation, but whatever your goals, you never use your gifts against another human being.

You deeply care about people and have an overwhelming desire to rehabilitate them. Because you are so kind, compassionate, and concerned, you continually find yourself listening to a lengthy list of problems. In any position of power, it's likely that those whom you administrate think of you as a "father figure"—but one whom they respect and admire. As a friend, you are cherished for your kindness and generosity. And as a husband or lover, you are appreciated for your loyalty and devotion.

You are active, full of life, and never let anything get you down. You can overcome any obstacle and enjoy the challenge. You can suffer any degree of pain, but not burden others with it, and you can achieve any far-ranging goal, because you have the greatest perseverance.

You are rational and passionate, deeply philosophical,

and have a scintillating mind interested in probing life's deeper mysteries.

You have a unique and uncanny ability to mesmerize the mind of another. In history there have been assorted Scorpio individuals who have used their charisma to influence the masses. Such men as Martin Luther and Billy Graham have chosen religion as a pathway to the minds of the public; others, such as Theodore Roosevelt, used politics. All felt the Scorpio need to rise above their own limitations, and they dedicated their entire lives to the attainment of this ideal.

Both morally and intellectually you're a perfectionist, and hold the highest standards for those to whom you are closest. You have great powers of concentration and a mind that is perceptive, intuitive, and emotionally aware. Mentally you are strong, independent, self-reliant, and a silent warrior in times of difficulty.

In romantic relationships, you find satisfaction from a deep, lasting commitment. Once in love, you are loyal, giving, supportive, nurturing, and sensitive to the needs of your partner. However, you never feel comfortable giving lighthearted compliments, and sentimentality only sickens you.

You have a mind that is so highly complex that you see nothing as simple. Comedies make you want to cry. Melodrama makes you want to chuckle, since an awareness of the absurd saturates your soul. In college, you probably failed all of your multiple-choice tests, because you tried to read three answers each into being the right ones, and after a while got so dizzy you just passed out. You communicate in convolutions of thought and feeling —feeling through thought, feeling plus feeling, then thinking plus thinking—because it's easier than just feeling.

Because you are so emotionally intricate, you are often emotionally misunderstood. At times you may appear to be cold, aloof, and noncaring. However, the truth is that you are really self-sufficient, private, and cautious. You mind your own business, and you expect others to do the same. Unsolicited personal questions thrown in your direction only get the cold shoulder.

You are quiet but forceful. You are also strong, willful, and courageous. You have deep inner convictions and hold high ethical codes. Your essence is the high-soaring eagle in flight, the symbol of the highest attainment. Like no other sign, you have invisible wings that will take you anywhere. It's all a part of your tremendous power, and you're not afraid to use it.

Unfavorable

As a child, your toys were whips and chains, your favorite hero Al Capone, and your secret career goal to become a spy or a gangster. Since then, your head hasn't changed much, but success has either brought you to the top of some multimillion-dollar corporation, made you president of the entire country, or put you in the front-page headlines as a murderer.

Gaining success was never a problem, since you have such secret scruples that even *you* haven't the faintest idea what they are. You take great pride in your position of power, which is understandable, since you probably poisoned several people to get it.

You are shrewd, selfish, and sarcastic. Your ears curl around corners, your memory is vaster than a warehouse of microfilm, and your mind is like a laser beam. You have a frightening habit of unraveling people's minds and motivations, while remaining inscrutable and remote yourself. But it's just as well that you stay mysterious, since to know your mental machnations is far more anxiety-producing than it is illuminating!

You are the greatest of all game players. Whatever the stakes, it's a given that you always win. You have more emotional maneuvers than any fiendish mind could manage to think of, and when your mind is intent and highly motivated, it's easier to reason with a hired killer than to talk *you* down.

You are a metaphor of the fire and the ice, and any woman who has experienced your Scorpion "kiss of death" will verify that it's one memory that is never forgotten. Even in love, you always calculate your options, previewing your opponent's moves, so that the entire relationship is like a chess game you've already won. Emotionally, you come close to being downright dishonest, and when your seduction tactics are worn thin, emotional intimidation always works. Then you wander out the door, leaving your lady wondering if she should have had your horoscope done just to understand your motivations.

The key to your soul is that you are terrified of the intensity of your unbridled emotions, and so you either repress or displace them. The day you fall in love, you might become bitter and sarcastic, since you know that you're caught in the tides of some dangerous feeling and you're losing all control, and then your killer instincts emerge. At this point, the action gets terribly complex. If you trust deeply, your feelings of love will overcome your sense of fear and then the recipient should just consider herself lucky. However, if you stand on shaky ground, you'll become emotionally obsessed and end the relationship to get a better view. Should the woman have her tentacles deeply entwined in the sexual area of your tormented soul, then the scene gets a trifle sadomasochistic, and in a very sordid way you may become addicted to the intensity of the entire situation.

Emotionally, your changing moods are like a Ping-Pong tournament, where the action is so fast you kind of forget who's winning. The turbulence takes you from some euphoric place far beyond the clouds to an inferno of the most violent feelings. At such times, your gaze becomes icy, you demand to be alone, and God help the poor unfortunates who stumble through your path. If they happen to be the supersensitive sort, chances are even if they emerge alive, they'll never be the same. For the rest of their lives, they'll probably just mutter to themselves a lot and stare into space.

To help you over the hurdles of such savage moods and to ensure that state of euphoric intensity, you may have drunk too deeply and have relied on the divine highs of drugs. Since you seek the lofty peaks and so often get lost in the valleys, you can put your body through a self-inflicted beating that some might consider a slow suicide.

Your sexual magnetism is like a weapon. You have more mystique than a personality created by a publicist, but because you are so subtly self-destructive, the women who get caught in your web usually come out bleeding. You have a strong tendency to test your loved ones so hard that you can turn them completely off. Part of the test is to push people down and then humiliate them when they can't come up. Your deepest respect is won by another's mental strength and intelligence, the kind that puts you down as it puts you in your place. Your response, however, is the deepest kind of cruelty. Maybe a slow smile, where your mouth twists down at the corners and with one well-chosen phrase you try to sear the most tender places of the soul. Needless to say, before people take you on, they should definitely have not only their wits about them but also a couple of weapons.

While you operate from the shadow of your personality, you are more of a menace than a dedicated psychopath. As a lover, you are totally lacking in compliments, quick with criticism, and so jealous, possessive, and controlling that you could easily move a mild-tempered woman to murder you in your sleep. You could sacrifice love and happiness for your pride and feel more comfortable destroying a relationship than entering into it. You heartily enjoy the act of ferreting out someone's feelings so that you can use them against him, and then you sit back, feel superior, and sport the sliest smirk. If you are the unruly sort, you are suspicious, cold, and can easily be moved to violence. Only in being totally out of control do you feel you can control those around you. It's interesting psychology, since it usually works.

When it comes to something you want, you know the most indirect way to get it, but it's something else altogether if you know how to keep it. That is a choice that is only up to you, and it's one that somehow takes your shrewd, all-seeing mind most of a lifetime to figure out.

DECANS

Every sign in the zodiac can be broken down into three subdivisions, called decans. Each decan roughly corresponds to 10 degrees—the first third, second third, and last third of the sun sign's time span, which is approximately thirty days.

As each of these periods has different subrulerships, the personality of a person is slightly modified by the specific decan it falls in. For instance, an Aries born in the second decan would be ruled by Mars, but subruled by the Sun. Therefore, he would tend to display a greater sense of pride, boastfulness, egotism, and optimism than an Aries born in the third decan, which is subruled by Jupiter. This Aries would tend to be more freedom-loving, flighty, travel-oriented, and interested in subjects of a philosophical nature. An Aries born in the first decan would be the most aggressive, but not necessarily the most productive and accomplished.

Decans are important, since they do account for a more detailed assessment of an individual's personality characteristics. They also show how two people born under the same sun sign can be markedly different.

If you were born between October 24 and November 2, your sun falls in the Pluto decan of Scorpio, and your characteristics most exemplify your sign.

You are very ambitious, driven, and often highly successful. Your mind is a battleground for your emotions, and you play them out through your career. You have an uncanny mentality that is shrewd, probing, psychic, and far-seeing, but also subject to turbulent mood swings.

Since you have tremendous ego needs, a formidable storehouse of energy, and a devastating desire for power, your emotions can often be effaced in the grueling, impersonal struggle to get to the top. Your desire to dominate, as well as your intuitive sense for business situations involving "big money," has inspired your mind to seek the highest executive positions, which you run with expertise once you get there.

In your being can be found all the elements for fulfilling the American myth of success. You are self-sacrificing to the company, cool to your personal needs, tenacious, dedicated, and highly organized. You work things out to form systems where procedures start to run themselves. Meanwhile, you're laboring till midnight to discover a newer, more efficient way to aid your monetary input to multiply itself.

You enjoy the games of competition, since you're so self-confident, clever, and enamored of challenge. However, you're so ambitious that your spouse sees less of you than your secretary, who has probably come to think of you as family. You have a special power over her mind, since you are magnetic, manipulative, and in your terse, cold way, kind and caring.

It is rare that you actually lose your temper. Instead, you resort to sarcasm and cutting comments, and that is enough to keep people away when they think about moving in on your emotional territory. You have a facade that is more frightening than you like to think, but at the same time, these sly, nonverbal intimidation tactics have gotten you many places.

At a certain point in your life, the experience of death has deeply affected you. You tend both to speculate on its significance and to be repulsed for fear that death is only synonymous with annihilation. There is a tendency for you to be drawn to occultism for uncovering the answers to some of your more unsettling questions. However, for those of you born in this decan there is a greater tendency that heavy commitments to the material aspects of your life will retard and inhibit an involvement with the mysteries.

In the later years of your life, you could gain much from an inquiry into some phase of occultism. As your perspectives alter, you will see that your satisfactions from living will become more profound and expansive.

If you were born between November 3 and 13, your sun falls in the Neptune decan of Scorpio. You are more emotionally vulnerable than Scorpios born at other times of the month and have a tendency to cling to the past. Although you hate to admit it, you are also more sentimental and tend to hold on to situations that should be over. In general, you feel more comfortable in the contemplation of any action than in its execution, and tend to fantasize a lot about how you would like life to be, rather than doing something about it.

Artistically, you have far more talent than you know what to do with. Although you have both writing and musical ability, you have a difficult time channeling your energies to gain the kind of fame you might otherwise draw to yourself.

You tend to be an escapist, and have a need for either drugs or alcohol to take you to some faraway place. More so than Scorpios born in the other decans, you seek the peaks and find yourself on a constant quest for the distant ideal. However, once an attainment becomes real, its excitement seems to diminish.

Your relationships are highly charged with a kind of narcotic romanticism that sometimes takes your soul to peculiar places. You are highly passionate and sensual and seek the same qualities in the opposite sex. At times, you tend toward obsession and get caught up in sex games.

At other times, you tend toward emotional self-sacrifice, and seem to come out of relationships losing.

Your nature is deeply sympathetic, compassionate, and concerned, and at the same time, you tend to be introverted and find it difficult to demonstrate your feelings openly.

You have a tremendous healing ability, which should be developed for your own benefit as well as for the benefit of others. For this reason, you could excel in the field of psychology and medicine and gain that meaning to your life for which you have long been searching.

Since you are also psychic, occult endeavors have always had a special appeal. With your sensitivity and insight, you could combine a knowledge of both fields to offer a great contribution to mankind.

Your special key to satisfaction in this lifetime comes in forgetting yourself and concentrating more on the needs of others. Chances are, your younger years brought you intensely sorrowful situations that are still not resolved in your consciousness. However, as long as you allow yourself to dwell in the miasma of your own emotions, they will definitely bring you down. Always remember that you were born under the sign of Mars and Pluto, which means self-directed action sustained over time. Dreams are wonderful, but allow them to take you somewhere. The longer you contain them within, the quicker your life will pass you by.

If you were born between November 14 and November 22, your sun falls in the moon decan of Scorpio. Your mother has had a profound influence in your life and may strongly affect your subconscious behavior patterns for many years to come. Chances are that on some level this relationship has brought you a great deal of pain, but until you work out your ambivalent feelings, you may unconsciously be perpetuating this relationship in your affairs with the opposite sex. There may be times when you take on some of what you feel to be her negative qualities, and at other times you may find them in the people with whom you choose to become involved.

There is a very strong nurturant aspect to your personality, and those who are close to you will attest that you seem to gain a great deal of satisfaction from taking care of them. In turn, you need the same kind of nurturance in your close relationships that you offer to others, but it is another question altogether whether you will allow yourself to accept such offerings, and it is close to impossible for you to ask.

When it comes to feelings, you are the supersensitive sort, though you rarely show it. When hurt, you are more likely to seek solitude within the confines of your home, and once you feel secure there, analyze your pain away so that you can coolly cut the cords.

In general, you are difficult to get to know and are more emotionally distrustful than Scorpios born in the other decans. This is because your emotional needs are greater. Unlike the Scorpio born in the first decan, you have a far more difficult time channeling your emotions into your career and coming out gratified. This is not to say that you are not ambitious, but worldly success is not that meaningful if you are lonely and lacking a trusting, intimate relationship.

It is likely that you would either marry young or would spend a good portion of your life living with assorted lovers. As sex is a deeply emotional experience for you, you can incur psychological harm if you try to detach your feelings to protect yourself and take the promiscuous route. In marriage, you seek a person with a perfect combination of emotional strength and vulnerability, as well as someone who can both understand your feelings and respect them.

On a professional level, you could gain through real estate and high-priced auctions. Your mind is extremely shrewd when it comes to money, so you know how to make even a little work for you.

LOVE

If you are a female Scorpio, you may be both more mysterious and more vulnerable than your male counterpart. While he can sublimate his emotions through career, sexual manipulations, and athletic undertakings, you're generally not satisfied with less than an intense, more meaningful kind of love.

You are loyal, giving, and can appear to be placid even when your emotions seem to be ripping your mind into bite size pieces. At the same time, you are reluctant to lose control until you have shrewdly assessed the odds in every romantic situation. Unfortunately, sometimes your desires get the best of you, and you may find yourself emotionally tied to a brutal affair with no clear recollection of how you really got there.

Your sex appeal is quiet yet exciting, and emanates from your eyes. Your direct gaze and smile are imbued with a sensuality that can move a man to lust in less than a minute. Yet unlike your Scorpio brother, promiscuity is not your emotional forte. You seek security, tenderness, and trust, and for what you desire, you're willing to give all of yourself in return.

You are both more sensual and more sexually inventive than the Scorpio male, who may be more interested in the ultimate orgasm than in the total experience of lovemaking. However, due to your need for control, it may take you years to experience your sexual potential. Because your intense emotions enter into every act, a subconscious fear of abandonment may block both your emotional and sexual responses for quite some time.

Once in love, you tend to be both possessive and jealous and drown in unresolved emotions long after an affair is over. You often tread a very thin line between love and hate, passion and violence, even if the feelings are merely confined to your private fantasies.

At a very early age you realized that sex is power and that it will get you wherever you want to go. The Scorpio experience of loving will take you in many emotional directions in one lifetime. Just remember at each crossroads and impasse that you made the decision to be there.

The Scorpio male is a warrior, especially in love, but unlike his Martian sibling, Aries, usually battles against his partner rather than for her. If you are a male Scorpio, you probably operate all your romantic endeavors from a mental control panel whose emotional switch is often on "off." You are so inscrutable and emotionally maddening that a bad involvement with you is enough to send some sweet thing to a mental institution. Although you have a lot of loyalty, in affairs of the heart you are really no prize. You seldom compliment, rarely communicate, and keep your feelings carefully closeted until the object of your affections is ready to sign her life away. You want it all in writing, her signature in blood, and someone so far-

sighted she can't even read between the lines. Should she
ever betray you, despite the legitimacy of the contract,
she's in for the kind of murder that's so quick and silent
that it's really quite painless. The worst possible penalty is
if you let her live, because what she faces then is the horrendous three C's: emotional cutoff, calculated revenge,
and the cold glance of death. Your eyes can create such a
frigid ambience that she will nervously contemplate changing to her ski underwear.

Although you expect a kind of active devotion that
exceeds the ground rules of the Mafia, you often em-
ploy a double standard in regard to your own behavior.
Emotionally, you are still being loyal to your loved one
when you are in bed with someone else only for sex. Of all
the signs, only you can separate your emotions from
your sexuality and come out the winner. However, God
help the loser, especially if she finds herself suddenly emotionally involved.

Not only can you tread over someone else's emotions, you have a unique way of dragging your feet as you
go. Although you are an intensely emotional human
being yourself, you have an uncanny ability not to let that
get in the way when you want something. You can be the
most remorseless exploiter of a sexual situation and the
most glacial participant in a moment of afterglow. When
you've gotten what you want from someone you sexually
desire rather than feel for, the first order of business is that
the body be removed. You have only one objective: getting your own or your lover's body out the door—quietly.

Unless you are deeply involved and emotionally committed, any woman who tangles casually with you just may
get her heart torn out. You are the most maddening kind
of enigma, especially to the Taurus woman, who watches
her telephone rather than her television, agonizing about
whether she's ever going to hear your voice again.

Being the sly, silent type, you never volunteer any
kind of commitment until the other person has sweated it
out far more than just a little, but you are most likely to
get caught up by the challenge of someone who is as sly,
shrewd, and sexually cunning as yourself.

What you like most is being stimulated on several
levels—the more, the better. You heartily enjoy an insightful intellect who sees through your emotional machinations. You adore a woman who can look you straight in

the eye, smile, and titillate you with prolonged visual contact. But what really carries you away is someone with all of the above who seems to have a power over you: a special knowledge, or an experience in a Scorpio subject, such as medicine, psychology, or some phase of the occult. Ideally, you would like to learn from a profound love experience and fantasize about a situation that is limitless in its levels of excitement.

Although you need love, falling in love is not an easy experience. Your need for total control as well as your critical nature can often lead you to impose limitations on many love experiences and to kill them slowly before they can come to fruition. Although in your silent way you usually wear down and overpower those around you, what you want most is to be overpowered—but through subtlety rather than force.

At this point, your extreme jealousy can evoke many sickening moments, much to your specious sense of regret. Since what you crave most is intensity, if you can't find it in pleasure, you'll finally settle for it in pain. Much like Leo, you tend to mentally dramatize the more emotionally intense moments of your life, and once you feel that your sense of pride is succumbing to a debilitating state of affairs, you cut loose with one quick blow. When you wish to end an affair with someone you're losing feeling for, you have a way of becoming invisible, so that the poor woman might wonder if you were murdered on your way home the last time she saw you. But if your desire is to withdraw in a position of power, you can derive particular glee, even if you're in pain, by informing your former friend that you've suddenly decided that it's curtains.

The most lethal trait of the Scorpio nature is the ability to make a former lover feel that she's swimming around an island in shark-infested waters. Emotionally, the Scorpio man can easily be a foggy island in the middle of a deep dark sea. The undercurrent is so strong, it can draw in unsuspecting souls. The only survivors in these waters are other warriors. Even good swimmers should beware, since life jackets have a way of getting torn apart.

MARRIAGE

Although you may feel that marriage is a necessity, your partner often feels it to be a situation that must be gotten out of. Why? Perhaps because your spouse has been chained to the four-poster too long and developed both welts and bedsores.

Your need to use marriage as an emotional base out of which you operate for all of your other activities may cause you to choose a partnership you later regret. Although in all of your other dealings you are such a shrewd and far-seeing fox, in the area of marriage your emotional, sexual, and material needs can easily overcome you.

The inherent paradox of your personality is that your pride screams that you should be a self-sufficient loner, while your tumultuous drives, desires, and nurturant needs can drive you into a connubial situation. It is true that Scorpio can weather any storm (you usually create most of them), but what luxury to leave the rain for a womb-like room with a roaring fire!

Although you do not hesitate to be unfaithful when you feel a falling off of the relationship's original intensity and stimulation, deep in your peculiar heart you would most like to remain a satisfied stay-at-home. Despite your actions, in your mind, marriage has a certain sanctity, and the violation of it often leaves you more saddened than satisfied. When you admit to yourself that a fast fling in the night has no value aside from the pleasure it gave you at the moment, and you could care less if your partner disappeared from the face of the earth, you are moving steadily toward promiscuity, which you use as emotional armor.

The only other extramarital activities that could excite you, outside of sex, are mind games. You like to slowly lure your victim in and then disappear. Alas, after a time such games become boring and so tedious you tend to want to be alone.

At the same time, if the spouses of Scorpios dare to engage in extramarital dalliance, they might as well dig their own graves, because when their misbehavior is uncovered, they'll wish they were dead (if they aren't actually helped along).

Even when you are being cool, you can be more persuasive than a champion wrestler. You realize that the key to power over another human being is in the mind, and you know how to put it through more unmerciful contortions than any hallucinogenic drug.

Because you put such an emphasis on mental mechanisms, you are extremely selective about the facts you communicate to your partner. In brief, your credo is: "What they don't know won't hurt them." It is very rare that you can envision an affair breaking up a "solid" but boring marriage, where daily support and nurturances sustain you through outside career pressures. The trick is that although you screen, censor, and consider some of your life definitely X-rated, from your marriage partner *you* demand total truth. When applied to you, the convenient little maxim of "What they don't know won't hurt them" changes to "What you don't know will tear you apart."

What you don't observe, you sense, and even when you're not sensing something, you're just downright suspicious at the least provocation. Knowing all the facts, you feel you can have everything in control and can then proceed with an "appropriate" action.

Your ideal marriage partner is intelligent, stimulating, sexual, ready to serve, and very myopic. You take up the total range of vision, and after that, everybody else is just a blur. Heaven forbid that your spouse should get glasses for distance and discover that outside of you there's a big exciting world with a lot of creatures called people. That might be the first step toward divorce—unless, of course, you bribe the optician.

MONEY

Money is power. You know it and feel it, but find it hard to admit it openly. Your sense of survival is paramount, and you know how to make a dime take you as far as a dollar. However, while you can live on next to nothing, you don't necessarily enjoy doing it. Poverty is hardly one of your favorite pastimes, yet your inordinate pride and self-sufficiency can force you to compromise a lot of little conveniences just to preserve your dignity.

There is a stern, stolid side to your character that makes you choose to suffer in silence rather than humble yourself in asking for financial aid. Of all the signs, you have the most patience to sacrifice present indulgences for future financial realizations. Deep down, you see the process of gaining wealth as gaining supremacy in a power struggle, and struggle is not only you against the establishment, but the conscious you against the unconscious element in yourself.

You heartily enjoy being associated with money, but only because it symbolizes a certain level of achievement, not for its intrinsic value. For you, money has no importance in itself. Its pursuit is merely a personal challenge, and as a possession it is only a means to an end. What you gain most from money, beyond the little luxuries and the creature comforts, is the sense of satisfaction from having attained it. For you, gaining wealth is a game called "test your personal power." It's a challenge, like chess, but with higher social stakes. You know that you'll always win. The key is in staying cool and refusing to let it control you.

CAREER

Success means a great deal to you, but what you actually consider to be success can be many different things.

If you are the more business-oriented kind of Scorpio, success means having immense power. You are driven, shrewd, organized, hardworking, and highly focused in all professional undertakings, but unlike the Leo or Aries business tycoon, you don't have to shout from the top to prove your position. Instead, you are quiet, calculating, and content to pull all the strings from a place of luxurious privacy. There have been more United States presidents born under the sign of Scorpio than under any other sign in the zodiac. This is not at all surprising, since the Scorpio mind is at once shrewd, willful, tenacious, controlling, success-oriented, and highly intelligent.

Such a combination by itself is overwhelming. However, when you add to it the element of strong-willed patience, you have one human being who is unbeatable at anything he or she strongly desires.

If your proclivities pull you more toward the spiritual than the material, success becomes a kind of Faustian quest into the ancient mysteries. At this point, success is assessed from the more abstract perspective of values, ethics, and moral objectives. Some of the greatest spiritual figures of our time have been Scorpios or have had this sign prominently configured in their horoscopes. Also, many of the most brilliant occultists who have contributed valuable esoteric knowledge to those minds ready to grasp it have the planet Jupiter placed in the sign Scorpio.

On the other hand, you could be anything from a hired killer to a surgeon, from an international spy to an insurance salesman, from a mortician to a psychoanalyst. And after you've run through all of those, you just could very well end up a preacher. But whatever you do, it's soul-inspired, even if you're the murky, moody, depressive sort who sits around and does nothing.

At the very most, you're inordinately ambitious; and at the very least, you're sedentary but think big thoughts. Since you've always been interested in the more penetrating issues, such as man's inner motivations, you could be a superb psychiatrist. You have an inner desire to pierce the veil of pretense and a more apparent desire to grab all the power you can get. When you manage to harness your energies, you're a menace to all competitors.

Your mind is sharp, shrewd, and sly. When threatened, you're a killer of the inconspicuous, quiet type. When stimulated, you're a free-flowing force, defiant of those who cannot channel their energies.

In business professions, your motivation is power. In people and philosophic professions, your motivation is the "why." You are both highly organized and extremely adept. Your Mars co-ruler gives you the courage of the warrior; your Pluto co-ruler, the power of penetrating all obstacles. Inherently, you have all the attributes needed for success. The only hindrance you must overcome is your fear of it. Once you relinquish your need to let your fears control you, all the forces of the universe become attuned to your commands.

FRIENDS

You can be counted on in a blizzard if the friendship is intense enough, but in return you ask for nothing less than total trust. You're so cautious, secretive, and generally suspicious that your friends are carefully screened, watched, and scrutinized before you become committed.

Your loyalty has no limits; neither does your capacity to sever feelings and nurse slights. Should you ever feel betrayed in a friendship, it's your tendency to cut the cords very quickly. First your voice becomes glacial; then all communication comes to a standstill, and your friend is turned to foe so swiftly that he almost wonders if the entire friendship was just a figment of his imagination.

Since you have little or no patience for people of the superficial sort, you tend to be attracted to personalities by whom you are stimulated and with whom you feel an intense rapport. Since you feel that this kind of chemistry happens infrequently, it is not surprising that you have very few close friends. Those who are privy to the more intimate details of your life never leave, even if they move away. There is just no getting away from a Scorpio, once you make the decision that you want someone to be there.

An acquaintance may know you for years, but never even know if you're married, if you have a pet rabbit named Neville, or if you like to sleep in a pile of leaves on the floor. If people should be invited to your home, chances are they won't get any further than the foyer and notice uncomfortably that most of the adjoining doors are shut.

If you should pass someone on the street who smiles, nods, and asks you where you're going, you'll say that you're on your way to buy some toothpaste when you're really going to the post office to mail a letter. Alas, sometimes the Scorpio mind is so convoluted that it's just lost all concept of what is straight.

The first thing the best friends of any Scorpio will affirm is that they can't remember where and how the friendships began. That's because they grew so slowly that there was no noticeable beginning. Besides, who would immediately consider friendship with such a strange, silent person who stares and breaks the silence only to ask a question? Either another Scorpio or just some curious soul who's not easily intimidated by a pair of piercing eyes, but at the same time has an abundance of patience.

However, years after, ask that same person who they can really trust and call upon in the middle of the night to take a pet frog to the veterinarian because he seems to be having psychic problems. Obviously, old Scorpio, since even sheer insanity is not enough to break the trusted bonds of friendship.

HEALTH

Because you must bottle up your mind in the confines of your body, tension often tyrannizes your visceral energies. Plenty of physical exercise will cool out the constricted places and allow your mental processes more free flow. Tennis is an excellent way to refocus mental energies into a physical outlet, but if you can't make it to the courts, try jogging, jumping rope, or running in place. Visualize your anger flowing from your brain, down your spine, and into the soles of your feet, and with each movement, feel it leaving your body.

Whenever you are emotionally charged, your mind tends to work overtime, and your obsession can become a demon that destroys a good night's sleep. Learn how to let go and not be a victim of your own energies. Try hatha-yoga for total relaxation, and T'ai Chi to get in touch physically with a state of mental balance. Transcendental Meditation will get your mind moving on a slower frequency so that you will no longer be a slave to your own thoughts.

Since you are prone to extremes and excesses, you often overextend yourself in indulgences of the sybaritic sort. Too much drinking, food, drugs, smoking, sex, and too little sleep are guaranteed to be both aging and anxiety-producing. You were the inventor of "divine decadence" and also the progenitor of degenerate diseases. Since you like to push each experience to the limits, it's a good idea to know first just what yours are, before you wake up in a strange white bed behind bars.

Your mind and body can take only so much intensity before you drive yourself crazy and take everybody around you with you. Drinking to get high can be especially dangerous, since you tend to blur out on your emotional controls, and if provoked, might find that your hands are wrapping themselves around somebody else's throat.

Since you have a special weakness for sex, overindulgence may bring on anything from mononucleosis to bladder disorders to those infections referred to politely as the nonspecific sort. Take special pains to keep everything nonspecific, even if that means you have to keep renewing your prescription for penicillin. Celibacy may make you break out in a rash, so if sudden eruptions should occur, visit your doctor first. Just remember to brush your teeth at bedtime with a germicidal toothpaste, since you might cause an infection to occur when biting.

HOME

Since your mood cycles make you seek solitude, your home must psychologically satisfy those hermitic urges. Chances are you like it quiet, very cozy, and your telephone taken off the hook. Compulsive phone friends who call at all hours make you twitch and think of murder.

Since your sense of privacy is paramount, you prefer your guests to come only when they're invited. Home entertainment is not one of your greatest pleasures, unless you're feeling particularly inclined.

You like a lot of space in which to roam around and think. In terms of decor, you gravitate toward dark wood and fish tanks that you can stare into for hours. Your walls are lined with books on such subjects as sex, the occult, politics, and psychology, and stretching the length of your living room is an indecently sensuous crushed-velvet sofa that seems to invite you to lie down as you pass.

The bedroom is your retreat from the impinging clamor and chaos of the world. You're a nocturnal creature and crave large, drooping swivel lamps for those times when you read until the sun comes up.

Since you're a person who hates to go to sleep, your bedroom has a particular effect on your emotional outlook. Potted palms that seem to tower toward the ceiling make you think you're Tarzan (or Jane) leaping about for some action under the banana leaves.

Your ideal fantasy house is a secluded oceanside retreat with high hedges, sprawling lawns, and floor-to-ceiling windows that overlook the foamy surf. In such a place, you revel, even on gloomy afternoons that call for a fire, an enticing book, and maybe a cup of tea with lemon.

Your dining room would be large, long, and wood-paneled. Since eating and drinking are one of your fortes, you would have a banquet table where each meal would be nothing less than a celebration. Silver chrysanthemums would adorn each setting, and a crystal carafe with a full-bodied Burgundy would sparkle in the candle glow.

The morning after your evening of self-determined overindulgence calls for ten laps in your indoor swimming pool, a little daydreaming in the sauna, and a very competitive foray on your private tennis court.

But whatever its decor, your home reflects your desire to keep both mentally and physically active, and wherever it is, it will be your very private retreat away from the world. It is an abode with an ambience that is stimulating, reclusive, cozy, and most definitely sensuous.

COSMIC CHALLENGE

The glyph for Scorpio is the letter M with a tail at the end. At its highest, this shape represents the ability to overcome emotional vicissitudes reflected in life's ups and downs. The tail at the end of the glyph symbolizes the destructive sting that Scorpio is capable of inflicting both on himself and on others when strangled by his own emotions.

The challenge of this sign is balance and internal harmony. It is not enough for Scorpio to control the roar of the ocean. In addition, he must master the movement of the tides. Scorpio symbolizes the water element at its most dangerous. Intrinsic to its nature is the challenge of dying to rediscover life. This experience can be either a quiet, fearful drowning or a relaxed ride on the crest of every wave.

Emotionally, Scorpio must master the highest lessons

of the previous sign, Libra, that is, loving from a place of inner balance. Scorpio can be either passion-motivated by selfless commitment or perversion-motivated by selfish egotism. However, the key to attaining balance comes in sacrificing the constricting sense of pride that often cuts off the emotional flow. To experience love in its most expansive state, Scorpio must become emotionally adaptive to all situations, like the sign Sagittarius, which follows it. It must free itself of rigidity, and challenge itself to experience a love that is beyond its own controls. Then it can claim: "I have sought; I have found; I have purified; and I have joined together through harmony." In gaining a state of inner balance, it allows itself to have All.

INSPIRATION

Scorpio represents the most potent power in the universe. Its underlying process is the alchemy of life through death. At your highest, you are the master magician, liberated from the limitations of the incarnate soul.

When you relinquish your ego, you relinquish your suffering. When you become selfless, you become the self of everyman. When you achieve emotional calm, you become the healer of all turbulence. And in that, you become the giver of life through love, and you also become its scepter and its sword.

Your psychic tool to self-attainment is selfless love. Your task is the correct and righteous use of your emotions. Your torch along the path is your vision of the All. You are the seer past all sense forms, and the one who searches in the silence. At this point, the structures of your environment no longer delude you; nor do they shackle you with tensions that have tentacles of control. Your mind has moved beyond surface successes to seek the timeless meaning of existence. Alone, you have passed through the dark night of the soul to be filled with heat and light. It radiates from each cell as you continue your journey. In this one brief life, your soul has led you through several thousand deaths, until finally you've allowed yourself the joy of rebirth.

WHAT HOLDS YOU BACK
AND HOW TO OVERCOME IT

You're hooked on control, despite your claims to the contrary. In the dungeons of your mental machinations, control is power, and power is a parasite outgrowth of your emotional pride. You would rather be caught without clothes than be out of control. But when you do lose control, watch out, world! Here's one Scorpio uncomfortably close to either murder or suicide.

Your greatest fear is feeling like a fool, and your second greatest is appearing frail and vulnerable. Chances are, you can't even cry in a closet. Since you're so closed, you have to hide your sorrow even from yourself.

In moments of emotional crisis, you tend to cut off all feeling. Friends may mumble among themselves about the frigid state in which you seem to function, but what they don't understand is that your self-preservation instinct is rapidly sending out a signal ordering instant anesthesia.

You are more emotional than even *you* realize, and without such protective ploys, you fear that a merciless emotional tide will just sweep you somewhere out of sight. However, after a few months pass and the pain starts to surface, your dreams and mental flashes are startling and merciless. The question arises: "Where do you go from there to escape what you were never willing to face in the first place?" Good question.

Some Scorpios will try alcohol; others will become workaholics. Overeating only makes you more miserable in the long run, and suddenly you realize that you are creating your own dead end, and the more you try to escape, the tighter the bonds become.

As odd and foolish as it may seem, the only way for you to acquire real emotional control is to learn how to cry, even if you have to stick a pillow over your face and stuff towels under the door to make sure that no one will hear you. If what you're afraid of is hearing yourself, use earplugs. Plunge into the pain intensely, and you'll quickly come out on the other side.

The one lesson you have to learn in this lifetime is the balance between your conscious forces and your subconscious fears. Once you tread that thin line, you are no longer a man or a woman; you are a magus who reaps the secrets of self-mastery. However, when you use suppression as a form of control, you teeter on a tightrope. And once you fall, the trip down is much faster than you think.

LOVE AND
COMPATIBILITY GUIDE

Scorpio with Scorpio

This may be love at first sight, but whether the love will be long-lasting depends on the maturity of the two individuals.

Both are intense, jealous, possessive, and dominated by the principle of pride. She is warm, sensual, and often self-sacrificing. He is sexual, demanding, and definitely ego-oriented. Unless they can come to a middle understanding and make it last, hostilities may brew heavily under the surface.

Although to the outside world he is at best an enigma, to her his mind is like an open book. Unfortunately what she reads may not always please her.

He wants to be boss, to set down the rules, and may try to circumscribe her life. Since she wants to be securely loved, for a while she'll give in and seethe under the surface. But when the resentment really starts to smolder, he may find himself in the divorce courts quicker than he can count to one.

If both are moody, it may be a very stormy situation, where suspicions rise and fall as quickly as the tides. After the afternoons of sarcasm come the evenings of tumultuous passion, followed by the mellow mornings of sensual splendor. Whatever you wish to say about the combination of Scorpio with Scorpio, there are so many emotional ups and downs that things never get a chance to get boring. However, they may get so violent and exhausting that after twenty-four hours both people feel they have just run the four-minute mile.

If both are more highly evolved, this match is an excellent one, where psychotherapy will undoubtedly have a place. Both may be so overly sensitive to the moods of the other that each may walk around reanalyzing the other's comments until they start dreaming about them. Although there may be many sleepless nights during which one member of this partnership stays up till dawn in the effort of making a simple scene complex, there can also be much sharing based on the mutual desire for personal growth.

In this relationship, togetherness may be taken to such an extreme that the couple starts to take on the attributes of Siamese twins. The danger is that one day one or both may feel the need for separation surgery.

All Scorpios need to understand that there really is a midpoint between autonomy and total possession. Only when they make a sincere effort to tread that thin line do they relinquish the need to be dominated by their own controls.

Scorpio Woman with Aries Man

He'll sweep you off your feet and carry you over the threshold, and for once, your mind will stop trying to figure whether you're going in the right direction. However, since you're both coming from such opposite places, this passion is short-lived, and in any prolonged involvement you'll start to think of him as selfish and silly.

He's all energy, passion, vitality, and promises. He runs rather than walks, but often the direction is in circles.

Sexually, he'll take you by storm and you'll love it, since deep down inside, you've always wanted to be conquered. He'll lift up the bed with you in it, just to show off his physical strength, and for about five days you'll think you've found your ideal. He'll dazzle you with his courage, vitality, and super-macho stamina. But when you notice that it's a much-repeated repertoire and that he's treating yours as one of a thousand faces, suddenly the starry-eyed passion dwindles.

Since he adores the idea of charging around to the tune of "My Hero," and so many women are waiting to be overcome, Mr. Aries is a busy man. However, a friend in need, he definitely is not—unless he's going to get something out of it. If you're looking for loyalty, you'd be a lot better off opening your pocket dictionary to L.

At first, his aggressive enthusiasm will win you over, but after you've seen his act a few times, he holds neither secrets nor rewards.

After a while, his arrogance will leaden the light-hearted tone of the relationship, and then you'll find yourself listening to self-centered speeches that tend to sicken you. For Mr. Aries, the entire world is a private audience that has assembled just to admire him. As long as you stay quiet, admiring, sensuous, and supportive, you're in —along with anyone else who is also that blind. If you should decide to hang on here longer consider sending him a bill for your services.

Scorpio Woman with Taurus Man

Regardless of what you've heard, he's no delight unless he's cooking you dinner, and he's probably doing that only because he's too cheap to take you out. If you break a tooth on the bread, it's undoubtedly because he bought it on sale. And if the milk in your coffee separates, it's only because he wanted to use up last month's before he opened a new bottle. Should the steak have muscles stronger than yours after six months of jogging, you know that he bargained with a discount butcher.

His conversation is great if you've been having insomnia problems, and his interests are extremely varied, if you like to watch six TV channels in one evening.

He's terribly sensitive—when it comes to his own feelings. But should you desire him to comprehend a subtle emotional situation, you may have to lean over and shout in his ear. Just don't expect him to understand the first time around, or the fifth, or the tenth, or the sixteenth . . .

To tolerate this man, you need enough patience to fill that time period called a lifetime. Yet he does have one distinctive attribute—he's faithful. That's because, in essence, he's too lazy even to move from one room to another. And besides, even if he were seduced by your worst enemy, you should thank the stars for such a stroke of luck. Only make sure that you move next door so that he'll never find you when he comes trotting back.

Mr. Taurus gets in ruts, so to get rid of him for good, you have to dig him another and push him forward.

Scorpio Woman with Gemini Man

At its best, this combination is friendship. At its worst, it's a quiet but very painful kind of immolation.

Although he thinks he's very clever, you sometimes

see him as simpleminded. He seems to be going in every direction but getting nowhere, while you stay in one place but travel very far.

He gets himself exhausted seeking constant amusement, while you can find entertainment while reading in solitude. He is indiscriminately friendly and freedom-loving, while you are cautious, reserved, jealous, and possessive. He chatters on about banal trivia, while you wonder if he's really that superficial or if he's just talking in code.

His thoughts create a kind of theater, which you find fun until it gets too boring and obvious. On the other hand, he likens your mind to a French film with a lengthy script but no subtitles.

Even if he took a course in Scorpio psychology, he could never understand you, and even wearing your dark glasses, you sense that his perceptions are merely superficial.

It is true that his sense of the ludicrous always keeps you laughing, but his constant lateness ignites your Scorpio temper.

His behavior is so erratic that it would be easier to depend upon the words of a man mumbling in a coma. At the same time, your sulking when he fails to see what you're purposely not saying, forces him to leave you for a chat with a girl who knows how to giggle.

There is no doubt that you intrigue him more than any other woman, but there are many times when he finds you to be too much trouble. He's the man who can make you jealous, insecure, and close to suicidal, but your tight emotional control never lets you get that far. When the relationship starts to get heavy, you will inform him vaguely that you are too busy, that you're madly in love (even if you're just spending evenings with your cactus), or that you just want to be friends. (That's if you're already too hooked to cut off.) Deep in your heart, you hope to hear a stifled sob as a response from the other end. Instead, you hear a cheery sound that seems to be telling you good-bye. You put down the phone, stare at the wall, and admit that even in the end he got you.

Scorpio Woman with Cancer Man

For you, he's a package deal—a man with the qualities of Mother. He'll understand your moods, kiss you on the forehead, bake you apple pie, and serve you tea with lemon.

This combination is highly compatible, especially if you were born in the last decan of Scorpio. As long as you respect his feelings, he is kind, caring, and loves to be controlled by your feminine power.

He'll feel flattered by your jealousy and return the feeling fourfold, which will make you feel all the more secure. You are his constant source of inspiration, and he is your constant bastion of support. Together, life can be a team effort offering many satisfactions and memorable experiences.

He is supersensitive and nurses his bruises. However, you're so adroit at handling fragile feelings that he never has the opportunity of rolling over and playing vulnerable. Since both of you communicate largely through what you don't say, conversation is never a problem. On full moons, you may resort to sign language interspersed with periods of self-imposed solitude. As long as you both don't live together in one room, the situation is salvageable.

At times, his sexual passivity may annoy you, though since you obtain a sense of power from being sexually controlling, this is not a major problem. With Cancer, the most efficient way to control is just to command.

Once you make him feel secure, he is loyal, loving, proud, and possessive. He'll romanticize your personality and give you total power in the relationship. He'll let you take him wherever you want to go, and make it known that you're the trip that he wants to be taking.

He'll put you on a pedestal and seduce you with this new self-image. Any way you look at it, you have a lot of needs and Mr. Cancer has a lot to offer most of them. Chances are, you'll find him easy to love, and almost as easy to spend a lifetime with.

Scorpio Woman with Leo Man

You'll make him wonder if you're speaking a foreign language that sounds like English. That's when you're communicating! As long as you open your mouth, he's always foolish enough to think he actually has a chance of understanding you. But when you close it and stare at his lower lip, forget it! All hope is lost, and so is a fleeting sense of his sanity.

At your most lucid moments, you are an enigma. But if he's trained in palmistry, face-reading, and phrenology (interpreting the bumps on your head), he might have a higher success ratio, provided he's not already too emotionally exhausted to notice.

You don't verbalize; instead, you expect him to read your eyebrows (through the sunglasses). You are intense, intuitive, and intelligent in a way he never thought of. You are aloof, while he practically overwhelms people with his presence. You live in the realm of the internal, while he exhausts himself hogging center stage. You are secretive, while he gives his loyal listeners an auditory overload.

Needless to say, the compatibility here is not compelling. And in terms of rapport, it would be easier to just mumble to your cat. When he asks you what's on your mind, after a ten-minute pause, you'll reply "nothing." That, of course, means "everything." Next step. Tell him not even to think about it. This is one game where he never even gets up to bat (or notices that there is one), because he's so dizzy wandering around the outfield.

At first, his pulse raced at the sight of your mysterious figure, but after he realized that he didn't even know the plot, the drama got a little obscure. When he tries to intimidate you, you just drift away. When he tries to make you laugh, you look at him, puzzled. After he "seduces" you, he realizes that he's the one who's been seduced. And when he tries to make you jealous, you devastate him with a look that makes him run for the center of any crowd, as he wonders nervously if you're carrying a concealed weapon.

There is no doubt about it; you have a lot of power. With both eyes closed, you can see right through his mind; and with both eyes open and a pair of bifocals, he can only get eyestrain staring at the furrows in your forehead. If he's so bored that he's lusting after the ultimate challenge, he has it here. But if it's mystery he's really after, he should do himself a favor and settle for Alfred Hitchcock. In the long run, it's a lot safer.

Scorpio Woman with Virgo Man

Since he's the nervous sort, try not to stare, or else he'll break out in hives. He is attracted to your depth, your intensity, and your sensuality. You appreciate his stability, earthy sexuality, and sense of purpose. He may not understand you, and think your emotions silly, but he'll stay up all night listening to your problems. Even if you're repeating your point twenty-five times and going over the same sentence every hour, he will try his best to listen. At the same time, he may drown himself drinking gallons of water because you've made him so nervous.

The basic difference between the two of you is that you feel the world through your emotions and he sees it through his logic. And you both overanalyze, until the original point no longer matters.

Your moods make him shake his head in wonder. His logic on the subject of your moods makes you sulk. You feel he doesn't see the forest for the trees. He thinks that you'll only get lost in the forest.

Despite the verbal banter, he is kind and nurturing, has the best intentions, but sometimes seems to ruin it all by being so critical. Should you suddenly get sick, he'll have a ready supply of nasal spray; but while you're coughing, sneezing, and spraying, he'll scold you for leaving the cap off the toothpaste. Share with him your greatest lifetime accomplishment, and he'll find the fatal flaw. Ask him if he likes your new haircut, and he'll tell you you should do something about the split ends.

Quite unintentionally, this man invites the most pointed sarcasm, while feeling that you invite a constant restructuring of your life. Initially, this relationship may kindle a few favorable sparks, but for the most part, consider it to be one that you are just passing through. Otherwise, you can expect a lifetime of index cards and multivitamins on your birthday.

Scorpio Woman with Libra Man

One look and you'll have him, but it will be quite some time before he feels secure that he has you.

He is a charmer, but you see through him. Sometimes you think he's superficial and lacking in substance. At other times you appreciate his sense of romance and the fact that he prefers Bach's organ music to a song by the Rolling Stones.

He'll try to woo you with lilacs, champagne, and perfume. If you prepare dinner for him, he'll bring you fresh basil for the salad. But when he wins you, it's only with an offer of a lasting relationship.

Should he take forever to make the commitment and you find him flirting on the side, he might as well bring over a wicker basket and take back his trinkets. Suddenly you don't want him, any more than you want a case of food poisoning.

Although a highly evolved Libran is certainly a lovable creature, the daily garden variety tends to daydream a lot about whom he doesn't have. He is taken in by the superficials, while you probe and patiently wait for the substance. He flies around to do a "Mr. Friendly" routine, but only with the beautiful faces. At the same time, you stay in one place and look aloof, pondering about what he could be saying that's taking so long. Should you notice that he's leaning over some lovely who's writing down numbers, it's curtains for him and more time with your own company for you.

Give him a lifetime, and he'll still never understand you. However, he may desperately fall in love, moan over your cooking, and keep referring to a future of connubial bliss. Just make sure that that future is with *you* before your heart gets carried away. He may already be a newlywed whose wife is visiting her mother. Mr. Libra hates to be alone, and at such times can be mawkishly sentimental. So when the spout turns on, just check to see that the water is flowing in your direction; otherwise, leave your picture on his pillow, have your phone number changed, and let him suffer.

Scorpio Woman with Sagittarius Man

You'll meet him on a tour to King Tut's tomb. He'll be riding his camel as if it were a Cadillac. You'll be clutching yours and smiling as if you were wearing a pair of tight shoes.

He is a character, and one that is guaranteed to initially charm you. He has the kind of sense of adventure that can transform a New York shopping spree into an African safari, and a formal sitdown dinner into a discotheque.

You'll find him funny, friendly, and fantastically silly —especially when he takes you to the zoo to introduce you to an orangutang.

He loves sports and the outdoors to such a degree that he goes mountain climbing just to ski down. On your first date, he'll be late because he was jogging. On the

second, he'll be late because a tennis game destroyed his
sense of time. And on the third, he'll be late because he
misplaced his appointment book, forgot which woman he
was going out with, and ended up at the wrong address.

Alas, Mr. Sagittarius likes a lot of women, is exceptionally freedom-loving, and is very disinclined to settle
down. He always seems to be in a state of much coming
and going, and sometimes doesn't himself know in which
direction. His attentions are extremely scattered, and so,
unfortunately, are his affections.

Quite unintentionally he has been known to stand up
a few damsels in his lifetime. So if he should invite you on
a canoe trip that never happens, and you find that he
took a last-minute jaunt to Afghanistan, just take it all in
stride. The key to this man is that his strides are long and
he seeks to cover as much territory in each one of them as
is possible. Just walking beside him, you feel you have to
catch up. That is allowable, but you have to seriously ask
yourself what you think you're catching up to.

Scorpio Woman with Capricorn Man

You admire his ambition, but get lonely when you
never see him. He respects your devotion, but at times
tends to take it for granted. At worst, this union can turn
into a bitter emotional battle. At best, it can be a situation
of mutual respect, much support, and a shared sense of
responsibility.

One thing to remember is that you hold the power.
Although he may appear to be stern, staunch, overbearing, and even critical, you can turn him into a melted
marshmallow with your warmth, emotional sensitivity, and
sexual passion. If he grumbles around a lot and works
till one A.M. on your birthday, it's only because you've
allowed it. You can get this man to stand on his head
and wave his feet in the air, if that's your desire.

He is highly disciplined but very insecure. And what
you read to be coldness is merely an emotional play,
since he cannot tolerate rejection. Therefore, you have
to be patient, understanding, and sometimes manipulative,
which isn't at all difficult. And what you will have in
return is a man who is highly devoted.

He tends to be depressed, especially when his career
is going more slowly than anticipated, because he is only
a corporate vice-president at the age of twenty-eight. If

you are supportive of his maniacal power drive and listen to his daily problems about how his secretary forgets to dot her *i*'s, he will develop the deepest attachment to you. However, do not expect that in return he will appreciate, tolerate, or try to understand your moods or deepest feelings.

No matter how much he loves you, this man will leave you lonely at times and give you the feeling that the universe comes cut-and-dried. You may stay up all night listening to his tales of thwarted ambition, but if in his presence you cry your eyes out, he'll inform you he's going to the store to buy eggs for breakfast. Although he may complain till your ears start ringing, he is terribly uncomfortable with your unsolicited emotional displays, and at times, is downright terrified.

Once committed, he is faithful, enduring, patient, and paternalistic. His inordinate ambition will vicariously bring you the power you so appreciate. But he will never even begin to explore your inner being. No matter how much you love him, you may always feel that there is something missing. Just remember that if you have enough personal power to discover what it is, you have enough personal power to create it.

Scorpio Woman with Aquarius Man

He will never forget you, because you are that elusive woman. Regardless of the amount of time he spends with you, he will feel so close and yet so far, and that is the key to his amorous idealism.

With this man, you had better be aggressive or else make yourself a pot of coffee, because it's going to be a very long night. He is extremely opinionated and has at least five thousand theories on the universe. Be prepared to hear each one of them or else be prepared to commit an act of rape. Granted, it may not be the most exciting scene to seduce him as he's staring blankly into a fish tank and thinking. However, if you wait for him to stop talking, you might as well wait for bronze to turn to silver. It's not going to happen.

He loves your mind, your sexuality, and your perceptions. Your emotions are quite another matter; those he finds interesting when they don't become confining. He has no idea of where your feelings are coming from or where they're going or what they're really doing there, but he has a lot of interesting theories. As a matter of course, none of the theories usually apply, but they are provocative just the same.

You like his mind, find his gestures dryly amusing, but have to make some heavy emotional adjustments before you are ready for more than a friendship.

Sexually, he is not that satisfying to you, since he would rather think about sex than act. Emotionally, he is not that gratifying, since he is best friends with the world, and often his world includes women. He is freedom-loving and detached; you tend to be possessive and attached. Unless he makes you understand that his detachment does not obviate feeling, and unless you make yourself feel that you can have him without forcing yourself to possess him, this relationship is best kept on a lighter level.

Karmically, your love lessons bring you to opposite poles of experience. You must learn to put yourself out of an experience, but still be in it; he must learn to put himself into an experience without still having to be out of it. If both of you are open, you could help each other grow, and from this perspective, the relationship has no limits. It will take you as far and as fast as your mind and emotions want to move.

Scorpio Woman with Pisces Man

He'll treat you like a drug. The problem is that you're a woman. The essence of this irreconcilable fact is the essence of your problems with Mr. Pisces.

In regard to sex, this man is the passive sort. In regard to love, he is a garbage pail of emotion, and as to romance, he prefers the druglike dream of your distant approach far more than your personal appearance.

Aside from that, you are pragmatic, while he is the drunken idealist. Emotionally, you are serious, while he is mawkishly sentimental. And you are the strong survivor, while he is weak, sniffling, and whiny.

It is true that Mr. Pisces is as frail as his fantasies. In a time of crisis, he'll just cry on your shoulder, but don't let all this flimflam fool you. When caught in an emotional dead end, he can be cruel, sadistic, and cunning. Although, emotionally, he may understand where you're coming from, don't expect him to appreciate it—especially if you should assail him with a human need.

In a woman, he's looking for both a movie star and a

mother. If you happen to fit both roles and want to play them, you've got him—as long as you don't mind sharing him with a few other faces. But remember that when he's being unfaithful, he may even be tacky enough to let you trip over the evidence.

Although at times he sees himself as mysterious, you can see through him. Despite what he may think, he never created subtlety. He learned it somewhere from a Scorpio. And judging from his behavior, that's only a fraction of the learning he still has in store.

Scorpio Man with Aries Woman

This combination is passion personified, but one that involves a primitive kind of power struggle in which egos will clash so hard that you both get bruises.

You'll get miffed at the fact that she's talking about herself rather than musing about what a mysterious man you are. And *she'll* get mildly outraged at the fact that you don't seem to be assenting to her self-congratulatory comments.

She'll boss you around, and if you don't do as she says, she'll step on your foot. You'll snarl and throw out a few viciously sarcastic comments, but the worst part is that she is so self-centered that she won't even be listening.

She charges around like an Amazon warrior, and although you admire her strength, you can't stand her lack of subtlety. You like to be the aggressor, but somehow she always beats you to the punch.

She is strong, ambitious, and the prototype of the liberated woman. You respect her ambition, her worldly accomplishments, her vitality, and her stamina, and she wants you to. But does she respect yours?

The first question is: Does she even notice unless you trip her? Only her bruises will tell.

Scorpio Man with Taurus Woman

You'll take her in and make her travel places she's never been before. In one evening, she'll find you alluring, mysterious, magnetic, sexy, and dangerous. You are—and you'll be glad this woman is smart enough to know it.

You'll find her warm, sensual, domestic, insecure, and very vulnerable. You can see right through her asparagus quiche straight into her soul, and what you'll see is a tremendous sense of need and longing to be needed.

At first, this may scare you, and during dessert you may calculate how many giant steps it will take you to get beyond the front door, but something besides the second cup of coffee and Grand Marnier will keep you seated. You have no idea what it really is, and that's because it really is a lot of things.

For Ms. Taurus, this is a fatal attraction. Her heart will get caught up in your contradictions, and you'll enjoy the power you have in just watching her try to get out. She is like a fly under the furry foot of a tarantula, and in whichever direction she chooses to walk, she's going to get stepped on.

To her mind, you're a kind of three-ring circus without sound. She never knows what show goes on next, and half the time she doesn't even know what she's watching. What you do and say and desire and want and hate and need are all beyond her. From her perspective, the mechanics of your mind are more obscure than an Arabic translation of the Bible.

Her greatest desire is for an honest relationship without games, and the kind of passion that comes without pain. You find such scenes comforting only in the dark night of your soul, when you feel sad and lonely. At all other times you want your attention to be galvanized by some sort of challenge. In the long run, you'll only leave Ms. Taurus feeling cold and hungry.

Therefore, the outcome of this encounter is most likely to be that of two people who pass in the night. If she's smart, the first thing she should do when she sees you is just keep on walking. She'll save herself a lot of heartache, and you'll save yourself a few inches on your waistline from her cooking.

Scorpio Man with Gemini Woman

She'll play havoc with your emotions, and when you act moody and macabre just to scare her, she'll giggle in your face and chatter on as if she didn't see you.

There's no way you can control her, because she's a law unto herself. Bombard her with your mysterious airs, and she'll grin and call you "Operation Overkill." She is flip, funny, and always has the last word. Attack her with your savage sarcasm, and she'll smile and get you back with an instantaneous retort. She is quick with the comebacks and can hold her own in any situation. And at moments, you want to dismember her because you're jealous of her blithe detachment.

Neither of you is operating on even related wavelengths. She could give you an auditory hernia from her talking. At the same time, you could give her a suicidal sense of boredom when you seldom say anything. She is mental; you are emotional. She is a spendthrift, while you are a money-maker. She is motivated by casual flirtations; you are committed to intense encounters. She is detached and freedom-loving; you are serious and jealous. You'll dismiss her on the grounds that she's superficial. She'll dismiss you on the grounds that you're predatory.

At first you find this woman refreshing, but after your energies have had a chance to blend, what you both need is a psychic purgation. Gemini with Scorpio is like trying to cross an Afghan hound with an irascible Chihuahua. It's better off just to buy a bloodhound.

Scorpio Man with Cancer Woman

She'll nurture all your needs, make you fat and happy on her cooking, and try to be understanding when you're being surly. She is kind, giving, compassionate, and more sympathetic than a Red Cross nurse. She'll listen to your problems, pay you more attention than you desire or deserve, and make you feel like you're "the greatest show on earth."

All that she asks in return is *love*. She wants to be smothered in it. She wants to be drowned. She needs to be possessed, cherished, and suffocated in order to feel secure. She wants to hold you, consume you, devour you, and digest you. And what will remain, remains to be seen.

You appreciate her love and affection, but something deep within you makes it difficult for you to totally accept it. You need to keep your own space—not necessarily because you want it, rather because you have a fear that if any woman gets too close and you start to need her, she just might be taken away.

You have a hard time trusting, and she has a hard time holding back. Your moods may make her feel unloved, while her needs may make you feel you're in a prison.

On the other hand, you could find her very nice to come home to, as she is loyal, sensual, supportive, and a positive witch at conjuring creature comforts.

She'll fall in love, practically at first sight, though she'll be too shy to say so. However, you'll be able to read it in her eyes as she smiles at you over your chicken soup shimmering in the candlelight.

This could be a great match, should you be ready to settle for some connubial bliss. However, should you have only a good fling in mind, after she tells you her sun sign, just keep on walking.

Scorpio Man with Leo Woman

If her ascendant, moon, or Venus is in water, and even better, in Scorpio, this combination spells sexual Sturm und Drang. Here is the drama that you dreamed of, but the question is, how long can you stand it?

This vibration is passion personified. Exciting, yes. But as the emotions condense into steam heat, just stand back and watch your sanity go up in smoke.

If there are no water signs prominent in her chart, this encounter will start off like a lusty Italian movie and terminate like a French film where nothing really happens and even the characters are so bored they walk away.

You are an enigma—even to yourself. But if she has Scorpio strong in her chart, emotionally she'll understand you, because you'll both be starting from the same place —total obscurity. The key to you is that you talk in code. "I like your ambition; there's a great project I think we could collaborate on" means "I know you don't want to waste any time either, so let's roll down the sheets." "I'm really angry!" means "I'm hurt, but won't realize it until two weeks from next Sunday." "I'm really hurt!" means "Now, I've got you!" Silence means "What did she *really* mean by that, and why?" or "In ten seconds, two hands will be wrapped around your throat." 9, 8, 7, 6 . . .

You are not an easy one to love, but this will not intimidate her. But when you communicate in convolutions of thought and feeling—feeling through thought, feeling plus feeling, then thinking plus thinking—because it's easier than just feeling, she'll either tell you you're boring her or inform you she just remembered she has another date.

At her most powerful she's only playing with a few parts of you—until you decide that you desire *all*, and then, watch out for Old Inscrutable. Your sense of power screams that you must be impervious to pain, but since you know you seldom are, you will have her under constant surveillance with omnipresent eyes that see around corners.

You are wildly jealous, and she is a compulsive flirt with a queen complex. Her consuming sense of drama may turn you around until you're facing the wrong direction. Then she had better watch her step, since aimless anger is not your style. You can go from cold control to violence and back again in ten seconds. If she bruises easily, she had just better behave herself.

Sexually, she'll find you a turn-on. Yet, her gaze tends to drift a lot when you turn off emotionally. She heartily appreciates that you're the most intense sort of man, but when you're so self-absorbed, she'd rather find someone shallow. Chances are, she'll have your total attention. And chances are, you'll try to dominate her with her own frailties, compliment her only on special occasions, and possess her in a kind of steaming sensuality. You are a pro at the game of power, and in this one she will have no hope of winning. Your rule is control at all costs. She knows it well; it's hers—but this time, she's the slave. She's always fantasized about someone strong enough to fearlessly force her about. With you, she's found him. And now that that's over, she'll probably tell you she's going.

Scorpio Man with Virgo Woman

Although at first she may appear cold, in point of fact she is just fragile. You will appreciate her mind, her stability, and her services. Together you can have a companionship that is quiet and comfortable. The problem is that you desire one that is noisy and intense.

Here there is a lot of talk but very little action, and passion simply does not reign supreme. Together you can analyze your feelings until you both fall asleep, but it is highly unlikely that you can get the matter to reign over the mind.

She has an aspect to her personality that is healing, and there is a portion of your personality that needs to be healed. However, there is another aspect that thinks it needs a consummate kind of passion, and because of this, you are willing to take what she offers, but let the relationship pass you by.

Basically you're attracted to a woman who calls the shots and galvanizes you with one passionate glance, and Ms. Virgo tends to follow the shots in an effort to be kind and pleasing. With all the women in your life who have forced you to passivity through sheer sensual impact, niceness was never a consideration. That is why, rather than putting her hopes on you, Ms. Virgo is far better off with her pet turtle. You'll always be looking for what isn't there, but a turtle just looks and looks. . . .

Scorpio Man with Libra Woman

She'll give you a sense of balance, and in return, you'll give her a taste of intense love. She has a special sense of the beautiful and can create a setting of the most seductive creature comforts.

You'll appreciate her good sense of humor and the fact that she is airy and easy to be with. She'll clear away your murky moods and fill your life with the little loving acts that take your heart away.

She is sentimental and romantic, but with you she might as well die and be reborn waiting for a little murmur of love. She fantasizes about the day when you'll bring her flowers, but if she searches your pockets for a trinket, all she'll find is a corporate financial statement.

She is so dependent that she hates even to go to the bathroom alone, and you are so independent that you can't understand her dependency. She is open and wants to share every part of her life. You are closed and want to share only selected moments.

She is sensual and loving, while you are sexual and possessive. But despite her faults, she is everything you want and need.

The question is: Are *you* everything *she* wants and needs? But since her needs overtake her desires, she'll be able to settle and make herself enjoy it.

Scorpio Man with Sagittarius Woman

You'll fascinate her, though she'll find you murky. And in five minutes she'll have you falling in love. Ms.

Sagittarius loves to laugh and just wishes that you did, but if you stick around long enough, she'll be willing to teach you. Despite personality differences, she is wise, positive, philosophical, and has an energy and enthusiasm that overwhelm you. Her personality is expansive, while yours is constrictive. She is adventurous and freedom-loving, while you are cautious and possessive. She knows how to fuse her mind and her body, while you often separate yours.

She'll find you charming, interesting, and sexually powerful, but she'll have a hard time understanding your emotions. Basically she is open and frank, while you are closed and indirect.

She is athletic and daring and could spend the entire day playing tennis in 100 degrees where her peppy enthusiasm will keep you on the courts until after sundown. Her personality is so zealous and romantic that you feel you've finally found your rhapsody at dawn. You have—as long as you behave yourself.

When you crowd her space with your jealousy, she'll laugh it off and call you crazy. That's because once she's committed, she's committed. You'll probably want to keep her in the broom closet, because you'll think that everybody wants her. But that's the first way to lose her, because she has to have her freedom.

Her wisdom will force you to travel in new directions, and her optimism will encourage your expansion. She will help you rise to the heights and share your revelations once you've returned. Together you could take each other to a place each of you has never been, and through a deepening love, regenerate as you realize even greater joy.

Scorpio Man with Capricorn Woman

In this relationship, there is a lot of talk but very little emotional understanding. However, in many ways the attraction is so irresistible that it borders on being fatal. From the very start, she will be bewitched and you will be turned on. The ensuing situation could be definitely erotic but in the long run emotionally deadening.

In the throes of her enchantment, she will end up giving more, and you will end up taking it. Your enigmatic behavior brings out all her insecurities. At one point she is swimming in them with her head above water but at another point she is drowned.

Although you appreciate her vulnerability, patience, understanding, and the fact that she would travel to the ends of the earth for you, you still make her suffer. You don't want to, but you get caught up in such a vortex of emotion that you can't help it. She brings out the intensity you always try to sit on, because it comes down to the fact that either you control it or it controls you. You hate losing control; and having an intense sexual, emotional, intellectual experience is just the thing to cause it.

You have a hard time accepting all she has to give, because somewhere you feel you don't deserve it. Therefore, you love the idea of her, but the actuality makes you nervous, and you may try to restrict it to brief encounters.

Your behavior will puzzle her, pain her, and put her into an emotional space where she starts doubting herself. The danger comes when she begins to believe that she deserves what little you give her. At that point, she should either withdraw or confront the fact that she's looking for misery.

You have the uncanny way of eluding your problems and making other people suffer for them. It's such an unconscious compulsion that half the time you don't even know that you're doing it until three days later, and then you may feel morose, guilty, disgusted, and deeply saddened. Until you find some way to change the pattern of your consciousness, you have to take responsibility for the pain and disruption. You have a special talent for bringing upon yourself what you fear most, and in this situation you may find that there will come a day when Ms. Capricorn will leave you. Unless, of course, you leave her first, so that you're not left hanging.

Scorpio Man with Aquarius Woman

You'll want to make love, but she'll want to go to the movies. When you *are* making love, she'll be musing on why the film ended without music.

Just forget trying to control her; she is so detached that she'll end up controlling you because *you* find it such a challenge to control *her*. She has about five thousand friends and takes on the personal problems of each one of them, and you sometimes feel like you're competing with the crowds at opening night.

She is so easy to be with that in a peculiar way you

find her irresistible. She is like a breath of fresh air, but if you stay around her too long, you may start feeling cold. You are passion personified, while she is mental and remote. You embrace direct experience, while she prefers having hers vicariously. After ten years together you may tell her you want an open marriage and she'll tell you she thought it always was.

If you're unfaithful, she'll be too involved in other people's lives to notice, so forget the pernicious apologies used just to get her attention. She'll give you a remote smile and say that whatever you want is fine with her, and would you excuse her, the phone is ringing.

Living with her is like having a roommate. Marriage to her is like having a friend. You'll never get tired of her, because you'll seldom see her—she's so busy living through everyone else's life.

So if it's freedom plus pleasantries that you're looking for, you have it here. From you she has financial stability and the knowledge that you'll never leave her. For in her eyes a marriage is never marred by an affair if the marriage fulfills a man's most primal needs. She's so agreeable, cheerful, undemanding, and such a vacation from yourself that you can't help but need her. Despite your efforts to the contrary, expect to have a happy life.

Scorpio Man with Pisces Woman

Sexually, this combination is so powerful that you may both end up on the floor. She'll control you through her desire, and you'll devour her through your control. You may both expire through the sheer exhaustion of the situation, but what a way to go.

As this kind of physical chemistry is narcotic, expect to get hooked. When you are together, it may come to the point where you stop eating, sleeping, and thinking, and start losing weight. However, just how many banana-cherry splits can you really eat?

The same philosophy applies to you and Ms. Pisces. Although her abandoned sensuality sends you beyond your fantasies, her passivity will ultimately begin to bore you. A little splendor in the afternoon is energizing, but too much passion is sheer dissipation.

Your moods will drag her down, and her dependence will irritate you. You like your emotions to be challenged, while she likes hers to be gratified. You like a woman who is ambitious, self-possessed, and successful. She is looking for a man who is all of the above so that she can be taken care of.

Any way you look at it, this is a short-lived affair. Indoors there are no limits, but what do you do when it's snowing and you're standing in silence on the street? Chances are, you'll do something to make her start crying so that you can take a deep breath and walk away. If there's anything you despise, it's phlegmatic females. Back to work. The world is waiting.

SAGITTARIUS

Dates: November 23—December 21
Ruling planet: Jupiter
Element: Fire
Mode: Mutable
Qualities: Masculine, positive
Planetary principle: Expansion
Primal desire: Liberty
Color: Light blue
Jewel: Turquoise
Plant: Begonia
Day: Thursday
Archangel: Sachiel
Magical number: 6
Material factor: Growth

SAGITTARIANS OF FAME AND FORTUNE

Woody Allen	David Susskind
Harpo Marx	Jean Paul Getty
Winston Churchill	Beethoven
Mark Twain	Maria Callas
Walt Disney	Lee Remick
James Thurber	Sammy Davis, Jr.
Noël Coward	Mary Martin

Betty Grable

THE SAGITTARIUS FEMALE

Favorable

You have the personality of Pollyanna, the charm of an unforgettable character, and the intelligence of a highly intelligent but absentminded professor. Your welcome anywhere is always a little overwhelming. That's because you're a blithe and friendly spirit that everyone gets more than a little satisfaction out of being around.

As a schoolgirl you were probably voted "Most Popular." And as a woman your reputation still reaps loads of attention and affection. This is most likely elicited by the sparkle in your eye, your winsome laughter, and the way you magically light up a room.

You don't demand attention, you just draw it in unintentionally. Your sense of humor is a stellar force in any social situation, and your gregarious good nature gives you a following of friends who constantly encourage you to frequent their company.

All the same, you are the independent sort and do as you please without feeling you have to please any group of people. Quite strongly you rebel against possessive persons and pattern your life according to your own laws, which predicate personal freedom and privacy.

In addition, your interests are so varied and consuming that you really haven't time for idle chatter. It seems that the quintessential dilemma of your life is that you perpetually wonder where the time goes. That is because there are so many things you want to do and there's so little time in which to do them. However, you have to admit that you have the sense of timing of a person traveling through a series of time zones. Somehow, you feel that after five minutes, only one has elapsed. Therefore, not only do you have a problem getting everything you have to do done, you also have a problem being punctual.

The foremost things that interest you are travel and sports. You could be the first woman to go around the world on a bicycle and the first person to bring indoor polo to the arctic region. Your favorite fantasy object is a swimming pool, and your favorite fantasy occupation is to be an explorer.

You love the lure of far-off places, as well as the excitement that occurs in the process of getting up and going. However, if you find you are lacking the funds for an international expedition, you could be almost as happy hiking, or taking a few sailing lessons and arming yourself for a sea adventure.

When it comes to romantic matters, your attitude is "I don't care about love—just give me the sun and the wind." However, although you are the undisputed queen of the elements, you are also far more romantic than most people think.

For instance, how could any stranger suppose that that girl in a sweat shirt playing touch football believes in an ideal kind of love?

Well, you do. And your ideal is a man strong enough to hold you, yet flexible enough to let you fly around. And when you find him, you won't drown him in saccharine love statments, and you might giggle in his face if he assails you with a few. However, you will be ardent, devoted, faithful, and at the very least a best friend who inspires love.

At your most candid moment, you're a natural person who is honest, forthright, spontaneous, and believes heartily in self-improvement. You love life, loathe pessimistic people, and righteously embrace the optimistic philosophy that "everything is for the best in the best of all possible worlds." Your mind overflows with wisdom and insights that expand your life and bring you that youthful quality that can't even be bought by the "beautiful people."

Your intelligent sense of humor and buoyant belief in the betterment of tomorrow give you an enviable and undeniable beauty. You know that the world is yours to make of it what you wish, and you do so. Fears do not make you falter, nor do they retard your growth. Your basic creed is that today is the beginning of the rest of your life. And like no other sign, you know how to get the very most out of today without waiting for a string of tomorrows.

Unfavorable

Even at your worst, you're lovable. You're one of those rare human beings who is so devoid of malice aforethought that people feel they have to sneer and get a little suspicious.

More miserable individuals probably mistake you for someone insipid, because you smile all the time. But they'd most likely hate you if they knew that you know how to make the best of everything. Nobody can believe that you can take so much bad with the good and still come out grinning like a cheerleader.

You should really write an inspirational book on how you do it. However, you scatter your time and your energy so badly that you might end up back where you started—wandering in circles. No, you are not the most organized and orderly of people, and sadly you have to admit it.

However, there's really no crime in keeping your income-tax receipts in the freezer next to the ice cubes (especially if your accountant likes to drink a lot). And who can blame you for putting your plane ticket in your medicine chest? After all, you get to look at it every time you use your nose drops. You have a unique way of putting important things away in very safe places. The problem is that the places are so safe that you never set eyes on those important things again.

However, there's no denying that your intentions are always the best, even if your confusion quota sometimes consumes you. Quite cheerfully you'll offer to baby-sit for a friend's gorilla and realize at the very last minute that you've been invited away for the weekend. Oh, well, a quick call to ask your hostess if you can bring a guest, with no mention of whether it's animal, vegetable, mineral, or by any chance human.

There are undoubtedly moments when someone would like to slap you on the back and beg you to volunteer to no longer volunteer for anything anymore. In one exuberant burst of enthusiasm, you will offer to address an entire mailing list of Christmas cards for some charitable organization. But when the time comes, those five thousand cards have somehow slipped your mind, and instead you've already taken off for a ski trip.

Although you mean well, you suffer badly from foot-in-mouth disease and have a maddening way of offering "helpful hints" and left-handed compliments: "I love your new sunglasses because I can see so little of your face."

. . . "Don't you think it's kind of cute that you and your bulldog are starting to look alike?"

Chances are that some people might consider either paying you or killing you just to keep your mouth shut. And it's not unreasonable to wonder why.

On the other hand, you do redeem yourself by being consistently generous and good-natured. You have no idea where your money goes, because often you spend it spontaneously on the gifts you love to buy for people. However, because you're lucky, your finances always seem to miraculously multiply themselves at the very last minute.

One item that you're most likely to spend money on is a cleaning lady. Due to your disorganization, lack of time, and almost reverent disinclination for such meaningless chores, your abode often looks like it was the scene of a jewel robbery. You're often lucky if you can find the telephone in less than five minutes. And your way of cleaning up after a dinner party is called leaving your dishes in the sink.

However, despite your messy ways, you're one person who is definitely endearing. Those people who resent you because you appear to be so happy would rather spend their time remaining miserable. So, keep on grinning and let the world worry on around you.

THE SAGITTARIUS MALE

Favorable

Some might consider you a kind of three-ring circus, others, a man who carries his own light. However, wherever you go, you bring such a robust attitude that your fans want to touch you just for good luck.

Even at the age of fifty-five, you're like a buoyant boy scout who bitterly resents rest periods. You have the spontaneous enthusiasm of a holy innocent, and the wisdom of an ancient sage. You have a simply irresistible sense of humor and an intelligence that takes you far beyond logic. You are a combination of a metaphysician and a restless excitement seeker. Your credo is expansion, and your power is positive thinking.

Your personality displays an insouciance that causes

people to lend you their total attention. You are a wonderful, witty bon vivant who makes everyone feel at least a little better. You are generous, kind, benevolent, endearing, and a friend in need, even to the furry creatures.

Women who come your way are quickly bewitched. You have a charm that could tame serpents, and a *joie de vivre* that makes one wish you could be rented for an evening.

In matters of love and romance, you are something of a sly devil. Although women overwhelm you and seem to materialize simultaneously at the most embarrassing moments, in your ebullient way you would rather remain uncommitted. You love the adventure and conquest of romance far more than any secure, sedentary situation. Preferably, you would like your life to be a kind of changing room where each woman allows you the challenge of the chase. However, you really don't want to catch up with any of them, because then all the fun would seem to slip away.

You are a freedom-loving fellow who is highly disinclined to make a marital commitment. However, should you find a woman who is far more fun to be with than to be without, and who will also pose no threat of confinement, then you might decide that marriage can be far more meaningful than you ever would have thought.

Because you are so impulsive and impressionable, idealistic and spontaneous, you have a high incidence of divorce. However, later in life, when you are a trifle more sober and a little less reckless, there is a strong possibility that you will marry for all the right reasons.

At any given time, life around you is never at a standstill. Whether you're taking off for a weekend at a balloon ranch, or planning a hike in the Himalayas, or attending a two-week Yoga retreat in Calcutta, you're never bored, and consequently, never boring.

You're one person who is always active, intensely alive, and ever eager to deal with life head-on. You love to travel, play around at sports, and pursue a path to greater growth and development.

Your philosophic attitudes can take you anywhere from a post as a philosophy professor to an expedition into the ancient mysteries. Your entire life is a quest that you follow with a kind of widespread wanderlust. The greatest part about it is that you never know where it might take you, and you really don't care. With your positive attitudes, any experience can be transformed into a kind of triumph, while all time becomes a passage into greater teachings. And you remain a most insatiable student, ripening in wisdom, love, and life's deepest joys.

Unfavorable

You're an international ne'er-do-well with a personality that could almost pay your plane fare. Because you elicit laughter, people will follow you anywhere. However, it's for only a short time period that you can even remember their names.

Your attention span flashes away in front of one's very eyes. And what's left is a man who can't even sit still because the call of greater good times is always upon him.

You love to frolic and have fun. And you take spontaneity to the extreme. You are an impromptu explorer into the far reaches of pleasure. And whatever fails to qualify, you lose little time in leaving behind.

From a Gstaad après-ski to the beaches of Biarritz, you're the man of the moment, making the most of every scene. You never settle for less than total satisfaction, because your momentary desires always dominate.

Your mind seeks immediate gratification, and then it's soaring on to something else. Meanwhile, in the dust sifting behind you often sits a person sunken in emotional pain. You are a taker who doesn't linger long enough to consider what you are leaving behind.

At your most charming, you're more like a little boy than a man. In your sad moments, you appeal to a woman's mother instincts and know exactly how to manipulate her with a carefully placed head on her breast. During gayer times (and these are more often than not), you give her your Dennis the Menace grin before you slip out of her life to find some new face in an anonymous crowd. You're a kind of playboy of the western world who seeks the sublime sexual situation. And when you make love, love has nothing to do with it.

Any female who gets to stick around is forewarned that you're a freedom-loving fellow who insists on a no-strings kind of situation. Love 'em and leave 'em is your motto, because you view variety as the plasma of romantic pleasure. The less any woman lingers, the more you feel assured. Your fear of being tied down is really a facade that poorly conceals the fact that you're just too selfish to share yourself with any person.

The fundamental core to you is that you are narcissistic, unreliable, irresponsible, and committed to noncommitment. Your attention span extends beyond yourself only far enough to scan other faces. And your interest in them is only a matter of what they can bring to you.

Your boyish charm is your ticket to those women who think less of themselves than they do of you. Their attitude is that a little charisma is worth a week of suffering, and they make themselves sick wondering who you're with, whether the phone will ever ring, and if they will ever get to gaze again into your twinkling eyes. If, for some reason, you feel that you'd be gaining so much that maybe you should marry, you would never be faithful. You're a restless rogue who likes to run around and follow the conquest of each new face. Your love of travel takes you from person to person as well as from country to country. And wherever you go and whatever you decide to do, it's totally on your terms.

Needless to say, you're about as mature as someone in mid-adolescence. In the sincerity of the moment, you can offer the world, but when it comes to a delivery, it's somehow slipped your mind and you're nowhere to be found. You're as easy to lean on as a tall twig, and more immature than an infant who sits and stares at his navel. Your life is one continual search that leads you in circles, with all experience filtered through a superficial value system. Your idea of adventure is to avoid responsibility for any of your actions. And your version of spontaneity is to do what you want when you want, with no human considerations in mind. Although you love to jaunt from country to country, ironically the world begins and ends with you.

After a while, you will pave the way for a playboy burial. At this point, your smile will no longer be your love light, your women would rather burn your postcards than read them, and your charisma will be so powerful that you'll be stood up by an indifferent female who decides she would get more out of cleaning her apartment than from another nighttime passion that has passed away by midmorning. Good luck, lover. Here's hoping that you're lucky enough for the "good life" to linger.

DECANS

Every sign in the zodiac can be broken down into three subdivisions, called decans. Each decan roughly corresponds to ten degrees—the first third, second third, and last third of the sun sign's time span, which is approximately thirty days.

As each of these periods has different subrulerships, the personality of a person is slightly modified by the specific decan it falls in. For instance, an Aries born in the second decan would be ruled by Mars, but subruled by the sun. Therefore, he would tend to display a greater sense of pride, boastfulness, egotism, and optimism than an Aries born in the third decan, which is subruled by Jupiter. This Aries would tend to be more freedom-loving, flighty, travel-oriented, and interested in subjects of a philosophical nature. An Aries born in the first decan would be the most aggressive, but not necessarily the most productive and accomplished.

Decans are important, since they do account for a more detailed assessment of an individual's personality characteristics. They also show how two people born under the same sun sign can be markedly different.

If you were born between November 23 and December 2, your sun falls in the Jupiter decan of Sagittarius.

You personify the principles of sagacity and swiftness and have an extraordinary sense of humor. You also possess a philosophic attitude toward life and a sense of joyfulness that you impart to all undertakings.

At your most unfettered, you are a highly spontaneous person who exists in the impetuosity of the moment. You love adventure, far-off foreign places, people who make you laugh, and the everyday experience of living. You know how to make the best of a situation and bring a kind of exuberant enthusiasm to every moment.

Travel is one of your greatest pleasures. However, a variety of sports also have a special appeal. Chances are, you like to ski, swim, play tennis, hike, camp out, and go canoeing.

Your energy is limitless, and your interest extends to everything around you. Basically, you see life as a learning experience that you get a lot out of. It's no wonder that people love to be around you.

If you were born between December 3 and December 12, your sun falls in the Mars decan of Sagittarius.

You are impulsive, aggressive, and strongly action-oriented. You have a highly restless nature and can be spontaneous to the point of carelessness. You have strong drives in whatever you undertake. However, often you lack a sustaining force and leave half-finished projects in midstream while you momentarily abandon yourself to something new.

Sports of all kinds are highly appealing, especially such competitive athletic activities as tennis and football. Bicycling, hiking, running, and camping also keep your energies in balance and your enthusiasm flowing. At the same time, such endeavors as karate and judo can give you the experience of a mental discipline through a physical form.

Once you learn how to control and direct your energies, your life will be an experience without limits. Your enthusiasm, aggression, and sense of daring can take you to the top of so many professions that you could end up being one of those people with a degree in each area of interest. You could easily become a veterinarian, an athlete, a philosophy professor, or maybe somehow combine all three.

Sagittarians born in this decan often have a high degree of sex appeal, so chances are that the only problem you will ever have in regard to the opposite sex is in choosing which person to spend time with. It is highly likely that you will be surrounded by many eager and susceptible souls who are avidly seeking ownership. However, your time is taken up by so many interests, activities, people, and places that you will be rather disinclined to put many emotional restrictions on your life. You have the most fun when you are just living in the moment, and you heartily enjoy the experience of knowing as many people as possible. Any way you look at it, you are not an easy person to carry away and confine. The requirements of your freedom-loving nature always come first, and until they are satisfied, you just can't be your joyous, ebullient self. For every Sagittarian who fails to smile, the world is surely missing something.

If you were born between December 13 and December 21, your sun falls in the solar decan of Sagittarius.

Deep within you is a drive toward creative self-expression. Chances are that you will fulfill this need either through some form of the arts or teaching. There is a strong desire for success in your personality, and concomitantly, a very positive attitude toward all that you undertake.

Of all the Sagittarian decans, you have the greatest determination, fortitude, and willpower. You are more highly organized, more disciplined, and have a deeper appreciation of the role that structures play in the process of goal attainment.

This is a truly powerful position for the sun's placement, since faith, hope, courage, and patience exert a most active influence.

You have a strong personality, and one that can take you anywhere, from the stage to the classroom, to the spotlights of the screen, to the pages of the world's most appreciated books, to the realm of comedy, to the kind of economic power that runs a country.

You have a magical kind of charisma that most people find so enchanting that they just can't get enough of it. Your overwhelming popularity comes from your sense of humor, warmth, and vitality.

Wherever your travels take you, you are most heartily welcomed and duly appreciated. That is because you are the personification of *joie de vivre* and your laughter lives on in the minds of many, long after you have moved on.

LOVE

You are independent, freedom-loving, and forever looking for a challenge. Your romantic reverie is far more an excursion into the exotic than an earthbound evening of champagne and roses. You would rather share a slow boat to China than confine yourself to a candlelit restaurant with a piano player. Because you are so restless, impulsive, and looking for the wildest kind of excitement, you're not an easy person to be in love with.

If you are a male Sagittarius, you can be maddening when it comes to making a commitment. You are a freedom fanatic and a philanderer, and you run rather than walk into the lives of a plethora of women. Each one of them you view as a kind of adventure—like going sailing without your life preserver.

In general, your interest is instantaneous but has the life span of a flash cube. That is because your attention is so short but your mind so overstimulated. In a most exuberant way, you yearn to embrace all experience. But because your arms reach out so wide, it all seems inevitably to slip through.

There are some who might accuse you of being adverse to love. However, this really isn't true. The fact is that you tend to be too insensitive to even consider being considerate. You live for what you can gain in the moment, rather than for what you can give, and see love as a floor show that comes straight to you.

Because you are always searching and hoping, but haven't the faintest idea of what you really want, you can go through more women than a greedy sultan. Love is something you can never seem to understand, because you can't sit still long enough to think about it. Each woman in your life is no more than a rushed experience fitted in between a few others.

Since your love life is busier than the office of a casting director, you have a hard time being monogamous or faithful. Therefore, marriage is not exactly your answer to attaining bliss. You loathe confinement and regard emotional commitment as menacing.

Until you grow up and take the time to acquire a sense of responsibility, you'll remain a roving playboy who always wonders if he could have done a little better. And your view of women will be nothing more than that of a side trip on the way to a circus.

If you are a female Sagittarius, you are less consumed by the chase and more by the quality of an experience. While you are also impulsive, independent, and enamored of adventure, you are capable of making a commitment, should the right man come along.

You prefer an exciting man who respects your independence and sparks your interest with his enthusiasm. It's not at all necessary that he have a private airplane. Merely a strong sense of humor and an assertive nature will do nicely.

You are a passionate person who doesn't find a loving situation a compromise to your sense of freedom. Instead, you find that it's even more fun to have a permanent tennis partner, or a hiking companion.

In love, you're not looking for a millionaire who will place a diamond bracelet around your wrist. You're looking for a funny friend who's a joy to be with. You could care less if he arrives in hiking boots. What you do care about is his sincerity and his soul.

In the end, any man you finally love has to become aware that he's very lucky. You are loyal, loving, and have an invincible life force that could raise the Druids from their resting place. Living with you is like taking a trip far beyond where the normal mind can see.

MARRIAGE

When it comes to marriage, you may have more than many. You are an adventurer with a freedom-loving philosophy that can take you through many places and many people.

In your younger years, you embrace "the chase" and travel alone from face to face. You're the last person on earth who feels that love has to light the way.

In your youth, you look at marriage as the most primitive kind of trap and avow that you much prefer the experience of many people. However, after a period of almost too many experiences, you can concede to sensing a persistent hunger for a soulmate.

In marriage, you need a clever, fun-loving companion far more than a breathless lover. You see a successful marital union rooted in a strong friendship that is both dynamic and nonconfining.

You need to be able to take an impulsive jaunt to the health club without having to face a jealous mate on your return. And you need to have the knowledge that your spouse wants to share experience with you rather than rid you of it.

What you find most enjoyable is a light action-oriented situation with a lot of laughter and many good times. However, if you start to feel the progressive lack of illumination, your mind and body begin to wander, especially if you're the male of the species.

Even then, you're prone to play around long after you've settled into a matrimonial sanctuary. The allure of the adventure always gets you off and going in search of an experience of greater intensity. To rationalize your need for extramarital dalliance, you have the convenient quip that all the world's a friend. However, the truth remains that at times you are irresponsible and fabricate your excuses to fit the occasion.

When a Sagittarius decides to make a commitment to be faithful, marriage is a most sacred soul union. However, when the mate spends more time outside the marriage than within it, a trip to the divorce court is imminent.

Every Sagittarius must be clear about what he or she really wants before marriage is even considered. Otherwise, the feelings trod upon will one day be paid for in kind, and often the price is a lot more than you think.

MONEY

Unless you have a heavy influence of Capricorn in your chart, you're a spendthrift who doesn't know when to stop. However, no matter how much you have, you never let money consume you.

You're generous to a fault and love to lavish presents on those people to whom you feel most affection. In addition, your voice is always foremost when it comes to picking up dinner tabs in a spontaneous fashion.

Whenever you let money control you, it never makes you happy. However, at the same time, you need to have enough to be able to feel free. Any kind of confinement is a *bête noire* to your basic sense of bliss. And you like to live each day in emotional ebullience.

When it comes to your spending habits, you're more likely to purchase a private airplane than a Rolls-Royce. Unless you're so wealthy that you no longer notice that you have money, you'll make sure that you get the most pleasure out of anything you pay for. Of course, one morning you may wake up to a mysteriously empty wallet after having withdrawn a very large sum the day before.

However, you do have a lot of fun when you're spending. You're one of the few people who know how to translate money into experience, and every experience that is forthcoming is sure to be truly fantastic.

CAREER

Because Jupiter, the planet of good fortune, is your ruling planet, success often comes your way with a modicum of effort. However, the importance you attach to it is quite another matter.

Unless you have a lot of Capricorn planets in your horoscope, you don't need a Rolls-Royce, a chinchilla, or a castle in Spain to make you feel comfortable. A humble beach house and a fluid bank account will do nicely.

Success is important only if it ensures your sense of freedom. However, if you feel you have to sell your integrity as well as your free time to gain a few societal power privileges, the situation ceases to be attractive, no matter what the trappings.

Because you find confinement and coercion most distasteful, you would prefer a spontaneous Spartan existence to a shackled form of opulence. Your mind is far too philosophical to allow you to barter your life for the facade of a successful existence.

Happiness means more to the Sagittarius mind than any amount of money. And while you wouldn't mind several homes scattered throughout a few countries, and maybe a private plane to take you to them, you're not willing to include sleepless nights due to anxiety attacks. Because your mind is independence-plus, you could just as easily walk away from a situation as into it. And if the situation brings you neither inner meaning nor inner joy, you will be quick to quit it.

Basically, you're an adventurer and hate being confined and closed in, so you might take a multitude of jobs before you find the one that best suits your sensibilities. There are Sagittarians who like to jump around from place to place to satisfy their wanderlust. Others prefer to devote their life to drifting, dreaming, and taking experience as it comes.

In terms of that special choice, you could be anything from a guru to a travel agent, from a philosophy professor to a comedy writer, from a philanthropist to a publisher. Not to mention an athlete or a sportswriter.

Since your ruler, Jupiter, governs education, teaching is always a strong possibility. However, because travel has always appealed to you so strongly, you could also find working in some foreign service most exciting. On the other hand, if you are still entranced with the lure of far-off places but would rather live at home, the import-export business gives you the drama of international traffic while you maintain the roots of a domestic milieu.

However, whatever you decide to work at, your commitment is to the *now*, not to what might happen fourteen years into the future. The last thing you would ever take a job for is future economic security. Your first priority is always to your present happiness. What happens after that depends on where you want your life to take you. And usually it takes you to exciting and wonderful places.

FRIENDS

You have more friends than you know what to do with. You're ridiculously popular, but that's not at all surprising, considering your joyous personality.

You're the kind of person who is in demand for every dinner party, and highly appreciated as a friend. The combination of your warmth, generosity, and arresting sense of humor is something that people can't get enough of. Despite the fact that you may seem scattered at first sight, you're a steady shoulder to lean on and a lovable person to be around. Your personality is like a sunshine pill that puts solar light into everyone's life.

You're a gregarious, strongly outgoing person who likes best to spend your time around positive people who are also on the go. While you will offer sincere and sagacious advice to the downhearted, people who dwell in self-pity are to be avoided at all costs.

Subconsciously, you select your friends on the basis of liveliness, agility, and sense of adventure. You don't have the time to be taken down by characters who prefer to stay gloomy. The drama of life is drawing you in from all directions, and you have to heed its call. One thing you realize is that your life just won't wait.

HEALTH

You're as healthy as an astronaut, but tend to overdo the sleepless-night scene. You hate to go to bed, because not all that much is really happening there. Therefore, you'd rather play Ping-Pong, do some deep knee bends, or play a few games of backgammon than face the land of counterpane.

Because you stay so active, you're usually physically fit. Your body makes the most of every moment, and you seldom give it a chance to stop performing.

The kind of exercise that most people do as a physical-fitness duty, you revel in as a form of relaxation. You're a natural athlete and fervent lover of the active life.

Because you drive a car like a blind man who got his license from a mail-order house, auto accidents are always a possible nemesis. Try to keep your mind on the road rather than on your latest trip to the Azores. Otherwise, if only for the sake of others, just stick to riding your bicycle. It's often safer to drive with a gorilla than with a Sagittarius, even if the company isn't as good.

HOME

You're a perpetual nomad who gets a little grumpy every time you have to settle down. Therefore, ideally, several houses well scattered about the globe would best suit you.

However, since you spend most of your money on airplane fare, it is highly likely that you can afford only one domicile at best.

Since you are flighty, freedom-loving, and always prepared for a rapid departure, your home sometimes looks like a changing room in an airport, with clothes scattered conspicuously about the floor.

Since it's difficult for you to find the time for decorating, a professional decorator would be the best solution.

You prefer clear, uncluttered space, with as many windows as possible. Because feeling close to nature is of prime importance, you could live in a tent and be happy. However, if your preference for a country dwelling must be compromised for a city sanctuary, there are always ways to make the ambience cozy and rural.

Select a dwelling with high ceilings and invest in a few fig trees for the living room, a majestic palm for the bedroom, a creeping philodendron for the kitchen, and a geranium for the bath.

Instead of sinking your money in expensive furniture, use colorful floor pillows and low plastic tables to create the illusion of greater space. In the long run, they'll also make your moving tasks more hassle-proof.

To create an outdoor effect, string a hammock from your living-room ceiling and try using this as your special retreat from the world. Padded window seats are a must for making daydreams, and white louvered shutters are wonderful gates separating you from the outside world.

In the bedroom, a touch of white wicker here and there set off by a few ferns could make it a room you love to enter. Beautifully framed travel posters on the walls will evoke that romanticism of far-off places.

Wherever you choose to live, you illuminate it with a vitality and joy for living that provide an enviable luster.

COSMIC CHALLENGE

Regardless of the fact that you have the best intentions, what happens despite them can be quite disconcerting. A rush of momentary enthusiasm often leads you to promise far more than you fulfill. Therefore, not infrequently you are considered capricious, self-centered, and inconsiderate. The challenge in your lifetime is to rise far enough above the whim of the moment to recognize the rights and feelings of others.

Until you take responsibility for your behavior, you may find yourself paying certain painful prices that you really resent. Try to realize that your compulsive need for expansion sometimes creates limitations that can be overcome only by a personally aware outlook. Allow your individual perspectives to extend to the people around you, and you will gain experiences that are richer.

The more considerate you are of others, the more caring they will be of you. And in the long run, your life will take you through fewer tentative places.

INSPIRATION

You are the sign of higher philosophy and wisdom. Intrinsic to your being is the force of expansion at its highest.

Your ruler, Jupiter, imparts to you optimism, jubilance, and beneficence. From within your higher self, sagacity overflows, lighting the way for those souls with less illumination.

You are highly respected for your insights, awareness, and faith in times of turmoil. Your love of life, your trust of your fellow man, and your philosophical aspirations can bring you to the heights of human experience. The radiance you exude is a divine force that links you with the higher planes. You represent the precept that to know thyself is to know God. And from within the deepest reaches of your questing soul rises a truly divine emanation.

WHAT HOLDS YOU BACK AND HOW TO OVERCOME IT

Because you tend to be in a constant state of coming and going, you often get little accomplished, and less finished. Your flighty, confused behavior can impose severe limitations on your productivity. It's wonderful to have a multitude of interests, but when they become so numerous that they take you in too many directions, you become a victim of your own diversity.

Set goals for yourself in what you want to accomplish, and see to it that you stick to them. It is important both to finish what you set out to do and to stand by each promise and plan that you make. Your karma requires you to get in control of your aspirations and to give as much attention to the tiny details as to your more expansive quests. Once you consider your commitments more seriously, you will be regarded with a deeper appreciation by all who deal with you. And as a result, you will come to love your life a lot more.

LOVE AND
COMPATIBILITY GUIDE

Sagittarius with Sagittarius

You are an enviable couple who typify all the romanticism of the good life. Together you will engage in pleasure jaunts to the jungles, side trips to the mountains, and prolonged seaside stays. Life is nothing less than a consuming adventure without interludes. That is because you both know how to make the best of every situation and can create your good times without waiting for them to come to you.

You love laughter, surprises, and the feeling of freedom that allows you to pick up and take off when the urge overcomes you. Together, you pursue a quest to a place without limitation. And your extraordinary sense of humor, along with your spontaneous imagination, is your greatest means of transportation.

Two Sagittarians don't even need an airplane, because they can create their own setting through their thought forms. You are two highly active principles who can get off on anything from a rugby match to a course on Eastern religions, from a canoe trip to a weekend Yoga retreat. You are both ebullient forces supported by a high degree of optimism and an unrestrained exuberance for life. And although you never sit still for long, it's a tremendous treat to be around you, because, at the very least, one can learn a lot.

Sagittarius Woman with Aries Man

You will consider his ego problems silly, and he will consider your behavior flighty. You have a lot of energy but in the long run never seem to have very much to show for it. However, you can ruin his self-image on the tennis court and can outdo him in stamina on a bicycling trip.

Once he overcomes his basic self-centeredness, the chemistry here can catalyze in a very intense kind of love.

Basically, you are both freedom-loving, friendly, and very optimistic. Your good-natured support will help him get his ideas off the ground. His active sense of competition will spur you to do something with your life and not just talk about it.

You'll laugh at his bossy behavior and make him see himself for the first time from the outside. At the same time, you will respect the power he feels from being a superachiever, and he will admire the way your philosophical attitudes always seem to support you. He likes the way you never let anything get you down for long. And you like the way his enthusiastic approach seems to get him everywhere.

He finds your sense of humor contagious, and you find that you like to make him laugh. You love the way he makes decisions off the top of his head, and he loves the way you have of making him see only the sunny side of life.

You both like to engage in more activities than there is time for, and you share a sense of spontaneity that can take you to the most peculiar places.

You fascinate him on cozy nights with your endless tales of traveling adventures. He fascinates you by demonstrating how you can have adventures without physically going places. In a very short period of time, you realize that you love being together far more than you like being apart. At this point, he will move in and ask you to marry him in a manner that's about as romantic as a holdup. You will be overwhelmed but not surprised. You're just too smart for that. If he really wants to delve into things, he will notice that you've already packed half of your closet, and it's not because you've planned a prolonged voyage.

Sagittarius Woman with Taurus Man

Your idea of fun is lots of physical activity; his idea of physical activity is either sex or overeating.

You'll get up at dawn just to work on your backhand, while he would rather spend the day eating pasta than playing tennis. You love to travel from country to country, while he rarely moves from room to room. You prefer a spartan life-style to the lap of luxury. He prefers a sybaritic setting to one where he has to rough it.

You have a sense of adventure that leads you to exciting places. He has a sense of fear that entrenches him in the same spot. You are fascinated by Eastern philosophy, but the only meditation he's ever done is on money. He'll sulk when he doesn't understand your sense of humor, and you'll be impatient with his overwhelming possessiveness.

Needless to say, the chances are highly unlikely that you will bring each other a lifetime of untarnished bliss. Instead, he would be much better off returning to his simmering pot of ragoût and you to a solitary shopping spree for some new sweat bands.

Sagittarius Woman with Gemini Man

In this combination, there is a magical kind of compatibility. He loves your laughter, and you love the way he always makes you laugh. You both find everything funny, have a strong need for freedom, and share a basic enthusiasm that could lighten up any room.

He amuses you with his spectacular knowledge of trivia; you entertain him with your tales of voyages to peculiar places. You are the only person he ever met who can be later than he is. He is the only person you have ever met who can beat you at backgammon.

You are both restless, impatient, friendly, and fearful of getting too close too soon. He'll help you balance your checkbook and show you how to save your tax receipts. In turn, you will teach him Transcendental Meditation and how to dive seven feet off a springboard.

You are both adaptable, adventurous, good-natured, and a little crazy. Together you can make every act an affirmation of the best life has to offer. Your life knows no limits, and neither does your imagination.

Sagittarius Woman with Cancer Man

He needs you beside him, but you need the space to be by yourself. You'll undoubtedly inflict a mortal wound when you ask him why he's so dependent. But you'll bring him to the verge of suicide when he hands you a love poem and you laugh and shriek "You've got to be kidding!"

You'll never understand his sensitivities, and he'll never understand your need for freedom. He'll become so infatuated with your vitality and sense of humor that he'll want to follow you to the supermarket and spend time with you while you stand in line. He'll get emotional over the way you butter your English muffin, and when you're not looking, he'll fondle your tennis racket.

However, the more he candidly expresses his feelings, the more you mutter "Yech!" and ask him to shut up and pass the mustard. You're a swell person, but he needs you like a hole in the head. You're a menace to his tenuous ego, and a deflated balloon to his romantic reveries.

Most of the time he spends with you he'll sulk in conspicuous silence, feverishly hoping that you're eating your heart out. However, when you cheerfully slap him on the back and ask him if he has indigestion, all hope is lost and he suddenly decides he wants to go home, even if he *is* home.

You don't have to love him, and it's more likely than not that you won't, but be nice to Mr. Cancer and don't batter and shred his ego. Otherwise, you may become a Cancer too in your next life. That thought should be enough to make you keep your mouth shut in the present one.

Sagittarius Woman with Leo Man

He'll meet you in an airport, where you seem to be going in both directions. You're coming from South America, and you're headed for Egypt, a little boat trip down the Nile, and then a night flight to the Azores. You spend more time in the air than most pilots.

To hold your attention, he might have to become a travel agent, a traveling tycoon, or a multimillionaire with a private plane in every color. He'll need them all just to keep up with you.

Far more than romance, you love the lure of adventure. He'll take you on an African safari and watch you wave to the boa constrictors. On a desert island he'll watch you swimming with the sharks. You are a terror to travel with, since he'll never know if it's the last time he'll ever see you. Undeniably, you'll give him all the excitement he can stand—and he can stand a lot.

You are an athlete par excellence, and at times your physical prowess can overpower him. You'll beat him at tennis, badminton, and bicycling. On the ski slopes you'll race past him, in the water you'll exhaust him, and at the end of a twenty-mile hiking trail you'll wonder why he's tired. One fact he'll soon realize is that if he tries to outdo you, he might wind up worse than dead.

He'll find your personality funny, your behavior flighty, and your mind strangely philosophical. You face

each day with a smile and a basic credo that everything
is ultimately for the best. Your laughter uplifts him, and
your ideas arouse him.

Like never before, he'll feel fantastic and full of
love. You have a primitive power called vitality. It's guaranteed to capture his soul and to seduce his sensibilities. He'll
never be the same. That's because he'll never want to be.

Sagittarius Woman with Virgo Man

He is overwhelmed by the fact that your bedroom
looks like the aftermath of a great jewel robbery. You
are fascinated by the fact that he records in a pocket
notebook the number of soda crackers he eats.

You are like a cyclone to his sensitivities. You seem
to be both coming and going simultaneously, whereas he
moves with caution from place to place.

He has never seen a human being who is so disorganized, and you have never met a man who is so ineffably ordered. His idea of fun is to go shopping for
file cabinets; yours is to sign up for a safari on the spur of
the moment. His idea of a pleasant evening is to sit in silence reading; yours is to try to take three trips at once.

You live your life without any conception of limitation, but he lives his through restrictions that he struggles
to rise above.

If there is any meeting of minds here, it will probably
be one in passing. Your life-styles are so incongruent that
the chemistry is the kind that can strangle you. Therefore, it's best to keep all your commitments on a less intense and more friendly basis.

Sagittarius Woman with Libra Man

Your exuberant enthusiasm has a magical way of
conjuring up his wildest romantic feelings. Your sunny
personality will sweep him off his feet, and your philosophical attitudes will inspire his deepest admiration.

When he's with you, it seems that there's action in
every corner. You'll take him tramping in the woods to
look for wildflowers, and he'll teach you the difference
between rococo and baroque music.

You're a panacea for his loneliness, and he's an electric awakening to those sentiments you never even knew
you had. Your jovial sense of humor will incite him to
throw all caution to the winds and to come on as the im-

petuous romantic who has lost his mind and doesn't even want to get it back.

He'll tell you twenty times a day that he loves you, and you'll giggle good-naturedly and inquire if he's gone a little crazy. However, he shouldn't expect you to bat your lashes and read love poetry to him. That's not your style. Your way of saying "I love you" is to laugh uproariously and tell him that he's an incredibly funnny character.

There are simply no limits to where this love could take you. But he shouldn't be surprised if, in the process, he has to buy a sturdy pair of hiking boots. Life with you is constant movement—up and down rivers, over mountaintops, and flying across oceans. However, although he may develop frostbite and get sore feet, he's guaranteed to love every minute of it. A bicycle trip in a blizzard is more fun with you than a dinner party with a hundred people, and that's because quite naturally you are a party unto yourself.

Sagittarius Woman with Scorpio Man

He'll fascinate you, but you'll find him murky. In five minutes you'll have him falling in love. You love to laugh, and just wish that he did. But if he sticks around long enough, you'll be willing to teach him.

Despite personality differences, you are positive, philosophical, and have an energy and enthusiasm that overtake him. Your personality is expansive, while his is constricting. You are adventurous and freedom-loving; he is cautious and possessive. You know how to fuse your mind and your body, but he often separates his.

You'll find him charming, interesting, and sexually powerful, but you'll have a hard time understanding his emotions. You are open and frank, whereas he is closed and insidious. This situation could be most intense. Between talking all night and making love, you'll lose a lot of sleep. However, you'll have the golden key to his soul.

You are athletic, daring, and could spend the entire day playing tennis. At one hundred degrees your peppy enthusiasm will keep him on the courts until after sundown. Your personality is so zealous and romantic that he'll feel he's finally found his rhapsody at dawn. He has —as long as he behaves himself.

When he crowds your space with his jealousy, you'll

laugh it off and call him crazy; that's because, once you're committed, you're committed. He'll probably want to keep you in the broom closet, because he'll think that everybody wants you. That's the first way to lose you, because you have to have your freedom.

Your wisdom will force him to travel in new directions. Your optimism will encourage his expansion. You will help him rise to the heights, and share his revelations once he's returned. Together you could take each other to a place each of you has never been, and through a deepening kind of love, realize great joy.

Sagittarius Woman with Capricorn Man

On the inside he is as vulnerable as your pet beagle, but on the outside he is unbelievably bossy.

He'll tell you what time to go to bed, state that you have no handle on your own life, and imperiously remind you that he does.

If he takes you to the movies, and you insist on bringing a book but forget your glasses, don't expect him to grin and tell you it doesn't matter. And if you cook him dinner and the stuffed chicken breasts come out resembling steamed broccoli, don't expect him to laugh and say he wasn't hungry anyway. But if he arranges to meet you at a street corner and forty minutes later he finds you staring into traffic ten blocks away, do expect him to proclaim to the immediate public that you should be put away for your own good.

Mr. Capricorn is dutiful but terribly intolerant, with a will that could easily make you forget that you're a free person. Because, generally speaking, your liberty means more to you than your love life, it might be best to let him try controlling someone else.

Greater communication has been shared by two foreigners speaking different languages simultaneously.

Sagittarius Woman with Aquarius Man

He'll teach you how to solve quadratic equations and relate to you the history of glycoproteins. You'll teach him how to play backgammon and beat him at table tennis.

You'll find him to be one of the most curious and eccentric men you've ever met. When he wears his aviator glasses, he reminds you of Einstein; but when you go hiking together, he bears a resemblance to "the boy next door."

You will be challenged and enchanted by his brilliance, and he will be enamored of your enthusiasm and philosophic approach to the most trying situations.

You will help him slow down his mind by teaching him Transcendental Meditation. And you might even cure him of insomnia, since you'll get him so tired on the tennis courts.

You'll find him a most exciting anomaly with a mind that is like a trip worth taking. He will find you to be a truly lovable woman from whom he can learn a lot.

Together you can enjoy a future of far-off places. Whether you travel by land or through your minds, a multitude of marvelous things will come to you. Every day will be a greater adventure than the day before.

Sagittarius Woman with Pisces Man

He is dreamy-eyed, sentimental, and totally divorced from the realities around him. You are impulsive, chaotic, and conscious that there must be something that you are missing. Well, look a little longer, because it's not him.

You are so flighty that you need a strong hand to grab you by the neck and ground you. His hand is limp, probably clammy, and so flexible that it feels like it's made of foam. Together you can take many sensational side trips into the world of the paranormal. You'll appreciate his complete collection of William Blake, soar to the ceiling when he invites you to your first séance, and then treat him like a guru when he reads your tarot cards correctly.

However, in the daylight, under the burden of such responsibilities as paying the rent, Mr. Pisces is of little or no help. Be best friends with this man, but don't consider marrying him unless you want to play Mama. He is looking for a firm shoulder to lean on.

He is sure to fall in love with your life force, the way you make him laugh, and the freedom-loving way you live your life. He sees you as a challenge, and you should be, unless you want to live your life in chains. He will share your dreams and fantasies and delight in your far-off travels. The two of you can have a lot of fun doing foolish things and dwelling in the romantic superficials of falling in love.

However, the price you will have to pay for all of these good times is supporting a weak man who has been known to wander sexually. So allow him to satisfy your need for adventure and then spread your time thin until you have gained a sensible perspective. Mr. Pisces can make you believe that he has the world on a string. He has, but the string is in his head, where all cobblers can be kings if they dream enough.

Sagittarius Man with Aries Woman

While this could be a delightful adventure, she may consider you too capricious for her tastes.

Surely you are charming, exciting, and have the sense of humor that arrests her total attention. However, at the same time, you could make her feel so insecure that she might wish she'd never met you.

She needs to be first but feels that she is merely one of your many interests.

You will bring on bouts of jealousy that will send her to bed—with another man, of course. (Somehow, even if you don't know about it and never will, she feels that she has avenged her mangled pride and inflicted enough pain to make you suffer a lifetime.)

Although you may take her skydiving, ballooning, and shooting the rapids, you will also tread on her ego so badly that it may need a long time away from you in which to recuperate.

She likes your outspokenness, but she hates the way you speak the truth. She *knows* she's gained five pounds over the past week, but there really must be something wrong with your eyes if you see it. For her birthday you'll give her a bottle of mouthwash, and for the day that she considers to be your "anniversary," you'll take out her best friend.

She is both charmed by you and challenged in a way that she has never felt before. You will cause her to lose control of her coercive tactics. She'll have to put her ego in the corner, be her most charming, and call upon her complete supply of patience. She has always come to life in the face of competition, but what she has here is a basic battle of her needs and wishes against yours. Inevitably, to gain what she wants from you, there's something she has to lose.

Sagittarius Man with Taurus Woman

You are a man of adventure; she is a cozy stay-at-home. You like to battle the elements, but she likes to watch the world from her four-poster. She is controlled by her creature comforts; while you love to rough it.

You are a fanatic for every kind of sport and have a hard time sitting still when you're eating. She prefers a sedentary life-style and keeps all athletics restricted to the bedroom.

Your sense of humor overshadows every situation, but hers takes twelfth place to her needs. Your idea of romance is to arm-wrestle; hers is to sniff peonies and wear silk.

On a night that she wants to lounge by the fire and cuddle, you'll want to play backgammon. So early in the morning that it seems like the middle of the night, you'll abandon her for a tennis date. Every time she starts to kiss you, you'll tell her she needs more exercise.

The outcome of this love affair is that you'll probably leave her for some girl who works in a gym. How can she compete with a woman weight lifter who jogs to relax? Forget it and find someone who appreciates your exuberant vitality. Life is just too short to force yourself to be something that you're not.

Sagittarius Man with Gemini Woman

You make everything an adventure that she wants to be a part of. She'll be friendly and funny and at times silly and lacking in sense.

You can talk her into a hike through the Himalayas, where she has to go for days without reading material, or an African safari, where the lions act as if they've always known you.

With you, she comes to expect the unexpected. Unfortunately, a good portion of this is your lack of follow-through. You will heartily promise her the heavens, but when it comes down to it, she's lucky if she gets a little moonlight.

She can depend on the fact that you are undependable and will probably never change in the course of your lifetime. However, one thing she might try is a kind of shock treatment to inform you that despite appearances, she does have feelings. Although it may set you back to learn that she is more than the mask she projects, certainly in the next hour you'll forget it.

You consider her a constant amusement, but if you have to stop and consider her emotions, the lively moments suddenly start to drag.

You think of yourself as extremely freedom-loving (which is code for the fact that you hate responsibility), so if any woman comes too close too fast, you consider taking a trip.

Therefore, if she holds it all in and lives off your laughter, no doubt she'll have you—as long as you don't suddenly decide that you want somebody else.

Sagittarius Man with Cancer Woman

You'll see her as a drag on your defiant independence, and she'll see you as a threat to her tentative sense of security. She'll be hurt and hostile when you don't even finish your dessert because you have a twilight tennis game. And your patience will be provoked if she would rather sit by the fire than go skiing.

She wants a one-woman man, but you are a restless roué who wants to sample as many pretty faces as time will permit. She needs a lot of security; you need a lot of space. She wants a man who is somewhat settled, whereas you have the vagabond nature of a ne'er-do-well.

She seeks a quiet kind of romance with someone who will provide an array of creature comforts. You seek a short-lived affair that is more like an animal chase. Your charm will probably rip into her soul like a grenade going off in a sleeping village. And because she often wants what she can't have, she will undoubtedly obsess, agonize, and drive herself into a depression over the fact that you don't seem to want to settle down to a cozy existence.

Any way you look at it, the two of you are about as compatible as pickles and ice cream. Unless you both feel you want to become fast friends, forget it!

Sagittarius Man with Leo Woman

She's like putty in your hands, and you can't help but know it. Her smiles and laughter never stop—even when you're not saying anything.

Yours is a funny world where humor frames an underlying philosophy: optimism. She cherishes it and wants to put you in a golden box for rainy days. The problem is that you must keep moving, and sorrowfully, sometimes the movement is out of her life.

You are the traveler of the zodiac. Your terrain usually transcends her control. But for once, she chooses not to make this a problem. In your presence she is delighted with even your wildest schemes.

You are so good-natured that she accuses you of being from another planet. She is so glamorous that at first you think she's from the gods. From there, if she can make it camping in hurricane country in the middle of a midsummer rush of rattlesnakes, she's on the way. At that point, when the brute forces of nature intercede and make marshmallow of her granite will, she's more than glad that one of you can still summon a sense of humor. Any deaf, dumb, and blind intruder could swear it isn't her.

She's always wanted to rub twigs together in forty degrees of wind, rain, and sleet. As she grinds her teeth in time with the saturated sticks, she'll wonder aloud if ballooning over a burning field might not be better. Then, when she's reinstated in her cherished creature comforts, having wrenched all of the pine cones out of her hair and masked the mosquito bites on her nose, you'll propose a trip to shoot the rapids.

And that's not the worst. You are a flighty individual who blanches and balks at the idea of suggested restrictions. "It's freedom that encompasses the most fortunate of men," you'll preach, before jaunting to a tropical island with an Olympic swimming star who looks more like a Swedish sex goddess. You tell her that you'll be back on Sunday. You arrive three Fridays later, suntanned and smiling.

Should she tell you to kiss off because she'd rather clean her apartment? It all depends on her degree of control. She may decide that anyone who's drifted higher than the heights should be able to acclimate to the sedentary side of daily living. Well, almost anyone. Not you. Good luck in the Himalayas.

Sagittarius Man with Virgo Woman

She may fall madly in love with your sense of spontaneity and invincible charisma. However, she won't appreciate your capriciousness or the way you treat her like a cross between a cook and a Red Cross nurse.

Your charm is like a cheap cosmetic that doesn't hold up under closer scrutiny. She'll be overwhelmed when you bring her to the airline ticket office and tell her that you're taking her to the Fiji Islands, but when the time comes and you've forgotten your original promise and instead take her best friend, then somehow you lose first place on her list of lovers.

You want challenges and excitement to take you to the clouds while she seeks an earthbound kind of love. You prefer quantity to quality, while she seeks plain and simple consideration.

Ms. Virgo needs to be needed, but you are so self-sufficient that you could survive being stranded in the desert. You both seem to be coming from such incongruous places that it's too difficult for you to come together. In the long run, you are far better off with someone who is so flighty that she acts like she has wings rather than feet. Ms. Virgo is too deeply entrenched in the earth to meet you in the clouds.

Sagittarius Man with Libra Woman

She will find you cute, charming, witty, and lovable. How long she can tolerate your terrible table manners is quite another matter.

You are Dennis the Menace breaking into adolescence. And that's a heavy load for a woman who favors maturity, sophistication, and graciousness. You have about as much *savoir faire* as a forest ranger. You burp in public, make noises when you swallow, and wear a T-shirt and combat boots to her most elegant dinner party.

You are a most spontaneous guy who likes to be left alone to do his own thing and to tread about *au naturel*. You are a law unto yourself, and written into that law is a clause that forbids a sense of responsibility. You have the most adventurous ideas, but when it comes to carrying them out, you are not to be counted on. At one moment you are like a child looking at his first Christmas tree; the next moment, all the toys under it are broken and strewn asunder.

If she takes you at your word, she'll probably be waiting a lifetime. Your memory is conveniently short, and so are your relationships. You see women as a kind of entertainment almost as good as a great western. You'll give her your entire attention when you're having fun. But if she needs a man who's willing to be a responsible friend as well as a lover, you are not to be considered. Unless you learn to grow up, she should think of you as an outlandish escort who is highly amusing but not a romantic stopping place.

Sagittarius Man with Scorpio Woman

She'll meet you on a tour around King Tut's tomb. You'll be riding your camel as if it were a Cadillac. She'll be clutching hers and smiling as if she were wearing badly fitted dentures.

Your sense of adventure is guaranteed to initially charm her. You can transform a New York shopping spree into an African safari, and a formal sit-down dinner into a discotheque.

She'll find you funny, friendly, and fantastically silly —especially when you take her to the zoo and introduce her to an orangutan.

You love sports and the outdoors to such a degree that you're the kind of person who goes mountain climbing just to ski down. On your first date, you'll be late because you were jogging. On the second, you'll be late because of a tennis game. And on the third, you'll be late because you misplaced your appointment book, forgot which woman you were going out with, and ended up at the wrong address.

Alas, you like a lot of women, are exceptionally freedom-loving, and are very disinclined to settle down. You always seem to be in a state of much coming and going, and sometimes don't even know in which direction. Your attentions are extremely scattered, and so, unfortunately, are your affections.

Quite unintentionally, you have been known to stand up several women at the same time. If you should invite her on a canoe trip that never happens because you took a last-minute jaunt to Afghanistan, she'll just have to grin and bear it.

Your strides are long, and you seek to cover as much territory in each one of them as is possible. Just walking beside you, she feels she has to catch up. That's all right if she knows what she's catching up to.

Sagittarius Man with Capricorn Woman

Your basic attitude is "Don't sweat the small stuff." Hers is "I have to worry about it, because nobody else will."

The two of you are coming from opposite directions. She will appreciate the way you make her chuckle after a dreary day at work, but should she also expect some sophisticated and dignified behavior along the way, she'll be sadly disappointed.

You'll accidentally bump into her as you try to get through the door first. You'll borrow her dinner napkin after you drop yours on the floor, and although you've been invited for cocktails, you'll show up in time for a midnight movie.

She is serious, sensitive, and expects some substance to issue from a love situation. At the same time, you're merely looking for a little fun.

Therefore, it is not surprising that she will look upon you as funny but frivolous. And you will look upon her as someone whom you respect but to whom you also feel responsible. She loathes lateness, and you never seem to be on time. She expects a certain amount of follow-through, but you have a hard time remembering what you've promised fifty minutes earlier. Capricious behavior makes her cold and aloof, while you often seem to be confined by it.

Although you are attracted by her warmth, you'll probably find it too much of a strain to make her feel satisfied and womanly. And since you spread your love light so thin, chances are that she will never take you seriously. Expect your scintillating smile to work better on a far more confused woman.

Sagittarius Man with Aquarius Woman

This is a most compatible combination that supplies many exciting moments.

You will be riveted by her multifaceted interests, and she will enjoy your overwhelming enthusiasm. The two of you are freedom-loving, easygoing, fun-loving, and adventurous.

You will teach her how to ski, and she will teach you

Transcendental Meditation. You'll keep her blood churning on the tennis courts, and she'll impress you with her progressive projects.

She will delight in your spontaneous propositions; you will delight in her humanitarian idealism. She is stimulating, yet undemanding; caring, yet unconventional. When you're with her, you are unfettered, fascinated, and frank about your deepest feelings. You find her easy to talk to, and she finds you fun to spend time with.

Together you can travel to a multitude of places and heartily enjoy yourselves along the way. She makes you feel that you have a best friend as well as a lover, a most unconventional traveling companion as well as a deeply caring woman. Quite happily, you can expand through each other and live your lives forever growing toward greater experiences.

Sagittarius Man with Pisces Woman

She'll fall in love with your boyish charm and wild enthusiasm. But after a while she'll realize that your warmth is casual and impersonal.

You will be seduced by her steamy sensuality, and delight in her daily do-good attitudes. However, the deeper differences between the two of you are enough to create a substantial conflict.

Her emotions are profound; yours are playful. Therein lies the problem that may bring her a lot of pain. Mistakenly, she often chooses a flashy fellow who hands out lots of surface excitement but who holds back when it comes to caring. And that pretty well describes you.

You are friendly, cheerful, and charming, but when it comes to women, you're like a car salesman who lives in anticipation of next year's models. In addition, you're so perpetually busy that when she sees you she has the feeling of being fitted in.

If she can clearly view this encounter as a brief but fantastic affair rather than a future marriage prospect, then no pleasure will be lost. However, if she decides to wait until you've seen the world and want to settle down, she will first find herself in a geriatric clinic.

It is perilous for Ms. Pisces to mistake you for her knight in shining armor. You're more likely to run her down than scoop her up into the saddle.

CAPRICORN

Dates: December 22—January 20
Ruling planet: Saturn
Element: Earth
Mode: Cardinal
Qualities: Feminine, negative
Planetary principle: Crystallization
Primal desire: Attainment
Colors: Charcoal gray, black, green
Jewel: Emerald
Plant: Apple tree
Day: Wednesday
Archangel: Cassiel
Magical number: 4
Material factor: Materialization

CAPRICORNS OF
FAME AND FORTUNE

Elizabeth Arden	Benjamin Franklin
Helena Rubinstein	Humphrey Bogart
Richard Nixon	Joan of Arc
Howard Hughes	Issac Newton
Martin Luther King, Jr.	Marlene Dietrich
Mao Tse-tung	J. D. Salinger
Edgar Allan Poe	Al Capone
J. Edgar Hoover	Janis Joplin
Muhammad Ali	

THE CAPRICORN FEMALE

Favorable

Your motto is that you can never be too rich or too thin. On a strict diet you're the kind of person who would cheat by eating less. That's because you have the discipline of an individual who does not know how to dally.

At times you seem frigid and glacial, but that's only to fool people. Your feelings are very much at the forefront. However, so is your sense of duty, and with this nothing dares interfere. There are moments when, in getting done what you have to do, you may appear cold, impatient, and condescending. The fact is that you simply have no time for frivolity, aimless chatter, or the kind of interference that might disrupt your day.

You are a highly organized superachiever who works like someone who is wound up. Idleness is an ugly word that should never even be thought about. Continual activity not only makes you come alive, it keeps you going. With a certain éclat you are capable of energizing even a mononucleosis victim.

Your pace is go-go-go, push-push-push, through sickness, depression, physical displacement, and nonspecific disruptions of any nature. In short, you are the most hopeless kind of workaholic who thinks of vacation as a different kind of work.

Due to your goal oriented behavior, you usually get wherever you want to go. And that's to the top, naturally, since you have no tolerance for being second best. However, despite your extraordinary success quotient, you're so self-critical that you can barely believe it once you get there.

On the outside, you smile and bow with a devastating dignity as you stoop to scoop up another success symbol. However, on the inside, you feel that you're simply fooling your public and that it's just a matter of time until the truth comes oozing out. In one deadly anxiety attack you weigh your attributes against your fatal flaws, which you duly inflate and then anguish over.

You have such a wilted sense of self-worth that it's almost a daily ordeal for you to try to deal with it. It's probably why you work so much, since you need something to take up your attention, or else self-criticism would consume your ego. If someone gives you a compliment, you smile self-consciously and thank the person for being nice. If praised for a splendid piece of artistry, you feel obliged to point out the flaws and then murmur that it was really nothing. If wooed by an ardent lover whom you admire, you tell yourself it can't be true, because, after all, what does he see in you?

You are kind, faithful, responsible, and possess the sort of integrity that makes people want to stay in your life. You are usually a friend of long standing who takes over in painful and needy moments. You can be depended on for your loyalty, sincerity, and constant support.

In matters of love, you are often as emotional as your astrological opposite, Cancer. However, your feelings are rarely evident because you exist under such tight controls. Nevertheless, you are very vulnerable and frightened of having your feelings made fun of. For a relationship to be successful, you have to gain a profound trust, a tremendous emotional reassurance, and a substantial amount of physical affection. You are most easily thawed out by a mature love that is giving, committed, and deeply caring.

You need a very strong man with, preferably, a sense of humor, who is free with his feelings rather than confined by the fear of them. Popular astrology chides the Capricorn woman for being a status seeker who would rather marry for money than love. Not true. What you really want is a man who is adept at making you feel like a woman. The "little boys" who pass through your life never have much luck in the long run; you're too solemn and dignified for their superficial sensitivities. Rather, you seek a man whose character you can respect and whose faults you can laugh at. And when you find him, you will become exalted in the embodiment of another Capricorn dream that has once again materialized.

Unfavorable

You're like Lady Macbeth on her bad days. You tend to be cranky, critical, and consumed by superficial contrivances. Your emotions are tainted with a kind of intolerance that leaves little room for human understanding. You are narrow-minded, niggardly in your sympathies, and not willing to look at an issue from anything but an impersonal perspective.

Fundamentally, you're very cold and care little about other people's feelings. When you do perform a personal service, you do it out of duty and then consider yourself a kind of martyr to a cause—the cause being that you have to make yourself look as if you care, even though you have more feelings for the fabric on your new sofa.

Because you're so status conscious, you'd love to be a countess who roams through a castle overflowing with priceless trinkets. Not only do you care what other people think, you try to create it by pretending to be something you're not.

You work very hard at your upward-mobility endeavors by giving fancy parties that you really can't afford, with the "right people" whom you really can't stand. Basically, you're all show and no substance. Therefore, it doesn't take a shrewd mind to see that you are not what you appear. However, what's even worse is that your behavior is as offensive as a fit of giggles at a funeral. You are a name dropper, a jewelry flasher, and a dedicated seeker of the "right" names and places. You wouldn't be caught dead going to Acapulco in December if *Town and Country* claims that the "in" spot is Gstaad. In any social situation, the first thing you inquire of a man, even before his first name, is what he does. If, perchance, you encounter a poor soul who happens to be merely the hostess's houseboy, you swiftly dismiss him as if he were a spilled drink.

In terms of men, you are interested only in those who really "make it." And within this group, you take full inventory of their lives to find out if they went to prestige colleges and whether they have homes in the country. When telling a friend of a new love, you might refer to him as Harvard '65 or London School of Economics '67.

Your almost obscene preoccupation with the material makes you in more candid moments appear emotionally desiccated. Congratulations. You are. You're the type who would treat a husband like a bank account that is collecting interest. But because you'll go to demented lengths for appearance's sake, after a long day's work you probably won't even let him sit on the furniture, because he might make things messy. It's highly likely that, instead, you would graciously offer him a tidy chair next to the dog's bed in the kitchen.

Because you're a woman who sees things in black

and white, and good and bad, you often have a bleak attitude toward life that creeps through your personality, despite your capped-tooth smile. Basically, you hope for the best but believe in the worst. And that often brings you severe bouts of fear and melancholy. Because you're so lacking in self-insight, you create nothing within yourself to alleviate your pessimism. All you can ever think of doing is having your hair done.

If you would complain less and cultivate expanded attitudes, you could ultimately feel more vital. It may come as a shock to your nervous system to find that the meaning of life cannot be found in a Cartier bracelet. And if you ever realize that all this time it's been lurking within you while you've been cavorting around town, you might even give up having your eyelashes dyed. Instead, you'll decide to find the most "prestigious" guru around and tell everybody you're taking breathing lessons.

THE CAPRICORN MALE

Favorable

You're a man of true grit and exceptional endurance. And because you exhibit such strength, authority, and ambition, you're often looked upon as a tycoon type.

Whether or not you become a tycoon, it's true that in your undertakings you seldom falter. You have a commanding personality that delights in taking charge as it climbs slowly but surely to the top.

In the throes of ambition, you can drive yourself past an average person's limits. That is because, when you seek to reach a goal, nothing deters you, distracts you, or slows you down. With a will of steel you move ever onward to greatness, regardless of the hardships you have to endure to get there.

Because of your dedicated drive toward achievement, you usually reach the pinnacle of success and become a person who is both well known and well thought of. You have a tremendous concern for your reputation and heartily appreciate the prestige you gain from being prominent.

Emotionally, you are intense, yet, to all superficial appearances, cool and stiff. Fundamentally, you are shy, insecure, and romantically reserved. Until you're sure of a woman, your approach is often more laconic than flowery. Your presence may loom in professional matters, but in romantic situations you are often far more self-effacing.

Because your personality is more suited to serious relationships than to casual dating, you are more comfortable in marriage than many other signs. For a wife, you seek a woman who can offer you security, stability, and a deep sense of trust. However, you often grow roots in relationships that should terminate after a time. And due to your inherent sense of discipline that urges you to try to make the best of a bad thing, you'll stick to a situation until it starts to destroy you.

In most matters of your life, you are shrewd, prudent, mature, and know when and how to capitalize on a situation. You aim high and have the endurance to accomplish what you set out to do.

However, you must gain greater flexibility in your relationships and understand that they can't be run by the same rules as a corporation or the diplomatic corps. You have a stalwart constitution that may eventually give you a towering stature. However, at times it makes you rigid and resistant to seeing the other side of a situation.

Learn to apply your sense of realism to your emotional goals. Are you seeking to satisfy a self-imposed ideal that doesn't really work? Or is emotional growth as strong a priority for you as personal power? The answer is to be found in your own feelings of satisfaction. If you can't feel gratification behind an office desk, then probably something in your personal life is not working. In the long run, pointing your finger at the other person really doesn't get you anywhere. Therefore, why don't you take the responsibility of examining your own behavior with a trifle more integrity? Remember that it is only your own resistance that holds you back. Eliminate that factor, and every facet of your life will flourish.

Unfavorable

You're a condescending man with a king complex, who is content only when controlling others. You live in bondage to your own will and suffer an aching discontent if forced to subdue your power plays.

Due to your tremendous ego problems, you feel a need to always be on top. One of your favorite experiences is telling other people what to do, as if they were deaf, dumb, and blind cretins who wouldn't have a chance otherwise.

You are arrogant, patronizing, commanding, and so careless about the feelings of others that you treat people as if they were office furniture. You're a snob who is ingratiating to superiors but abrupt or barely civil to lower-echelon personnel. You disdain those beneath you and blindly emulate those above you. Through your cloud of self-obsession, you endure each day because it brings you closer to playing the lead in power games.

Some people might call you a sourpuss, others a wet blanket. That's because you treat yourself as if you were a trophy, yet have an alarming way of taking others down. Your ruthless motivating principle dictates that in order for you to prove your superiority, you have to demonstrate another's inferiority.

You delight in playing the devil's advocate to such a degree that at times you may put your life in danger. Your personality is so maddening that you could bring a saint to consider murder. After a period of listening to you, people will do anything to shut you up. You're a windbag who never gives up trying to convince the world that he is something he isn't.

When it comes to romance, your attitude is: I'll take that one. You have a way of making a woman feel like a horse who is saved from the glue factory by a generous offer. The most fascinating detail is that when you make up your mind that a certain woman is chosen, you regard her opinion as strictly secondary.

Your basic attitude is that women are meant to serve, should be sensitive enough to keep their mouths shut and listen, and, last but not least, be proficient at taking orders. Thinking is totally unnecessary, since you always know best.

Because a woman is something you need like a pair of socks or a well-stocked refrigerator, it is important to make sure that you get the kind that looks the best but costs the least. However, if after a certain period of time it dawns on you that your chosen just doesn't want you, you become defensive, morose, and hostile. After all, it's only *your* feelings that count, since she certainly doesn't have a right to have any.

However, because you have as much tenacity as a hungry dog who bangs his dish on the floor, you just can't consider giving up. Therefore, you'll use the same tactic that got you the presidency of the college debating club, your present job, and your new promotion. It's called pressure. When you apply it, you have a way of obliterating resistance and reducing people to sweating, mewling creatures begging for peace. However, all such pleas fall on deaf ears. You have no patience with peace. All you care about is power, the kind that carries enough propaganda to prepare the unenlightened for your second coming.

DECANS

Every sign in the zodiac can be broken down into three subdivisions, called decans. Each decan roughly corresponds to ten degrees—the first third, second third, and last third of the sun sign's time span, which is approximately thirty days.

As each of these periods has different subrulerships, the personality of a person is slightly modified by the specific decan it falls in. For instance, an Aries born in the second decan would be ruled by Mars, but subruled by the sun. Therefore, he would tend to display a greater sense of pride, boastfulness, egotism, and optimism than an Aries born in the third decan, which is subruled by Jupiter. This Aries would tend to be more freedom-loving, flighty, travel-oriented, and interested in subjects of a philosophical nature. An Aries born in the first decan would be the most aggressive, but not necessarily the most productive and accomplished.

Decans are important, since they do account for a more detailed assessment of an individual's personality characteristics. They also show how two people born under the same sun sign can be markedly different.

If you were born between December 22 and January 1, your sun falls in the Saturn decan of Capricorn.

You are achievement-oriented, often successful, and have a solemn, somewhat aloof personality. You are also hardworking, disciplined, and suffer from depressive mood swings.

The opinions of other people matter greatly to you. That is because you are fundamentally insecure in yourself. Therefore, you tend to socialize with individuals whom you respect, since you see your self-image as a reflection of your relationships.

You tend to be critical, status-conscious, and prefer that people don't take up your time. At the same time, to those people to whom you are committed, you are loyal, dutiful, and often devoted.

Because you have an earthy personality, you have little patience with flighty people who never seem to know whether they're coming or going. You most admire the qualities of strength, stability, honesty, intelligence, and accomplishment. In other words, you possess the highest personal ideals.

In terms of love, you are most attracted to people of prominence. However, due to your deep-seated insecurities, you often become involved with people beneath your own level of accomplishment.

Because your own drive to create a praiseworthy existence is paramount, you ultimately eliminate from your life those people whom you feel bring you down. It is very likely that by the middle of your life you will have proved your own supremacy in a highly competitive society.

If you were born between January 2 and January 11, your sun falls in the Venus decan of Capricorn.

You are charming, sociable, and often highly creative. In business, you have an exceptional shrewdness in money matters, and in social circles you display a gracious *savoir faire*.

You are a highly productive person who works a lot and sleeps very little. You are diplomatic, understanding, adaptable, sincere, and kind. An individualistic value system determines your life goals. And toward these you climb with a courage and tenacity that are never dissuaded. Capricorns born in this decan have a tremendous need to create the materialization of their desires, despite the strength of any opposition. And they do it with such a determination that others look on with perplexity and fascination.

Inherent within this decan is the ability to subdue the pleasure principle for a situation of long-range profit. In addition, there is a sense of tremendous dedication to career duties as well as a conscientious attitude toward details.

Romantically speaking, early in your life there is often heartache and disappointment from a destroyed marriage or love relationship. However, if you do not become embittered, it is likely that this experience will be followed by an extremely happy one with a loyal, devoted partner.

Capricorns born in this decan have an extremely powerful will, and the moment they come to depend on it is the moment their lives become limitless.

If you were born between January 12 and January 20, your sun falls in the Mercury decan of Capricorn.

You are an idealist caught between a logical and emotional framework. As a result, you often suffer severe anxiety when faced with choices that will heavily affect your life. You tend to take to brooding about past decisions and often bring on your own states of melancholy.

Your mind is highly disciplined when it does not control you through depressions and negative mood swings. You are a mental person with a steadfast nature and a strong sense of purpose.

Although you excel at details and have strong administrative faculties, you often have a sideline interest in some form of the arts that could easily become an occupation. However, first you must discipline yourself against your own fears, because they can severely retard your expansion.

Because you are shy, you sometimes have problems either communicating or making yourself heard. Although your ideas are forceful, at times your means of channeling them are weak. As a result, they often suffer from lack of exposure.

There is potential writing and oratorical talent in this decan. However, first you must be able to trust yourself to be the powerful person that you are. The world may very well be waiting for your insights. Consider the fact that you might be doing everyone a favor by projecting your personality and more strongly participating in the universe around you.

LOVE

Although you're a barracuda in the business world, you're shy and vulnerable when it comes to loving. A deepseated sense of insecurity can often make a love situation far more painful than pleasurable.

Despite the fact that you possess a remarkable sense of realism in most areas, in matters of romance it is not unusual that you go through an initiatory period with the wrong people. Because you get sidetracked by stunning surface qualities, you often set yourself up for a bad hurt. And because you're not the most resilient human being, emotional pain can hang on long after an affair is over.

Often you have to endure many difficult love situations before you come to the conclusion that "Love is all." A less than total love might be great for a freedom-loving Aquarius or for a Sagittarius with a short attention span. However, the compromise of a partial love for you, despite the satisfactions it may bring in the beginning, will, in the long run, only make you morose.

Because you have deeper emotional needs than an Aquarius or a Sagittarius, it's important from the onset that you don't sell yourself short. You have a terrible tendency to be too patient and to settle for unsatisfactory conditions in the present rather than create change by making clear, forceful demands. What holds you back is the fear that your demands may not be met and you may lose all. However, you should learn with age that there can be no loss of that which you didn't want in the first place.

When you do fall in love, you are serious and, in turn, need to be taken seriously. You find games loathsome, and immature behavior only turns you cold. As a rule, you tend to be faithful, and demand the same from the one you love. When your trust is violated, bouts of jealousy can make your mind constrict in pain.

A warm, stable, affectionate person is your best choice for a happy relationship. It would also help if the person works as hard as you do. However, the most important factor is that in any relationship you must never neglect your emotional needs. Remember that for another to respect your needs, you must first show a little respect for yourself. Only you create your romantic limitations, and once you grow beyond the need to do this, you are ready for the kind of love that will flourish.

MARRIAGE

Although you're definitely the marrying kind, often you don't marry until you're a mature adult. Ideally, you seek a partner who represents a bastion of security and stability.

While some Capricorns have been known to marry for money, the vast majority seek a kind of emotional nurturance. Although you are undeniably self-reliant, you also need some support to boost your feelings of self worth.

In marriage, you are capable of total loyalty, and, of course, expect the same. You are a person who trusts, and, in turn, one who can be deeply trusted. Once you make a commitment, you are responsible, dutiful, and determined to make a marriage work.

What you need most is a partner whose feet are on the ground and whose head is in the air. Someone who sparks your enthusiasm and adds a little laughter to your life will also do wonders.

Because you carry some of the qualities of your polar opposite, Cancer, a rich marital relationship can serve as an important foundation for your other activities. The expansion you gain from a connubial union will bear fruit in all aspects of your life. In the long run, you will find a wealth of emotional happiness far more meaningful than one based on money.

MONEY

You're so shrewd about money that you could be an economic mogul. You know how to make it, keep it, and multiply it. You have the tenacity of a tycoon and the wits of a financial wizard.

When it comes to money, you're hardheaded, realistic, and willing to work hard for it. Regardless of the size of your income, you always manage at least a moderate savings. Most of the time, you tend to be frugal, and can even be stingy and cheap.

However, if you are the more luxury-minded Capricorn, you can spend a small fortune in an hour on a shopping spree. Yet, because you appreciate beautiful things, you seldom spend aimlessly. Each purchase, regardless of its price tag, will bring you a lot of pleasure for a long time to come.

At the same time, there are certain Capricorns who live just to work, and consider money strictly secondary. Rather, their foremost consideration is achievement and recognition. Money is merely a by-product of an overactive work period. What is sought primarily is the prestige of accomplishment.

Whatever your preference in your private monetary matters, you're one sign that will surely never starve. You're much too smart for that, and usually too successful. However, because you tend to be a worrywart, you'll probably never believe it. What you consider a modicum of money, a Sagittarius might consider a small fortune. However, the important point to remember is that, in the end, it's all relative. Try not to get so engrossed in the figures that you forget how to live your life.

CAREER

Because you're one of the most success-oriented signs in the zodiac, you follow a path straight to the top. And on the way, nothing deters you. With a grit-hard determination, you could drive yourself over a bed of nails if you felt that the pain would give you more power.

At five years old you were as self-assured as a teenager. You're the classic superachiever who never stops trying to do a little more. You are honor-oriented, status-conscious, and titillated by the idea of supremacy.

You'd like to be president of a thousand organizations simultaneously and wouldn't at all mind the work involved. You find it a challenge and a source of satisfaction to be able to collapse after the completion of a rare accomplishment.

You're the most assiduous kind of worker who sustains a steady output. What you're working toward is total recognition that expands your sense of self-worth. At a certain point in your life you decided that you are what you do. Therefore, you try to do all those things that are praiseworthy and guaranteed to make your name preeminent. Because you battle daily with a deficient ego, your drive toward prominence is often an act of overcompensation. If you show the world that you are worthy, maybe the applause in turn will be able to convince you.

In the long run, it's not a matter of how well this works, but a matter of how long. Meanwhile, in those murky moments, when you begin to doubt your own foundations, you can always duck into some unfinished business and clear it up right away so that you can begin your next project. You are the embodiment of the capitalistic ideal, and after your ambition has brought you to the zenith of your career, what you want most from your life is simply to keep achieving.

Quite often your sign signifies people who seek social and political attainment of the highest echelon. Government positions, from the presidency to the diplomatic corps, are common among Capricorns. Because your approach is highly organized, your mind shrewd, and your personality authoritative, you make an excellent administrator of any kind. However, you're definitely the type to be chairman of the board, president of your own company, or a corporate executive striving to gain control of the entire country.

Other vital areas to which your ambition could easily take you are urban planning, archaeology, architecture, and law. Because you tend to be devoted to your work, you have the potential of being a high-powered corporate money-maker.

However, should your aspirations take you even higher than material activities, your quest for the heights could carry you into the occult. A number of formidable astrologers are born under the sign of Capricorn. They satisfy the curiosity of an adaptable, deductive mind by burrowing into the profound depths of an ancient esoteric teaching. The result is an attainment that has taken them into nothing less than an in-depth understanding of the universe.

Whatever your specific career choice, what you bring to your profession is your total self. The combination of tenacity, drive, and sheer endurance is a winning one that most people are too weak to compete against. In terms of your professional goals, you know what you want and you always get it. You're a hard worker who never waits for opportunities to open up. You create your own props to get you closer to each goal. And because you take total responsibility for your own success, you are both a monumental and praiseworthy person who deserves the authority for which you have so sedulously striven.

FRIENDS

You're the proverbial friend in need who is always there, no matter when the call. Friends admire your sturdy supportive shoulders when the earth underneath them feels like quicksand.

Your sense of realism, your organization, and your no-nonsense approach assure that you'll always be a person who is much in demand. You're an individual whose promise is not taken lightly, because it's offered from a generous and steadfast place. At the same time, your composure in a moment of crisis is controlling in a positive way and, likewise, very comforting.

You're a brick who knows how to take the good with the bad and treat both as if they were some kind of blessing. You're strong, highly responsible, loyal, and have a sense of duty that is everlasting. Those you call friends will remain friends, unless, of course, they do something dishonest to destroy your feelings.

In that case, no Eskimo could know such coldness. You're capable of cutting loose quite quickly, although you may still be haunted for a long period by the pain of being betrayed.

However, in general you are too shrewd to be taken in so and don't usually waste your time with people who aren't taking you anywhere. Those people who remain in your life give you their highest appreciation and deepest love. A friendship with you is a hallmark of the highest human values. And your exemplary character confirms it.

HEALTH

Depression can devastate you if you let your gloomy moods get out of hand. Therefore, try to control your worry quotient and let as much sunshine into your life as possible.

Negative thinking can bring on a variety of psychosomatic disorders, with painful stomach ailments being foremost. Therefore, when anxieties become excessive and overwhelming, consider a kind of therapy that will help you live your life with less sadness.

Nervous tension can create tightness in the neck, migraine headaches, muscle spasms, intestinal problems, and a multitude of other menacing disorders that are totally unnecessary. Indulge yourself in massages, and if the physical tension is still too great, invest in regular visits to a chiropractor. In the long run, you will see the worth of this.

Your teeth can potentially be a problem area, especially when Saturn transits your sign, so make sure you find a friendly dentist and discipline yourself to have regular checkups. Ask him for some preventive tips on teeth care to help you avoid the need for a lot of work at a later time.

Because the condition of your mind is intrinsically linked to the physical state of your body, make sure that you optimize your energy. Stick to low-carbohydrate foods that are rich in protein to keep you going at a good pace. Avoid mucus-producing foods that cause energy blocks that leave you emotionally listless and low in physical vitality.

Disciplined breathing exercises combined with some of the basic yoga postures can improve your mind, your emotions, and your muscle tone. This is an excellent way to get the kind of relaxation you so need but somehow never allow yourself.

Although you're a tiger in the material world, sometimes you should close your eyes and let it slip away. Once you learn how to just "be," you can lift off the chains that you place around yourself. Consequently, you will live a long life that is free from restrictions and focused on greater health and happiness.

HOME

You've got a lot of taste. Therefore, your ideal abode is one of dazzling sunlight and patrician splendor.

Since you tend to be traditional in your tastes, you love nineteenth-century chandeliers, marble fireplaces, sterling-silver candelabra, and crystal vases.

Bunches of the brightest flowers adorning each room dispel the beginnings of a Saturn gloom. In the entrance foyer, a priceless cloisonné umbrella stand cheers you up even on those drizzly days.

At a very early age you decided that beautiful things had to belong to you. And since then, you have striven to have them. A dark, spartan setting only brings you down. Therefore, color is a definite requirement for controlling your murkier moods.

Use wall space to experiment with a mélange of vivid splashes, all created on canvas by your own genius. If you never considered yourself creative, you're in for a big surprise when you stand back to survey the outcome.

You're an elegant entertainer who has an all-or-nothing attitude to culinary undertakings. You love indulging in candlelit dinners of poached salmon *mousseline*, chilled Pouilly Fuissé, raspberry mousse, and *café filtre*.

Since you're something of a snob when it comes to luxury, you appreciate quality far more than quantity. Rather than buy a clutter of furniture, you might indulge yourself in a four-thousand-dollar set of ivory bed legs. And since comforters are getting more and more expensive any way, why not invest in one made of the finest silk?

In the springtime, keep a fragile bouquet of sweet peas by the bedside so that you can lean over and smell them as you turn off your alarm. In your bathroom, hang some English ivy from the ceiling to take away the starkness and add a warm, provincial look.

At all times, let your living quarters be a haven for your soul and a foundation for your more positive feelings. Make it a place of pleasure and unlimited delight that you adore coming home to. And you will see that, in the long run, your life will have the luster of luxury.

COSMIC CHALLENGE

You tend to place heavy limitations on your life by negative thinking and giving free rein to your fears. Try to rise above all points of restriction by programming your mind to more positive thinking.

The only obstacle you really have to overcome in this life is yourself. All other challenges become automatic as you rise with ease to bring about the results you want.

Dwell emotionally on your good points, your strengths, and your satisfactions. There are always more than you would spontaneously be able to cite. Let living be more of a celebration than an endurance, and do whatever you feel you have to do to get to that point.

Your cosmic challenge is experiencing joy without worrying about what will happen when you don't feel it anymore. Gain mental flexibility so that you can float with the flux and flow of the Tao. Learn to live in the *now*, so that you can ride the upward tides rather than fearing that you should cling to the bottom.

View change, not as loss, but rather as what it is, expansion. And let your mind lift toward the sun that shines upon your life.

INSPIRATION

You are the sign of strength, power, and accomplishment. You make your aspirations materialize through the mastery of your will. The achievements of your lifetime reflect a personality that never falters. Your fame is the result of your total trust in yourself, and your success a sign of your material evolvement. From this point onward, the upward path beckons.

WHAT HOLDS YOU BACK AND HOW TO OVERCOME IT

A sense of pessimism often prevents you from experiencing a more joyous existence. Instead of abandoning yourself to the "now," you torment yourself with the obsessive question of "What will happen if . . . ?"

In any unpleasant occurrence you have a strong tendency to dwell on the negative aspects rather than view the situation with detachment reinforced by your sense of humor. You are a serious person who will never take life lightly. However, you can try to conjure up a little laughter to alleviate a bad situation and remind yourself that tomorrow is another day.

In any matter that is giving you a lot of anxiety and grief, ask yourself what is the worst that can possibly happen. After you have answered this question, look upon this possibility realistically but not tragically. Keeping your emotions out of it, analyze the options open to you. Then consider which ones will be the most pleasant. It is not unlikely that one of these options will be far better for you in the long run than the present situation to which you are so strenuously clinging.

Look back on your life to what you consider the most horrible experience. At the time, the pain was so great that you were sure that you could never live through it. But you did, didn't you?

Inherent in all magic (the art of bringing about something that you want to happen), there is a concept of sacrifice. And intrinsic to this concept of sacrifice is the idea that you have to give up something in order to get something better. However, this does not at all imply that what you give up is really worth having. As a matter of fact, it is often something that is holding you back.

Therefore, it is important to understand that it is this negative attachment in Capricorn that is causing the pain, not the act of relinquishing. In order for a practicing magician to become a more powerful individual, he must give up his self-delusion and self-restricting neuroses. If he can't, he can seriously weaken himself by essentially resisting what he wills to bring about. And his resistance is motivated by the fear of parting with something that he doesn't need in the first place. Thus the personality gets caught in the abyss of confusion, depression, and defensiveness.

One of the most important axioms of occultism is "Fear is death." It kills hope, change, expansion, and happiness. Once you get in touch with your fears and see them with detachment as merely passing emotions that do not have any inherent hook-up with reality, then you will no longer be controlled by them.

Remember that you tend to move toward that within which you dwell. Therefore, why not try to dwell in only the happiest things that can happen? If you gain proper control of your mind, you will never be a victim of the objective world, because you will understand that things are neither good nor bad. They just are. It is only you who give them any color.

LOVE AND
COMPATIBILITY GUIDE

Capricorn with Capricorn

This is more a primitive power struggle than a starry-eyed romance. In the better moments, you can understand where the other person is coming from, but it's another thing trying to tolerate it.

Basically, you both want to be boss and possess an unquestionable assurance that your way is the right way. In such a conflict, it is difficult for either of you to concede. Therefore, there issues a time of much mutual scowling and sulking.

Because you both struggle with a gnawing kind of pessimism, it is far better for you both to be with more cheerful people. Since it is a Capricorn characteristic to think the worst and to worry about imagined unpleasant happenings, what you really need is someone to slap you on the back and make you giggle.

Although this could be a relationship of deep friendship, loyalty, mutual admiration, and much trust, if you get the drearies at the same time, it will only take you both down.

All Capricorns need to learn how to cavort with life and to be less cautious, so a steady but blithe spirit would bring you a lot more sunshine. When Capricorns learn that they haven't forgotten how to laugh, out comes the sharpest sense of humor.

This is not a bad combination, but neither is it one to open up the skies. If you want to remain earthbound, this relationship can accomplish just that. If you want a little levity, look elsewhere.

Capricorn Woman with Aries Man

On the surface, you are cool and steady, but on all levels he is a crazed madman who means well. Therefore, he'll be enthralled by the way you carve your way to greatness.

You will be a little overwhelmed as he comes dashing into your life and almost knocks your door off its hinges. You'll think he's nice but maybe from another planet when he moves about your living room like a Mexican jumping bean and in the middle of a conversation starts doing pushups. He will excite you with the way he gets enthusiastic over an ice-cream flavor, and he will make himself unforgettable in his repertoire of bedroom activities. However, if he wants you to really warm to him, he has to exercise a little patience. You want a man who is dependable. Unlike him, you don't seek a circus where the action in the main ring never ceases.

You don't believe in love at first sight, although you do believe in liking someone a lot. However, there has to be more than surface activity to make you want to stick around. Since you are seeking a situation of substance and a human being who will not violate your trust, capricious behavior only leaves you cold, glacial, withdrawn, and looking elsewhere.

You're extremely ambitious, and unlike him, more concerned with perfecting your work than merely initiating new projects. He is attracted to your lists of accomplishments, but sometimes might feel a little competitive if you work your way into too much of the limelight. You are driven, persevering, and probably spend more of your personal time at the office than he does. In terms of his work, you will be interested, supportive, and understanding. However, you really don't have time to polish his ego like an apple and stay up all night listening to him tell you how great he is.

If he wants a woman who is real, then you are for him. However, if he is more interested in pursuing a challenge than in giving of himself, go elsewhere. You have no tolerance of little boys who try to make the world believe they're men. You're too sensitive to live with a facade, and sometimes he is insensitive enough to prefer it.

Capricorn Woman with Taurus Man

You'll find him better than a Christmas present on a cold, rainy morning. He'll find you to be the kind of competent career woman he's always gotten a crush on.

You are strong and dignified, yet have a lot of feeling underneath a cool surface. He is warm and cuddly, with an earthiness that makes you feel at ease.

You will inspire his career goals, while he will make you feel loved for yourself rather than your title of vice-president. Your encouragement will help him drive himself to greater places. However, in the end, his pace will help you to slow down and live longer.

Together, you will linger over romantic candlelit dinners and find each other so stimulating that you forget to have dessert.

You'll develop a glow and a tenderness in his company. He'll announce to the world that he's fallen in love.

Capricorn Woman with Gemini Man

This is definitely not a match made in heaven, but it just might bring you to that well-known place called hell.

Neither of you can really understand where the other is coming from, but even if someone told you, it wouldn't be much of a help. You need assurance in a relationship, and the only kind that he can give you is that he's one person you'll never get it from. He heartily enjoys frolicking from one woman to another, while you are capable of sitting still if there is something to sit for.

You appreciate the finer things in life while he can be a happy-go-lucky living hand-to-mouth. You are hardworking and persevering, while he perseveres at not working hard. You view your life seriously, but he sees his through an insipid sense of humor.

You have a deep sense of loyalty and commitment; he is capricious and undependable. His witty comments have a way of winning your heart, but his kinetic avoidance of commitment cools your propensity for passion.

You may consider him fun, but certainly not your ideal for the future. Once you get past the persiflage, your deepest desires will direct you straight to a man who is a model of stability and graciousness. You value sturdiness and accomplishment while he is the fanatical free spirit whose vision of stability is change.

At best, this can be a friendship; at the very worst, it can be a marriage. In general, you are too sane, stable, and successful for his tastes. He needs a woman who, after he torments her with a grin, will still look up to him because he's so witty.

However, after a few of his choice performances, you will give him the cold shoulder and inform him that what is really so amusing about him is that one day his capricious antics will make him very sad.

Capricorn Woman with Cancer Man

You'll be touched by the way he seems to care for your welfare. But you'll have a hard time taking his moods.

He seems to invent slights and then sulk about them. And no matter what you do, you can never discover what you've said wrong.

He'll wonder why you spend so much time at the office. In turn, you'll resent his suspicions and the way he makes you feel guilty.

However, despite these minor considerations, you need a lot of love, reassurance, praise, and support, and he's just the person to provide them. Although he may be impressed by the fact that you're president of a corporation, he'll love you for your total personality, not for your title. With him you can strip away your soul and stop worrying that he will find you less worthy. He doesn't care if you gain five pounds, don't have time to wash your hair, and cook him a dinner that self-destructs on the way to the table. He wants the woman, not the gilded superachiever.

Therefore, if you can look at him from a less superficial standpoint, you may find a man who is very much worthy of your attentions. However, the price you have to pay for his sympathy and services is some of your own. The more you let what happened at the afternoon's board meeting get in the way of your better moments, the more you will be prying apart a potentially happy union. Remember that in order to get, you have to give. Therefore, decide whether you want to pay the price for a successful private life.

Capricorn Woman with Leo Man

He'll meet you at a tennis club. You won't be playing, only watching, but your outfit will be more smashing than his backhand.

To all appearances you have class. If you didn't originally have it, you've paid a lot to get it, and what you're seeking is a reward, the bigger the better. You're guaranteed to love him the minute you see him put down that hundred-dollar bill. And to keep your eyelashes aflutter, he'll keep producing more, even if he has to politely excuse himself to do a little counterfeiting.

Together, you could make an awesome-looking twosome. And at a party, you look as if you were hired for appearances.

Quite easily he can charm you, but if he wants to keep you, he'll cut out the casual flirtations. Since you seek control, in your mind nothing is casual. So when you cut him cold, you're just being cautious. Again, his narcissism has made you very nervous, so if he doesn't want to be abandoned, he'd just better behave.

You are serious, supportive, faithful, and trusting. In addition, you are usually successful. Your credits will exalt him, and your concern will overwhelm him. If he gives you enough Leo love, you'll forget you ever wanted a chinchilla.

Capricorn Woman with Virgo Man

Since neither of you knows how to sit still, you'll indulge each other's tendency to workaholism. He will applaud the discipline, tenacity, and drive that take you straight to the top. You, in turn, will approve of his Sundays spent at the office to make his projects perfect.

You will find him to be a man with two feet on the ground but with a heart that is always happy to be of service. He is shy but loving, at times fearful, but always faithful. He is the fellow you can depend on when your friends' lives are filled up with their own misfortunes.

You will be touched by his shyness and terribly impressed by his strong resolve. He has the discipline to get up at six A.M. to take a self-improvement course. That is because, every day, in every way, he somehow tries to be a little better.

He will offer realistic suggestions for your problems, and will know how to bring up your mood level when you get the gloomies. Living with him is like an exercise in organization, but one which you welcome heartily.

You like a man who has his life under control. He likes a woman with much drive and ambition. Together, you have great rapport and compatibility. This is a marriage that could last a lifetime.

Capricorn Woman with Libra Man

Any way you look at it, he is not as intense as you are. While you sit back and smolder with a quiet zeal, he analyzes what he should be feeling.

You will appreciate his approach to aesthetics, but when you just want somebody to grab you, he generates as much heat as an air-conditioner.

You are perfectly capable of appearing frigid, but it's all a big show, and what you really want is a lot of love. So does he, but he has a hard time initiating any action in that direction.

He is endlessly impressed by your superachievements, enamored of your appearance, and attracted to your warmth. However, there is something about your stability that is a little overwhelming.

It takes him half an hour to order three courses on a menu, while you make up your mind with just one glance. He lets his insecurities overcome him, while you keep yours coolly under cover. He is amazed at your consistent sense of self-reliance, and you marvel at how he needs assurance on where in the room he should hang his spider plant.

You will hold his hand on gloomy days, tell him ten times in one hour that you approve of his latest ski boots, and give him your solicited opinion on his most recent career conflict.

However, when you need a shoulder to lean on, you'll have to look elsewhere, because he'll probably be too distressed over some trivial problem of his own. You are the kind of woman who is solid, enduring, and devoted. He is the kind of man who is ephemeral, fickle, and self-indulgent. If he can overcome these traits and decide to dwell in his higher being, this relationship could become a close one. If not, consider it another Capricornian rhapsody that ends up battered and blue.

Capricorn Woman with Scorpio Man

In this relationship there is a lot of talk but very little emotional understanding. However, in many ways the attraction is so irresistible that it borders on being fatal. From the very start, you will be bewitched and he will be feverish. The ensuing situation could be definitely erotic but in the long run emotionally deadening.

In the throes of your enchantment, you will end up

giving too much. And he will take it. His enigmatic behavior brings out all your insecurities. At one point, you are swimming with your head above water; at another point, you are drowning.

Although he appreciates your vulnerability, patience, understanding, and the fact that you would travel to the ends of the earth for him, he still makes you suffer. He doesn't want to, but he gets caught up in such a vortex of emotion that he can't help it. You bring out the intensity he always tries to control but that frequently controls him. He hates losing mastery over himself, and having an intense sexual, emotional, intellectual experience is just the thing to cause it.

He has a hard time accepting you as you are, because he feels he doesn't really deserve you. Therefore, he loves the idea of you, but the actuality makes him nervous and he may try to restrict the relationship to brief encounters.

His behavior will puzzle you, pain you, and put you into a position of doubting yourself. The danger comes when you begin to believe that you deserve what little he gives you. At that point you should either withdraw or confront the fact that you're looking for a lot of misery.

Like no other sign, he has an uncanny way of eluding his problems and making other people suffer for them. It's such an unconscious compulsion that usually he doesn't even know that he's doing it. If he finds out, then he may feel morose, guilty, disgusted, and deeply saddened. Until he finds some way to change the pattern of his consciousness, he has to take responsibility for the pain and disruption. He has a special talent of bringing upon himself what he fears most. And in this situation, he may decide that there will come a day when you will leave him. Unless, of course, he leaves you first so that he's not left hanging.

Capricorn Woman with Sagittarius Man

His basic attitude is "Don't sweat the small stuff." Yours is that you have to worry about it because nobody else will.

Fundamentally, the two of you are going in opposite directions. You will appreciate the way he makes you chuckle after a dreary day at work. However, should you also expect some sophisticated and dignified behavior, you'll be grievously disappointed.

He'll accidently bump into you as he tries to get through the door first, he'll borrow your dinner napkin after he drops his on the floor, and although he's invited you for cocktails, he'll show up in time for a midnight movie.

You are serious and sensitive and expect some substance to arise from a love situation. Unfortunately for you, he's merely looking for a little fun.

You'll see him as funny but frivolous while he will look upon you as someone to respect. You loathe lateness, and he never seems to be on time. You expect a certain amount of follow-through, but he has a hard time remembering what he's promised an hour earlier.

He is truly taken by your warmth, but he'll probably decide it's too much of a strain to try to make you feel satisfied and womanly. Since he spreads his love light so thin, the chances are that he will never take you seriously.

Capricorn Woman with Aquarius Man

He's a bit more unconventional than you could ever imagine. And more freedom-loving than you may feel comfortable with. However, because he is more fun than a circus, he may make you lose some of your Capricorn control.

You'll swoon at his startling intelligence and ponder on his peculiar ideas. He'll delight you when he shows up at midnight with a bottle of champagne and the next day sends you roses. He's quite the romantic, though you'd never know it to listen to his theories on the universe.

However, because he often tends to be all theory and very little practical action, you may become impatient with his approach to the world. He is not the superachiever that you always dreamed of. Nor is he the man who will rush into your life and simply take command. It's far more likely that in a moment of crisis he will sit back and throw out some fascinating fact on the eating habits of the Eskimo.

Mr. Aquarius is a little impervious to considerations of the present, since his mind is like a satellite of the future. You, on the other hand, prefer to live in the now.

If you can put up with his physical passivity and don't mind taking total charge of life's menial details, then this could very well become a happy relationship or marriage. He may expand your earthy mind and cure you of your persistent melancholia. In turn, you may ground his eccentric ideas and help to make them materialize. If the two of you can deal with the friction caused by your differences, you can learn much from each other and, at the same time, gain a lot of love.

Capricorn Woman with Pisces Man

At first he will seem romantic and sentimental, at second glance, weak and wishy-washy. He has a hard time dealing with the day-to-day world while you thrive in a competitive corporate milieu.

His mind is floating somewhere above the clouds, whereas yours is rooted firmly to the earth. You find his ultimate objectives vague, his emotions inconstant, and his approach definitely escapist. He spends more time trying to get out of something than he does in ultimately doing it. And when you ask him what he wants and what he thinks he's looking for, you get an answer so nebulous that it assures you he hasn't the vaguest idea himself.

You are a no-nonsense person who doesn't have time for adolescent instability in an adult whose hair is turning gray. Your attitude is: Either shape up or ship out. His is: Take me or leave me, but just don't bug me.

He fancies himself a poet in a world of worry. You find him to be a spineless escapist who would prefer to vegetate until he is "discovered."

Any way you look at it, his way is not your way unless you like a lot of giving and very little getting.

Capricorn Man with Aries Woman

You'll worry that she works so hard she'll destroy her health. She will angrily retort that you are being overcautious. Deep down, you are a good soul who means well, but she may at times find you to be a bit gloomy.

It's true that you could have written the original disaster movie. And at times she might consider you to be something of a sourpuss. However, if she disregards your propensity toward pessimism and concentrates on your sense of responsibility, she might find you to be a man worth meeting, knowing, and perhaps loving.

If you make a commitment to her, she will remain uppermost in your mind, and you will never try to evade what you feel you have to do. However, you are controlling and chauvinistic and embrace a double standard that she may have to break down before she goes any further. You have advice to offer on every subject, which she might find somewhat irritating, since she is not used to listening to unsolicited opinions. However, often your insights are deeply based in realities that she could learn a lot about.

You will find her exciting, stimulating, and provocative, but at the same time a little crazy. You'll admire her for her drive, determination, and ambition, but you'll question the way she goes about getting what she wants. She is headstrong, while you're stodgy. She is unorganized while you cling to your structures. She is blunt and tempermental while you are defensive, supersensitive, and sometimes outspoken.

If she steps on your feet, you'll be sure to let her know she's standing there and that you need the space. And if you get too bossy, she won't waste any time telling you to look for someone else (which might not be a bad idea).

However, if you can both relinquish your individual needs to supervise and control, and instead put your energies into trying to understand each other, this relationship could take you anyplace you might want to try going. It's worth the battles that will come about as a result of your efforts. Just keep in mind that it's not the fights that matter, but the resolutions that really count.

Capricorn Man with Taurus Woman

You are the archetype of the ambitious breadwinner, and the kind of man she would like to take command. She is the fertile earth mother, and the kind of woman you would like to serve.

Both of you share a sense of practicality and purpose that will draw you together. You are responsible, dutiful, loyal, and loving. She is solid, stable, devoted, and nurturing.

She admires your ambitious, hardworking nature. You respect her resourcefulness and understand her security needs. Together, you could build a business, a marriage, a family, or a corporation.

You have a shrewd sense about making money, and she has an uncanny way of making it multiply. You are dignified and fatherly; she is unassuming and motherly.

While you may appear cool and aloof to others, she has a way of warming you up and getting your total attention in record time. She has a special way of fulfilling your needs, and you have a special way of fulfilling her expectations. Together, you enjoy a certain amount of material security, along with a taste for those little luxuries that often make life worthwhile.

Much mutual support, understanding, and compatibility make this combination one that is especially meaningful. Together, you could move mountains, or maybe just a big place in each other's heart.

Capricorn Man with Gemini Woman

She'll think you're a terrible bore because you would rather work than go dancing. You'll think that she should be locked up when you see the scattered way she runs her life.

She is willful and defiant; you are commanding and bossy. You can dedicate your life to one sense of purpose, whereas she has no idea what that means, since she changes her mind every other minute.

You seek stability and security, but she would throw her life away for the right kind of excitement. You make decisions slowly while she agrees to anything off the top of her head. You are possessive and want to settle down, while she is freedom-loving and likes to wander. You are controlling while she's like quicksilver running through a fork.

Your personality is sober and often gloomy, hers lighthearted and full of laughter. She loves a man who makes her laugh, but you can make the corners of her mouth turn down. You never know if she's serious or if she is just trying to torment you. She never knows how you can be happy but always look so grim.

She lives for the moment while you plan your life past the point of old age. You are brilliant at conserving money, while she has a gleeful enthusiasm in spending it.

She'll make you feel uneasy, since you've never met anybody quite this crazy. You may find her so foreign to your sensibilities that you ask her to marry you because you think her more entertaining than going to the movies. Now, you're not exactly her definition of mind-shattering excitement, but you are warm, supportive, sincere, and willing to put up with all of her insane behavior. Besides loving her, you are the man to help her to get her life together and to give her a lot more than she could ever think to ask for. So don't be surprised if she giggles in your nervous face and accepts your proposal by muttering —maybe.

Capricorn Man with Cancer Woman

You are the security that she's always longed for; she is the woman who can give you the warmth you so need. Between you there is an undeniable attraction and a very basic understanding.

Fundamentally, she needs a strong man she can care for, while you need a woman who knows how to care. Her vulnerable femininity will melt your cool veneer, and your competence and ambition will win her highest respect.

She is a woman who can be so nice to come home to. She will nurture you and never allow you to feel neglected. In turn, you will be her bastion of material security and buy her the kind of creature comforts that make her life worth living.

Together, you can live a cozy existence, showering lots of love on each other and sharing many close moments. Within the depths of her feelings you will be able to see the same insecurities that bring on your own melancholy moments. The more you allow your sensitivity to expand, the more emotionally rich your life will be. And once you've experienced this, you can never deny that it is the greatest kind of wealth.

Capricorn Man with Leo Woman

You take everything in life seriously, so if she really wants you, she'll have to keep her temper in check and tread lightly. If she smiles sweetly and speaks softly, you'll walk the dog, take out the garbage, and forget there are other women in the world.

Your price for such supreme fidelity is control. Like Mr. Leo, you love telling women what to do at every waking moment. You were the original model for male chauvinism, and your ideas haven't changed much since the term was coined.

Due to your Saturn influence, you tend to be rigid, cautious, and occasionally cold. Actually, it's all a front for a pervasive sense of insecurity. And the more she brings this out through maniacal manipulations, the less likely you'll care to stick around.

She'll admire your ambition, drive, and tenacity. Your goals are highly focused and your target is power. The more you have, the more she wants you.

Together, you share an appreciation for the very best. You can be a snob, a materialist, and an idolater. But unlike her, who views her trinkets as her toys, you view your objects as a measure of self-worth. She can't really blame you, since you've probably killed yourself to get them and they represent a drive past endurable limits.

Your pace will never be as fast as she would like it, but your durability outdoes all. You are strong, sincere, honest, and loving. If she's smart, she'll shut her mouth, exert her warmth, and maybe cajole you into supporting the vagaries of militant women.

Capricorn Man with Virgo Woman

Even if you're president of five different corporations, on the inside you're just a little boy who wants to be taken care of. Because Ms. Virgo needs to be needed, appreciated, and applauded, this combination could work out very well.

She'll handle you when you get bossy, and in turn you will make her life better by your constant care and concern.

On the job you are a most aggressive kind of go-getter. However, at home you are just a happy man who likes to spend time with the woman you love. Ms. Virgo appreciates your feelings, offers you a kind and sympathetic shoulder, and has an almost magical way of allaying your insecurities.

On dreary days, she will cook you a beautiful dinner and then offer you her critical advice for the problems that seem to be pressing. She is considerate, warm, and the kind of woman you wish you had always known. Her intelligence will stimulate you, her affection will open you up, and her fidelity will give you a sound strength in more trying moments.

This combination has the makings of great happiness, mutual trust, responsibility, and love that can create a mature kind of marriage.

Capricorn Man with Libra Woman

Deep down inside, you're both so insecure. However, you have a much stronger personality and a tendency to be controlling. At first, she may feel it divine to be so loved; however, on second thought, she has to admit that you are truly bossy.

You are that tree she can lean on, but the harder she leans, the greater the price. At your most primitive self, you are the most outrageous kind of male chauvinist who will tell her what to eat, when to cross the street, and what to cook to keep you happy. You'll reorganize her life, inform her how to live it, and pat her warmly on the head while you point out her feminine foolishness.

Fundamentally, you like to play Daddy and have her be the giggling little girl. That means she must obey you because you know what's right for her. If she does as you say, and doesn't give you any lip, you'll refer to her as a "good woman." But then, with you breathing over her shoulder, when would she get the opportunity to be bad?

Whatever you do, you mean well. However, your self-awareness is somewhere around the level of a willful gorilla. You are typically the kind of person to exit from a self-awareness seminar feeling sorry for those other people with the problems.

If Ms. Libra happens to favor a man who is seeking to transform a free woman into a slave, you are most definitely the man for her. What she will get in return for such subjugation is the assurance that you love her. With love like this, she'll need all the assurance she can get.

Capricorn Man with Scorpio Woman

She'll admire your ambition but get lonely when she never sees you. You respect her devotion but at times tend to take it for granted. At worst, this union can turn into a bitter emotional foray. At best, it can be a situation of mutual respect, much support, and a shared sense of responsibility.

One thing to remember is that she holds the power. Although you may appear to be stern, staunch, overbearing, and even critical, she can turn you into a molten marshmallow with her warmth, emotional sensitivity, and sexual passion. Although you may grumble and work till midnight on her birthday, it's only because she's allowed it. She can get you to stand on your head and wave your feet in the air if that's her desire.

You are highly disciplined but very insecure. Since you cannot tolerate rejection, what she reads to be coldness is merely an emotional panoply. Therefore, she has to be patient, understanding, and sometimes manipulative, which isn't at all difficult. What she will have in return is one man who is highly devoted.

You tend toward depression, especially when your career is going more slowly than anticipated and you are only a corporate vice-president at the age of twenty-eight. If she is supportive of your maniacal power struggles and listens to all your trivial daily problems, you will develop the deepest attachment. However, she should *not* expect that, in return, you will appreciate, tolerate, or try to understand her moods or deepest feelings.

Therefore, no matter how much you love her, at times you will leave her lonely. She may stay up all night listening to your tales of thwarted ambition, but if in your presence she cries her eyes out, you'll inform her that you're going to the store to buy eggs for breakfast. Once committed, you are faithful, enduring, patient, and paternalistic. Your inordinate ambition will vicariously bring her the power she so appreciates. But no matter how much she loves you, she may always feel that there is something missing.

Capricorn Man with Sagittarius Woman

On the inside, you are as vulnerable as her pet beagle, but on the outside, you are unbelievably bossy.

You'll tell her what time to go to bed, state that she has no control over her own life, and imperiously remind her that you do.

If you take her to the movies and she forgets her glasses, you won't grin and offer to skip the film. And if she cooks your dinner and the stuffed chicken breasts come out resembling cinder blocks, you won't laugh and say you weren't hungry anyway. If you arrange to meet her at a street corner and forty minutes later you find her staring into traffic ten blocks away, she can expect you to proclaim to the immediate public that she should be put away for her own good.

You are dutiful but terribly intolerant, with a will

that could easily make her forget that she is a free person. Because, generally speaking, her liberty means more to her than her love life, she would be better off to let you try controlling someone else.

Greater communication occurs between two foreigners speaking different languages simultaneously than between Mr. Capricorn and Ms. Sagittarius.

Capricorn Man with Aquarius Woman

She is somewhat eccentric and very freedom-loving, while you are pragmatic and a little insecure. This is where the differences begin, and where they end is infinity.

She is a dreamer while you are a man of the material world. She is fascinated by a multitude of people, but you are more concerned with yourself. She is a woman who lives in the future while you are consumed by matters close at hand. She views life through an unconventional framework, while you hold tightly to tradition. She abandons herself to her mental interests while you spend your time merely making money.

The two of you are not the least compatible combination imaginable. However, you do manage to come pretty close. Ms. Aquarius's desire to spread her energies among so many people will only, in the long run, peel away your feeling of control. In turn, the time you invest in capitalistic activities may make her decide to look for a man who wants more out of life than money.

Not only are you both coming from different places, you're both willful enough to bring the other along. Well, it won't work. Therefore, you must either learn to accept each other or both take a walk and look for somebody else.

Capricorn Man with Pisces Woman

You will be the father figure she's been searching for, and she will be your woman of romance. She needs a strong man she can depend on, and you need a woman who knows how to need. She'll bolster your ego when she comes running to you raving that she longs for your counsel as well as your shoulder to cry on. In turn, you'll tell her what to do and demand that she follow your instructions implicitly.

Emotionally, you'll never understand where she's coming from or where she's going. She cries over things that you could not care less about, like sad stories in the news, the problems of people whom she'll never even meet, and her own enigmatic moods that seem, to your sensitivities, silly. At times, you have the uncomfortable feeling that there's a part of her that will always be a stranger. You're probably right. However, there are also those times when her womanly warmth just sweeps you away and the impending matters of the outside world no longer seem so important.

You imbue her with some practicality; she imbues you with a poetic sensitivity that you never knew you were capable of. Together, if you are determined to learn from your differences, you can create a love relationship that will put you in touch with yourselves as well as with each other.

AQUARIUS

Dates: January 21—February 19
Ruling planet: Uranus
Element: Air
Mode: Fixed
Quality: Masculine
Planetary principle: Truth
Primal desire: To know and understand
Colors: All colors of the spectrum
Jewel: Opal
Plant: Myrrh
Day: Saturday
Archangel: Uriel
Magical number: 22
Material factor: Investigation

AQUARIANS OF
FAME AND FORTUNE

Angela Davis
Paul Newman
Jack Lemmon
Charles Darwin
Clark Gable
Charles Lindbergh
Galileo
Franklin D. Roosevelt
Jeanne Moreau

Abraham Lincoln
Jules Feiffer
Virginia Woolf
Sergei Eisenstein
Emanuel Swedenborg
James Joyce
Norman Mailer
François Truffaut
Thomas Edison

THE AQUARIUS FEMALE

Favorable

You're like Alice in Wonderland, skipping through the forest making friends with all the furry creatures and asking a lot of questions. Questions are to you what complaints are to a chronically depressed person. You are the most curious female in the zodiac, and look upon life as a combination of Disneyland, the Hayden Planetarium and the Bronx Zoo.

"That's very weird," you say to yourself, shaking your head with a gleam in your eye. This means, of course, that you're impressed, enthralled, mystified, and most of all excited. You love out-of-the-way things that make other people turn their heads, trip even when they're walking slowly, and wonder if they might be momentarily going mad.

The more bizarre the incidents in your life, the better. One of your favorite things is to stay up all night analyzing and speculating, until, in the morning, your eyes look like a night-shift proofreader's. Totally incongruous situations stir you up and make your blood boil over. Nothing would delight you more than to be introduced to a tuxedo-clad Bela Lugosi look-alike whose teeth resemble weapons and whose pale-faced girlfriend sports blood on her neck. Your first inquiry would be whether she needs a tissue; your second, whether she's a hemophiliac.

You are definitely the unforgettable-character type that scares certain people but delights others. Sometimes you ask so many questions that one would think you're taking a survey. A Scorpio or Taurus might get defensive and mutter, "What do you want to know for?" The simple answer is that you want to know just to know. You find people fascinating, especially when they have a lot of quirks and eccentricities. You can have a great time listening to a story about a friend of a friend if that person happens to be peculiar enough. Even if you never meet the individual, you'll never forget the story, and the next time you see your friend, you'll be sure to ask for any new details.

You are the best listener in the zodiac and thrive on

gossip, especially when it's interesting enough to make you guffaw and giggle. Chances are, you know the details of everybody's business so well that you could be an FBI agent who works overtime. Because your mind is so alert and your memory so vast, you remember details for days that other people forget in five minutes. It's not above you to have total recall of a year-old conversation with a twice-encountered acquaintance. To the question "How did you remember that?" you only shake your head and mutter to yourself about people's memories.

Fundamentally, you're the friendly sort who seeks constant stimulation and excitement. However, what you call excitement might make the next person a little wary. Numerology, magic, mind control, higher mathematics, molecular biology, palmistry, acupuncture, and an assortment of other highly unusual subjects are likely to attract you. You probably have a brilliant, original, farseeing mind that dares to look at the world differently and delights in discovering new alternatives in thinking, feeling and being.

You thrive in a situation of mental challenge and gravitate to people who embrace constructive change as much as you do. Sluggish, narrow-minded souls are what you want to avoid at all costs, along with people who let their limitations enclose them. You're a free spirit whose versatility is seldom matched. You love to take on a lot of things at once or deal in intellectually competitive situations that demand your entire attention.

In terms of romance, you're enigmatic, detached, changeable, idealistic, and more vulnerable than most people ever imagine. You dream of a man of all-embracing intellect who will have a firecrackerlike effect on your emotions. Because you have Leo on your natural seventh-house cusp, you like being courted and greatly appreciate a dinner-by-candlelight romance. However, should his be a bohemian life-style, then Portuguese wine and a candle in a bottle will do if accompanied by a great rapport and a lot of human consideration. You are hardly a fortune hunter who dreams of the cozy comforts of chinchilla. Underneath, what you are looking for is a man who can be your best friend as well as your lover.

In love and marriage, you are both highly trusting and worthy of trust since truth is extremely important to you. Honesty is one of your ethics, and since you adhere to it so strongly yourself, you simply assume that the situation is the same on the other side.

However, if you discovered that the person you felt so secure with was dishonest and unfaithful, the first thing you would do would be to sit down and find out why. While another woman might scream, yell, throw things, or sob her heart out, you would calmly say, "I just don't understand." It's not that you have no feelings, it's just that in any situation, conflict, or disaster, *why* always takes precedence. Since you are neither a judgmental nor vindictive person, you feel that you must understand a situation before you can be in accord with any aspect of it, especially the feelings of the transgressor.

When there is no further communication flow in your mind, there is no longer a reason for a relationship. Because your personality is basically nonattached, breakups never devastate you, although sadness may overcome you in solitary moments. You face endings as calmly as you face beginnings, but with less expectation or enthusiasm. Because you realize that there is really no security except yourself, and no stability except change, your life force does not ebb with the loss of a love. Rather, you exist in the excitement of the new, and you know how to make your life a creative outgrowth of your own inner resources. Because of this, you are a fascinating person and an inspiration to those around you, who would never, in a lifetime, be able to fathom your feelings.

Unfavorable

Although there are Aquarian women who are militant torch burners and bomb throwers, for the vast majority, anarchist activities are not even a temptation.

On the contrary, you tend toward conformity because it's most comfortable. Unlike your iconoclastic sister who is more influenced by the Aquarian co-ruler Uranus, you are more an example of the limitations imposed by the lesser co-ruler, Saturn.

Chances are, your ego is as fragile as a robin's egg. You're terribly shy, insecure, and sure that you're not going to get what you want, so you don't bother asking in the first place. You'd like to like people, but you have as hard a time trusting them as a spy from Red China. Therefore, you are aloof and wary of spontaneous interactions and friendly entanglements.

You tend to submerge your individuality in whoever happens to be a stronger influence at the moment. In the event that there are no stronger influences, your attitudes are wishy-washy, and your mind embedded in both sides of the question.

Your intelligence is superficial and your ideas scattered. You have a tendency to be emotionally unstable and to make those around you suffer because of your own dissatisfactions. Although your sign has a reputation for being fervently humanitarian, you may reserve your ideals to your private life and adhere to a profitable system of getting rather than giving. You are far more a sly usurper than a self-sacrificing soul dedicated to a cause.

The cause that you serve is usually yourself. Your greatest desire is to marry and move to security land, where domestic trinkets and treasures will surround you. You're more likely to marry a man for his money, his last name, or his credit cards than you are for his smile, his personality, or his soul. However, after twenty years of middle-class tedium, you often think that it might be a better deal alone, and so you break it up and start to rough it, only to find out just *how* rough it is.

You forgot that life outside was a strain when you stopped reading *Time* magazine. A solitary Aquarian who no longer wants to be alone can be a very crabby person.

In general, you have very few interests outside of gossip, getting your hair done, going to bed, getting advice that you know you're never going to take, and reading your husband's mail. Television, "Dear Abby," and listening in on the party line are what you consider entertainment.

You're a person more boring than bored. You live in the shadow of life around you, like an eagle watching its prey. But instead of pouncing, you stand back and wait until your last chance is gone.

THE AQUARIUS MALE

Favorable

You're a prophet disguised as a bearded electrician, or a Nobel Prize-winner who spends his life speculating on life on an asteroid. Whatever, your mind is so far beyond its time that often people haven't the vaguest idea what you're talking about. However, sometimes they have the suspicion that even if someone were kind enough to translate, they still wouldn't understand. You speak in your own language, make up your own words, and could create your own dictionary, Bible, religion, and society. You're the only person walking on the face of the earth to know that science fiction isn't fiction, but more likely fact.

You have the mind of the mad inventor, the brilliant mathematician who can never find his glasses because they happen to be hanging around his neck, and the eccentric scientist who seems to be creating something so very strange that one is rather afraid to ask him what he's been doing lately.

As a general rule, people are timid when it comes to the new, and that is the realm that you live in. Your mind is so progressive that from the time you were about two, you considered becoming the first astronaut to visit Venus. Now you daydream about building a summer home on some planet that scientists haven't even discovered yet.

While other precocious children merely played with microscopes, you were busy inventing one that magnified to a higher power. Your mind is ever active and sometimes controls you in those moments of insomnia when a certain quadratic equation keeps running through your brain like a hit song.

You are cerebral, scientific, individualistic, and eccentric. You love new ideas, new games, new concepts, and new areas of knowledge. However, most of all, you love testing them out, and finally thinking beyond them.

On a personal level, you are idealistic, sincere, honest, dispassionate, and very humane. Outwardly, your disposition is serene. However, inwardly you pass through more emotional spaces than most people are aware of. But because you possess a certain amount of self-detachment, you don't dwell on your emotions long enough to allow them to drag you down. That first stab of pain or sadness is always swiftly replaced by a thought that tells you that it's really not that important in the long run.

Because you can live in the now without getting stuck in it, you have far greater control over your life than most human beings. Your mind allows you to see beyond the restrictions of the present to a place where the future will unfold further opportunities. And in the long run, should things not work out as well as you had hopefully planned, then you chalk the whole thing up as an experience worth having, only because you would never take back even your "bad" moments.

Basically, you have an unbiased mind that sees beyond good and bad to what *is*. And from there, you always find something about the experience that is interesting and worthwhile.

One of the few negative things that gets to you is having your trust violated. You like to think that the people you consider friends feel the same way about you and share the same idealistic principles. As a friend, you are generous, giving, kind, and often altruistic. However, should someone sell you out, you are saddened but not spiteful. You can feel the pain but have no problem relinquishing it, and ultimately take on the attitude of "Oh, well . . ."

Although you're never mawkishly sentimental, you're still a romantic who believes in an ideal kind of love. It's true that Aquarius is a freedom-loving sign. However, freedom for the more highly evolved Aquarian does not imply nonattachment. As a matter of fact, the presence of people is intrinsic to the satisfactions of this sign, and the right kind of relationship can be a most definite asset.

What you seek most in a woman is mental rapport, kindness, an innovative intelligence, and a respect for your space. At times you need to be alone, if only in your own head, and the woman who becomes too confining can bring on a consuming attack of claustrophobia.

Fundamentally, you're a friendly type of person who shares himself with many people. Because you find comfort in groups, you could live in a commune, provided you still had your own private space for those moments when the collective mood level closed in on you. You enjoy the give and take of a group experience because you find people to be interesting entities when their fears don't force them to be passive to their own lives.

You consider life to be a playground that provides infinite possibilities. You're not afraid of discovering them, and before it's all over, usually come out creating a few more.

Unfavorable

You have a fickle mind and a heart like a refrigerator. You talk fast but fake the follow-up. Your friends tolerate you, probably because you grin a lot and can come up with the quickest punch lines.

Your personality is erratic and anxiety-producing to those people who have to depend on you. Working for you is like signing your soul over to a psychopath. Being married to you is less satisfying than curling up next to a microwave oven that is missing its "on" switch. And being your friend is like creating a playground for the criminally insane.

The adjective most frequently uttered to describe you is "crazy." In the honor of truth, you'd be the first to agree—except that you really don't honor truth. To avoid being called a liar, years ago you forgot the definition.

You live your life in a state of emotional uninvolvement camouflaged by the fact that you're almost constantly in a frenzy. Sometimes you have a nervous twitch that makes it seem that you're grinning. You're so anxiety-ridden that one has to look twice to be able to distinguish a smile from a spasm.

Your greatest pleasure in life comes through mental manipulation. When you push and pull people's thoughts and fears, you obtain a sense of power that gets you through life one moment at a time. For excitement, you prefer the nefarious to the nice-guy route, bcause you know that good guys finish last.

You want to be out in front, even if you have to mangle a few minds to get there. Mind games are your forte, and you play them like a jaded gambler who no longer seeks the secrets of the casinos. You find them to be infinitely gratifying because not only do they get you what you want, they give you some entertainment at the same time.

Standing back and staring at the reaction of your victim is one of your favorite things. It beats vacationing in Florida and even outdoes watching someone dying. There's nothing like that flicker of the eyelash, the constriction of the pupil, and the wringing of the hands to tell you that, once again, you've made your point beautifully.

At your most engaging, you are cheerfully diabolical.

The boyish grin and the innocence in your eyes conceal a personality that is as innocuous as a cyanide pill.

When it comes to marriage, the most a woman can hope for from you is a divorce. You're obsessively unfaithful and even force yourself into affairs because you have no other way to fill up your time. You're the kind of father to make a child believe he's an orphan, and the kind of husband that is a challenge to a bored and decadent mind.

In the end, your mind games imprison you and make you grow old, only to appear a sad man who seems so pleasant. Only those who have suffered through you know for sure that your body is at the mercy of a malevolent mind.

DECANS

Every sign in the zodiac can be broken down into three subdivisions, called decans. Each decan roughly corresponds to ten degrees—the first third, second third, and last third of the sun sign's time span, which is approximately thirty days.

As each of these periods has different subrulerships, the personality of a person is slightly modified by the specific decan it falls in. For instance, an Aries born in the second decan would be ruled by Mars, but subruled by the sun. Therefore, he would tend to display a greater sense of pride, boastfulness, egotism, and optimism than an Aries born in the third decan, which is subruled by Jupiter. This Aries would tend to be more freedom-loving, flighty, travel-oriented, and interested in subjects of a philosophical nature. An Aries born in the first decan would be the most aggressive, but not necessarily the most productive and accomplished.

Decans are important, since they do account for a more detailed assessment of an individual's personality characteristics. They also show how two people born under the same sun sign can be markedly different.

If you were born between January 21 and 30, your sun falls in the Uranus decan of Aquarius.

You're a very versatile human being with a restless mind and a nervous, high-strung nature. This decan often implies both genius and notoriety. However, there is also a tendency toward rebellion inherent in the personality that can make natives feel at odds with the structures they have to live in. More aggressive individuals of this decan display subversive iconoclastic behavior, rioting, social uprisings, and armed attempts at the destruction of the status quo.

Change, innovation, and progress are key words to the ideals that this decan represents. Often you are so farsighted that you see beyond your time into future conditions that should be either improved or obliterated.

You have humanitarian impulses and a social consciousness that is pervasive, intensely aware, and often unconventional. As a general rule, you restrict your attitudes to the realm of analysis rather than action, and have a tendency to speculate on situations rather than actually do anything about them.

Your personality is friendly, curious, freedom-loving, enthusiastic, impersonal, and very independent. You're fascinated by many things but committed to few. That is probably because your mind is so quick and creative that a plethora of projects can easily overtake you before you have the time to complete any one of them.

You're a people person who enjoys crowds, parties, social gatherings, and most of all, new faces. Because of your lively personality and seductive sense of humor, you're often ridiculously popular. However, paradoxically, you're a loner in the midst of a million friends and even more acquaintances. You love people but need your space, and when a situation gets too confining, you find a way to remove yourself—mentally, if not physically.

You have universal sympathies that sometimes take over, yet you're amazingly detached from events closer to home. Romantic endings hardly overwhelm you, yet you're likely to feel melancholy watching the evening news.

Any way you look at it, you're a law unto yourself. People may not always understand it, and sometimes they may not like it, but chances are they'll respect it. You ask nothing from the world except honesty and justice, which is another way to say that you ask everything. However, that is your privilege in this Age of Aquarius, provided you also acquire the patience to learn the practice of waiting.

* * *

If you were born between January 31 and February 9, your sun falls in the Mercury decan of Aquarius.

You're all mind and very little emotion. Your greatest interests and aptitudes are of a scientific and mathematic nature. Computers, engineering, medicine, marine biology, and scientific research are vocational areas that appeal most to your analytic mind.

You are open, honest, gregarious, and highly talkative. However, because your mind is so rapid and restless, you often have a hard time coordinating your words and your thoughts.

Probably, for a long period of your life the idea of engaging in some form of writing has highly appealed to you. However, you first have to develop the discipline to deal with the tedium of the experience, or else you will never complete any project. You expect things to happen fast or not at all, and have a hard time proceeding at a methodical pace. When you do master the rapidity of your own mind, you can become the creator of some brilliant and very innovative writing.

Any way you look at it, your mind is definitely beyond its time. Sometimes you may suffer for this, because people are not willing to accept your new ideas, structures, and forms. However, with persistence your genius will be able to crumble all resistances and ultimately win the recognition it deserves. One of your greatest pleasures comes in communicating your ideas to other people and then testing and analyzing their reactions. In the more lowly evolved Aquarian personality this decan can indicate the game player who psychopathically plays with people's minds and then coldly stands back to observe how the game is going.

On the positive side, your personality is kind, sincere, and considerate. Optimism, self-confidence, and tenacity are characteristics that ultimately bring you a great deal of success. Deep within your mind there is a belief in man as a limitless being, and your actions are an outgrowth of this attitude.

You most often know precisely what you want and work for it, rather than waiting around for it to take you by storm. Defeat never gets you down, because you know how to use it to create a far more substantial success. You are the magician who holds the powers of the universe within your mind. You are not afraid to use your power and never forget that it's there.

If you were born between February 10 and 19, your sun falls in the Venus decan of Aquarius.

You are more romantic than Aquarians born in other decans, and tend to get persistently involved with the wrong people. The distance factor is a force that seems to affect your relationships to a considerable degree. This takes the form of falling in love with someone married, someone who lives in another country, someone whose emotional problems prevent involvement in mature relationships, or someone who simply does not share the same attraction.

Romantically speaking, you seek excitement rather than substance, and have a restless nature that swiftly spurs you on. You have a pleasure-loving personality that is impulsive, changeable, and sometimes fickle. In your more youthful years you see love as an exciting kind of game whose components are ever-changing.

On the positive side, you are generous and idealistic, emotional and more sensitive than Aquarians born in the other decans. Your personality is charming yet mysterious, affable yet elusive.

People are sometimes wary of getting close to you because of the contradictory elements in your personality. It's often difficult to understand what you really feel, because you change your mind so often. And in a moment of truth, when your deeper feelings come to the fore, you often use your ludicrous sense of humor to obfuscate the entire situation.

Fundamentally, you're someone who's very easy to know yet very difficult to understand. Your personality is a paradox that is very intriguing, quite entertaining, and at times a little maddening. If someone should abruptly ask you what you want most, you'd probably respond with fifteen answers off the top of your head, then say that you take it all back because you really want none of them. Then you'll explain that you just *thought* you did. At this point, the questioner is totally confused. But that's all right, because, as a matter of fact, so are you. However, you're quite accustomed to having your mind play tricks on you. In the long run, it's part of what makes life so ineffably exciting.

LOVE

You're the truly independent sort who creates a comfortable space and stays at a safe distance. Therefore, your attitude toward love is just like you—unconventional.

Your feeling is: "The more I don't see you, the more I want you." You stay away from predatory people who might close in and cut you off from that feeling of freedom that is so precious.

Soft lights and mood music don't move you half as much as somebody intelligent to talk to. The more interests, the better, since you're seeking the mental stimulation that arises from a vital, inquisitive person. Because your attitude toward love is more cerebral than emotional, you have to like the idea of a person before you can come to the point of loving. Admiration is a key factor to your emotional makeup and the more someone gives you reason to feel it, the more responsive you spontaneously become.

Basically, you're looking for someone to share your passion for photography, body painting, and nuclear physics. Or, even better, you'd like someone who also has many passions to share. Falling in love for the Aquarius means having a mind so stimulated that the body is forgotten.

Even in love, you're detached and freedom-loving, which may madden and confuse a possessive lover. You probably see your lover as your best friend and find flowery language and effusive romanticism excessive. Basically, you find so much drama and excitement in the details of daily life that you don't feel the need to impose grade-B-movie standards on your love relationship.

Because you're an idealist, in your own idiosyncratic way you're also romantic. However, most people neither see this nor understand it. When you do love, you embrace all a person's faults and virtues, without illusion and without a compulsion for reform. Your attitude is that the greatest gift you can give a human being is respect for individual freedom. When the lovelight shines in your eyes, it seems to say "I accept you as you are, and I know what that is." In return, you require the same mental, emotional, and physical space. But if the moment should come when your lover seems to be encroaching on your space, with no intention of moving, it is time to say in that characteristic Aquarian way, "Let's be friends." Alas, the door is reopened, the air is cleared, and once again you can feel your energy moving.

MARRIAGE

Because you're such a freedom-loving person who enjoys crowds as much as one-to-one situations, marriage is certainly not the end-all and be-all of your existence. Many Aquarians marry late in life, and some not at all. However, those who do settle into a connubial state cannot be confined if the marriage is to last.

You require absolute freedom to come and go as you please and to have a solitary space set aside to pursue your own interests. Jealous, possessive partners who follow you everywhere make you anxiety-ridden, suffocated, and depressed.

What you seek most in marriage is a solid companionship based on communication and rapport. However, you don't want it badly enough to pay the price of heavy restrictions.

You're a people person who can never get enough of new faces. This doesn't mean you're looking to fall in love with them. However, the fascination you hold for other human beings can be downright threatening to an insecure marriage partner.

You're a person who cannot be controlled by jealous threats or accusations; your spontaneous response is a cool counterchallenge. Infidelity on the part of your partner would not crush you. In fact, it might be something that you, one day, might experience yourself. Because you tend to think in terms of "What would happen if . . . ?" you can take a simple personal encounter to a place more intimate than you might have ever expected. However, this need not threaten your marriage unless the marriage is already so weak that it's on its deathbed.

Although you could probably live your life alone and like it, provided your social calendar was filled, marriage can also provide many satisfactions if you find the right person. In a situation based on a sharing of interests, ideas, ideals, and attitudes, you could find a lot of stimulation, happiness, and personal pleasure. However, you do require a mutual respect of privacy. Ultimately, the freer you feel in marriage, the more faithful you will be; when you're caged, you slowly lose consideration for any marital commitment.

MONEY

You don't value money for itself; however, it does help you do those impromptu things that pop into your head in an hour of insomnia. You're not the type to hoard a lump sum in your sock that you count every full moon. At the same time, you do have the ability to think far ahead, which means you'll have the spending money needed for your first trip to Uranus.

You do appreciate the finer things in life and have a level of practicality that people who love you are consistently surprised at. How can someone who is so up in the air come so far down to the ground when it comes to something as mundane as money? There's no doubt about it—you're full of surprises.

In general, you're as generous as Santa Claus. When the restaurant check comes, you grab it as your best friend travels swiftly to the bathroom.

If you're a highly evolved Aquarian, the only value you can find in money is in giving it away. You'll hand out your next-to-last dollar to someone who has only fifty cents, and thereby come out with less money than the loser. It makes you happy to give even if the object of your charity needs the money less than you do.

Money could never control you, since you see its value as transient in a very fast-moving time span. Whatever you decide to do with it, you make sure that you enjoy it, even if that means just getting rid of it.

CAREER

You don't long for that chunk of corporate power in the sky. However, you do demand the freedom to do as you please, without constant interference.

Because of your antipathy for controlling structures,

you're often happier working on your own. Your mind is like that of a mad scientist who sleeps in his laboratory so that he won't miss anything.

Although you enjoy your creature comforts along with those little priceless gadgets, you don't need them enough to spend your life working to get them.

Rather, success is the mental gratification that comes from discoveries, breakthroughs, the feeling of progress, the unfolding of a new truth. You must be stimulated by what you're doing in order to consider it a successful undertaking. When a certain kind of work bores you, it leaves you unmoved and lacking in motivation.

Because you're terribly idealistic about what you do, you're sometimes willing to sacrifice monetary rewards for greater personal satisfaction. You're easily taken in by new schemes that are not particularly security-oriented, yet prove to be a provocative kind of adventure.

You hate to feel tied down to any work situation, especially when you can't seem to see beyond the burdens it imposes. Therefore, the greatest success is doing your own thing and getting paid fairly for it. When you wake up in the morning to what you consider a consuming interest rather than a job, you're on the road to the kind of success you've always been searching for.

Because you're such a free spirit, you're often happier doing free-lance work or owning your own business. However, a profession that is a challenge to your mind or one that requires you to work with a lot of people can also provide the kind of satisfaction your restless mind keeps searching for.

You have a scientific mind with a mathematical nature. Therefore, everything from nuclear physics to computers to accounting could appeal to you. Medicine is also a distinct possibility, or perhaps scientific research or psychiatry.

Electronics or engineering could offer the kind of stimulation your mind requires. Aviation, astronomy, and astrology are other possibilities, since you love to speculate on the limitless.

Basically, you have the mind of an inventor who looks at the world in new ways. Your progressive proclivities and innovative ideas can bring you both fame and fortune, should you decide to put them to use.

Because you have humanitarian urges and are a people person, social work and psychology could be especially satisfying, particularly group therapy. However, interest groups based on change and social betterment could also appeal to you.

You often have a tremendous amount of creativity that finds expression in a profession. And because you're so uncannily able to get behind people's minds, your writing, painting, and poetry could be extremely reflective of more profound human truths.

Since your mind is so original, so independent, and often so far beyond its time, chances are you can invent a few new professions to suit your fancy. At least one might be located on another planet; another could be an interplanetary commuter system that runs on thoughts. As long as your thoughts keep coming, universal world progress should never know a stopping point.

FRIENDS

You're a person who finds excitement in new faces. People fascinate you so much that you sometimes spread yourself too thin and become friendly with a lot of people but close to very few.

You're a gregarious group person who circulates and makes fast associations that are not necessarily long-lasting, intimate, or intense. You probably have a lot of friends and even more acquaintances that come and go like various phases of the weather, only to be replaced by new ones.

The people who do stick in your life are the friends with whom you have most in common. Your idea of the bosom buddy is someone who is close but not a person who hangs on or smothers. Your best friendship is one that affords you space for other people and at the same time the deepest rapport.

Your first and foremost tendency is to befriend everyone and to bestow favors on all. However, sooner or later something tells you that your idealism is a little self-defeating. There aren't enough hours in the day to fulfill everyone's expectations, so the time arises when you have to discriminate. Your humanitarian tendencies can too easily get the better of you, to the point that you're on the verge of turning your home into a hostel. You're the kind of person who brings dogs, cats, rabbits, and people in out of the storm, only to create a fiercer one indoors.

Because you think beyond good and bad and find something wonderful in everybody, a lot of people love you and want to follow you around. However, the story of Aquarius is "so near and yet so far." Even in the same room and sitting on the same sofa, you can be light-years away from the person next to you, although you're looking him straight in the eye and smiling. There aren't many people whose minds move on your frequency, but because you can adjust to anyone's mind for a while, you get a taste of the world without having to go anywhere or give anything up. That is the privilege of being the sign of universal brotherhood. Within your zany individuality, you are really all men and all women and can recognize yourself in the experience of each person you encounter.

HEALTH

Your nervous system is on such a high frequency that chihuahuas start howling whenever you walk near. Because of your overworked mind, insomnia is often a problem, leading to physical exhaustion and sometimes mental depression.

An erratic nature and emotional instability are typical Aquarian pathologies that can be easily avoided with rest and regular meditation. Prolonged unrelieved stress can set your entire system up for an ultimate breakdown that begins insidiously when you're least aware.

Muscular spasms can also cause discomfort if you're the type to neglect the needs of your body in the interest of the activities of your mind. Regular exercise and especially yoga are excellent ways to keep your body young and smoothly functioning.

Later in life, high blood pressure may menace your cardiovascular system, so avoid an excessive use of salt, as well as foods high in cholesterol. A course in deep breathing, regularly applied, can ultimately slow down your heartbeat and prolong your life.

Finally, when an onslaught of nervous energy starts to make you irritable, calcium-magnesium tablets can slow you down and cool you off. Because they have a cumulative calming effect, a regular morning dose with your orange juice can prove more than worthwhile in the long run—especially when you notice that the chihuahuas have shut up and started staring in silence.

HOME

Because your mind is ahead of its time, you most naturally want your home to be modern. Ideally, you need a lot of light and space in which to wander about.

Walk-in closets big enough to be disco parlors are definitely best.

Since you probably have as many sleep-in guests as a motel owner, your best bet would be a sprawling A-frame with more rooms than the White House. That way, as an after-dinner game you could play hide and seek when backgammon begins to get boring.

Naturally, electrical gadgets would be found in every corner, cranny, ceiling, and wall. Earphones would be attached to all the chairs for those people who prefer to tune out the conversation. And, of course, you need a wall phone in the bathroom for when friends call with last-minute party invitations. On the phone in the study, you've installed a mini screen so that you can watch the expression of the person with whom you're speaking. And should you happen to be preoccupied with staring into the phone when the doorbell rings, on the wall in the entrance hall you have an electric hand that will admit guests and give them a handshake.

In the den, where you spend a lot of time, you have a special telescope for watching your neighbors, and another one for watching the stars. One entire wall is your TV screen, which you can operate by remote control when you are lying on your vibrating couch.

In your kitchen are a microwave oven, an electric dishwasher, a ten-speed blender, a five-speed juicer, and a robot who operates all of them simultaneously. Since most of your acquaintances have no idea that a robot makes his home in your pantry, it comes as quite a surprise when they come down to raid the refrigerator and suddenly feel a steel hand on their shoulder.

Your bedroom is the best room in the house, because that's where you think a lot. With a flick of the wrist, you can sunbathe on your bed as solar rays shine down upon you from the starlike fixtures in the ceiling. One entire wall is a tropical fish tank that you stare into in those moments of insomnia. The wall opposite your bed is covered with a floor-to-ceiling mirror so that your curiosity can keep up with your lovemaking.

Adjacent to your bedroom is a photography workroom where you can set up some equipment to capture those spontaneous moments on film.

COSMIC CHALLENGE

Your cosmic challenge is to develop a deeper compassion for others. At times, you tend to treat people not as complex human beings but as curiosities that are a constant entertainment until they try to get too close. Your level of detachment sometimes denies the consideration of deeper feelings. People come to think of you as cold, remote, and removed from a more intimate and satisfying interaction. You have a strong tendency to take what you need and then walk away, without stopping to consider the response you've generated.

Until you develop a less ruthless attitude in your interactions, you may be undermining your own efforts at friendliness. In the long run, a deeper awareness of your own behavior will help bring you closer to the Aquarian ideal of universal brotherhood.

INSPIRATION

You are the sign of universal love. You have a mind that transcends the personal to merge its energies in the highest truths. Through your quest for knowledge, you come to bear the fruit of Hermes, and contain within the source of your being both wisdom and awareness. You are the patient truth seeker who has sacrificed the limitations of ego to enter into the ancient mysteries. Wherever you go, your presence is venerated, and you are known by the name of Wise One.

WHAT HOLDS YOU BACK
AND HOW TO OVERCOME IT

There is often a temptation to get too involved in vicarious experience, with a less active involvement in your own life. Sometimes, your detachment overtakes you and your attitude toward your relationships becomes ambivalent at the same time your curiosity about the feelings of your friends increases.

It is important that you confront your own feelings and come to a deeper understanding of them. Because it seems that there is always so much happening around you, you usually find it easy to avoid your own emotional confusion.

Until you get accustomed to looking into yourself to satisfy that emotional part of you, you may suffer severe frustrations that could get the better of you. Try to become as comfortable with your feelings as you are with your intellect, and you will gain a far more integrated personality that will ultimately lead to a deeper sense of satisfaction.

Knowing what you really want is the first step you have to take before getting it. And the more time you invest in knowing yourself, the more you will develop your will, so as to become a far more powerful human being.

LOVE AND
COMPATIBILITY GUIDE

Aquarius with Aquarius

You're best friends, soulmates, and something of an ideal companion to the other. You're both busier than four people put together, yet you still have time for those late-night talks that cover all topics in the universe in three hours.

You give dinner parties several times a week, go out at least two or three nights, and spend the rest of the time helping drop-in friends with problems. Even snowbound, you seldom clutter each other's space and have an uncanny way of letting your interests insulate you.

You love to trade ideas, theories, speculations, and

curiosities about everything from politics to your best friends' eating habits. You share the same needs, desires, devotions, and attitudes, and when nobody else wants to listen, you know you always have an eager sounding board.

This relationship could easily be one of super mental stimulation and emotional devotion. You both like being together, and somehow this even makes being apart a little better. Together you're like tourists in a land of endless sights. The points of interest are never-ending, and the company itself never ceases to be an entertainment. This is the kind of attraction that long-term marriages are made of. Consider it to be one that is always changing but never confining.

Aquarius Woman with Aries Man

You awe him with your humanitarian idealism, and he overpowers you with his list of achievements. You're the kind of woman he loves to talk to, and he's the kind of man to whom you like to listen.

Beyond this, the basic difference is that he is a talker while you are a giver. He's absorbed by self-interest; you have an interest in every person who crosses your path.

With him, chances are that you'll end up giving far more than you're getting. You are so good-natured that you have a bad habit of sacrificing your own inclinations to other people's strong desires. In a most aggressive way, Mr. Aries is demanding, jealous, and possessive, although he fully expects the freedom to do as he pleases. He will scowl and make waves in his soup when he feels that you are being too friendly to the waiter. And when you leave him in the middle of a sentence to go see a friend in need, he comes close to having temper tantrums. When the phone rings after midnight and you murmur in your amiable way, "Oh, hello, Harry," suddenly you have one phone that is no longer attached to the wall.

However, if he can manage to give you the benefit of the doubt, the two of you could have a fantastic thing going. You will give him the most extraordinary ideas for his new projects. You won't complain when he works so hard that he rarely sees you. And if he has a little affair here and there, that, in a moment of gut-wrenching guilt, he has to confess, you'll tell him with a detached smile not to trouble himself.

Any way he looks at you, you are an unusual woman

who is an experience unto yourself. Chances are, he'll consider himself lucky to have found you.

Aquarius Woman with Taurus Man

Any way you look at it, the two of you together are like strangers from different planets. He eats different things, he sees different things, and he wants different things. Any interaction between you will probably be no more than one in passing. If you try to make more of it, frustration can approach the level of paralysis.

You have more interests than there are days in your lifetime; Mr. Taurus restricts his to TV channels. You live your life giving to people around you; he lives his in taking. You are inflamed by the future, whereas he somehow gets stuck in the past. You are fervently dedicated to progressive ideals, he to gratifying his present desires. You have an eccentric mind that is ahead of its time; he has one that has a hard time keeping up.

He likes to hoard his money, and you like to give yours away. You get carried away by causes; his favorite cause is personal gain. He is enslaved by the material, but your needs are on the ethereal.

When he starts babbling about football, you'll smile politely but won't understand a word he's saying. When you start talking about unions, strikes, and grape pickers, he won't understand a word you're saying, but he won't be quite as polite. It was someone just like him who created management and it was someone just like you who created revolutionary uprisings.

The communication gap is like a cosmic crack in the universe. If he hangs around you too long, he may fall in. However, what he loses in the process may do him a world of good.

Aquarius Woman with Gemini Man

He'll never meet a woman who's as easy to get along with. And you'll never meet a man who's quite as crazy.

You'll love the way he makes you laugh until your sides split. However, you won't appreciate the fact that he's always late and sometimes doesn't show up at all.

Your secret is that although you're good-natured and will go along with a lot of insanity, you still have feelings. And although you won't mention it, being stood up is not your favorite way to spend an evening.

He'll respect your basic attitudes and the way you're committed to your sense of freedom. However, when he sees that you're as nice to your mailman as you are to him, for the first time in his life he may sulk and feel a little slighted.

You are one woman who can teach him a lot if he shuts his mouth for a while and just watches you. While he is critical, you are accepting. He delights in constant change; you benefit from both change and stability.

He'll respect the way your mind works and the fact that it operates in so many directions. And it's not unlikely that you'll capture some place in his heart that he never even knew he had. Mr. Gemini may stay up all night trying to figure out what's really happening to him, and why. However, if he just allows himself to forget both time and reason, he'll figure out in the end that it's not really the why that matters. It's only how he feels that counts. Good luck!

Aquarius Woman with Cancer Man

He craves closeness, but you feel more comfortable with distance. He prefers cozy tête-à-têtes while you embrace crowded settings. He enjoys quiet evenings at home while you prefer mass riots. Any way you look at it, the differences here are distance-producing.

He needs a woman who will nurture his strengths and overlook his insecurities. You need a man who has fewer insecurities and a greater degree of emotional detachment.

You'll become impatient with his supersensitivities, his mood swings, and his possessiveness. At the same time, he'll feel morose and sulky when you give some meaningless stranger as much attention as you do him.

You are a freedom-loving, freethinking woman who creates her own spaces. And he tends to close them off with his first attempts at getting your total attention.

At first, you may respond enthusiastically to his romantic gestures. However, if he moves in too far too fast, you may take a giant step backward for a quick breath and another look.

Since you are adaptable to most personalities, you could also come to love his. However, if he drowns you in a swamp of mawkish emotions and makes too many demands too soon, you'll leave him to his sentimental dreams and memories of an affair that never really was.

Aquarius Woman with Leo Man

If he marries you, he'll have his own private social worker, psychotherapist, and recreational director. But that's only if he ever gets to see you.

Chances are, you know more people than a politician —and they all occupy a special place in your heart. When it comes to people, you have an insatiable attention span and a penchant for helping the problem souls. The phone probably rings till dawn and the doorbell till twelve-thirty. At ten o'clock he'll find you lavishing warmth on the lovelorn; at two A.M. you desert him to aid a "friend" just jailed for inciting a protest riot in a geriatric clinic. Sometimes he feels that he's sleeping in a social-welfare unit. At such moments, he yells, frowns, grumbles a lot, and sometimes kicks the sofa. On your way out, you'll inquire if he's not feeling well, and he knows he's got sixty seconds to answer before he hears the door slam.

Your mind is so far out that he stops going to the movies. What Mr. Leo would call a human zoo, you refer to as the rudiments of utopia. Your thoughts are in the future, while his heart is in the present. With patience, he can combine them into one loving and totally insane time span. But with force, he'll only instigate a state of nonfeeling.

Despite your outward friendliness, you are frightened of human proximity. You are at once loving and kind, freedom-loving, and impersonal. He shouldn't try to figure you out, just experience you. Through his love and encouragement, you will gain a sense of ego; through your infinite patience and understanding, his feelings may unfold into universal love.

Unlike many of his habitual heartthrobs, you generally rate low with the superficials. You have little or no interest in personal appearance and usually look as though you dressed in the dark. However, you are so different, but genuine, that even he can occasionally overlook the fact that you wear an embroidered work shirt to a dress-up dinner party.

Aquarius Woman with Virgo Man

When he looks at your life, he feels he should take care of you. However, the hardest part comes in trying to

convince you that you need someone. You're a free
spirit who feels claustrophobic when anyone gets too
close. He's an orderly, controlling type who means well
but may not always have the best ideas.

He may love your mind but resent your detachment.
He'll get cross when you forget to do the dishes (even
though there's only one fork). However, when you wake
him up in the middle of the night with a theory on the
movement of electron particles, he'll sit up in bed and
give you his full attention.

You appreciate the fact that he's a good soul who
tries hard. At the same time, he makes you feel like a cork
on a corkscrew. His mind is willful and imposing, while
yours is universal and used to doing what it wants.

No matter what you do or how you do it, he has a
suggestion to improve the overall efficiency. Since you
care more about the experience than the outcome, his
ideas fall on deaf ears. You really don't want to hear his
opinions, or to do it his way, but when you tell him, he
doesn't hear you. He merely makes a new suggestion.

He has a way of taking up your space with his expectations that makes it seem cluttered and confining. On
the other hand, you have a way of making him feel like
a third sock that has less than an even chance of finding
the mate. The way he lives his life by a thousand systems is not the way you want to live your life. The last
thing you need is someone to follow you around and tell
you what to do. The first thing you need is freedom. Since
this is not something you'll find forthcoming from Mr. Virgo, it might be best to look elsewhere and to keep this
relationship one of a merely friendly nature.

Aquarius Woman with Libra Man

You will understand his ego needs and listen to all
his problems (even with other women). He's never gotten
such a degree of undivided attention, and naturally, it can
be habit-forming.

You don't make bells ring, lights go on, or candles go
out. However, you do make him feel like he's never felt
before. It's a lot deeper than starry-eyed; it's more like
devastated.

One day, Mr. Libra comes to understand that he
needs you a lot more than you need him. For months you
have been a sturdy sounding board, but what has he

been besides an amiable escort? Suddenly panic sets in, and he becomes possessive. But it doesn't work, because you're everybody's person, but not one person's plaything.

You have an unlimited capacity for being selfless, while he has an unlimited capacity for being selfish. You can give a lot, and you don't ask for much while he can take a lot and doesn't really look around to give. Because there is this peculiar congruency, the two of you could be quite compatible.

You will bring him to lectures on meditation and numerology, while he will teach you how to play the guitar. And because you have a million interests and know a million people, he'll rarely see you, will never have a chance to get sick of you, and will remain sufficiently insecure to maintain a consuming interest.

Besides the fact that he seeks security, he also seeks the excitement of a challenge. And you, just being your honest, natural, everyday self, will be the kind of conquest to intrigue him.

Aquarius Woman with Scorpio Man

He'll want to make love, but you'll want to go to the movies. When he *is* making love, you'll be musing on why the film ended without music.

He'd better forget trying to control you; you're so detached that you'll end up controlling him. You have about five thousand friends and take on the personal problems of each one of them. Therefore, he feels like he's competing with a crowd on opening night.

You're so easy to be with that in a peculiar way he finds you irresistible. You're like a breath of fresh air, but if he stays around you too long, he may start feeling cold. He is passion personified, while you are mental and remote. He embraces direct experience, but you prefer yours vicariously. After ten years together he may tell you he wants an open marriage, and you'll tell him you thought it always was.

If he's unfaithful, you'll be too involved in other people's lives to notice. Tell him to forget the pernicious apologies used just to get your attention. You'll give him a remote smile and say that whatever he wants is fine with you, and would he excuse you, since the phone is ringing.

Living with you is like having a roommate. Marriage

to you is like having a friend. He'll never get tired of you, because he'll seldom see you—you're so busy living everyone else's life.

So if it's freedom plus pleasantries that he's looking for, he has it here. From him, you have financial stability and the knowledge that he'll never leave you. In your eyes, a marriage is never marred by an affair if the marriage fulfills a man's most primal needs. And you're so agreeable, cheerful, undemanding, and such a vacation from himself that he can't help but need you. Despite his efforts to the contrary, expect to have a happy life.

Aquarius Woman with Sagittarius Man

This is a most compatible combination that can provide many exciting moments. He will be riveted by your multifaceted interests, while you will enjoy his overwhelming enthusiasm. You are both freedom-loving, easygoing, fun-loving, and adventurous.

He will teach you parallel skiing, while you will teach him Transcendental Meditation. He'll keep your blood churning on the tennis courts; you'll make his mind marvel at all your progressive projects.

You will delight in his spontaneous propositions, and he will be taken with your humanitarian idealism. You are stimulating yet undemanding, caring yet unconventional. When he's with you, he feels unfettered, fascinated, and frank about his deepest feelings. He finds you easy to talk to, and you find him fun to spend time with. He'll take you to the Caribbean for a cup of midmorning coffee, and let you take him on a tour of the natives. You're probably very curious about the economy and will try to inquire about the custom of voodoo.

You can take each other to a multitude of places, and heartily enjoy yourselves along the way. You make him feel that he has a best friend as well as a lover, a most unconventional traveling companion as well as a deeply caring woman. Quite happily you can expand through each other and live your lives forever growing toward greater experiences.

Aquarius Woman with Capricorn Man

You are somewhat eccentric and very freedom-loving, while he is pragmatic and a little insecure. This is where the differences begin; where they end is an infinity away.

You are a dreamer; he is a man of materialization. You are fascinated by a multitude of people, but he is more concerned with himself. You're a woman who lives in the future, but Mr. Capricorn is consumed by matters close at hand. You look at life through a most unconventional kind of framework, whereas he holds tightly to tradition. You abandon yourself to your mental interests, but he spends his time making money.

The two of you are not the least compatible combination possible, but you do manage to come pretty close. Your desire to spread your energies among so many people will only, in the long run, peel away his feeling of control. In turn, the time he indulges in capitalistic activities may make you feel that you want a man who requires something else from life.

You both come from different places and are willful enough to try to bring the other along. Well, it won't work. Therefore, you must learn to accept each other as is or both take a walk and look for somebody else.

Aquarius Woman with Pisces Man

You live in the future; he often gets stuck in the past. You are friendly yet detached, but he is aloof and sentimental. You scatter your feelings among many people, while Mr. Pisces nurtures his in private places.

Basically, the two of you are so different that you seem to be traveling in separate directions. You require change and constant activity, whereas he is content with the status quo. You get inflamed over social injustice; he prefers to pass the time dreaming about a utopia. You demand honesty for any committed relationship, but he is of the opinion that honesty is not always the best policy.

You're about as romantic as a cheerful dentist extracting a wisdom tooth; he is intensely sentimental and sometimes a little sappy. You have no patience with his armchair observations, and he has no tolerance for your perpetual curiosity. Any relationship closer than backgammon partners is bound to result in mutual irritation that is more than a little electric.

Aquarius Man with Aries Woman

You are the ultimate challenge, and she hates to admit that you've got her. She thinks you have a beautiful mind, while you think she has a beautiful body. She feels she can't get enough of you, but unfortunately, you aren't caught in the same vortex of emotion.

You like women, men, dogs, cats. You're not a snob; you'll speak to anybody. Naturally, this bothers Ms. Aries, since she wants to overwhelm you to the point that you'll beg to follow her anywhere. However, in this instance she's the one who's doing the following, and without planning it, you're the leader. Because your basic attitude is that you have nothing to lose, and because hers is that she can get seriously hurt, you hold the key to her heart.

If she loses her temper, you'll walk away; if she threatens to leave you, you'll calmly say, "Go ahead." If she tries to make you jealous, you'll mention that maybe she would be better off with another person; if she tries to coerce you, you'll tune her out and give your attention to another woman.

The basic difference here is that you are detached from your ego and she is too attached to hers. You are fascinated by many people, but she is interested in herself. You are friendly but impersonal. She is friendly but very personal. Because of this, you won't appreciate her possessiveness or recognize how easily her ego is threatened. To reassure her, you won't hold her to your heart and touch your lips to her temples. You'll give her something to think about, then wander off in wonderment at why the earth tilts on its axis.

However, this is why you stimulate her; you're always caught between a bizarre set of questions and answers. If she can manage her out-of-control feelings, this could be an exciting and rewarding love match. But if she feels your nondiscriminatory friendliness causes more pain than she's willing to confront, then it's better that she just be your friend.

Aquarius Man with Taurus Woman

You're far more interested in what's out in space than in what's right in front of you. And when it comes to those little sensual pleasures that make her life worth living, you have a way of reducing them all to a thought.

You'll torment her possessive proclivities and put her jealousy through a kind of trial by fire. Communication between the two of you is like a bad phone connection.

Your deepest desire is to have wings; hers is to have an anchor. You are attached to nonattachment, but she has an infinite capacity to own. You see love as an idea, while she sees it as the stuff that life is made of. And you consider the connubial commitment an open marriage, whereas she would love a husband she can lock up.

Needless to say, this is not a compatible arrangement, and you would be better off bypassing it without expectation. The two of you are like backgammon pieces going in different directions—except when you stop to bump each other.

To her mind, you are strange, weird, bizarre, perhaps a little crazy. To your mind, she is confining, conventional, rigid, and foolishly willful. You're the grand humanitarian; she believes that good deeds should begin at home.

There is only one thing to do in the face of this encounter: quit while you're still ahead, shake hands, slap each other on the back, and come out calling yourselves "friends" (a favorite Aquarian term). That way, on lonely Sundays she can call you and tell you her love problems, and you'll leave your girlfriend and be over in five minutes to cheer her up.

Aquarius Man with Gemini Woman

She'll stay up all night talking, and you'll unfold to her the secrets of the universe. You are on a perpetual quest of "why" and never cease searching—even in the middle of making love.

She is intrigued by your genius and by how you seem to make the most simple things complex. You are curious about how she makes the most complex things simple, and think her sense of humor is a scream.

You will share with her your inventions, your universal theories, your friends, and your need for freedom. Ms. Gemini offers you a superb sense of the ludicrous, and she teaches you how to write down your theories so that you don't lose them somewhere in your head.

She shares your enthusiasm for meeting new people, going to parties, and discussing the personal habits of the hostess. You are smitten with her sensational mind, respect her independence, and thrive on her infinite repertoire of witty lines. In turn, she is intrigued by the fact that your unpredictable nature is almost as intense as hers and that you don't make her feel like she's suffocating.

Although the sexual passion here is not likely to make either of you pass out, the ideas that are mutually inspired are enough to steam up the windows. This could be either a match made in heaven or a platonic love with the luminescence of the stars.

Aquarius Man with Cancer Woman

She lives through her emotions, while you rely on your mind. And from here comes the kind of friction that may be more than either of you can handle.

She may think she has to knock you out with a swift karate chop and then hypnotize you with the right words just to get a little romance going. Otherwise, she'll work up the courage to tell you she loves you, and you'll respond that that's really quite fascinating. Then, just imagine her reaction when you stop and ask her why.

When she makes you an ice-cream pie, you'll take it apart, stare at it for a while, ask her what's in it, and then forget to eat it because you're too busy talking. Needless to say, you get more pleasure in finding out how the whole thing works than you do in the actual experience.

The same goes for your relationship. You may spend agonizing hours analyzing her feelings and your thoughts, until finally she concludes that you're falling in love. Impatiently she proposes, and cheerfully you inform her that all relationships are merely illusion. At that point she savagely attacks another piece of ice-cream pie. You smile at her, sip your coffee, pass her the cream, and tell her that she's much too sentimental.

Although you are the good-hearted sort, you sometimes get so entangled in your theories that you remind her of a mad scientist who sleeps with test tubes under his pillow. If Ms. Cancer wants a man to hug her, make passionate love, and remind her how much she means to him, she'd better start looking in another direction. To show your affection, you are more likely to slap her on the back and hand her a slide rule to illustrate some recondite point to which she's only pretended to listen. Although you mean well, you're just not her type, and for her to try to adapt to your emotional level is like skinny-dipping in the middle of February.

Aquarius Man with Leo Woman

You are the detached humanitarian, and she is the emotional narcissist. Your desire is to be friends with the world; her desire is to make sure that "the world" doesn't include women.

At parties, you thoughtfully observe, while she slinks about to see *what* you're observing. She just may find that she's spilling her drink over someone's sleeve when your bright-eyed curiosity keeps you too long in the company of a stunning blonde. With one obtrusive giant step forward, Ms. Leo moves in to detract your attention to an atrocious wall hanging. "Isn't that unusual?" she gasps, pointing her empty glass.

"No," you cheerfully reply. "But did you notice the man in the corner with the balloon tie? Isn't it interesting that he's wearing two different colored socks?"

Your sign is a people-watcher, and Leo is a sign used to being watched. She cannot understand why you cannot be content watching her. But according to you, the blonde's attraction was merely a split earlobe.

"This man is crazy!" she mumbles as she turns her back to think out her plan of operation. But as she decides to calm down and forgive you, she notices you talking to a gorgeous brunette. She tosses on her coat, twists her lower lip, and crisply informs you that she's leaving. You look at her wide-eyed. The brunette was only some electrical engineer with whom you were arguing about the polar state of the universe.

Swiftly she moves for the door. As she leaves, her soul twists toward the morose. You didn't even run after her to beg, she sputters to herself. You must think she's grotesque, and you're glad that she's gone.

At the party, you sink slowly into the nearest sofa. "She certainly is a strange one," you mumble in critical scrutiny. But your ideal is a three-ring circus, and so far, she's come the closest. However, the salient question arises: Will you always have the energy to be a lion tamer?

Aquarius Man with Virgo Woman

When she tells you her deepest problems, you'll ask her a lot of questions and then offer her a diet root beer. You're far more curious than sympathetic, and somehow it doesn't sit well.

She is sensitive, supervulnerable, and needs someone who will make her feel more secure. You love her mind but have no patience with her emotions. It's your opinion that she worries too much. It's hers that you don't worry half as much as you should.

She'll never understand how you can get more involved with foreign aid to Fiji than with balancing your own checkbook. You'll never understand why she worries because she has two cents in her bank statement that she can't seem to account for.

Her penchant for order sometimes irritates and distracts you. Your comfort amid chaos can send her mind reeling. You love to party, whereas she is a shy stay-at-home who would rather have you all to herself than lose you to a group.

Because she takes everybody's feelings to heart, including her pet iguana's, she has a hard time understanding how you can be so detached. At the same time, her obsession with her cat's sinus problems makes you impatient, restless, and ready to take a walk.

Mentally, there is much mutual stimulation; sexually, there is a lot of talk. This relationship is best kept on a just-friends level.

Aquarius Man with Libra Woman

She'll think you're a little strange and eccentric, but also kind and understanding. You hang out in your head, while she tends to get stuck in her heart.

She'll meet you at a party, where you seem to be talking to everyone at once. You are a people person, and love to touch as many lives as possible.

You come alive in a crowd, but she is tantalized by an intimate tête-à-tête. You are detached and warmly impersonal, while she is terribly attached and personalizes the world with which she comes in contact.

You are loving, but not necessarily in the way she needs it. You can be loyal, devoted, and most delightful; however, you need your space. She has a way of feeling insecure when the person she loves would rather be by himself than with her. And she tends to need the kind of attentions that you might not always be around to give.

She feels a need for shared experience, but you need a feeling of freedom. That does not mean that you will abandon her because you've found someone better. Rather, that you need to spend a day in solitude with your astronomy equipment or attend a seminar on quadraphonic amplifiers—alone.

If Ms. Libra can discipline herself to enjoy her own company, there need not be a problem. But you need a woman you feel is an equal in terms of developed individuality. You'll be her best friend and help her with all her problems, but when she starts treating you like a pillow, then suddenly the fun ends. You're a man who is warm and human but also self-reliant and eager for new experience. If she can develop the same attitude, there are no limits to this relationship. But if she wants a man who is more a cushion than a thinking being, she'd be better off avoiding you.

Aquarius Man with Scorpio Woman

You will never forget her, because she's that elusive woman. Regardless of the amount of time you spend with her, you will feel both close and yet far away. However, that is the key to your amorous idealism.

You are extremely opinionated and have at least five thousand theories on the universe. She should be prepared to hear each one of them or else commit the act of rape. Granted, it may not be the most exciting scene for her to seduce you as you're staring blankly into a fish tank and thinking. However, if she waits for you to stop talking, she might as well wait for bronze to turn to silver. It's just not going to happen.

You love her mind, her sexuality, and her perceptions. Her emotions are quite another matter; you find them fascinating when they don't become confining.

She likes your mind, finds your gestures wryly amusing, but has to make some heavy emotional adjustments before she's ready for more than a friendship.

Sexually, you're not that satisfying, since you would rather think about sex than do it. Emotionally, you're not that gratifying, since you're best friends with the world, which often includes women. You're also freedom-loving and detached while she tends to be possessive and attached. Unless you make her understand that your detachment does not obviate feeling, and unless she makes herself feel that she can have you without possessing you, this relationship is best kept on a light level.

If both of you are open, you could help each other grow and from this perspective, the relationship has no limits. It will take you as far and as fast as your mind and emotions want to move.

Aquarius Man with Sagittarius Woman

You'll teach her quadratic equations and the history of glycoproteins. She'll teach you how to play backgammon and beat you at table tennis.

She'll find you to be one of the most curious and eccentric men she's ever met. When you wear your aviator glasses, you remind her of Einstein; when you go hiking together, you bear a resemblance to the "boy next door."

She will be challenged and enchanted by your brilliance; you will be enamored of her enthusiasm and philosophic approach to the most trying situations.

She will help you slow down your mind by teaching you Transcendental Meditation. She might even cure you of insomnia, since she'll tire you on the tennis courts.

She'll find you a most exciting anomaly with a mind that is like a trip worth taking. You will find her to be a truly lovable woman from whom you can learn a lot.

Together you can enjoy a future of far-off places. Whether or not you travel by land or through your minds, a multitude of marvelous things will come to you. Every day will be a greater adventure than the day before.

Aquarius Man with Capricorn Woman

You're a bit more unconventional than she could ever imagine. And more freedom-loving than she may feel comfortable with. However, because you're more fun than a circus, you may make her lose some of her Capricorn control.

She'll swoon at your startling intelligence and ponder on your peculiar ideas. You'll delight her when you show up at midnight with a bottle of champagne and the next day send her roses. Underneath, you're a romantic, though she'd never know it by listening to your theories on the universe.

However, because you often tend to be all theory and very little practical action, she may become impatient with your approach to the world. You're not the superachiever that she always dreamed of. Nor are you the man who will rush into her life and simply take command. It's far more likely that in a moment of crisis you will just sit back and throw out some fascinating fact on the eating patterns of the Eskimo.

You are a little impervious to considerations of the present, since your mind is like a satellite of the future. On the other hand, Ms. Capricorn prefers to live in the now, since it depresses her to consider the passage of time.

If she can put up with your physical passivity and decide that she doesn't mind taking total charge of life's menial details, then this could very well become a happy relationship or marriage.

Aquarius Man with Pisces Woman

Although she respects your intelligence, it wears her nerves a little thin when she yawns at midnight and you're still babbling on about electron microscopes.

You have absolutely no idea where she's coming from, but you have a wealth of theories. However, each of them, while interesting, somehow misses the mark by a long shot.

You filter the world through your mind; Ms. Pisces sifts it through her emotions. She's a romantic sentimentalist, while you're a restless man of many interests. You're the humanitarian who feels a lot for everybody in general but very little for any person in particular. On the other hand, she's the angel of mercy with the kind of emotions that bring the world right into her living room.

She is so deeply feeling that she's fearful of her own emotions, while you're so cerebral that you have a hard time making the two connect. As friends, you could probably take each other to delightful places. She could teach you how to appreciate poetry and how to use meditation to slow your mind down. In turn, you could imbue her with a little Einstein theory and explain the importance of polyisomers.

As a serious love affair, this probably won't be long-lasting. Both of you are lovable people, but the emotional differences are enough to drive you apart.

PISCES

Dates: February 20—March 20
Ruling planet: Neptune
Element: Water
Mode: Mutable
Quality: Feminine
Planetary principle: Sacrifice
Primal desire: Unification
Color: Heliotrope
Jewel: Chrysolite
Plants: Seaweed, moss
Day: Thursday
Archangel: Asariel
Magical number: 11
Magical factor: Love

PISCEANS OF
FAME AND FORTUNE

Elizabeth Taylor
Philip Roth
Rudolph Nureyev
Chopin
Handel
Elizabeth Barrett Browning
Ted Kennedy
Michelangelo

Nijinsky
Auguste Renoir
Meher Baba
Edna St. Vincent Millay
W. H. Auden
George Harrison
Maurice Ravel
Irving Wallace

Buffy Sainte-Marie

THE PISCES FEMALE

Favorable

You're a little like Snow White before she married the prince—delicate, vulnerable, soft-spoken, and sensitive. You cry at tender love stories, sniffle at wondrous weddings, and choke up when it comes to the moment of good-bye.

Your innermost secret is that you need to be cherished, needed, and nurtured, even if, to overcompensate your feelings of vulnerability, you behave more like Tarzan than Jane. At the same time, if you are worshiped, you still have a tendency to feel unloved in tiny ways, and often force your lover to prove his feelings. In doing so, you sometimes bring a situation of pleasure far closer to one of pain.

Even if you wear overalls and sport a black belt in karate, you're still a classic romantic who gets off on Grimm's fairy tales. The problem is you keep waiting for the prince, except that he's usually a modern version called a playboy. And, unfortunately, this individual is far more likely to run you over with his horse than he is to scoop you into his saddle and hand you a white lily.

Alas, Ms. Pisces, you often pick the wrong people, although they seem so good at the time. However, five years later, when you start to feel like Cinderella, who never goes anywhere except to see her stepsisters on weekends, you might stop and reconsider your options. It seems that everyone else in the world is at some kind of ball, while all you do is stand in front of the mirror and peer at your enlarged pores. If, as time goes by, you never find answers, only perhaps a few pimples, then you know your life is in for some heavy changes. Essentially, you want to be superwoman, but if someone should give you a gold pin initialed SW, you're the first person to think that it's all a cruel mistake. Likewise, you're not very convincing when it comes to graciously accepting the love you so need. It's far easier for you to be lonely than it is to believe that you deserve such unsolicited attention.

Your self-image is not only hazy, it's hazardous! And although you're devoted to the act of self-improvement, you're the last one to see where and how you have improved. As a result of your own insecurity, you are often supersensitive to the feelings of friends. You are the savior of the crumpled souls and an inspirational force for those unfortunates who feel forsaken. One hour with you is more uplifting than yoga at dawn, and that's because you too have known what it's like to feel lost and alone.

Basically, you have a beguiling personality and a sense of humor that can be seductive. During your more relaxed moments you are a dreamy-eyed sensualist who loves making love all night long, languishing in scented baths, reading magazines in bed, and spraying yourself with expensive perfume. You also love sipping hot wine on winter nights, seeing incandescent Christmas trees, and, of course, hearing the sound of the sea at its wildest.

You are an intense, vital human being with the captivating charisma of a sex siren and the emotional purity of a virgin love goddess.

You are touched by the changing seasons and thrilled by the winter holidays. You probably keep your birthday cards for years at a time and take your Christmas tree down in April. Your creative nature bubbles over at the little things that most other people never notice. And you translate these feelings into poems, paintings, musical compositions, screenplays . . .

Despite what you may, at times, feel, you are not at all weak. Rather, you are deeply feeling and afraid of your own emotions. The experience of personal sorrow has brought you to a place of profound compassion and universal understanding. Essentially, you have the soul of an artist. And your vision is one that could resurrect the consciousness of the world.

Unfavorable

You're a perpetual damsel in distress who never tires of high drama. Friends become fatigued with the repetition of your problems. However, you keep making the same mistakes and never seem to learn from them.

You have a passive-aggressive personality that expresses anger in the most indirect ways. Sarcasm, sulking, hysteria, and hypochondria all prove their point— but do they really get you anywhere?

You like to go off in a corner and lick your wounds, hoping that someone is looking. However, since this is not the most effective attention-getting mechanism, you usually end up sitting by yourself and feeling slighted and abandoned.

You fly high on self-destructive experiences, moments, and people that ultimately bring you down, to drown in self-created sorrow. Then you roll over, play loser, and weep your heart out.

You have a special talent for bringing on those experiences that you need most to avoid. That's because you are a slave to your self-destructive tendencies and find a subtle sensationalism in sadness. You drown and choke in sentimentality, get taken in by fake profundities, and are moved by the most melancholy clichés. Therefore, it is not surprising that your idea of love is nothing less than a grand finale that comes complete with a total enchantment—a kind of package deal.

Due to the degree of your emotional immaturity, you often fall in love with the wrong people. Your men are usually married, sedentary ne'er-do-wells, suave playboy types, criminals that you can rehabilitate and control, macho hit men, or men who simply prefer their mothers. The pattern is that there is always a distance factor excluding the possibility of closeness.

However, this really doesn't matter to you, because you create what you want with your mind and never listen to anybody anyway. The fantasy factor is so strong in your personality that sometimes you don't need a man —a mere mind trip will suit you nicely.

Your rapport with reality is so poor that quite easily you can prevent yourself from seeing anything you don't want to. After you cut yourself off from what is going on around you, then you begin to feel lonely, alienated, and depressed.

At the same time, you are truly possessive about such depressions, mood swings, and morose moments. You want solitude, not solicitous advice. And if you get it anyway, chances are you won't hear it or show gratitude.

Like a coward, you would rather hide than stand up and confront the world. You have no idea what you want, although you make a lot of noise about the fact that you can't have it. Until you confront your own passivity courageously, you should stop the complaining and self-analysis that never get you any further than a short-term tranquilizer for a permanent anxiety attack.

Although you like to live your life as a victim, remember that you're really your own worst enemy. No one else could ever play the role as well.

THE PISCES MALE

Favorable

At your best, you're a man who not only loves life but also respects it. You are sensitive, intuitive, spiritual, and ever searching for a more transcendent experience.

You are the sign of the mystic, the psychic, the monk, and the clairvoyant. Often you are a man of musical genius, artistic sensitivity, and strong scientific aptitudes. You have a mind that is interested in a multitude of areas, and you possess enough talent to master most of them.

Obscure esoteric subjects have always appealed to you. So have medicine and some of its more progressive offshoots, such as acupuncture, chiropractic, and such mind-body practices as yoga, the Alexander technique, and T'ai Chi.

Because of your lively imagination and trenchant sense of humor, you're a delight to spend time with. However, regardless of the crowd of your admirers, there is an enigmatic part of your personality that remains distant and unknowable.

You have a dual personality and at times play the gregarious bon vivant and at others seek serious moments in solitude. You tend to be secretive and private. However, unpredictably, you can also be open and indiscreet.

At the highest level, you possess a luminous intelligence and a personality that is self-sacrificing and self-effacing. Your mind is receptive, thoughtful, and meditative. Often it is feverish with spiritual or philosophic aspirations.

Underneath, a penetrating shyness and an extreme sensitivity prevent you from openly speaking your mind. When the shyness seeps through, your personality appears diffident and unassuming. At such moments you may retreat within yourself and simply put an end to all conversation.

At times, Pisces is the least accessible sign. However, when it comes to matters of romance, it can be ebullient, vulnerable, and very submissive. You are a romantic in the deepest sense of the word and can get carried away by nature, springtime, soothing music, and, of course, scintillating women.

At the higher levels, you are a devoted lover with a sense of sympathy, compassion, and caring that comes from a most profound place in the heart. Your love is reverent and religious and exemplifies a need for union with God or the higher self.

It is likely that you are strongly artistic and have a passion for music that could bring you a place of fame and fortune, if you decide to make commercial use of your talents. However, when it comes to the competitive corporate world, unless you have a lot of fire or earth in your chart, you are far more content not competing. Your idea of satisfaction is to have the security of sitting back and not being forced to strain your sensitivities.

Your life is a constant search for more meaningful mental, emotional, and spiritual foundations. And as you grow through the expansion of these new structures, you gain in the kind of wisdom that elevates your consciousness and uplifts your life to an ever higher plane.

Unfavorable

You are a self-destructive anomaly who languishes in Byzantine fantasies and hungers after bacchanalian delights. You live your life according to a kind of primitive pleasure principle and will embrace anything that brings you pleasure, no matter what the pain.

In your personality there is a kind of sadomasochism operating, if not saliently, then on more subtle levels. You adore being dominated by strong, sharp-tongued women who sport a streak of cruelty. Of course, it also helps if they're beautiful and can berate you with a seductive but elusive body.

The key to your personality is that you always want what you can't have. Therefore, you are often enslaved by the memory of faded love affairs and beautiful faces who come close enough to get your attention but stay far enough away to hold it.

You are a passive person impassioned by escapes. Drugs, alcohol, sexual forays, and, of course, an overworked fantasy life all imbue your existence with the kind of luster you so long for.

You are a fervent excitement seeker who is easily bored, highly critical, perpetually discontent, and forever searching for the sublime. What you want most is to be swept off your feet in a semicomatose emotional fever.

Often you exist in a state of psychic pandemonium, seeking to create a decadent kind of drama. Quite easily you can turn your life into a masquerade that you stand back and watch, reverent and misty-eyed. Because your energies are inert, you wait for what you want. And as you watch your life pass by, through undercurrents of distilled anxiety, you just keep waiting and watching.

In marriage and more serious love relationships, you are dishonest and compulsively unfaithful. Because you are a slave to your sensibilities, you're easily seducible and just as easily discarded. The strong-willed women to whom you are so highly attracted become quickly fatigued with your farfetched schemes and dreams that always seem to disintegrate before they materialize. On the other hand, less willful women, who may hang on tightly and ultimately hook you into a marriage, end up lonely and unloved. One of the inherent paradoxes of your personality is that a man so emotional can also be capable of such coldness.

Because there is a duality to your nature, you need two kinds of women: one to alleviate your loneliness and one to give your life a romantic luster. In the conflicts that can arise from such a situation, you are the kind of coward who can cut someone so deeply that, many years after, the damage still remains.

The continued intensity that you try so painstakingly to create in your life comes from an awareness that you are withering away and going nowhere. On the lower levels, Pisceans cannot come to terms with the inevitability of the aging process, and, due to an anxiety over death, attempt desperately to make life more vivid. When taken to the extreme, this tendency can take you to a point of self-destruction, ironically bringing on what you most want to avoid. Embedded in such a miasma, life becomes more of a forgetting than an awakening.

At this low point, you may become a cripple searching for a cocoon. However, all that exists is the self-created bedlam that emotionally beguiles you.

On the most primitive level, this sign can become an institution unto itself. The consciousness is locked into place and permits no freedom. Loneliness, alienation, and fear force their way into a far-reaching fermentation that starts in the mind and ends by incapacitating the body.

Life continues its self-induced surrealism, and there is no sanctum that is long-lasting. In moments of solitude, sorrow submerges the mind and truths are avoided. And thus, another cycle of self-pity followed by a new resignation to find another refuge.

DECANS

Every sign in the zodiac can be broken down into three subdivisions, called decans. Each decan roughly corresponds to ten degrees—the first third, second third, and last third of the sun sign's time span, which is approximately thirty days.

As each of these periods has different subrulerships, the personality of a person is slightly modified by the specific decan it falls in. For instance, an Aries born in the second decan would be ruled by Mars, but subruled by the sun. Therefore, he would tend to display a greater sense of pride, boastfulness, egotism, and optimism than an Aries born in the third decan, which is subruled by Jupiter. This Aries would tend to be more freedom-loving, flighty, travel-oriented, and interested in subjects of a philosophical nature. An Aries born in the first decan would be the most aggressive, but not necessarily the most productive and accomplished.

Decans are important, since they do account for a more detailed assessment of an individual's personality characteristics. They also show how two people born under the same sun sign can be markedly different.

If you were born between February 20 and March 1, your sun falls in the Neptune decan of Pisces.

You are a classic romantic who loves to turn life into a pageant of poetry. You live in far-off dreams, plans, schemes, and self-induced drama. You are wistful, sentimental, highly emotional, and sometimes melancholy. Your mind is creative, often artistic, and always overactive. Relentlessly you search for divine highs, fantasies come true, and fabulously romantic situations. However, when troubled, you require solitude in which to sort out your more puzzling feelings.

While the circumstances that induce your momentary gloom seem hazy, so, quite often, is the state of your mind. Emotional confusion can sometimes lead to a withdrawn condition, and one day you realize that you just can't get out of bed—mainly because you don't want to. Sinking deeply into a maudlin mood is often a temptation. And during such times, you try to create a protective cocoon in which to withdraw, ruminate, and muse about your emotions.

However, despite your need to retreat into a more passive role, you usually have more internal resources at your disposal than most people. Your problem is that sometimes you don't know how to use them, and they get ignored and left untended.

It is likely that you have psychic sensitivities, a tremendous creative talent, and an inventive, original mind that could flourish in occult study.

However, the problem is that your emotions sometimes cripple you to the point that you are too fearful to carry out your own desires.

Once you rise above your tendency to take yourself down and hold yourself back, life will become more of a pleasure than a problem. However, first you must decide that you are more interested in trying than you are in giving up and passively accepting dissatisfying situations.

If you were born between March 2 and March 11, your sun falls in the lunar decan of Pisces.

You are more impressionable, changeable, and emotionally vulnerable than Pisces natives born in other decans. You are also highly imaginative, considerate, and caring.

Although you tend to be idealistic, you also possess the means for making your dreams materialize. You are tenacious, intuitive, intelligent, and struggle to overcome negative emotional states.

However, mood swings often undermine your feelings of self-confidence, and because of this, you should work assiduously toward greater self-discipline and emotional balance.

Deep within your nature is a conflict between your effort to make practical ideas materialize and a tendency toward inaction. Although your mind is highly original, your dreamy-eyed attitudes can stall your progress and put your plans into a state of dormancy. You have a keen sense of timing, but your tendency to wait things out often retards and restricts your ultimate results.

In general, you have an optimistic attitude toward life and express a deep enjoyment of life's more sensual pleasures. In the extreme, your sybaritic sensibilities can bring you more trouble than you care to anticipate. Until you learn to balance your impressionability with a more resolute pragmatism, you are in danger of becoming a victim of your own desires.

Once you establish an equilibrium between heated inspiration and cool, lucid logic, you will have the key to accomplishment at your disposal.

If you were born between March 12 and March 20, your sun falls in the Pluto decan of Pisces.

This is the most powerful decan of this sign, because its association is with the concept of death and rebirth. It is likely that you have heavy karma from which you have to free yourself by calling upon the highest spiritual forces. Painful subconscious memories are pulling you back into the past. However, it is important that you reexperience these memories long enough to finally resolve them and ultimately free yourself of them forever. New cycles of experience are awaiting you. However, first you must purify your consciousness of its dross material.

Intrinsic to this decan is the alchemic concept of change in its most profound manifestation. Either on a psychological or physical level, it is likely that you have undergone many deathlike experiences. At times, the torrent of upheaval has seemed almost more than you can bear. However, each time, you have transcended your pain through the power that exists within you.

Because of this decan's association with Pluto, your soul must undergo the fire of transmutation before you are ready to go on. This experience can be very painful, because it always brings about some kind of loss. However, once you have helped yourself evolve to the higher levels of consciousness, then you will understand automatically that what you are losing is merely a negative situation or experience that will only imprison you if it continues to exist.

If you resist the change that occurs organically within your life, and you prefer to get stuck in past habits, memories, experiences, and relationships that you no longer need for growth, then you will be creating tremendous pain for yourself. For at a certain point in your life, all such experiences will be leaving you, whether or not you like it. And to resist is to go against the Tao, the inherent flux and flow of the universe.

If, instead, you use each experience as a door through which you can gain, first, greater self-awareness, and, second, greater spiritual awareness, then you will be moving toward the cycle of liberation and rebirth as seen in the following sign, Aries. The meaning of Aries is new beginnings created by the self-directed will. This is an unfettered will that is free to bring about the changes it so needs in its own experience. And, therefore, it implies a great deal of individual power.

Eminent in this decan is the idea of sacrifice. You must first be willing to sacrifice the old, destructive life patterns before new, constructive ones can reformulate experience. And if you are not willing to do this, inherently you will be sacrificing yourself to the chains of the past that are still pulling you down.

An extraordinary amount of psychic power can be developed if you are willing to march forward in devotion to the higher forces. And thus, within this decan can be born the spiritual prophet, the guru, the magician, and the monk, each of whom has been able to relinquish recidivistic patterns to the All. And for what they have given, they have gained nothing less than the highest power of the universe.

LOVE

Although you often loathe your vulnerable side, you're a wild romantic itching for emotional intensity. You want your soul to be swept away by nothing less than a grand passion.

You're a highly charged sensualist who'd love to live out a Rabelaisian fantasy. However, in such situations you often let your emotions get the better of you. You're an emotionally attached lover living in the dream of how exquisite your life could be if only . . .

Needless to say, you're an idealist who is both dreamy-eyed and devoted to the act of loving. However, the problem is that too often you become enslaved by negative situations and hang on to the past like a drowning swimmer embracing a sinking boat. When you really want someone, you'll sit back and wait interminably, feeling that time will be able to change conditions that you can't.

When your romantic life is really wretched, you get dreary and depressed, and feel lonely, unloved, and alienated. The next step is to seek escape through drinking, drugs, sleeping, eating, promiscuous sex, or overwork.

On your more devastating days, you seek solitude. One of your favorite things is to crawl under the covers and curl into a ball, feeling sorry for yourself and wishing the world wouldn't be so unsparing. At this point, the pain is so intense that it almost becomes a kind of pleasure.

However, when the time comes that you feel like a bitter, jaded, loveless victim, remember that it was you who made all the choices. In compromising a sense of total satisfaction in order to gain emotional security that existed only in your mind's eye, somehow you lost. On the other hand, maybe you learned something. In the end, your love life is merely a statement of what you *think* you deserve. Therefore, if you're not getting what you want, maybe you should just stop crying about it and decide not to settle till you get it.

MARRIAGE

Because you have a roving eye and a forked tongue, marriage is not always your best bet. Monogamy can be a problem, especially if you choose a mate who might murder you in a moment of sweet revenge.

At a certain point, when all the surface excitement seems to be calming down, marriage seems like a secure thing. Because you think in terms of beginnings rather than endings, you are loath to contemplate the termination of an affair.

You would prefer that you and all your lovers could remain friends forever. A civilized amount of distance combined with a number of friendly visits would suit you nicely and leave you room enough to roam.

However, at one time or another you usually sell out your visions of romantic splendor for marital security. And here is where the fun either ends or begins, depending on which direction you want to go. Married life would be ideal if you lived in a Zulu colony, where polygamy isn't considered a perversity. You often choose a very individual route of infidelity, especially when you have one of those alchemic attractions that make your pupils dilate or you get so drunk that anybody starts to look good.

Deep inside, you are searching for a kind of narcotic attraction that makes you feel like you're once again seventeen and heartbroken. But the fiftieth time around, it's surprising how that pain starts to feel familiar and kind of cozy. It has the kind of poetry in motion of which marriages never seem to be made (at least, to your thinking). However, on the other hand, marriage has something specific to say for itself. It's the security of knowing that somebody close loves you, even if your cheekbones start to sink and your teeth turn green.

Many Pisceans can remain faithful once they've made a marital commitment. However, it's the Pisces men who are more prone to wander around in search of more sensational thrills. In such situations, the deception is done with remarkable dispassion and astounding alacrity. Marriage, Pisces style, is like having two dates for the same football game. One person gets the grandstand with a front-row seat, the other a quick hot dog during intermission.

MONEY

Money slips through your fingers like quicksilver, and, quite clearly, you have no idea why.

You especially love to spend it on dreary days when you feel lost and abandoned to the doldrums. A few divine highs, regardless of the cost, can bring you back swiftly to a far more sanguine self.

Luxury gives you a plethora of pleasure. Some Dom Perignon can easily help you through the night—along with silk sheets and, of course, an elegant body to keep you company.

You really don't require a country estate with a team

of servants (although it would be very nice). However, what you do crave is comfort, and sometimes your version of it can be quite costly.

While a Sagittarian would be thrilled with the prospect of living in a barn, because it has that adventurous "outdoorsy" effect, you seek those little final touches that can easily take you into debt if you don't watch it.

On the other hand, the spiritual side of you can make a home out of a blanket and refer to the sky as the roof. On this level, the only interest you might have in money would be in giving it away.

However, it is likely that you have a long way to go before you get that far. Therefore, in the meantime, when it comes to spending, try to consider your priorities. Unless you can pay for a merry-go-round of pleasure, try to challenge yourself to find happiness with a little less.

CAREER

Unless you have a lot of fire or earth in your chart, it is highly likely that you're not exactly a barracuda in the business world. There are some Pisceans who are extremely ambitious. However, this has much to do with other factors in the horoscope and little if anything to do with the sun sign.

In general, Pisceans prefer a quiet life to one of corporate competition. They also look upon the anxiety-ridden superachievers with a sardonic disdain.

Therefore, if you are what is referred to as a typical Piscean, it is likely that you desire to be a comfortable bystander rather than a high-pressure mogul. Your mind probably seeks a haven from the nagging worries of the outside world, so the pandemonium of a business office would only exhaust and depress you.

You are the artist, the poet, the psychic, the mystic, and the musician. Because of your vital imagination and inherent need to escape the impinging world, acting and writing can provide a creative catharsis. Painting, sculpturing, and filmmaking are also fruitful possibilities that could pave your way to success.

Chances are you're so talented that you really don't know what to do with yourself. However, aside from artistic endeavors, you often have spiritual proclivities that could take you far away from the "madding crowd." You could be a mystic, a monk, a guru, a priest, or a magician living a solitary Spartan existence.

Because Pisces is a sign of exceptional psychic ability, mediumship, psychic readings, and psychometry are areas to which you are particularly well-suited. Healing is another, so you might consider either medicine or psychic therapy.

Even if you don't become physically involved in healing, you often have a desire to be of service. Therefore, psychology, criminal counseling, social work, and various areas of rehabilitation are excellent professions for imbuing your life with a sense of purpose.

In the end, whatever you choose, a paucity of talent will never be the problem. However, an inner lack of self-confidence, along with a tendency to be terribly indecisive, may be. Once you break down these barriers within yourself, the world at large will be more than happy to welcome your worthy contributions. And you will rise like the star you always yearned to be.

FRIENDS

You can never say no to a friend in need. Undeniably, your shoulders have developed a great muscle tone from all the dreary heads that lean on them. Because your solace is sought after in the most miserable moments, you are the kind of friend no one can ever forget.

You are loyal, understanding, kind, compassionate, deeply caring, and always happy to be of help. You inspire the love you receive and give even more back in the long run.

Although a part of your soul will always classify you as a loner, there is another part that loves to be with people. Lots of people contact helps you glide through those murky moods that can be so confining. It also enables you to take your own emotions less seriously when confronted by the presence of other bleeding hearts.

You keep your closest friends for years, and often for a lifetime. Such friendships illuminate your life with the deepest kind of meaning. Chances are, your close friends are as important as your family. No matter how famous you become or how many people surround you, your most important friendships will never lose their meaning. Rather, with the coming years they will grow much deeper, richer, and closer.

HEALTH

Your biggest problem is emotional instability and despondency, leading to drugs and alcohol usage. Such induced escapism is not only harmful because of its destructive effect on the body, it can also bring on astral experiences that may be more than the mind can handle.

The very young Piscean constitution is often weak and predisposed to illness. However, as an adult this can be overcome by vitamin supplements, a scrupulous diet, plenty of sunshine, and regular exercise. Stick to foods that are rich in protein to give you the energy that you need to take on the world. Excessive drinking and drug usage can leave you sluggish, listless, and feeling a little hopeless about handling life's daily challenges.

Also, because of an iron-phosphate deficiency, you may feel fatigue, headaches, glandular disorders, and depression. Research has shown that this is somehow a particularly Piscean ailment that can be easily eradicated by eating such foods as lettuce, cucumbers, almonds, walnuts, raisins, strawberries, and radishes.

Finally, because Pisces rules the feet, sometimes you can suffer peculiar accidents or maladies in that area. Shoes that serve a practical purpose are far more important than those that merely look good. If you have to, make sure that you can satisfy both conditions. Also, promptly see your doctor if foot pain seems to be putting you temporarily out of commission. A little preventive medicine is, in the long run, worth far more than any cure.

HOME

Ideally, your home is your love castle, complete with a sprawling view of the sea. Because you find your roots most easily in ocean soil, a beach house is best, with a front yard of sand castles to remind you of your dreams come true.

A living room with glass walls and a majestic fireplace is a perfect place for creating Piscean fantasies. In the middle, a white L-shaped couch sprawls on a lime-green wall-to-wall shag, giving the room a kind of forest effect.

Create bursts of indirect lighting on rheostats to synchronize with the changeable Piscean mood level. And place quadraphonic speakers in clever places to pick up the intensity of the treble and dramatize the total sound.

In the spacious, sun-drenched kitchen, allow the dignity of a fig tree to fill out some empty spaces. At the same time, the bedroom speaks of color, in luscious blues, lavenders, and pale greens—on the walls, the floor, the bed, the telephone . . . Dazzle the ceiling with hanging plants. Cover one wall with a mirror, but save one for a total sea view.

Create a sun room for those creative moments of painting, writing, thinking, daydreaming. Choose a desk of solid glass and keep a crystal vase of fresh flowers on the side as a silent token of welcome. Let your own paintings transform the barren walls, to remind yourself of your invincible talent. And, finally, place a towering palm in the corner to bring a touch of the faraway right into your more intimate thoughts.

In the bathroom, set up a cork bulletin board, and on it paste postcards, meaningful mementos, and birthday tokens you can't bear to part with. Go in and read them on dreary days to remind yourself how much you are appreciated, loved, and admired.

COSMIC CHALLENGE

Your cosmic challenge is to acquire a constructive use of your own free will. Too often, you fall prey to outside influences and fail to take responsibility for the consequences of your actions.

However, your violent recriminations are misdirected. You make your own choices and therefore must suffer the consequences of them.

Until you realize that you are not a victim, but rather a willful human being, you will always hold yourself back from what you think you want. Rather than wasting time on self-deception, try to be clearer about your choices. In the long run, it will save you from sorrowful situations and may also bring you something very precious that you never thought was possible.

INSPIRATION

You are the twelfth sign of the zodiac, the end of the circle of reincarnation. Within your being is the possibility of the greatest aspiration, the final unification of the Godhead. However, this is only possible when you transmute your emotions to the highest level and dwell in the universal love that your sign represents.

Because you carry the collective energy of all the signs, you have a great responsibility to yourself to act in accord with your higher self. However, when you misuse the energy of your soul in self-destructive acts, you create a prison of pain and confusion that simply closes in. At this point, Pisces becomes the sign of sorrows. However, the sorrows are of self-undoing, not of afflictions coming from the external world.

When you act from your higher self, you will bring on new beginnings that will better your life. Your mind will expand with each new experience in a state of oneness with the divine source of eternal light.

WHAT HOLDS YOU BACK
AND HOW TO OVERCOME IT

You tend to be an escapist who will use any means, whether it is your own mind, drugs, or alcohol, as a blinder against what you don't want to see.

Pisces is a sign known to have a high incidence of alcoholism and narcotics addiction. Unevolved natives born into this sign are also notoriously passive to the circumstances of their own life, while they create a miasma of misery for those close to them. They drown in a mire of self-destructive emotion that brings them further and further into the depths of despair. On the lowest level, these tendencies can bring them to the brink of suicide. This is why astrologers often flippantly refer to Pisces as the garbage pail of the zodiac.

Until you accept responsibility for your own actions, you will be battered about not only by the external elements but also by your own confusion and emotional chaos. The feelings of depression, melancholy, and alienation that you experience are the result of wrong choices and negative thinking. If you want your life to be different, you have to do something about it. Wishing it were so is simply not enough. Too often your daydreams displace assiduous efforts, and you deluge yourself and those you love in false promises of change and development. However, until you take control of your life and walk out from under your umbrella of illusion, your mind acts as a noose around your own neck. And the more you evade your earthly responsibilities, the more the noose tightens.

LOVE AND
COMPATIBILITY GUIDE

Pisces with Pisces

This starts off as poetry in motion. However, after you come in for a landing, then what?

Somebody has to pitch in with a little realism. And, chances are, neither of you really knows where to begin. You both smile, look searchingly at the other, and mutter, "Well . . ."

As time passes and you're still smiling, you could lead each other to the heights or to an indefinite stay in the depths. It all depends where you prefer to spend your time *and* your money.

At the very least, you can become best friends, although part of the time that's a little like the blind leading the blind. However, if and when you put your heads together and at least *one* of you can see where you're going, then the trip is really worth it.

Because you both can be highly confused creatures, you have to be clear about why you're tying your lives together. At first, you may feel that you've found your alter ego.

In essence, this is a warm, close relationship that could get very comfortable. However, both of you need a lot of strength and support, which you might find missing here. If you can provide it for each other without bringing the other down, this could be the romance of the century. However, if that is not an outcome of this coupling, do consider the possibility of other people. Life is too short to get lost in a dream that just keeps on re-peating itself.

Pisces Woman with Aries Man

For you it's almost love at first sight, whether or not you want to show it. But that's just for sexual starters. After the first few nights, he's still in the running for a total ravagement of your mind and body. However, after you witness how selfish he can be in the daytime with the sun shining in his eyes, then it's quite another matter if the love continues.

You are still searching for that knight on his white horse to come and whisk you away. Superficially, he'll fulfill your fantasies, but underneath, not only will he not understand you, he won't even have the patience to try.

You have a way of getting your feelings hurt at the most inconvenient moments, and he has a way of treading on them without either realizing it or wanting to be aware of it. He'll be inflamed when you withdraw and become sad and sulky. At the same time, it causes you to despair when you see that he can be so insensitive.

He acts first and thinks later, while you have a way of sitting still and just feeling. He needs a woman who will challenge him, support him, and make him a little in-secure. You need a man who will love you, support you, and make you very secure.

You need a lot of time and attention. He also needs a lot of attention, but he has very little time. In the end, this relationship is better off without expectations, yours or his. Just play it as it lays, and you may find in the end that you have more than you both bargained for.

Pisces Woman with Taurus Man

He is like a big house that you can lean up against; and only a Taurus man can stand the weight.

You are a fragile, vulnerable creature with a mental makeup that he'll never understand. He is a stolid force with a matter-of-fact philosophy that totally eludes you because it's so simple.

The compatibility here is not exactly attention-get-ting; however, the underlying needs that are satisfied are something else. You both tend to be enslaved by the sensu-al pleasures that quicken the pulse and speed up the bloodstream. You both like to sleep in the sun and sip cold drinks to the strains of melodious love songs. You both could adore a marathon of sex from dawn till the disappearance of daylight. And you both prefer a body that is naked to one that is nicely dressed.

At this point, the similarities start to dwindle. You are emotional and weepy, while he is practical and puts his emotions in a place where they don't show. Your sacred dwelling is in daydreams, while his is in a material dynasty rooted in the earth. You are an ephemeral creature of the clouds; he is a man of a multimillion-dollar corporation.

He finds you to be seductive, alluring, and at times more mysterious than his mind can take. You find him to be solid, stubborn, sensual, and someone you can depend on. Your inherent creativity can bloom under his love and protection. His sense of purpose can become inflamed under your support.

Together, you could become a worthwhile team if your divergent approaches to life don't get in the way.

Pisces Woman with Gemini Man

You are both enigmas; the difference is that you have depth. You are emotional, empathetic, compassionate, and moody. He is cerebral, self-centered, critical, and moody.

Despite the externals, deep down you are shy and unsure of yourself. More often than not, you will find him uncaring and he will find you confining.

You are sensual and winsome but don't exactly devastate him with the kind of logical comments that cut a space in his attention span. You are in touch with your feelings, but he hates to take the time to even think about the fact that he has any.

You remember your commitments and honor them, while he promises his life away but forgets what he's said within five minutes.

Deep down inside, you seek emotional security, while he seeks the perfect state of freedom. He can be callous and abrupt with you, and at the same time chummy with the world. Your feelings are badly bruised when he conspicuously ignores you at an intimate dinner party. But your feelings fly away when later he whispers clever love lines in your ear. In between, the heights of misery may make you feel that life's not worth living. It isn't, with him; you need a man with a lot of warmth to offer. And the warmth that Mr. Gemini has just doesn't seem to go very far.

Pisces Woman with Cancer Man

The psychic rapport of this match will leave you starry-eyed. He will sympathize with your mood swings, cry along with you in teary grade-B movies, and remember what you wore on the day he first met you.

You will marvel that he is a better cook than you are, that he is equally as sensitive, and that he seems to know not only what you're thinking but why.

You'll both find yourselves saying the same thing simultaneously; you'll finish each other's sentences and respect each other's ideas.

This relationship is one made for lazy weekends at ocean retreats, evenings of champagne and candlelight, winter afternoons of Bach, quiet talk, and a snifter of brandy.

Prepare for a lifetime of love on the beach under the stars or beside a bowl of roses and an open window that lets the moonlight peep in.

Pisces Woman with Leo Man

You'll whine around a lot, which can get pretty boring, but what you do in bed is something else altogether. You are the supersensualist. You talk through your body, and your language levitates his solar plexus. Naturally, he'll like to have you around, but, being the restless sort, it's a question of how long.

For a while you feed each other on dreams, and the air will reek of romance. In this relationship, neither of you cherishes the light of day. It's candlelight and love —all the way to the wedding. But after that point it can be loneliness if you start emerging from the mental mist unprepared.

In the long run, you are too passive for his patience level, and he is too self-centered for your sensitivities. You'll smother him with love, but you won't stimulate him, and he'll clutter up your life with trinkets to make you momentarily forget you have feelings. You'll mope about and lose your sparkle. He'll become abrupt and increasingly busy. You'll take a lover, and he'll spend eve-

nings at the office. One day you might collide in the kitch-
en, and each of you will see a stranger and not know how
the stranger got there. Neither will ask. But both of you
will wonder—all the way to the divorce court.

Mr. Leo must keep in mind that you are ultrafemi-
nine and frightened but capable of very deep feelings. If
he ignores you, you will wither. But if he expects you
to confront him, he'll spend a lifetime waiting. You'll
never challenge him with a strength of steel or stimulate
him with a dynamic independence. You'll lean on him if
you love him, and cry rather than command. Your sensitivity will be his shackle unless he alleviates your insecurity, and this comes from tenderness, not trinkets.

You represent one of the few signs that can let the
feelings flow. And although you may not be quite indestructible, you have strength through vulnerability. He
acknowledges only stiff-upper-lip strength, so he won't recognize this subtlety. Until he opens his head and his heart
and learns how to unite them, this man is better off bypassed.

Pisces Woman with Virgo Man

You find comfort in chaos, while he craves the kind
of order found from control. You long for a life of never-
ending emotional excitement. He prefers the kind of stability that could give you sleeping sickness.

You are emotionally moved by grade-B movies,
glamorous nights on the town, and ghost stories. He is
moved by the mechanics of his mind and the number of
shelves in his new file cabinet.

Basically, you are both so different that if you manage to get past the first five dates, then you may decide
you have something. However, a strong compatibility will
never exist, nor the kind of emotional rapport that obviates verbal communication.

He doesn't see the value of poetry, because it can't
be proven. You, on the other hand, can't see the importance of his structures, because they leave no room for
spontaneity. On a spring night he'll want to stay home
and put his tax receipts in order; you want to go out and
paint the town. You'll occasionally overdo the brandy
alexanders while he fidgets with his skim milk.

You both may grumble at the other's way of doing
things, but you are both cognizant of the good intentions

that motivate these actions. Although he may be critical and at times fussy, he'll try to take care of you to the best of his ability. And because of your sympathetic and intuitive nature, you'll be able to see through his systems and straight into his heart.

Your differences are entirely too great for a smooth-running relationship. And your sensitivities are disparate enough for the kind of divorce that seems to deny there ever was a love.

Pisces Woman with Libra Man

He will probably never understand your moods, your chaotic emotions, or the fact that you need far more reassurance than he wants to give you.

You are fearful of your feelings, while he has a way of enjoying his. He relies on reasoning to gather insights; you know that your intuition will get you anywhere. He sees the world as a sharply defined puzzle, while you feel it in pastel hues.

Sexually, you will sweep him off his feet, but emotionally he may feel that you bring him down. You have a way of seeing all the sorrow in the world; he sees only what gives him pleasure. You have a side that bubbles with a serious intensity, but he prefers joviality to sobriety.

You have a way of being selfless; he has a tendency to take and forget to say thank you. You will listen to his complaints and will understand his problems. On difficult days, you will nurture his needs and smother him with love. The problem is, can he do the same for you?

Unless he has a very high sense of awareness, this relationship is not an equal one. However, it can be happy, peaceful, and very calm. You have never felt that you deserve that much. And until you reach that moment of reckoning, it's not fair to expect him to give you what you won't even ask for.

Pisces Woman with Scorpio Man

Sexually, this combination is so powerful that you may both end up on the floor. You'll control him through your desire, and he'll devour you through his control. You may both expire because of the sheer exhaustion of the situation, but what a way to go.

Since this kind of chemistry is narcotic, expect to

get hooked. When you are together, it may come to the point that you stop eating, sleeping, and thinking, and start losing weight.

Although your abandoned sensuality sends him past his fantasies, your passivity will ultimately begin to bore him. A little splendor in the afternoon is energizing, but too much passion is sheer dissipation.

His moods will drag you down, and your dependence will irritate him. He likes his emotions to be challenged; you like yours to be gratified. He likes a woman who is ambitious, self-possessed, and successful. You are looking for those same qualities in a man—so that he can take care of you.

Any way you look at it, this is a sex-is-all kind of love story. Indoors, there are no limits, but what do you do when it's snowing and you're standing in silence on the street? Chances are, he'll do something to make you start crying so that he can take a deep breath and walk away. If there's anything he despises, it's phlegmatic females. So, look for someone else. The world is waiting.

Pisces Woman with Sagittarius Man

You'll fall in love with his boyish charm and wild enthusiasm. But after a while you'll realize that his warmth can be turned on quite casually and impersonally, at will.

He will be seduced by your steamy sensuality and will delight in your daily do-good attitudes. However, the deeper differences between the two of you are enough to create a substantial kind of conflict.

Your emotions are profound; his are playful. Therein lies the problem that may bring you a lot of pain. Mistakenly, you often choose a flashy fellow who hands out lots of surface excitement but holds back when it comes to caring. And Mr. Sagittarius falls into this category like a paperweight coursing down a manhole.

He is friendly, cheerful, and very charming, but when it comes to women, he's like a used-car salesman who lives in anticipation of next year's models. In addition, he's so perpetually busy that whenever you see him, you have a feeling of being worked into a crowded schedule.

If you can view this encounter as a brief but fantastic affair rather than as a future marriage prospect, then nothing will be lost. However, if you decide to wait until he's seen the world and wants to settle down, you will first find yourself in a geriatric clinic.

It is perilous for you to mistake him for your knight in shining armor. It is far more likely that he will run you down than scoop you up into a trusty saddle.

Pisces Woman with Capricorn Man

He will be the father figure you've searched for, and you will be his woman of romance. You need a strong man you can depend on, and he needs a woman who knows how to need. You'll bolster his ego when you come running to him for his counsel and a shoulder to cry on. In turn, he'll tell you what to do and demand that you follow his instructions implicitly.

Emotionally, he'll never understand where you're coming from or where you're going. You cry over things that he could not care less about, like sad stories in the news, the problems of people whom you'll never even meet, and your own enigmatic moods that seem, to his sensibilities, silly. At times, Mr. Capricorn has the uncomfortable feeling that there's a part of you that will always be a stranger. He's probably right. However, there are also those times when your womanly warmth just sweeps him away and the impending matters of the outside world no longer seem so important.

He imbues you with some practicality, while you imbue him with a poetic sensitivity that he never even knew he was capable of. Together, if you are determined to learn from your differences, you can create a love relationship that will put you in touch with yourselves as well as with each other.

Pisces Woman with Aquarius Man

Although you respect his intelligence, it wears your nerves a little thin when you yawn because it's midnight and he's still babbling on about electron microscopes.

He has absolutely no idea where you're coming from, but he has a wealth of theories. However, each of them, while truly interesting, somehow misses the mark by a long shot.

Basically, he filters the world through his mind, and you sift it through your emotions. You are a romantic sentimentalist, while he is a restless man of many interests. He is the humanitarian who feels a lot for everybody but very little for any person in particular. On the other hand, you are the angel of mercy with the kind of emotions that bring the world right into your living room.

You are so deeply feeling that you are fearful of your own emotions, while he is so cerebral that his feelings have a hard time getting through. As friends you could probably take each other to delightful places. You could teach him how to appreciate poetry and how to use meditation to slow his mind down. In turn, he could imbue you with a little Einstein theory and explain to you the importance of polyisomers.

However, as a serious love affair this probably won't be long-lasting. Both of you are lovable people, but the emotional differences will eventually drive you apart.

Pisces Man with Aries Woman

Her temper may give you nightmares, but what she does to your daydreams is quite another matter. You are destined to fall flat on your face in love, but she won't want to hear about it or see it.

You are too subjective for her sensitivities and have a way of making her feel like she's working in a clinic for the emotionally disturbed. You try her patience, never get to the point, and drive her to a state of insanity with your moods.

She needs a man strong enough to push her around after she steps on his feet. However, you will just let Ms. Aries stand there and play bus stop.

At the same time, she does need a lot of love and approval, and you can truly drown her with devotion. However, when your sentimentality starts to ooze, and she suddenly feels more suffocated than aroused, you should know you're nearing the beginning of the end.

You see her as a sadomasochistic kind of challenge. She sees you as a noose around her neck that keeps getting tighter. At the end, through your tears, you'll wish her the worst. But she'll be so happy that she'll wish you the best as she barrels her way out of your life forever, screaming.

Pisces Man with Taurus Woman

You are a fantasy addict while she prefers facing the facts. If she marries you, she'll take on the responsibility of a caretaker in a home for the convalescent.

You can't be bothered with day-to-day details, so she has to assume what you shun. You are overflowing with sympathy for the underprivileged. However, should she develop an acute case of bronchial pneumonia, you'll still expect her to bring in the car for the yearly checkup.

During bad times, you'll lean on her so hard that she'll fall over. But when she needs you, you'll be so far into fantasyland that you won't even know that she's there. Marriage with you is a kind of do-it-yourself existence, except that she's doing for two, not one.

Undoubtedly, you will feel that she's one fine person. The problem is that you think that about every woman on the street as well as your lovers on the side.

In the divorce court, you'll tell your lawyer that she taught you a lot. What you taught her is that marriage is not really the wonder that she hoped it might be.

Pisces Man with Gemini Woman

This combination is so incongruous that the only qualities you have in common are that you are both human (hopefully) and that you are both alive (even more hopefully).

In a remarkably short period of time, she will mutter to herself that you are just a garbage pail of emotion. At the same time, you will think quite secretly that she is nothing but a chatterbox and an emotional void. What you won't admit is that even if you can't stand her, she's also such a challenge that you fear you love her. Now, if she tries to understand all this, it means that already she's spending too much time with you for her own good.

You are like a damp blanket that makes her nostrils twitch. She is like a relentless buzzing sound zinging through your brain. You are mawkishly sentimental and regard your own melancholy as invincibly romantic. However, even when she's depressed, she's too detached to know she's sad.

You think her mind is a fascinating puzzle. She thinks your burgeoning emotions make you a self-obsessed bore. You feel that her personality is consumed by trivia, while she is convinced that you don't know the difference.

After a while, she will just wish you'd go off and drown yourself in your own emotions. However, you still daydream that her glacial heart will give you a chance. The only chance she's willing to consider is a peaceful parting. Her mind is just too restless to be forced to focus on such a sideshow of sentimentality. And to truly get her attention, you're not above weeping through a megaphone.

Pisces Man with Cancer Woman

You will find her so nice to cuddle with. In addition, she will create a plethora of seductive creature comforts and provide the emotional backup that you need to do your best.

Not only is she warm and sensitive, she has the kind of womanly strength that reminds you of Mother. She will understand your moods, listen to your problems, and lend you a lot of loving assistance for those projects you know you'll never finish.

In turn, you will write her love poems, send her daffodils in January, and bring her champagne to sip by the sea.

With rapturous enthusiasm you'll make her feel that she's a combination of Wonder Woman and Aphrodite. You'll lavish praises on her femininity and provide her with the encouragement she so craves.

Sexually, you'll both send up smoke signals, drums will start to beat, bells will start to ring, and you may find out that you are deeply in love.

In essence, this combination could be a divine exploration into the deepest experience of loving. The communication here may carry you to the farthest planes of feeling.

Pisces Man with Leo Woman

You fall in love fast and send her skyward with verbal splendors. Unfortunately, you go on talking too long.

The younger she is, the better this duo. If she's known a few Pisceans in her lifetime, she is probably wary and impatient. She'll tell you that she has time to listen for only a brief while.

At sixty, you still seek a romance more fabulous than your fantasies. Needless to say, you rarely find it. The sad part is that you never stop looking.

Last week, to attest to your love, you promised her your life. This week, she catches you clandestinely kissing someone else. She might try to accept your unbelievable explanation. More likely, she'll settle into a state of anger and silent sorrow. And swiftly, the mood music changes from "La Vie en Rose" to "Rhapsody in Blue."

Unlike her tenacious sister Ms. Taurus, she won't stick around for more of the same. One deceit scene, and she's out the door, her lover wishing he was dead, if he already isn't. With you, she might as well keep all exits open.

Although you mean well, you are deformed by a shriveled superego. In your fantasy world of ideals, guilt has no place. You are capable of being honest about many things, but not about yourself. You embrace an infantile idea of romance and dwell on the memories of your most divine love. You are addicted to your larger-than-life luster. The problem is that you can't tell the difference between love and addiction. The burden is on her, the blame on you. So if she chooses to get involved in your game of emotional Monopoly, at least be fair—make sure that she's the banker.

Pisces Man with Virgo Woman

She is quiet, shy, and very sensible. You are chaotic, dreamy-eyed, and consumed by farfetched fantasies.

You have a mind that seems to be traveling in too many time zones. On the other hand, she thinks straight ahead and doesn't get distracted by emotional side trips.

She may find your daydreams fascinating. However, she'll probably choke and sputter over the constant confusion you seem to live in. She loves to have her time organized, while you can't commit yourself seven seconds into the future. She feels secure when she can create a premeditated order; you take spontaneity to the most peculiar extremes.

She needs a warm, stable, enduring kind of love, whereas you seek the drama of a Russian play and a woman who is more of a daring dance partner than a human being who may make demands.

After a time, she will probably watch her patience dwindle as she starts to realize how easily you can turn the romance into a kind of riot. Meanwhile, your attention span has probably wandered past your fifth martini, and you're wondering how you'll ever get to meet Sophia Loren.

You're a man whose mind melts before breaking, while Ms. Virgo is the kind of woman who prefers immediate action to a lot of ethereal thinking. The differences here are entirely too awesome for a tranquil relationship. Trying to force this relationship to work is like an exercise in tormenting your soul.

Pisces Man with Libra Woman

You are a sentimentalist who will send her soaring past the limits of her logic. You will make her feel she's the first woman you've ever wooed and the only one you ever want to. Together you will enter into a dreamlike existence where love becomes a drug more debilitating than the fruits of the poppy.

However, one day she may wake up from her romantic interlude to note that she is lying next to a man who is weaker than she is. At this point she may slowly break out in an aggravated case of acne as she tries to decide what to do for the next lively episode.

Basically, she is an open person who loves to communicate her feelings. However, outside of a few effusive rhapsodies about the way you feel when the light shines on her hair, you are for the most part closed. She has a reverent attitude toward her own emotions, while you would rather keep yours in the closet. She loves shared experience, but there is very little of yourself you are willing to let loose. You exist pretty much in the vault of your subconscious fantasies; she can spend a lifetime trying to make her daydreams become real.

Emotionally, you both might be coming from similar places. However, how you approach life is different enough to create frictions of a minor sort. Fundamentally, Ms. Libra wants a man she can lean on. You also want someone to lean on, so if she leans on you, the two of you will topple over. However, if she is willing to bypass emotional support for simple companionship and doesn't mind enduring a regular assortment of murky moods, it may be worth a try. She may end up with a bad back, because you can really be a heavy load, but whatever makes her happy is worth a little physical sacrifice.

Pisces Man with Scorpio Woman

You'll treat her like a drug. The problem is that she's a woman and wants to be treated like one. That is the essence of the problems between you.

Sexually, you are the passive sort. In love, you are a garbage pail of emotion. And in regard to romance, you prefer the drug dream of her distant approach far more than her personal appearance.

She is pragmatic; you are a drunken idealist. Emotionally, she is serious, while you are mawkishly sentimental. She is a strong survivor. You are weak, sniffling, and whiny.

It is true that you are as frail as your fantasies. And in a time of crisis, you'll cry on her shoulder. However, she should not let all this flimflam fool her. When caught in an emotional cul-de-sac, you can be cruel, sadistic, and cunning. And although, emotionally, you may understand where Ms. Scorpio is coming from she shouldn't expect you to appreciate it—especially if she assails you with a human need.

In a woman, you are looking for both a movie star and a mother. If she happens to fit both roles and wants to play them, she's got you—as long as she doesn't mind sharing you with a few others. And she *will* know about the others, because when you're being unfaithful, you're careless enough to make her trip over the evidence.

You consider yourself to be mysterious, but even squinting, she can see through you. Despite what you may think, you never created subtlety. You learned it somewhere from a Scorpio. And judging from your behavior, that's only a fraction of the learning you still have in store.

Pisces Man with Sagittarius Woman

You are dreamy-eyed, sentimental, and totally divorced from the reality that is going on around you. She is impulsive, undeniably chaotic, and conscious that there must be something that she is missing. Well, she should look a little longer, because it's not you.

She is so flighty that she needs a strong hand to grab her by the neck and ground her. Yours is limp, probably clammy, and so flexible that it feels like it's made of foam. Together, you can take many sensational side trips into the world of the paranormal. She'll appreciate your complete collection of William Blake, soar to the ceiling when you invite her to her first séance, and then treat you like a guru when you read her tarot cards correctly.

However, in the daylight, under the bustling burdens of common responsibilities, such as paying the rent, you are of little or no help. She might consider being friends with you but shouldn't consider marrying you unless she wants to play mama or big strong woman. You are looking for a shoulder to lean on, and a very firm one at that.

You are sure to fall in love with her life force, the way she makes you laugh, and the freedom-loving way she lives her life. You see her as a challenge, and she is. You will share her dreams, her fantasies, and delight in all of her far-off travels. And together you can have a lot of fun doing foolish things and dwelling on the romantic superficials of falling in love.

However, the price she will have to pay for all of these good times is supporting a weak man who has been known to wander sexually. It's true that you can be extraordinarily charming, but unless you can also learn to stand up by yourself, your charm will inevitably lose its luster. You can make her believe that you have the world on a string. You have, but the string is in your head, where all cobblers can be kings if they dream enough.

Pisces Man with Capricorn Woman

At first, you will seem romantic and sentimental; on closer inspection, you appear weak and wishy-washy. You have a hard time dealing with the day-to-day world; she thrives in a competitive, corporate milieu.

Your mind is floating somewhere above the clouds, but hers is rooted firmly to the earth. She finds your ultimate objectives vague, your emotions inconstant and your approach definitely escapist. You spend more time trying to get out of something than you do in ultimately doing it. And when she asks you what you want and what you think you're looking for, she gets an answer so nebulous that it assures her you haven't the vaguest idea yourself.

Ms. Capricorn is a no-nonsense person who doesn't have time for adolescent instability in an adult whose hair is turning gray. Her attitude is: Either shape up or ship out. Yours is: Take me or leave me, but don't bug me.

You fancy yourself a poet in a world of worry. She finds you to be a spineless escapist who would prefer to vegetate until you are "discovered."

Any way you look at it, your way is not her way, unless she likes giving generously and getting very little back.

Pisces Man with Aquarius Woman

She lives in the future; you often get stuck in the past. She is friendly yet detached, whereas you are more aloof and sentimental. She scatters her feelings among dozens of people, but you nurture yours in private places.

Basically, you are both so different that you seem to be traveling in opposite directions. She requires change and constant activity; you are content with the status quo. She gets inflamed by social injustice, while you prefer to pass the time dreaming about a utopia. She demands honesty for any committed relationship, but you are of the opinion that honesty is not always the best policy.

Aside from all this, she is about as romantic as a cheerful dentist extracting a wisdom tooth; you are intensely sentimental and sometimes a little sappy. She has no patience with your armchair observations, and you have no tolerance for her perpetual curiosity. Any relationship more serious than partnership at backgammon is sure to create mutual irritation that is more than a little electric.

THE RESPONSIBILITY OF
THE ASTROLOGER

Ideally, the study of astrology should be analogous to the dual study of both physics and metaphysics. As a basis for an understanding of the science, we must first become familiar with its physical laws.

A practical understanding of the physical laws of astrology, operating in relationship with each other, is indeed a difficult task and the reason why accurate astrological analysis is such as complex and demanding undertaking.

However, the astrologer's work should only begin at this level. It should continue on an infinite plane of metaphysical analysis. For there is little use in the mere knowledge of an event, without an understanding of its philosophic meaning in the life of an individual, and there is no benefit in the forecasting of a planetary unfoldment if the individual does not understand how he must peronally adjust to be in accord with its vibrations.

BIBLIOGRAPHY

Further Reading on Astrology

Arroyo, Stephen. *Astrology, Psychology and the Four Elements: An Energy Approach to Astrology and Its Use in the Counseling Arts.* Davis, Calif.: CRCS Publications, 1975.

Bailey, Alice. *Esoteric Astrology.* New York: Lucis Publishing Co., 1951.

Bram, Jean Rhys, trans. *Ancient Astrology Theory and Practice: The Mathesis of Firmicus Maternus.* Park Ridge, N.J.: Noyes Press, 1975.

Busteed, Marilyn; Tiffany, R.; Wergin, D. *Phases of the Moon.* Berkeley, Calif.: Shambala, 1974.

Crowley, Aleister. *Astrology.* New York: Weiser, 1974.

Davison, Ronald. *Astrology.* New York: Arco, 1967.

Dobyns, Zippora Pottenger. *Finding the Person in the Horoscope.* Calif.: TIA Publications, 1973.

Goldstein, Ivy. *Here and There in Astrology.* Jacobson/Private Printing.

Green, Landis Knight. *The Astrologer's Manual.* New York: Arco, 1975.

Greene, Liz. *Saturn: A New Look at an Old Devil.* New York: Weiser, 1976.

Hand, Robert. *Planets in Transit.* Gloucester, Mass.: Para Research, 1976.

Jinni and Joanne. *The Spiral of Life (Psychological Interpretation).* Seattle, Wash.: Author Private Printing, 1974.

Jocelyn, John. *Meditations on the Signs of the Zodiac.* New York: Steiner, 1970.

Jones, Marc Edmund. *Astrology: How and Why it Works.* Baltimore: Penguin; 1971.

————. *The Guide to Horoscope Interpretation*. Wheaton, Ill.: Theosophical Publishing, 1974.

————. *How to Learn Astrology*. Garden City, N.Y.: Doubleday, 1976.

Leo, Alan. *How to Judge a Nativity*. London: Fowler, 1969.

Lewi, Grant. *Heaven Knows What*. St. Paul, Minn.: Llewellyn, 1976.

Mason, Zoltan. *Astrosynthesis*. New York: Emerald Books, 1974.

Meyer, Michael. *A Handbook for the Humanistic Astrologer*. New York: Anchor, 1974.

Oken, Alan. *As Above, So Below*. New York: Bantam, 1973.

————. *Astrology: Evolution and Revolution*. New York: Bantam, 1976.

————. *The Horoscope, the Road and Its Travelers*. New York: Bantam, 1974.

Pagan, Isabelle M. *From Pioneer to Poet or the Twelve Great Gates: An Expansion of the Signs of the Zodiac Analysed*. Wheaton, Ill.: Theosophical Publishing, 1969.

Rudhyar, Dane. *An Astrological Study of Psychological Complexes and Emotional Problems*. Berkeley, Calif.: Shambala, 1976.

————. *The Lunation Cycle*. Berkeley, Calif.: Shambala, 1971.

Sakoian, Francis; Acker, Louis S. *The Astrologer's Handbook*. New York: Harper & Row, 1973.

————. *The Astrology of Human Relationships*. New York: Harper & Row, 1976.

Schwickert, Frederick; Weiss, Adolf. *Cornerstones of Astrology*. St. Paul, Minn.: Llewellyn, 1972.

Suggested Related Reading

Blavatsky, H. P. *Studies in Occultism*. Pasadena, Calif.: Theosophical University Press, 1973.

Bucke, Richard M., M.D. *Cosmic Consciousness*. New York: Causeway Books, 1974.

Budge, Wallace. *The Egyptian Book of the Dead*. New York: Dover, 1967.

————. *The Gods of the Egyptians*, 2 vols. New York: Dover, 1969.

Burckhardt, Titus. *Alchemy*. Baltimore: Penguin Books, 1971.

Case, Paul F. *The Book of Tokens: Tarot Meditations*. Los Angeles, Calif.: Builders of the Adytum, 1974.

———. *The Tarot: A Key to the Wisdom of the Ages*. Richmond, Va.: Macoy Publishing Co., 1976.

Conway, David. *Magic: An Occult Primer*. New York: Bantam, 1973.

Cope, Lloyd. *Your Stars Are Numbered*. New York: Dell, 1976.

Crowley, Aleister. *Magic Without Tears*. St. Paul, Minn.: Llewellyn.

Duncan, A. D. *The Christ, Psychotherapy and Magic*. London: George Allen and Unwin, 1969.

Fortune, Dion. *Applied Magic*. New York: Weiser, 1973.

———. *The Esoteric Philosophy of Love and Marriage*. New York: Weiser.

———. *The Mystical Qabalah*. London: Ernest Benn, Ltd., 1957.

———. *Practical Occultism*. New York: Weiser, 1935.

———. *Sane Occultism*. New York: Weiser, 1967.

———. *The Training and Work of an Initiate*. New York: Weiser, 1930.

Jung, C. G. *Psyche and Symbol*. New York: Anchor Books, 1958.

Levi, Eliphas. *Transcendental Magic*. New York: Weiser, 1969.

Ouspensky, P. D. *In Search of the Miraculous*. New York: Harcourt Brace Jovanovich, 1965.

———. *A New Model of the Universe*. New York: Vintage, 1971.

Poncé, Charles. *The Game of Wizards*. Baltimore: Penguin, 1975.

Regardie, Israel. *The Tree of Life*. New York: Weiser, 1969.

Reifler, Sam. *The I Ching: A New Interpretation for Modern Times*. New York: Bantam, 1974.

Roberts, Jane. *The Nature of Personal Reality*. Englewood Cliffs, N.J.: Prentice-Hall, 1974.

Three Initiates. *Kybalion: Hermetic Philosophy*. Chicago, Ill.: Yoga Publications Society, 1908.

Trungpa, Chögyam. *Cutting Through Spiritual Materialism*. Berkeley, Calif.: Shambala.

Wilhelm, Richard. *The I Ching or Book of Changes.* Princeton, N.J.: Princeton University Press, 1967.

———. *The Secret of the Golden Flower.* New York: Causeway, 1975.

*Learn the secrets of the stars
and let them help you on
your road to success*

LINDA GOODMAN'S SUN SIGNS
Linda Goodman
____27882-7 $7.50/$9.99 Canada

SECRETS FROM A STARGAZER'S NOTEBOOK
Making Astrology Work for You
Debbi Kempton-Smith
____25849-4 $5.99/$7.50

ROBIN MACNAUGHTON'S SUN SIGN
PERSONALITY GUIDE
Robin Macnaughton
____27380-9   7.50/$9.99

ALAN OKEN'S COMPLETE ASTROLOGY
Alan Oken
____34537-0 $15.95/$18.95

SEDUCTION BY THE STARS
An Astrological Guide to All Stages of a Relationship
Rose Lexander
____37451-6 $11.95/$15.95